A FEMINIST HISTORY SOCIETY BOOK

Inside

A Decade of Feminist Journalism

EDITED BY
PHILINDA MASTERS
WITH THE BROADSIDE COLLECTIVE

Second Story Press

Library and Archives Canada Cataloguing in Publication

Title: Inside Broadside : a decade of feminist journalism / Philinda Masters with the
   Broadside Collective.
Names: Masters, Philinda, editor.
Description: Series statement: A Feminist History Society book | Includes
   bibliographical references and index.
Identifiers: Canadiana (print) 20190083506 | Canadiana (ebook) 20190084901 |
   ISBN 9781772601121 (softcover) | ISBN 9781772601138 (EPUB)
Subjects: LCSH: Broadside (Toronto, Ont.) | LCSH: Women's periodicals,
   Canadian—History. | LCSH:Women—Canada—Periodicals. | LCSH: Women's
   rights—Canada—Periodicals. | LCSH: Feminism—Canada—Periodicals.
   LCSH: Canadian newspapers—History. | LCSH: Newspaper publishing—
   Canada—History.
Classification: LCC PN4914.W58 I57 2019 | DDC 305.420971—dc23

Cover design by Michel Vrana
Edited by Andrea Knight
Book design by Melissa Kaita
Original series design by Zab Design & Typography

Printed and bound in Canada

*Second Story Press gratefully acknowledges the support of the Ontario Arts Council
and the Canada Council for the Arts for our publishing program. We acknowledge
the financial support of the Government of Canada through the Canada Book Fund.*

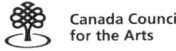

Published by
Second Story Press
20 Maud Street, Suite 401
Toronto, ON M5V 2M5
www.secondstorypress.ca

To those brave and brilliant feminists no longer with us — Broadside collective members Bev Allinson, Heather Brown, and Jacqueline Frewin; artists and activists such as Moira Armour, Sherrill Cheda, Maryon Kantaroff, and Kay Macpherson — to the others who helped lead the way, and to the now and future feminists who will continue to stand strong.

Broadside

May 1979

...ctory Issue

Broadside

A FEMINIST REVIEW

...me 2, number 4

February 1981

Credit Un...

Volume 5, number 5   **March 1984**

RISE U

February 1988

CONTENTS

EDITORIALS

179 **CHAPTER 3**

Features: Debates & Debacles

A NOTE TO THE READER: The articles reprinted herein are exactly as they were in the original publication. As such, they represent varying styles and may differ from each other in punctuation and forms favoured today. We have left them as is in order to keep the authenticity of the many voices contained in *Broadside*.

Broadside

Introductory Issue   May 1979 $-

Heads They Win, Tails We Lose

by Jacqueline Frewin, Judith Lawrence and Eve Zaremba

Three Mile Island near Harrisburg, Pennsylvania, was the site of a very 'significant event' on March 28th, 1979.

In the vocabulary of the nuclear industry, it was a 'significant event'. In our terms it was a potentially disastrous nuclear accident.

The worst of all possible disasters was slimly averted. The dramatic impact of *The China Syndrome* came perilously close to reality: the equivalent of a nuclear bomb destroying the surrounding area, making Pennsylvania uninhabitable and contaminating the water, air and food chain as far away as Ontario.

Now government regulatory agencies, power companies and the nuclear industry are falling over backwards attempting to reassure us and pacify our very real horror. Making the best of a bad situation, they are insisting that this 'significant event' merely proves how safe nuclear power is, since disaster was averted.

In Canada, we are assured that our own Candu reactors have an extra safety feature: a vacuum chamber surrounding the core. All is being made safer. We are not to worry. Meanwhile, more and more reactors are planned and under construction. Business is booming.

But there was human error. There was mechanical malfunction. What the Nuclear Regulatory Commission has now termed a 'transient accident' — transient because no-one knew what to do, it just came and went — was the exposure of large portions of the core for approximately fifteen hours. Improperly closed valves on the reactors, premature turning off of the emergency cooling system which is the principal method for preventing the overheating of the uranium in the reactor core, and poorly designed containment which did not isolate some of the water as it was meant to do. Magnetic valves failed to close properly and pressure level indicators were inaccurate at a crucial point.

Dr. Ursula Franklin, Professor of Metallurgy at the University of Toronto, consultant to the Royal Ontario Museum, ex-member of the Science Council of Canada (1974-78), Director of Energy Probe and life-long activist, has attempted to clarify some of the issues for *Broadside*. She affirmed some of our suspicions that nuclear reactors can never be safe, not with the best safety reviews and emergency back-up systems in the world. Furthermore, "whether one is satisfied with safety is completely a political consideration. The issue is not a technical one. The central lesson is the relationship between the triviality of the cause of the disaster and the enormity of the consequences. No amount of reviews will get that out of the way, that is the nature of the beast. Life just isn't a totally predictable thing.

There are all the possibilities within which one can operate, considering that human beings and machines have a certain rate of randomness, and the disproportionality between the size of the error or mishap, and the consequences. It's in the nature of the technology."

Because of the nature of the technology they say it will take two years to decontaminate Harrisburg. Have we even considered what this term 'decontamination' means? Dr. Franklin suggests that we misconstrue the term. "Radioactivity is irreversible. Nothing we do can destroy it!

"Decontamination only means taking the radio-activity from place A to place B and waiting until it has decayed naturally. Now, some things decay fast, and some things decay slowly. Iodine will be gone within weeks. Other things can take a thousand years. The things you worry about are the long-life things and those which might get into the food chain."

The basic issue then is not simply the 'safety' record of any specific plant or energy authority to date. Ultimately what we are seeing happen is the increase of radioactivity and the multiplication of sources of the deadly radiation. All we can do is attempt to hide it and move it around.

"Ever since one has been able to create artificial radio-activity something really very pro-

Continued page 3

Volley Number One

There hasn't been anything like *Broadside* — ever. It's been a long time coming, but finally it's here and it intends to stay and make an impact.

Broadside recognizes the need to cut across the left/right, good/bad polarities women usually face when we make the political and personal decisions that define our lives. We all need to cultivate a critical eye, a grasp and a tolerance for ambiguity combined with an intolerance of tendentious tripe. *Broadside* wants to create a dialogue among women — not only among politically active feminists — in a forum which belongs to us all, not to large corporations, or left wing sects or advertisers or even any particular feminist group.

We are not objective. We leave "objectivity" to the daily papers and other media which consider women as a "special interest" group. As it is, *Broadside* is uniquely and openly biased in favour of women. We are setting out to represent ideas and priorities that are not reflected in the mainstream press. We want to rediscover terms, words and concepts and define them for ourselves. For example, the battered term feminist must be rescued from media-conceived notions and given a new lease on life. We see our bias as an effort to counterbalance the unacknowledged bias of the mass media in general.

At the same time *Broadside* intends to play its active political role. The Women's Liberation Movement is alive and we intend to cover it as it develops — whether in

Parliament, in women's organizations or in the streets. *Broadside* offers a section dealing specifically with local women's movement activity, bringing readers news of women's services, meetings and the issues that the women's community confronts as we go to print.

We are not a house organ of women's liberation. *Broadside* will explore the world and be the eyes and ears of women as well as a provocative pro-woman voice. Often what we see and hear may provoke anger, anger which we want to express freely, creatively and with wit. *Broadside* will be a tough, vivid exuberant paper which, however it strikes you, will never be dull.

INTRODUCTION

A Decade of Feminist Publishing, 1979–1989

by Philinda Masters

Do you think you know everything there is to know about second-wave feminism? Do you think it's old hat, those early feminists just didn't get it? Or do you think they were awesome? Well, read *Inside Broadside*, then decide. It's all here in this book—the discussions and debates, the opinions, film and book reviews, the explorations of feminist art, the letters from readers, the editorials from the Broadside collective along with profiles of and interviews with some of those second-wave feminists themselves. It all makes us think, have things changed? How much? Or have things not changed at all?

The pieces in this book are a snapshot of ten years of activism, contemplation, creativity, and reporting on what was in the early days called the women's liberation movement. When the mainstream press caught wind of it, it came to be called "women's lib," and we became "women's libbers." It was their attempt to trivialize what was becoming an enormously threatening trend. And in case you're snickering at how dismissive and odd this sounds, consider what the movement is called now: #MeToo!

To see how it all began, how some things change, and some things don't change, read on.

• • • • • • • • •

Five of the many Broadside collective members
over the decade: (from left) Eve Zaremba,
Catherine Maunsell, Donna Gollan,
Phil Masters, and Susan G. Cole, 1984.

Broadside's first meeting ever was held on February 22, 1978, at the Toronto home of future collective member Eve Zaremba. We were there to begin the process of starting a new feminist newspaper. Some of us had known each other already, while others had met at meetings of WAVAW, or Women Against Violence Against Women, a group that had formed to protest the many forms of misogynist representations of women in popular culture. Still others of us had met at meetings of the International Women's Day Committee, the coalition that planned and orchestrated the annual rally and march in Toronto. So we already had shared views on feminist theory and activism, and felt that we were more than ready to take on the huge task of publishing. We had a lot to learn!

A few weeks before our February meeting, some of us had met at the Lesbian Organization Of Toronto (LOOT) building at 342 Jarvis Street, to discuss the possibility of taking over from *The Other Woman*, an established feminist newspaper that was first published out of A Woman's Place on Dupont Street in Toronto, and then at the University of Waterloo. Their collective had simply run out of steam and resources. In fact, they counselled us—in no uncertain terms—not to take on the stress and struggle of publishing a feminist newspaper. But we—in no uncertain terms—decided to do just that. For most of us, our publishing experience consisted of reading newspapers and having opinions on everything. But we did have some expertise: in magazine journalism, in newspaper pre-production, in research, in television and puppetry, and in graphic design. Looking back, we were a very talented group of women who set out to change the world. But we really had no idea at that point whether the whole endeavour would actually come together.

What was clear was the overwhelming need for women, feminists, to have a hub for events, information, and discussions of theory, as well as a place to take part in the many debates that were swirling around in those early days of second-wave feminism. We needed a structure of communications to support and maintain our sometimes fragile, sometimes enormously strong, political movement. A large network of newsletters had grown up during the 1970s. Most of them were published by women's centres, run off on Gestetner machines (remember those?), but there were also the slightly more elaborate versions published by status of women

A typical issue's Table of Contents.

councils throughout the country. These councils were supported by various municipal and provincial governments, and had more money to spend on communications. So a new web of resources was becoming available to feminist activists in both urban and rural areas of the country.

In the end, we decided to start a new feminist paper rather than take over from *The Other Woman*. For one thing, we wanted a new perspective and a new approach to editing. In those days, editing was frowned upon as "perpetuating patriarchal bias," thereby stifling women's true voices. There were grounds for this belief, considering the ways that mainstream media either wrote our stories for us — removing anything awkward, or overtly feminist — or erased our experiences altogether. But dealing with the issue by eliminating any editorial process was, from our point of view, also extremely problematic. There was clearly room for many different kinds of publications and we wanted something more along the lines of a review, offering opinions and discussions, rather than the news digest that most student and activist papers were at the time. In fact, our official name was *Broadside: A Feminist Review*, though nobody ever called it that.

COLLECTIVE OPERATIONS: EARLY DAYS

Our new publication began its life with an office overlooking College Street in the front room of another collective member, Susan Sturman. It was there that we plotted our business structure, PR initiatives, even our name. This latter was easier said then done. In the introductory editorial of our digitized version six years ago (see broadsidefeminist.com), we described how it went:

> It took us a while to find a name. We joked about calling it The Monthly Rag and the name Bias—which openly trumpeted our unconventional journalistic approach—almost stuck. But, inspired by a conversation between collective members Eve Zaremba and Susan G. Cole, we settled on Broadside. It conveyed our desire to be hard-hitting, it resonated with the old-school idea of a political flyer and, best of all, it was definitely not earnest.

We decided to incorporate as Broadside Communications Ltd. because we thought that our legal identity would protect us. From what? From being taken over by the sectarian left groups that were always on the lookout for more ways to fuel the revolution. Their revolution, I might add, was not ours. That kind of thing really did happen back then. But we never encountered that problem in all our ten years. We also wanted to ensure that our supporters could invest in us. A few generous women did donate serious money to the cause, for which we probably never thanked them enough. But we just ended up putting all those legal papers in the filing cabinet and carrying on. Most not-for-profit organizations in those days counted on government funding or foundations for startup and operating costs, not investors, and, for Broadside, being a for-profit corporation was never a good fit.

Our weekly meetings after that first one were devoted to hashing out the many aspects of publishing we had learned along the way, often accompanied by wine and cheese and baguettes. In early 1979, we met with two more experienced feminist publishers, Sharon Batt from Edmonton's *Branching Out* magazine and Eleanor Wachtel from Vancouver's *Room of Ones' Own* literary journal. This meeting took place in the home of Sherrill Cheda, executive director of the Canadian Periodical Publishers Association, and was extremely informative. Nobody told us not to publish, but we got a pretty clear view of what was in store for us from Sharon and Eleanor. We also talked to everyone we could think of, from editors at Women's Press and academic journals like *Resources for Feminist Research* (*RFR*) to author Margaret Atwood and journalist Michele Landsberg, among others. So we were well mentored and prepped for the realities of the venture when we brought out our *Broadside* Introductory Issue in May 1979. Our first regular issue came out five months later, in October 1979.

As mentioned, our original collective members had a range of rather impressive skills as well. They included women in mid-career like Judith Lawrence, Casey and Finnegan's puppeteer on CBC TV's *Mr. Dressup*; Bev Allinson, author, and writing and art coach for children and elders at the Toronto school board; and Eve Zaremba, author of a lesbian mystery that was about to become a series featuring the first-known lesbian sleuth; on the younger end of the career spectrum were Susan G. Cole, researcher for eminent Canadian investigative journalist Peter C. Newman; Susan Sturman, an excellent illustrator and graphic artist from a York University student magazine who became *Broadside's* first designer; Alex Maass, who had a printing press in the basement of her Cabbagetown house and was Toronto feminists' go-to printer for flyers, ads, and pamphlets; and Deena Rasky, member of a well-known Canadian documentary filmmaking and journalist family—at the time of our first issue she was trying to become a member of the compositors' union at the *Toronto Star*, a notoriously closed shop, and eventually succeeded—to two former teachers, Jacqueline Frewin and Heather Brown, who, as experts at carpentry and electricity, refurbished our first official newspaper office, a huge loft at Bathurst and King. As editor, I had publishing and production skills gained first at the *Varsity*, University of Toronto's student newspaper and then at the *Financial Post Magazine*, part of the Maclean-Hunter dynasty (now Rogers). These two disparate experiences probably combined to turn me away from mainstream journalism into what could be considered a marginal yet deeply feminist form of publishing. As the years went by, our collective complement changed as some left for other work or other parts of the country and new members joined *Broadside* to add their distinct voices to the mix. It was, all-in-all, a very healthy, productive group.

For the first five years, we had only one paid editor, who did everything from working with authors, editing the copy, teaching volunteers, overseeing the page designs on production weekends, dealing with typesetters and printers, and juggling our meagre finances to pay the bills. The other collective members worked on a volunteer basis, but it was an extremely committed and hardworking group who managed to produce a newspaper every month for ninety-six months. The collective, among other things, planned each issue, solicited articles based on what we had discussed at our weekly meetings, worked with the authors, proofread copy, and helped on production weekends and mailing days. We had to do most of this work in three weeks, produce the newspaper in the fourth, and then start all over again. Over the ten years of its existence, the newspaper was only late twice—once when there was a lengthy postal strike and once when our typesetter's electronic equipment broke down and we were forced to add a day to our production schedule. It is a testament to our feminist work ethic. As we wrote in the introduction to broadsidefeminist.com:

> The Broadside collective was a high-functioning collective for several reasons. First, each member understood what was required and met their commitment. And it was a serious one: two meetings a week—Mondays and Thursdays—plus both afternoons of one weekend a month for production. Incredibly, meetings always started on time. Second, we were able to operate via consensus. In the 10 years that Broadside published, not a single vote was taken. That's because we had a shared understanding that it made sense to step back from a discussion when someone else knew more. Most important, perhaps, was the fact that we kept the focus on what we were doing. Everything took second place to meeting deadlines and getting the newspaper out. What we were creating was always bigger than the group and we were always conscious of the fact that we were part of a whole movement that was bigger than Broadside.

In that first year, in addition to everything else, we had to fundraise to pay for our first few issues before the bulk of our subscription revenue kicked in. We sold pre-order subscriptions to everyone we knew, we leafleted every meeting we went to, and we approached our more affluent community members (i.e., those with a real jobs) for more sizable donations. We just talked up *Broadside* up whenever we could, so that when we started to publish, it was a well-anticipated event. And we were very lucky in our community support. Although we never had much money over the years, we always had just enough. At a feminist publications conference in 1986, all the attendees at one session were asked to write down our magazine's annual budget, listing both income and expenses, so we could discuss various publications' production and distribution costs. One woman who worked at a magazine supported by a university department was shocked that *Broadside*'s budget showed that we paid for rent, printing, phone, mailing, and supplies, plus staff, for $30,000 a year. It was shocking—even taking inflation into account, we worked with very little money. So much for incorporating as a for-profit corporation as we had originally and misguidedly done. We were happy, though. We had enough money to put out a pretty good paper, but we couldn't have done it without a lot of support from our community—the very engaged readers, the cultural producers, and the activists who provided the stories, debates, and debacles we reported on, interpreted, and analyzed.

Our collective process was very different from most mainstream and even activist work structures. It was feminist, which means that it was an amalgam of progressive organization with non-hierarchical, collegial, and consensus-reaching processes, and lessons we'd learned from earlier, often failed, attempts to operate in woman-oriented progressive environments. We had learned, for example, that editing a manuscript for brevity, clarity, or accuracy was not necessarily an act of cultural appropriation. We were careful about not overriding an author's intentions, but we believed in good editing, which is really more of a chameleon-like operation than an appropriation. But further, we had learned the lesson of what Jo Freeman called the "Tyranny of Structurelessness" (*Ms.* magazine, 1973, among other places). Her contention was that, in an attempt to avoid the top-down, hierarchical, directive, and competitive environment of most workplaces, feminists had become distrustful and had thrown everything out with the bathwater. As a result, we were left with rudderless organizations in which nobody was the boss so nobody was responsible; nobody's skills were acknowledged so nobody was credited for their work; and everybody had to do a bit of everything, even things they hated doing or were no good at. This approach clearly did not work and created toxic collectives, not healthy and productive work environments.

THE COLLECTIVE PROCESS

While we were working hard producing the newspaper, we did have a good time. The Broadside collective was a group of literate, intelligent, informed, smart women who operated with integrity and, particularly, with wit. Our headline process is a good example. Unlike in academic publications, where scholarly authors wrote their own article titles—some of which were clever but many of which were turgid or overwritten, the Broadside collective wrote all the headlines ourselves. And we sometimes managed a particular feminist, roguish flair. One headline for an Italian play about cooking was "Commedia dell'Artichoke"; another more serious one on censorship was "Censory Perception"; and "Instruments of Sculpture" was used for an art installation on lesbians and mental health. Occasionally things went horribly wrong as a result of typesetting errors, as when we wrote "Ritualized Mutilization" for an article on the practice of female genital mutilation and not one proofreader caught the mistake. These headlines were the last thing we did at the final meeting before our production weekends, when we knew for sure which articles would be in the paper. So when we came up with them, we were tired but pumped and the exercise was quite cathartic. Then we went out for Chinese food.

We had fun doing fundraising, too. In fact, *Broadside* led the way for a new brand of fundraising that seemed to catch on. We held a feminist cabaret, a bingo game, a strawberry tea, film nights, and any number of restaurant dinners. As we wrote in our broadsidefeminist.com introduction,

> We were very creative fundraisers, organizing benefits, some of which became templates for other organizations looking for

fundraising ideas. A cabaret at the now defunct Bamboo Club on Queen St. West set a precedent for many groups who later staged similar entertainments. Previously, feminist groups weren't looking to the bar scene for party venues. Other funders featured Shawna Dempsey performing her infamous and hilarious We're Talking Vulva, and a screening of Lizzie Borden's NFB film, Born In Flames, all indicative of the fact that *Broadside* stayed abreast of cutting-edge feminist art. There was also a champagne and strawberry brunch held at the Women's Cultural Building on Lombard St. (the former morgue), where collective members auctioned off personal artistic endeavours [mine was a watercolour sketch of a serrated knife, a tomato and a wilted daisy], a number of fundraising dinners at feminist-friendly restaurants, and even a successful bingo night at the Heliconian Club in Yorkville.

In other efforts to encourage community participation in *Broadside*'s activities, we held "*Broadside* Forums," where people could come and discuss the hows and whys of publishing a feminist newspaper, and find out ways to contribute, either through fundraising or through volunteering at our production weekends or monthly distribution (i.e., mailing) days. Over the years, a great many women's names showed up on our masthead (page two of every issue). We encouraged people to get involved in the actual hands-on production of the paper, even people without previous design and paste-up skills. It was all done manually. We'd type and edit manuscripts on paper, then have them typeset to produce galleys that were glossy on the front and waxed on the back (we waxed them ourselves). The galleys were then measured and cut with very sharp scalpel-like X-acto knives and rolled down on art boards with mini-rollers. We showed people how to do it all and only admonished them to make sure their lines were straight and didn't cut themselves with the X-Actos and bleed on the copy. We only had one mishap in ten years, when a collective member dropped an X-Acto knife point down on her big toe—the knife stuck straight up and vibrated until someone pulled it out.

Another important aspect of producing a feminist publication was to encourage interaction between the readers and editors (the collective), and among the readers themselves. We had a very interactive and full "Letters" section (a number of which are reproduced in this book—see Chapter 1, "Opinions: Ours and Yours"). Readers questioned us, critiqued the

articles, complained, praised, and generally made *Broadside* their paper. Some readers wrote article-length letters; it got to the point that we had to intervene and ask them to keep the letters short (or at least shorter). If they wrote well, we could always ask them to write an article for us.

We stumbled on another more unusual form of interaction when a dedicated volunteer, Ottie Lockey, suggested that we sell business card-sized ad space and place the ads together on one page, first for International Women's Day, then for other holidays, for *Broadside* anniversaries, and finally as a final farewell to the paper in 1989. It was a way to showcase various organizations and feminist-friendly businesses and allow them to be recorded in our history while making us a bit of money. We also started running classified ads, which were always informative and useful: for apartments, coming-out groups, yoga classes, retreats, country accommodations, and other necessities of feminist and lesbian lives. These ads complemented our "Outside *Broadside*" monthly calendar of events that was compiled by collective members Catherine Maunsell and, later, Layne Mellanby.

These ads and classifieds provided a very popular and important service and helped give the women's community a lived-in look and a sense of our reality in the face of mainstream resistance to accepting our place in the world. As a result, in the early 1980s, *Broadside* applied for and received a small municipal grant to hire someone to manage our circulation and sell advertising. Our first manager was Donna Gollan, a film student who doubled as a film reviewer for *Broadside*. She was followed by Ingrid MacDonald, another artist and writer, on a similar grant, and then Jackie Edwards, thanks to a

Card-sized ad pages were very popular, showcased feminist organizations and businesses, and were a valuable source of revenue.

grant we shared with the Canadian women's health magazine *Healthsharing*. Jackie eventually became *Broadside*'s coordinator.

It was at least five years before we started applying for and getting grants from government funding agencies. The first to give us annual support for our efforts was the Ontario Arts Council (OAC), followed by the Canada Council for the Arts (CCA). We decided to make the first OAC application a pleasurable activity and wrote the project description with a light and chatty hand. When we'd been awarded our grant, the OAC program officer called to thank us for submitting an application that was so pleasant to read. Most of them, she said, were painstaking and stiff. Lesson learned. *Broadside* was supported by the OAC for the rest of its existence. The Women's Program of the Secretary of State, one of the key funding supporters of women's groups in Canada during the 1970s and 1980s, was a little hesitant to fund us, probably because of our brazen and outrageous politics or perhaps because we were quite critical of government policies, particularly when the Progressive Conservatives under Brian Mulroney were in power. In 1990, The Rt. Hon. Mr. Mulroney and his sidekick the late Hon. Michael Wilson pulled funding from the Women's Program—blatantly and unusually in the Throne Speech—and directed that women's centres, feminist research centres, and research journals across the country be closed down. This move created a national outcry. The women's centres' funding, a mere $25,000 each but crucial to their survival, was eventually reinstated, but the feminist research centres and journals were never refunded. This happened just after *Broadside* closed, but the political climate that allowed for this anti-feminist agenda had already been in place for a number of years.

We were more directly affected by the emerging extreme right-wing anti-feminist organization, REAL Women of Canada—the acronym stood for Real, Equal, Active for Life. Following the tactics of the Moral Majority in the US, they began blitzing

Every issue contained a calendar of events. This example gives a hint of the breadth and depth of feminist activism in March 1985.

the government with letters in 1984, appropriating the language of the women's movement as they went, and acting very much like the church group they undoubtedly were. The government listened to them and they gave us a run for our money, not because what they said made sense (they were anti-choice, anti-LGBTQ, anti-women's rights, you name it), but because they were an excellent foil for the women's movement and mainstream news media could, and did, use them as the equal-and-opposite point of view considered essential in traditional journalism. The REAL women have largely faded from the landscape, but they were a harbinger of the kind of alt-right, bigoted, misogynist, and downright anti-feminist politics

Broadside **CLASSIFIEDS**

DUPLEX FOR RENT. One bedroom, ground floor with shared basement, yard, laundry. Two women with baby (expected November 12) living upstairs. Danforth-Broadview. $525 per month, utilities included. (416) 421-8227, evenings or weekends.

COMFORTABLE HOUSE looking for fifth woman, non-smoker, Queen and Strachan. Cheap'n'friendly. (416) 364-6067.

HALIFAX WOMAN needs holiday accommodation in Toronto December 11-30. (Non-smoking, women only.) If you need Halifax space then, or at some other time, consider a swap. I would also consider renting your place. Write, c/o Pandora, 5533 Black Street, Halifax, B3K 1P7.

BURNOUT WORKSHOP: coping with/prevention. 10-5 December 7th. Sliding scale. Facilitators: Susanne/Taylor. 964-1278.

BICYCLISTS NEEDED as couriers— year round— must know downtown and bicycle maintenance. Cooperative, professional environment. Call Barbara at Sunwheel Bicycle Couriers, (416) 598-0053.

DRIVERS also needed for reputable car courier service that collaborates with Sunwheel. Good earnings. Must provide own vehicle. Call Gerard at Gopher Express, (416) 252-9531.

INCEST SURVIVOR GROUP: Small group, creative approach, sliding scale, new members welcome. For more information, call Michele (416) 977-7609, Wendy (416) 977-7609 or (416) 598-4105.

THE WOMEN'S INFORMATION LINE welcomes new volunteers to operate feminist phone referral service. Call Ottie: (416) 920-9797.

YOU ARE COMMITTED to a crazy life, but you want to change your diet. Nutrition/cooking workshop— Grains and Casseroles, November 10, 11-4 pm; Soups and Stews, December 1, 11-4 pm; $40 per workshop. Queen Street West. Diana Meredith (416) 979-2319; Charna Gord (416) 593-6591.

WOMEN'S JOURNAL WRITING GROUP forming: Mondays 10 am to 12 noon, or 7 to 9 pm. $50 per month. Also journal writing workshop, Saturday, November 23, 9 - 4 pm. $50. For information, call Melinda (416) 759-7389.

GAY/LESBIAN RIGHTS RESEARCHER WANTED. Innovative, independent gay/lesbian rights researcher with office and interviewing skills required to research a brief to the Ontario Legislature. Full-time, Dec/85 - Feb/86. Toronto access required. Reply no later than November 15, 1985 to: Coalition for Gay Rights in Ontario (CGRO), Box 822, Station A, Toronto M5W 1G3.

DYKE DIARIES. Anthology of lesbian personal writings— diaries, journals, letters, thoughts— requests submissions of up to 20 pages. Pieces used may be published anonymously if the writer wishes; confidentiality will be strictly observed. Please include year of writing and age of writer at the time. Deadline: March 1, 1986. Send material to Frances Rooney, PO Box 868, Station P, Toronto, Ontario M5S 2Z2.

- 25¢ a word ($3 minimum)
- First word in **bold face**
- Ads accepted up to 20th of the month
- All classified ads must be *pre-paid*
- Fill out the coupon and send it with cheque or money order to:
Broadside, PO Box 494, Stn P, Toronto M5S 2T1

No. of words _____   Name _____

Amount $ _____   Address _____

☐ Cheque   _____

☐ Money Order   Telephone _____

AD COPY: _____

(type or print clearly)

we are experiencing globally and must fight every bit as hard against as we did in those early days when *Broadside* started to publish.

IMPACT: THEN AND NOW

Many people consider *Broadside* to have had a large impact both on the women's movement of the day and, therefore, in direct and indirect ways, on current feminist initiatives like #MeToo, #Yes, All Women, (a counter-offensive to #Not All Men), the Pussyhat Project and women's marches that took place across North America in January 2017 and were repeated in 2018 and 2019, and many other activities. Canadian feminist publications that emerged in the 1970s and 1980s, such as *Kinesis*, *Herizons* (still publishing), *La Vie en rose*, the *Northern Woman Journal*, and quite a few others, were all working to a similar end—to make the experiences of women during the period of second-wave feminism "discoverable." We were uncovering aspects of our lives that we had not been aware of before and the impact was huge. When we understood what was happening, we could work to change things. It was a useful formula for action. Then and now.

The impact of these publications, including *Broadside*, can also be measured by the extent to which people were threatened by them. A 1982 FBI report on communications, leaked to a feminist press conference in San Francisco, stated that the women's liberation movement was held together by its network of feminist presses, bookstores, and newspapers. It was probably the only time we ever agreed with the FBI—well, until Trump. A former high-school classmate from a fairly conservative environment asked me during that time what I was doing now, fifteen years after we'd been at school together. "Editing a feminist newspaper," I answered. "Oh," she asked. "Which one?" (as if she'd heard of any). "*Broadside*," I replied. "Bloodshed?" she exclaimed in horrified tones. That made me laugh, but she obviously equated feminism with something to be feared. And she was right.

As philosopher and leftist Herbert Marcuse said in one of his last lectures at Stanford in 1974, "I believe the women's liberation movement is perhaps the most important and potentially the

Left: Classified ads connected our readers with a multitude of feminist projects, everything from feminist-friendly housing to coming out workshops to incest survivor groups.

WOMEN

AGAINST VIOLENCE AGAINST WOMEN

P.O. Box 928 Station Q, Toronto

most radical political movement that we have." He got it. Most people still haven't. Time and again these days we've heard ourselves saying, "We were writing about this in the 1980s and nothing has changed." At this year's January 2019 women's march, March On: Toronto, one older woman held a placard we're seeing more and more: "I can't believe we're still protesting this shit!"

It's hard to respond when asked what impact we think *Broadside* had on its readers, on the women's movement, or even on Canadian society as a whole. For one thing, we can't look at *Broadside* in isolation—the impact came from the network of similar publications in concert with all the projects, protests, and organizations that made up the feminist activism of the 1970s and 1980s. So much changed in the decade we were publishing—not to mention the period from the late 1960s to the early 1990s—that it's impossible to condense it into a few paragraphs, or even a book. But one thing is clear: for those of us who lived through that intense period of feminist activism, we felt the changes in our bones. When you're on the front lines of any social movement, you learn that the perceptions of events are very different seen from a mainstream point of view (or "male-stream," as OISE professor Mary O'Brien put it). Feminist activists, including feminist publishers, didn't only work for changes to the abortion law or pay equity or childcare or labour laws—that is to say, the institutional infrastructure needed to maintain a discriminatory culture. We were hoping to change the way people thought about not only these issues but also about broader issues such as race, sexuality, gender identity, and popular culture. And that's tough because people don't generally want to change; more importantly, they don't always recognize that they're operating from unconscious biases because, by definition, they're unconscious. Our project as publishers of a feminist newspaper was to critique, analyze, and interpret what was happening around us and present the issues to our readers so they could decide for themselves how to respond—while offering our opinions as to how this might be done, of course.

It was not really part of our plan to measure the impact of our newspaper on the issues we addressed. We weren't terribly interested in our influence or in the effect we were having on the currently existing metanarrative of feminism/anti-feminism. We were writing and publishing from within a social movement, reflecting and interpreting our own perceptions of what was important—important to our readers and important to us as a movement. The only indicator of our success that we had to consider was our ability to attract subscribers. Our funders required this as well, but it was a flawed metric. Any true discussion of our influence was, of necessity, 100 per cent hindsight.

It is only now that it has become important to look back at our impact and I think it's fair to say that the impact of second-wave feminism on everything has been considerable. Although much of what we were working for in the 1980s hasn't changed appreciably, if at all, some things have changed enormously. While reading through the articles we published thirty to forty years ago, we couldn't help being surprised at what was concerning us back then, things we don't think about at all now. People don't talk about the "chairman" of the department, we talk about the "chair," but that was a big fight back then. We don't talk about mankind, or Mrs., or he (when we mean he or she, or just she), but those were big fights, too. Our place in the public sphere was much more restricted then. Our workplaces were different (check out *Mad Men*), as were our relationships (LGBTQ anyone?), and clothes, and slang. But more significantly, when we started out, abortion was still criminalized; men couldn't be convicted of raping their wives; women often had to have a man, any man, co-sign their loans; girls couldn't join soccer or hockey leagues; we were expected to laugh at sexist insults and put up with bad behaviour from men. This was the reality of our lives and the day-to-day struggles we faced.

And, of course, technology is vastly different from what it was then, which has affected us all in life-altering ways. It's hard to remember that everything that happened in the 1970s and 1980s happened before email, before cell phones, before the Internet, even before personal computers, as they were known then. Everything was, in a sense, manual. Everything from typesetting, to design, to cut-and-paste editing, to communicating—the only forms available to us were typewritten letters or the telephone—with no voice mail. It all took longer and was more complicated. Imagine that if you wanted to move a paragraph from one page to another, you had to physically cut the paragraph from one page and paste it in with glue, say, two pages later. Your only other option was to type the whole document over again every time you needed to make a change. It's all too easy to forget, but the way we operated on a daily basis changed completely in the 1990s, after *Broadside* had folded.

ENDINGS

As the 1980s came to a close, it became time for members of the collective to readjust and recalibrate our purpose and goals, both societally and personally. We had worked very hard for ten years to bring some important aspects of women's lives to the forefront. We had tried to explain various phenomena that had not been named before, or were taboo in polite circles, or were largely inexplicable in a culture where male behavioural norms and customs dominated and, in some cases, obliterated anything else. By the end of the decade, some things had changed appreciably, as demonstrated by many of the articles published in *Inside Broadside*, and many of us felt we'd given it our best shot—there were other women who could assume the mantle. We closed up shop after our tenth-anniversary issue (Vol. 10, No. 1, October 1988) with our final issue (Vol. 10, No. 5, May 1989). As we wrote on our broadsidefeminist.com website, in 2013:

> There is no simple reason why Broadside ceased publishing; several factors played a part. Some of it had to do with the changes going on in our own community. We were an all-white collective with an all-white sensibility, which in itself was making us less and

less relevant within a movement in which women of colour were seeking more voice and leadership. As it was we were a credible publication—almost an institution—with no money. Our subscriptions numbered over 3,000, which by Canadian standards was not low—at the time 85 per cent of publications in Canada had less than 2,000 subscribers. But we had reached maximum growth. And members of the collective were going through their own changes. Among them, after 10 years, Phil Masters decided to take a position at a long established feminist publication, the academic journal Resources for Feminist Research (RFR), published out of the Centre for Women's Studies at the Ontario Institute for Studies in Education (U of T).

I continued to work part-time for both *Broadside* and *RFR* for a couple of years, but my focus was split. So it was with great sadness that we dismantled our office of ten years at 455 Spadina Ave., in the Tip Top Tailor Building. Most of our papers went to the Canadian Women's Movement Archives—at the time in the same

The front-page image for *Broadside*'s final issue was chosen to reflect the diversity of our coverage.

10 years of Broadside!

building, on the same floor, so it was an easy move, though it now has a permanent home at the University of Ottawa. Some of the rest, such as light tables, back issues, art boards, and photo-negatives of the entire run, went into various basements (mostly mine), the furniture went here and there, and our subscription list went to the Black Women's Collective's newspaper, *Our Lives*. Again, from broadsidefeminist.com:

> When we announced that Broadside was folding we were flooded with letters from feminists from all over the country mourning the demise of the newspaper [read them in Chapter 1]. If we weren't convinced of Broadside's value at the moment we decided to cease publication, those testimonials assured us that it had played an essential role in gaining justice for women.

And as I wrote in our final editorial in May 1989 about planning *Broadside*'s last issue: "We started with the idea of a retrospective, ten years in the life of feminism in Canada. But this is a false category, based solely on the fact that *Broadside* published for ten years and is now folding. Feminism isn't folding." And now here we are, thirty to forty years later, in many ways still alive, hopefully providing another spark to ignite women's activism and aspirations for a future of exploration and empowerment, debates and discoveries, and in some ways just plain amazed at what we, collectively, have done with our lives.

CHAPTER 1

Opinions: Ours and Yours

Opinions, from our writers, from our readers—the ones who loved us, the ones whom we outraged—and the points of view of the Broadside collective. We begin our *Broadside* survey here, proudly and pointedly, because as feminist publishers, we never feared subjectivity. In fact, we embraced it. We saw that conventional journalistic standards of "objectivity" were actually fake and knew that mainstream newspapers and magazines—including the so-called women's magazines—for the most part upheld sexist values. Their editors were making choices that weren't objective at all and their contributors wrote with their own biases intact.

Although many publications open with letters to the editor, that isn't why *Broadside* began each issue with words from our readers. We made that choice because one of our essential commitments was to the voices of women who'd had few outlets to express themselves before *Broadside* began publishing. Proof of the importance of that strategy was that *Broadside* received many more letters to the editor per reader than the average publication. We never had to pad the letters section; women from all over the country were more than happy to give us their opinions. Our readers yearned to be heard and responded to almost every article with unusual fervour. *Broadside* readers often sent us three- and four-page letters responding to articles or introducing us to new issues—and new writers—a further testament to the need for *Broadside* as a forum. But at a certain point, as we mentioned in the introduction, these missives got so lengthy that we had to run a special editorial telling our readers that letters could only be a certain length to be considered for publication.

Often, as you'll see, readers wrote just to thank us for existing. Throughout our decade of publishing, these particular letters propelled us along in the face of constant financial worries and—given that the paper was driven almost entirely by volunteers—borderline burnout. When the letters started flooding in after we announced that we would stop publication, we were deeply moved. Throughout our decade of publishing, our readers proved themselves wise, angry—for good reason—and fully engaged.

Also in this section are opinion pieces from writers with powerful points of view. Their subject matter reflects the preoccupations of the women's movement during the 1980s. You'll notice, for example, that many of them are on pornography and censorship, the subject of fierce debate for five years. Others are from a section called Movement Comment. We were always committed to the idea that feminist strategies needed to be discussed and challenged. The opinion columns came from some of Canada's best-known writers and public figures—Grace Hartman, Sarah Sheard, June Callwood, for example—and often from activists on the front lines, either of women's services or the courts. We suspected that the women doing the work had more insight than pundits who were watching from the sidelines. It's no wonder all of these columns have a palpable passion.

A note about the editorials: they cover everything from free trade to Nestlé's baby formula and abortion law. Often, in the midst of a bitter debate inside the women's community, we felt the need to express a collective opinion. When we say collective opinion, we mean it. Surprisingly—miraculously, some might say—we came to the point of view contained in these editorials by consensus. We found ways to discuss our issues so that we could emerge fully capable of producing an opinion piece that we could all support. In putting together this section, we could sometimes not, in fact, remember who wrote even the most contentious of them.

Now for the fun part. Feminists—unfairly, some of us think—were mercilessly criticized for lacking a sense of humour. In a moment of defensiveness, we might have said that women's oppression is no laughing matter. But at the same time we wanted to dispel the myth of the grim feminist and welcomed contributions from writers who liked to play. Crosswords figured prominently. One of our most popular humour writers was Mary Hemlow, who wrote under a pseudonym because her caustic commentary seemed to come from right inside the government (it did). Sarah Sheard's piece, published here, about the problem of having big feet and finding shoes in stores was a big hit, and Judith Quinlan's chess game is a riot. Feminists are not actually a bunch of earnest bores.

So here's to powerful opinion—and fun and games. And remember, there's a lot more of this in the original digitized version of *Broadside* at broadsidefeminist.com. Check it out too.

Susan G. Cole

LETTERS

Introductory Issue (May 1979), p. 3

Dear *Broadside*:

I couldn't for the life of me figure out why you had chosen the name *Broadside* for your newspaper. I took it upon myself to seize hold of *The Compact Edition of the Oxford English Dictionary* (and my magnifying glass of course) to find out exactly what the word broadside means. Much to my surprise I discovered that broadside, in nautical terms, refers to a discharge of artillery from the side of a ship. I took this to imply that your newspaper intended to hurl a series of volleys at the varying bizarre turns of the world's events. How right I was, for indeed broadside also means a verbal assault, which I hope *Broadside* will continue to launch against those forces which keep members of our sex down.

Can you imagine my delight at reading that *Broadside* is also defined as a newspaper printed on one side of the sheet. After reading your introductory issue, I do hope that you continue to write your splendid prose on both sides. Did you know that a broadsider collects broadsides? My Oxford dictionary told me that too. And I'm pleased to report that I intend to remain a broadsider for many years hence.

Did you read your *Compact Edition of the Oxford English Dictionary* before you chose the name?

For broadsiding,
Ms. Sue de Nim
Toronto

[From the editors: yes, we did.]

Volume 1, No. 1 (October 1979), p. 3

Broadside:
You have no idea what joy I felt when I received your complimentary copy of *Broadside*. I have approached the regular newspapers with increasing despair and have felt there has been a crying need for a newspaper such as yours for a long time. Bless you! I have already got the Women's Resource Centre interested and will be doing some more groundwork at my church and some organizations I think might recognize the benefits you are promising.

Please hurry and get into (more) print.

P.S. I love your name.

Kim Naish
Peterborough, Ontario

Volume 1, No. 1 (October 1979), p. 3

Broadside:
I object strongly to the title of the newspaper (*Broadside*), but it's good work. Congratulations.

Lucinda Flavelle
Mississauga, Ontario

Volume 1, No. 3 (December 1979), p. 2

Broadside:
It's interesting that your name is so similar to ours (*Broadsheet*) and I note that you are getting very much the same criticisms as we did. Whence decided on *Broadsheet* it was partly an act of desperation, so many of the possible names had already been used. We like *Broadsheet* because it was reclaiming a word, was tongue

in cheek and also described the actual format of our magazine as it was when we started off. Sometimes I wish we had been able to come up with something stunningly original, witty, etc., but as you probably found out it's hard coming up with the goods.

Sandra Coney, *Broadsheet*
Auckland, New Zealand

Volume 2, No. 10 (August/September 1981), p. 2

Broadside:
Thank you for the letter reminding me I'd said I was interested in writing about pornography for *Broadside*.

When I thought the idea over I realized that I had too much on my plate to do a real survey of pornography and perhaps that wasn't what I wanted to consider anyway.

What worries me is a note of Grundy-ism entering into many considerations of sex by feminist magazines. Since some relationships with some men are bad, all have by extension become bad. Since some writing-about-sex is corrupting, all is corrupting, etc.

This of course denies us the freedom, newly acquired, to write about sex in our own way, and writers are worried. That this denial of freedom should come from a liberation movement is ironic.

It does creep into *Broadside* quite a lot, mostly in the form of a lack of charity towards women writers whose work the reviewers disagree with (*viz* the article on Sylvia Fraser, February 1981). Surely *Broadside* was never intended to be narrow-minded!

For further material on this theme I refer your readers to Jane Rule's essay "The Sex War" in *Outlander*.

Good luck and best wishes to *Broadside*, which I like a lot.

Marian Engel
Toronto

Women and Words
Volume 5, No. 1 (October 1983), p. 2

Broadside:

We read with interest and amazement your account of the Women and Words Conference (Eve Zaremba, "The Writing on the Wall," Aug./Sept., Vol. 4, no. 10). We make specific reference to the paragraphs on the participation of women of colour, immigrant women and native women. We would like to note that we are critical of this article and not the conference. The article is a misrepresentation of the participation of women of colour (indeed, we are not even mentioned), native and immigrant women and the issues we raised, issues which, by the way, were widely discussed both formally and informally at the conference.

It is patronizing and patriarchal to state that "it was not just that native and immigrant women from many backgrounds attended or even that they spoke up. What matters is that they were heard." This stinks. It stinks of men paying lip service to women so that they will not be accused of sexism. This is exactly what Zaremba is doing if we substitute the word sexism for racism and the word men for women.

Speaking up is a "courtesy" extended to one's social inferiors, minors, and women in the patriarchal mode of discourse. We gather from Zaremba's analysis that what we had to say was of little importance. What was important for her was that white women granted us the courtesy of "hearing" it.

"Admittedly," she writes, "it will take much more than patience and courtesy to break through the cultural chauvinism of the majority whose roots are in the dominant culture and whose ignorance of all else is often difficult to distinguish from racism." Difficult for whom? Patience by whom and with whom? Pray tell!

This dominant culture business. Please! The dominant culture in Canada is capitalism and white skin privilege plays no small part in propping it up. We belong to the majority—women—and our roots are not in the dominant culture, neither are Zaremba's if she takes the time to check.

It is not only "cultural chauvinism" which needs a breakthrough but also, and more importantly, the political analysis of Zaremba's so-called majority.

Zaremba is not alone in her rather shaky analysis. It brings to mind an encounter we had with a white middle class feminist critic who told us that we should not mistake dominant behaviour for racism. What crap. Are we also to think that rape is only a matter of dominant behaviour?

Give Zaremba her due, she does continue: "But those distinctions must be made and those qualities of mutual respect cultivated if we hope to go on and get anywhere." But her appeal here to "mutual respect" belies her paternalism on the subject. Given those terms of reference, who needs it?

We trust you appreciate our "speaking up" again. Please grant us your "attentiveness and good will" in having the courtesy to print this letter in its entirety.

In sisterhood nevertheless,
Makeda Silvera and Dionne Brand
Toronto

A What?
Volume 6, No. 4 (February 1985), p. 2

Broadside:
As a faithful reader and sporadic contributor, I appreciate the collective's continuing efforts to make *Broadside* a credible publication. But, alas, even the best of intentions cannot prevent the occasional error from slipping into the copy. I know it happens to every writer—their words, so carefully chosen, are misprinted in even the most expensive of publications. But in the December 1984 issue of *Broadside* ("Spooking the Snools: Scriptures According to Mary Daly,") it happened to my favorite word!

There I referred to Alfred North Whitehead's "asymptotic descriptions" or definitional structures in language. Asymptote is a wonderful word. It means "a line which approaches nearer and nearer to a given curve, but does not meet it within a finite distance." Ah, the anticipation in the infinite approach! What appeared was, "asymptomatic," which does not appear in the OED. Poor old Alfred would roll over in his grave.

The same day, an article on slips such as this appeared in *The Globe and Mail*. And it made me feel just a little bit better—at least I could give the demise of my favorite word a name. It read: "...linguists have been interested in slips for reasons of their own. Their main concern is to detect errors that creep into a test in the course of it being passed along from version to version; for example, by a typist or printer's mistake. One of the most common kinds of errors linguists have identified is what is called "banalization," the replacement of an intended word by an erroneous one that is more familiar or simpler."

Carlyn Moulton
Toronto

Father Tongue
Volume 6, No. 4 (February 1985), p. 2

Broadside:
I was intrigued and excited by the work that Betsy Warland and Daphne Marlatt are doing with language in their poetry or rather with the language of their poetry (*Broadside*, December 1984).

In the reported interview, Betsy Warland talked of discovering a "mother tongue" and Daphne Marlatt made the connection with "father land." The problem, i.e. of reclaiming language, has presented itself somewhat differently for me, a New World Black poet.

Although English is my "mother tongue," I have been aware for some time now that I do not in fact possess a mother tongue, and that English is my father tongue—the language of the male white colonizer.

The languages that my African ancestors would have brought with them to the New World were by and large destroyed along with their cultures, religions and histories. The English language, with all its references to the non-being of the African, was then imposed on them. This linguistic rape and subsequent forced marriage has resulted in a language capable of great rhythms and musicality—a language which is and is not English—and one which is probably one of the most vital in the English speaking world today.

I approach English as we know it in Canada—standard English—as essentially a foreign language. I know no African language, one or several of which would have truly been my mother tongue.

My quest is therefore to discover what is in fact my mother tongue, given that odd and brutal coincidence of events that has placed me here in the New World. One way would be to learn an African language; the other, which has more immediate relevance to me since I continue to write in my father tongue, is to execute by some alchemical process (alchemy from al-kimiya, the art of the black and Egypt), a metamorphosis in the language, from father tongue to mother tongue, and in that process some aspects of the language will have to be destroyed; new ones created.

At this time I have many more questions than answers but it is reassuring to see others involved in a similar process of change.

Marlene Nourbese Philip
Toronto

No Free Trade!
Volume 9, No. 2 (November 1987), p. 2

The following open letter was sent in September to organizations across Canada, and to all elected representatives of federal provincial and municipal governments:

Broadside:
As Canadians, we are approaching a fateful moment in the history of our country, as the federal government of Canada intends to initial a Free Trade Agreement with the United States. Such an accord will profoundly affect the social, cultural, economic, and political life of Canada. Yet free trade negotiations have taken place behind closed doors, without significant input from the Canadian people.

We speak as individuals and organizations from all regions of Canada: labour unions, farm organizations, church groups, women's organizations, cultural associations, aboriginal groups, community groups, professional associations, environmental groups, academic organizations, peace groups, seniors' organizations. We maintain there are grave dangers to our livelihood and our way of life in a Free Trade Agreement with the United States.

The potential costs of free trade include:

1) gradual elimination of agricultural marketing boards, tariffs and quotas, causing farmers to lose their farms and livelihood;

2) reduction or removal of federal assistance programs for regional economic development, with devastating effect on poorer provinces and regions;

3) diminished Canadian control over resource and energy pricing, discouraging diversification in resource-dependent regions like Western Canada;

4) greater US access to and control over Canada's oil, gas, and other natural resources, reducing our ability to conserve non-renewable resources for long-term development;

5) inability to protect Canada's environment via government subsidy and public regulation;

6) further undercutting of food processing, electrical products, textiles and clothing, and other vital, labour-intensive industries, with attendant job losses;

7) weakening of major manufacturing industries such as auto, through reduction of tariff and quota protection;

8) rights of "establishment" and "national treatment" for American service industries in Canada, posing a threat to workers in communications, financial services, advertising, data processing, health care, etc., many of whom are women; and undermining public provision and regulation of services in Canada;

9) removal of restrictions on US investment in Canada, and an end to screening for Canadian content, job guarantees and export levels;

10) erosion of social programs like Medicare and Unemployment Insurance (e.g. to fishers) on grounds of "unfair subsidy" or by pressure to harmonize taxes and business costs in Canada and the US;

11) flooding of Canada with even more US television, radio, publications, and entertainment, with further assimilation into mainstream American culture and undermining the achievements of Canadian artists; restriction of our ability to build Canadian culture through direct grants and distribution programs;

12) a strengthened, new form of continental protectionism— Fortress North America—preventing third world countries from seeking special trade relations with Canada;

13) closer ties to the US military-industrial complex, limiting Canada's ability to play an important role promoting peace and nuclear disarmament;

14) limitation of our ability to pursue an independent foreign policy for the promotion of human rights and the reception of refugees, especially in relation to countries dominated by US economic and military pressures;

15) erosion of our political sovereignty over territorial lands, waters and fisheries, especially in arctic and coastal regions;

16) "harmonization" of Canadian labour standards and collective bargaining rights with those of American non-union "right to work" states;

17) new emphasis on market-oriented values and priorities in our society and culture; especially values which reflect selfishness rather than community needs.

Some of these changes would immediately follow a US-Canada Free Trade Agreement. Others would come more gradually, as Canada harmonizes its policies and regulations with those of the US. Much has been said about a binding trade dispute mechanism. We do not believe such a mechanism would resolve the problems free trade presents. Even if it overrode all American trade remedy laws—an unlikely prospect—a binding mechanism might actually magnify some of the costs of free trade.

The coming months are crucial for our future. Yet at the level of federal politics, all we have been promised is a debate among members of Parliament. This is entirely insufficient. We favour extensive public hearings at all levels of government. These can serve to expand discussion, debate, and participation. However, hearings alone will not suffice for so momentous a decision. Only a general election centering on the issue of free trade can generate the public discussion and debate necessary at this moment in our history. The people of Canada must decide.

We demand a general election be held immediately to determine whether or not the people of Canada are prepared to give the federal government a mandate to sign and implement a US–Canada Free Trade Agreement.

Grace Hartman
Pro-Canada Network
Ottawa

Deliberate Decision
Volume 9, No. 3 (December 1987/January 1988), p. 3

Broadside:
In Margaret Buist's excellent article, "One Foot in the Door" (October 1987), she described the continued fight for women's equality and how the Charter of Rights and Freedoms is being used for and against us. It is important, I think, to clarify one essential point. The author states that just five years after fighting to have our rights entrenched in the Charter when it was first formed, it is necessary for us to do so again as a result of the Meech Lake Accord. She says that "in those few hours of bargaining at Meech Lake, it appears that the men did not even consider section 15, or worse, they considered it and rejected its significance."

I believe that the intention was far more serious. On the last day of its hearings, the Commons-Senate Committee on the Constitution heard from Senator Lowell Murray, the Minister of Federal-Provincial Relations, and Norman Spector, Secretary to the Cabinet for Federal-Provincial Affairs, who told the members that the first ministers examined and then rejected the idea of inserting equality guarantees for women. Spector said that this exclusion was not an oversight, and that the ministers had had their longest discussion over the relationship between the "distinct society clause," and the Charter of Rights.

The Prime Minister and the first ministers know full well that the Charter would be affected. Their decision was not only deliberate, it was critical to reaching agreement. Had section 15 been altered to include women, Spector testified, there would have been no deal. The ministers were motivated by "political reasons" as they believed that a distinct society subject to review of the Charter would be "meaningless."

Once again, women were used as a bargaining chip in a constitutional deal. Once again, women lost. It is critical that we know this, as it will inform our strategy in the upcoming months.

Maude Barlow
Ottawa

Women's Railroad
Volume 10, No. 5 (August/September 1989), p. 3

Broadside:
What can I say? I feel I can imagine the exhaustion and frustration that led to this conclusion. Like you, I hope it will be a necessary pause for rest, breath, and fresh energy and support.

I received your letter with such regret, such sadness and know that across the country women are taking stock and wondering what we can do to lead to other recharging of our newspapers. Please know that we'll all be thinking, meditating, ranting, and raving about it, hoping like you for a solution. The work of the last ten years has been more than an inspiration. It has been the women's railroad connecting us across the country, across our regional, racial, cultural and political spaces.

Sincerely,
Rina Fraticelli,
Executive Producer,
Studio D,
The National Film Board of Canada
Montreal, Quebec

Fairminded

Volume 10, No. 5 (August/September 1989), p. 3

Broadside:

I'm very sorry to hear that *Broadside* has suspended publication. I think it was wonderfully successful as a source of feminist views, that it was fairminded and conscientious. It will be missed, since there's nothing else like it (that I know of).

With best wishes,
Mary Meigs
Westmount, Quebec

Valuable Girder

Volume 10, No. 5 (August/September 1989), p. 3

Broadside:

I am sorry that *Broadside* will be no more. You have all produced a paper that has been a crucial and valuable girder of the women's movement. It has been hard to imagine the absence of *Broadside*. But I know it's important to take care of yourselves to be able to continue to move on at other times. My one voice of thanks, among many, for all collective members and *Broadside* contributors past and present that have made *Broadside* happen each issue.

In sisterhood,
Nikki Colodny,
Toronto, Ontario

Remarkable Accomplishment
Volume 10, No. 5 (August/September 1989), p. 3

Broadside:

I imagine I am among many women who are very sorry to hear that *Broadside* is suspending publication. I hope it is, ultimately, merely a suspension and not a demise.

I enclose a cheque as a contribution toward the 10th anniversary issue—to use for printing or champagne.

And I do think champagne (or a non-alcoholic equivalent) is in order to celebrate 10 years of toil, commitment, thought, creation, drudgery—10 years of women's words made tangible. It is indeed a remarkable accomplishment. And I hope, after some time for resting, there will be bursts of energy in various quarters of the women's movement as the revitalized women of *Broadside* disperse to continue their inciteful activities.

Thanks for your work,
Megan Ellis
Vancouver, B.C.

Outside the Mainstream
Volume 10, No. 5 (August/September 1989), p. 3

Broadside:

Congratulations on ten years of successful publication! I'm happy to hear that you are planning an anniversary issue, and I'm sad and thoughtful about the news that you've suspended publication. While living in Santa Cruz I saw *Matrix* struggle with issues similar to yours, as did *Plexus* in the Bay Area. I personally sympathize with the sense of financial insecurity so often linked to work outside the mainstream. So I'm sending what I can to support your effort and I'll look forward to receiving my copy.

I'd also like to pass on, to those of you who were on staff when I was writing a film column, a compliment that meant a lot to me. Adrienne Rich, with whom I worked while I was a member of New Jewish Agenda in Santa Cruz, said she first knew me as

Barbara Halpern Martineau in *Broadside*—she said "No one in the US was writing about the material you were dealing with—it was very important." The words tied my past to my considerably altered present—I was grateful to Adrienne and also to *Broadside* for giving me a forum.

Warm regards,
Sara Halprin
Haleiwa, Hawaii

Mainstay in the Community
Volume 10, No. 5 (August/September 1989), p. 3

Broadside:

To say we were saddened doesn't quite seem to do it. It's devastating news that *Broadside* is at least temporarily ceasing publication.

We certainly share your view that the political climate is a difficult one for us to survive in right now, let alone put up with the "normal" working conditions we've become accustomed to, like high turnover, burnout and lack of adequate resources to publish. I just hope that we haven't all been stricken with the same patriarchally-inspired disease; one that strikes unsuspecting feminist publications just when things appear to be going well.

If you don't agree with the conspiracy theory, there's the more healthy, optimistic outlook that says that a period of retreat can be a period of rejuvenation. After all, it's only normal that we get tired once in a while and take some time out to be introspective, distracted, lazy, indulgent even, or whatever strikes us at the time.

It was very hard for us to separate the stress, anxiety and general negativity that in difficult times pervades our environment, from the product we managed to create in spite of these factors. Now, looking back we have all felt incredibly proud and validated upon looking at our "product"...somehow those feelings are what fall to the wayside when crises in funding and woman power are priorities. We are hopeful that some of the inspiration you provided your readers over the last 10 year will be there now to sustain you, and in the future as well.

As feminist publishers, we continue as best we can and when we can, it seems. *Broadside* has been a real mainstay within this publishing community and we continue to have great respect for the women who have produced *Broadside*.

Wishing you the best of luck in your future efforts. Hopefully we'll both be at it again soon. In the spirit of sisterhood and co-operation.

Penni Mitchell for Herizons
Winnipeg, Manitoba

Well Earned Rest
Volume 10, No. 5 (August/September 1989), p. 3

Broadside:
We write to tell you how sorry we are that you are no longer able to continue. Believe me, we understand only too well your problems. We also have been looking, for some time, for another group to take over but, alas, with no success.

Congratulations for having done so much for so long. May your publication soon be revived—and may you enjoy a well earned rest.

With sisterly affection,
The Womanspirit Collective
Australia

Cheers
Volume 10, No. 5 (August/September 1989), p. 3

Broadside:
Here's for *Broadside*, and here's to *Broadside*. It has been a great publication and it will be mourned everywhere.

June Callwood
Toronto, Ontario

One of the Best
Volume 10, No. 5 (August/September 1989), p. 3

Broadside:
I was sorry to get this news, but I understand only too well from my own involvement with *Broadside* what you mean by energy drain and financial problems. If there is a group that can pick up the paper, great, but if not you and all of us who have been part of the paper over the years can feel proud of having produced one of the best feminist papers in the country.

Sincerely,
Jean Wilson
British Columbia

Heroic Enterprise
Volume 10, No. 5 (August/September 1989), p. 3

Broadside:
All in the same week these deaths were announced: the artistic director of the Royal Winnipeg Ballet, Abbie Hoffman, the wife of a friend in Warsaw, and *Broadside*. It's too much.

Although it's been years since I contributed as a writer to *Broadside*, I was a faithful subscriber and reader. I loved the paper. I feel awful about its demise, although I can understand the causes. What does it say about our struggle/movement when a feminist newspaper can no longer be sustained in a population of 13 million women/girls, 20 years into a revolutionary liberation movement? If I ever get my head out of eastern Europe, I intend to make my own answer to that.

In the meantime, please accept my donation with heartfelt thanks for a heroic enterprise which kept us all together, coast to coast, with verve, cheek, intelligence and style for so long.

In solidarity,
Myrna Kostash
Edmonton, Alberta

THIS IS BROADSIDE

Introductory Issue (May 1979), p. 2

This issue of *Broadside* is an introduction, a shadow of its future self. We hope these skeletal pages will give you an idea of what is to come, starting September 1979.

In many ways *Broadside* is a review: a review of the arts, a review of the news; all filtered through a pro-woman screen. Included in this issue are investigative stories, analyses, interviews with woman artists, columns, cartoons, local community events. We plan to continue in this vein. Sometimes we will run a feature for several issues, as we intend to do with our story on women in the media. This issue it's print media, next it will be broadcast media. Already we have commitments from well-respected, established Canadian women writers to provide copy for *Broadside*.

What is missing from this introductory issue is input from our readers. We want *Broadside* to be a dialogue, not just our own encapsulated view of the world. To stimulate participation we plan to hold public meetings every few months to discuss the content of the latest issues of *Broadside*, to exchange ideas, to keep in touch. We also want readers to feel free to submit letters for publication and to send ideas for future stories. And we plan to institute the habit of exchanges with other women's publications, for increased flow of news and views.

Although *Broadside* is based in Toronto and will cover local concerns, it is not in any way restricted to the Toronto scene. Through our exchanges we will keep our figurative eyes and ears open to the rest of Canada and the world beyond. We also will rely on a far-reaching network of contacts, women who will work for *Broadside*: by distributing the paper, selling subscriptions, writing copy. *Broadside* collective members have already begun to fan out and set this process in motion: we now have contacts in Vancouver, San Francisco and Montreal.

Which brings us to another point: *Broadside* is an English-language paper, although that doesn't prevent us from accepting copy written in other languages, to be translated. We will also run translated excerpts from other-language publications (duly credited). We hope *Broadside* stories will get the same treatment.

And now—the information you've all been waiting for: how to work for *Broadside*. (We've already had thousands clamouring at our doors.) It's a 3-stage process. Stage 1 includes any woman who wants to do anything for *Broadside*: write, layout, answer phones, sell subscriptions, solicit ads, distribute the paper, take out the garbage, set up systems to do all the above, etc. etc. Any woman is welcome. Drop us a line or talk to a collective member (readily identifiable by our arm garters and eyeshades.) We will be in touch with you.

Stage 2 includes those women who wish to become collective members. This involves a more consistent commitment of time and energy. The system has not been entirely formulated as yet, but we expect that a woman will work on the paper for a period of several months at which time a discussion will take place between the collective and the prospective member to explore the possibility (ie. she has to be able to work with us and we with her.) After that the process of formally joining the collective can take place.

That brings us to stage 3: although *Broadside*'s working structure is a collective, we are in fact a legally chartered business corporation. That means the collective members (11 of us) are also directors of the

Women Against Violence Against Women (WAVAW) cenotaph boldly refocused Remembrance Day.

NOVEMBER 11 — REMEMBRANCE DAY

Sixty-one years ago, on November 11th 1918 at 11 a.m. Armistice was signed and the First World War was over.

On that date every year since then, victory is celebrated and fallen men remembered in ceremonies at cenotaphs up and down this land.

For the past two years, Toronto women have attended the Armistice Day service at Toronto City Hall. They came in silent solidarity to lay flowers at the foot of a different cenotaph. A cenotaph created in memory of all women who are victims of wars past, present and future, the world over.

During this brief ceremony, a speech is read:

"On this day, when we remember the agonies which war brings to the lives of ordinary people, the women of this city remember too the grief, terror, and violence which have always been part of women's experience of war. It is in remembrance of these unsung women that we each bring a flower of compassion and solidarity to this place on this day. We remember expressly that the rape of women marches like a dark shadow in the ranks of every army and lingers long in every female consciousness as an inevitable reality of women and war."

Toronto women will be at the Old City Hall again this year at 11 a.m. Join us there. Bring a flower.

This tradition should continue. May the idea spread to other cities, towns and villages. People must not be allowed to ignore or forget that women are the spoils of war and the victims of both winner and loser.

company (Broadside Communications Ltd.—we have big plans). A prospective collective member must become a board member, complete with financial commitment and legal liability. We, the current collective, think the legal, profit-making business structure is to the advantage of everyone concerned. We want *Broadside* to be a successful business, with the possibility of paying staff and contributors as our revenues mount.

We also want *Broadside* supporters to have the advantage of investing their money rather than donating it. That way they can get it back, if they're so ill-advised as to want it back.

The *Broadside* collective is a motley crew (see masthead for our names). We include a few seasoned journalists, writers of various sorts, typesetters, a printer, some graphic artists, a few financial wizards, one or two social workers, a puppeteer and a closet taxidermist. (References on request.) That should provide a broad enough cross-section of the population to produce a unique newspaper.

Having now whetted your appetite for future words from *Broadside*, we hope you will fill out the subscription forms on the back page for yourself and 50 of your closest friends.

VOLLEY NUMBER SIX: A SUGAR-COATED PILL
Volume 1, No. 6 (1980), p. 2

In this issue we tell the story of the Nestlé corporation's attempts to encourage Third World women to administer the Nestlé formula to their young babies. The fact that these women haven't the facilities to sterilize the bottles, the fact that the instructions for the dilution are remarkably vague, the fact that this has caused a near epidemic of malnutrition among Nestlé-fed babies, has not prevented the huge Swiss multinational corporation from continuing its rigourous campaign to sell the formula all over the world. Nestlé has steadfastly refused to accept corporate responsibility for the abuse of their product.

The Nestlé case is not an isolated one. 1700 Puerto Rico women were plied with oral contraceptives in the early sixties. They were human guinea pigs, never aware of the dangers of the experiment. And this phenomenon of keeping women in the dark about such matters hit closer to home when the oral contraceptive, our supposed saviour, was placed on the market in North America. It was at least six years after the birth control pill's appearance on the scene that the rumblings about side effects were heard. Even then doctors insisted that their patients, complaining of depression and leg cramps, were hysterical and had read too many newspaper scares.

The drug companies forged on, flogging oral contraceptives, advertising that the pill was safe. Naturally, since two drug companies, Ortho Pharmaceutical (a division of Johnson and Johnson) and Wyeth (a subsidiary of American Home Products) monopolize 70% of the oral contraceptive market in Canada. The profits from the oral contraceptive in 1976 were two and a half times higher than the profits of the drug industry as a whole. What this means is that the pill is "marked up" two and a half times that of any other drug. This demonstrates very simply a cartel, a gentlemen's agreement among drug companies to keep the price up. So we can see why we have heard so many assurances from the pharmaceuticals that the pill is safe—it is not in their interest to tell us otherwise.

More on the drug front. Valium is the most heavily prescribed drug in North America. Its sales volume is the highest of any drug in Canada. It is prescribed to women two to three times as often as to men. Hoffman-LaRoche, the Swiss pharmaceutical that first developed the drug, boasts sales of well over two billion dollars for Valium and Librium alone.

What we are seeing through these examples of corporate irresponsibility is a syndrome in which women are actively infantilized. Nestlé knows that their consumers believe the bottled formula has magical powers, that the bottles are filled with soda pop by mothers who hope that some of the magic will rub off. Ortho and Wyeth at least have doctors administer oral contraceptives, doctors who press the packet into the hands of women and send them of with a pat on the back and assurances that all will be well. And how much more accepted a form of infantilization than when women are numbed by Valium into a false sense of calm so that no questions need come to mind?

The news is not all bad. In fact there have been developments that are promising indeed. The Nestlé boycott is an example of the efforts being made to make corporations accountable. And whereas in the past it was felt that women were so desperate for an effective birth control device that boycotting was not an option, the number of prescriptions for the oral contraceptives filled by pharmacologists in the US dropped 25% between 1975 and 1978. In particular, the number of prescriptions for Ortho's brand filled that same period plummeted 43%. (N.B. Prescriptions for diaphragms between 1975 and 1978 skyrocketed 140%). While Hoffman-LaRoche is struggling in court to defend itself against a charge of undercutting the price of Valium, that drug is on the decline as well.

What all this suggests is that in spite of the efforts of corporations to abdicate responsibility for the quality of their products and the way that they are used, women are finding out the crucial information, absorbing it, making choices and taking action. And we are hitting the multinationals where it hurts, at the bottom line. Ultimately that's the only way to put an end to the syndrome.

WIFE BEATING...

Volume 3, No. 8 (June 1982), p. 2

When we heard that Saskatchewan ex-Premier Allan Blakeney wanted to trade two women's rights for a Native right in the constitutional debate, the fact that we are governed by male caprice hit home to millions of Canadian women. The rights of women could be bandied about like a squash ball, or so our fearless leaders thought. You may have noticed that Allan Blakeney is no longer counted among our fearless leaders. We hope his quotable quote still haunts him.

During the constitutional debate many women came of age politically and consciousness was raised in unusual quarters. But the subject then was civil rights, an abstract principle that exercised theoretical ideas only. But the word "fearless" was wasted until our fearless leaders started laughing about wife battery. Now the issue of our physical safety is at stake.

By now all of us are undoubtedly aware of what happened in the House of Commons last May 12. Margaret Mitchell (NDP

Vancouver) asked why the shelter situation for battered women was so dreadful, and what was the Canadian government going to do about it.

A hearty guffaw rose from the house.

We'll never know exactly who caused the uproar. Parliament has its own ways of covering itself. Even Margaret Mitchell herself refused to identify the culprits, feeling that since the reaction in the House was so widespread (yes, a few NDP members harrumphed with glee), singling out individuals without naming every name would be unfair.

She sought instead, on May 13th, to secure from the House of Commons an apology to all the women of Canada. And the sorry saga continued.

Apologies pass in the House only if they receive unanimous approval. No go. Speaker Jeanne Sauvé heard some "no's" from the Liberal side of the house. The dissenting Liberals claimed that they *always* say no to motions for apologies that come from the opposition. Party politics will always have priority over the female constituency.

Marcel Roy (Liberal Laval) gave it a try. "Nos" were heard again, this time because Anglophone MPs had not put on their translation headphones fast enough. One can imagine the English-speaking Members languishing in their chairs while Roy went on in that foreign language. The respect accorded to Francophone MPs is probably only several cuts above the respect MPs can muster for the women of this country.

Finally, Ursula Appolloni (York South-Weston) wrenched out an apology to the women of Canada from the House on May 14th. It took two days chock-filled with furious telegrams and vituperative press for Members of Parliament to get the message.

One might well ask what the MPs were laughing about in the first place. Nervous laughter they called it. Did we hear the House snigger away at the deaths of seamen off the coast of Newfoundland? Did they howl at the hilarity of mercury poisoning of fishing waters natives rely on for their survival? Would they have got away with it if they had?

Then again, let's just deal with the facts. As one angry reporter put it, if one out of ten Canadian women living with her spouse is a battered woman, then that means that one out of every ten men living with his spouse is a batterer. Let's see. That means there would be about 25 Members of Parliament who beat their wives.

Isn't that a riot?

BUILDING BRIDGES
Volume 5, No. 7 (May 1984), p. 2

Broadside readers may recall an exchange that took place in this newspaper in the wake of the first annual Women and Words conference held in Vancouver last summer. Eve Zaremba reported on the events of the conference in an article and Makeda Silvera responded with a letter to *Broadside* taking Zaremba to task for her apparent racist description of the events. Shortly after, Annette Clough reviewed the *Fireweed* issue devoted to women of colour and *Broadside* received more criticism from Cy-Thea Sand in Vancouver who argued that the review did not do justice to the efforts of the women involved.

These two incidents, some of us felt, were symptomatic of a deeper problem that we believed had to be addressed. The "we" in this case, were members of the publishing community who were conscious of a lack of communication between the editorial collectives of various feminist publications. More important, it seemed that *Broadside*'s readership could be wider. *Broadside* collective members met with the *Fireweed* collective and representatives of *FUSE* and *This Magazine* to begin to discuss the ways that all of the members of the feminist press could reach out to subscribers and increase the range of contributors to the magazines. The process of discussing race and class does not begin and end in one meeting. Indeed, after an exhausting afternoon of coping with the problems of communication, outreach, style and content, many of the participants felt we had barely had the chance to clear our throats, let alone grapple with the real substance of the challenge we've set ourselves. Some participants have decided to continue to meet monthly, understanding that the process can be painful, but that the rewards are worth struggling for.

THAT'S ENTERTAINMENT!

Volume 6, No. 4 (February 1985), p. 2

From the Smothers Sisters to the Pillow Sisters, from Nancy Drew to Eartha Kitt, from Susan Cole singing "I Am Oppressed" to Lorraine Segato doing vocal warm-up exercises: all were part of the line-up at *Broadside*'s 5th Birthday Party in December at Toronto's Bam Boo Club.

For those of you who don't live in Toronto, or who had something more important to do that night—you missed a great show. If you like hot music, there was the Pillow Sisters (Lorraine Segato, Julie Massi and Lauri Conger of The Parachute Club). If you're into jazz, there was the too-seldom-heard Kye Marshall Jazz Band. For the memorabilia freaks, there was Ann-Marie MacDonald and Bev Cooper's thriller Nancy Drew & The Clue in the Fast Lane, and Jane Farrow's impersonation of Eartha Kitt. And for those who need a little feminist content in their entertainment, there was

Beverly Cooper (left) and Ann-Marie MacDonald play Nancy Drew and her boyfriend, Ned, at the Broadside Cabaret, December 1984.

our very own activist Susan Cole's two-chord rendition of her own original song "I Am Oppressed, I Am Depressed, etc."

After the jazz and the star acts, there was dance music (taped by Deb Parent of Night Moves—a great dancing tape) that kept the die-hards going till closing time. The Bam Boo Club's owners, who are a bit skeptical about the viability of private do's, were impressed by the turnout and the high energy. And although the evening was a celebration, not primarily a fundraising event, *Broadside* did manage to make a little money to help defray our production costs.

So everyone was happy.

THE MEDIUM AND THE MESSAGE
Volume 7, No. 1 (October 1985), p. 3

As feminism enters the mainstream marketplace with its imperatives, so the debate in our own community evolves regarding the wisdom or the foolhardiness of certain strategies. Varda Burstyn's interview in *Forum* magazine's September issue, has brought about a flurry of media interest as to the appropriateness of that action.

In our centrespread this issue, Burstyn herself evaluates the nature and the intentions of her interview. Regarding *Forum* as a "mixed bag," containing pornography "a lot of which is sexist, some of which is not," and thinking herself in good company with the roster of prominent sexologists on the *Forum* International Board, Burstyn offers a critique of pornography directly to the users of pornography. To her credit she was shrewd enough to demand control over the final content of her interview, which is feminist in content, and consented to the interview only on these grounds.

And yet it seems that the problem is not so much what Burstyn has to say as it is where it was that she said it. While a case could be made for addressing the problem of pornography in pornography itself, it remains to be seen whether Burstyn has conducted a media coup, or whether *Forum*, by manipulating the context in which the interview appears, has undermined her content.

Forum does Burstyn a disservice by associating her brand of anti-censorship with their own interests in anti-censorship. In the issue is a full page ad sponsored by *Penthouse* magazine which smoothly associates a pro-censorship position with fascism, nazism, and the threat of communism. Hitler, Stalin, the Ayatollah and Castro have their photos above a cut line, "The experts agree that censorship works." "Freedom is everybody's business" reads the ad. On the page before Burstyn's interview appears a cartoon which ridicules opponents of pornography, depicting a Woman Against Pornography as sexually hostile.

Not related to the topic of censorship, but indicative of the nature of the magazine is a "news" story lamenting that *National Geographic* magazine is publishing fewer photographs of naked third world women. "Either the planet is running out of primitives, or *National Geographic* needs more enterprising men in the field," concludes their report.

One can't help but be suspicious of *Forum*'s sudden interest in feminist and lesbian concerns. This season alone they have published excerpts from Naiad's *Lesbian Nuns*, reviewed the lesbian-produced magazine *On Our Backs*, solicited and published Burstyn's interview, and written an editorial on the controversy in the women's presses about the excerpting of *Lesbian Nuns*. "The feminist press denounces us for desecrating their preserve," reads the editorial.

It would seem that *Forum* is taking advantage of sexual liberation and courting a female, and also a specifically lesbian, readership, just as cigarette companies have done in purusing the female smoker. For *Forum*, as part owners of the dominant culture, to generously make themselves authorities on grassroot and alternative sexuality, they are no more than sexual imperialists. They allow their readership to know about alternatives in a controlled, self-interested manner. And then they pose as our champions. "I believe," writes their editor, "that *Forum*'s ongoing defense of sexual minorities and their concerns deserves attention from our holier-than-thou lesbian and feminist critics."

A male-dominated press, sheathed in the amnesty of self-proclaimed liberalism, is interested in making what is ours, theirs. They are also speaking for women again, when of Naiad's *Lesbian Nuns* they claim, "*Forum* was the first magazine to recognise the importance of *Lesbian Nuns*...We helped launch *Lesbian Nuns*." Whether it is true or not, this is their boast.

It is difficult to predict to what extent the best of intentions and a guaranteed control over text can be undermined by the placement of an article in the larger landscape of a mainstream magazine. For our part, we might consider the role that the fear of contamination plays when we criticize feminists speaking to certain presses and not to others. Would Burstyn's interview evoke the same interest were it to appear in *Vogue*, *G.Q.* or perhaps *Hot Rod* magazines? Just because Burstyn gave an interview to *Forum*, it does not mean that she has necessarily joined boys' team. In her own opinion, she has most certainly *not* done that.

Nonetheless, the appearance of the interview does suggest that a critical consideration of *Forum* as an appropriate venue is required. As well, it indicates the vulnerability of text, which, even when intact, can be greatly undermined by the relationship that its larger context brings to bear upon it.

One has only to look at the cover.

FREE TRADE: NO BARGAIN FOR WOMEN

Volume 8, No. 2 (November 1986), p. 2

As the federal government continues its pre-occupation with free trade agreements with the United States, interest groups have been left to sort out for themselves what the implications of the negotiations may be. At present the PCs are painting a rosy picture of future scenarios, but a paper drafted by Marjorie Cohen, a Vice President of the National Action Committee on the Status of Women, warns that free trade is going to have a specific and negative impact on women. The paper, entitled "The MacDonald Report and Its Implications for Women," traces the economic factors that bode poorly for women workers under the free trade regime.

Cohen begins by assessing the manufacturing sector, where women's labour is highly concentrated, and where, as the MacDonald Commission admits, there is likely to be the greatest vulnerability.

The Commission's report, Cohen writes, identifies the manufacturing sector as one of those which will become weakest if free trade talks are successful. The textile and clothing industries and four others are named as potential casualties: two-thirds of the people working in these sectors are women, constituting 42% of all manufacturing workers, whose work lives will be jeopardized if free trade philosophies prevail.

Cohen criticizes the Commission's report for its ingenuous speculation about what will happen to these women. The Commission explains that displaced workers will be retrained into more highly paid jobs which will work in their interests. But this, according to Cohen, is based on belief not fact. Already women are under-represented in job training programs, and the assumption that these workers, many of whom have been on the job for over thirty years, will be prepared for such a significant change of life, is actually quite callous. A garment workers strike recently settled in Toronto drove the point home, especially as workers complained that there were no other jobs to go to.

The Commission, when it is not talking about retraining, talks about other "adapting behaviour" which is a euphemism for re-locating, something married women with children do not find easy. A quick look at the manufacturing situation suggests that, if some economic sectors will benefit from free trade, others will pay for those benefits, and the ones paying the costs are going to be women.

Taken together, the vulnerability of the manufacturing sector, and the uncertainty similarly anticipated for the service sector where 80% of all women workers are employed, free trade begins to look less and less appealing. This does not take into account free trade's inevitable threat to Canadian cultural policies, Or even the fact that free trade could mean a virtual blizzarding of Canada by pornographers who are anxious to change the pornography-free (that is, relative to the US) conditions enjoyed by Canadians.

But what Marjorie Cohen and NAC have done is to begin a process that other women's groups would do well to join. Taking into account the interests of women, an entirely new body of material can be generated to garner opposition to the Mulroney strategy, and to subvert the free trade talks. *Broadside* is interested in any views of free trade that place women first on the priority list. We share with Cohen the view that free trade is going to be bad for women.

BROADSIDE AND BEYOND

Volume 10, No. 5 (August/September 1989), p. 2

A few years ago, a friend asked me if I was always going to want to work at such a marginal job as *Broadside*. *Broadside*, marginal? I had considered *Broadside* to be central. Not just because it was my job, one I loved doing, and therefore central to my life, but also because, in its function at least, I thought of it as a focal point for feminist activism. I saw it, and other feminist publications, as playing a key role in the reflecting and shaping of our political struggle.

I knew that outside in the "real" world, the main stream, it didn't count for much. Lots of people had never even heard of it; and if they had, they dismissed it as a "little" newspaper, put out by fringe fanatics. This, of course, by perverse feminist logic, merely served to prove how central it really was.

Again a few years ago, an old high school classmate I bumped into asked me what I was doing these days. I told her I was editing a feminist newspaper. "Which one?" she asked (as if she knew of any). When I answered "Broadside," she looked as if she hadn't heard right and said, "Bloodshed?"

How marginal can a project be which stirs up such fears in the woman-in-the-street?

Still, there are grey areas of marginality. If you're *really* marginal, you can get away with anything: nobody pays any attention. It's when people start taking you seriously that the trouble begins. And that's in part, I think, what happened to *Broadside*.

That's not to say it wasn't taken seriously all along by those of us who contributed to it and produced it, and by its readers and the feminist community at large. It was, very much so—to the extent that *Broadside* was considered, even expected, to have *the* radical feminist line on anything. It also very quickly was invested with the character of an institution which then, like any symbol of authority, had to be proven wrong.

We got into a lot of trouble (much of it probably deserved). First of all, we called the paper "*Broadside*," a pun not popular with everyone. We reprinted an article on discrimination against women poets from an in-house newsletter when we weren't supposed to and caused problems for its author. We ran an anti-Zionist (rather anti-Israeli imperialist) article and were criticized for our anti-Semitism. We printed a letter from a well-known feminist academic about what she considered the disturbing increase of Third World (i.e., not feminist) content in International Women's Day events, and were boycotted by immigrant women's groups. We ran an editorial calling lesbians the "clergy" of the women's movement and lesbianism the "psychic imperative" of feminism, and were called on to explain ourselves. The list goes on.

The generous thing to say is that we took risks, attempting to give space to diverse opinions, not wanting to censor or censure any feminist voice. So, sometimes what we did was deliberate, though usually it wasn't. At any rate, as Doris Anderson—doyenne of mainstream feminist journalism—has said, we printed our own internal controversies all over our pages. In mainstream circles this is something that is clearly not done. But for feminist newspapers, it's the crux of the matter.

Given all this positive energy, and delight in iconoclasm, what happened? Two questions immediately rise to the surface: Why exactly is *Broadside* folding? and what will happen without it? The answer to the first is not simply burnout and financial strain. The closing down of *Broadside* is part of a larger picture. Why did *Pandora*, *La Vie en rose*, *Herizons*, *Hysteria*, and *Cayenne* all decide to fold in the past couple of years? We're all part of the same phenomenon, some of it obvious (money and womanpower) and some of it not so obvious.

And what will happen without us all? There are still good feminist publications around—newer ones like *The Womanist*, *Our Lives*, and *Tiger Lily*, older ones like *Kinesis*, *Room of One's Own*, and the *Northern Woman Journal* (this latter a stellar example of sheer determination to survive) and academic ones like *Canadian Woman Studies*, *Atlantis*, and *Resources for Feminist Research*—and there will be others to come.

But with respect to *Broadside*, I think both its marginality and its centrality have contributed to its demise. We dealt with issues which were central to the lives of women (abortion, lesbianism, violence against women, for example) which are being increasingly marginalized as the result of the Conservative government's right wing agenda. This marginalization also makes it easier for those who are made uncomfortable by many of the implications of a radical feminist analysis to sweep issues under the carpet, to deal with some things and not with others.

Over the years, *Broadside* has been thought by many to be a lesbian feminist newspaper. Because we didn't hesitate to write about lesbianism (we used the L-word quite a lot), it was assumed we had to *be* lesbian (who else would dare, or bother?). In fact, there never was a time when the *Broadside* collective didn't include heterosexual women. So, we were a feminist newspaper which incorporated a pro-lesbian, anti-heterosexist perspective. Others of our readers thought we should just come out, period. Well, we were too lesbian in some quarters, not lesbian enough in others. We ended up realizing we couldn't please everyone, so we might as well just go ahead and do our thing.

Meanwhile, back at the Progressive Conservative ranch house, right wing lobbyists were gaining momentum. Anti-choice backbenchers had the ear of cabinet members and were applying pressure on the abortion issue. With the advent of R.E.A.L. Women and the pro-family agenda, it was a short step to realizing that lesbianism, too, was a threat.

Then things heated up for the Secretary of State's Women's Program, the biggest funder of feminist groups in Canada. Under attack from the right, the program was subjected to a parliamentary review. The resulting report, *Fairness in Funding*, guaranteed the Program's continuation, reaffirmed its commitment to women's equality, and recommended not only that the Program's budget be maintained, but that funds be found to support "doubly disadvantaged" groups.

That's the good news. At about the same time, the Program's funding eligibility criteria were quietly formalized. Now, we were told, applicants whose project promoted a particular lifestyle, or a view on abortion, would be ineligible for funds. Lest you think "a particular lifestyle" might possibly include the hetero variety, keep in mind that R.E.A.L. Women, whose printed objectives include the phrase "to reaffirm that the family (defined as two or more people living together, related by blood, marriage or adoption) is society's most important unit," *were* considered eligible to receive funds. R.E.A.L. Women are also explicitly anti-abortion.

Does this make sense? Well, yes. The Program's mandate to fund equality-seeking groups is being eroded on a number of fronts, including major budget cuts, which means the financial viability of many women's groups in Canada is at stake. The Program never gave *Broadside* operating funds (though it did fund us for a promotion project in 1984) so its recent history is not a direct contributory cause of our folding, although in applying for funds to produce this last issue we were asked to put in writing that the funds received from Sec State would not be used for the above-mentioned naughty activities.

But although the criteria are now written down, a subtler form of disqualification has always been in operation at the Program and elsewhere. Being considered lesbian, having unabashed lesbian content, obviously is enough to give anyone the heeby-geebies. The question is, how does the government get away with such a misogynist agenda? They get away with it partly because the very groups who could put up a fight have already been effectively destabilized. Feminist publications are a powerful tool in this respect, and the less support we get, the better for the status quo. *Broadside*, like any publication in Canada (given the geographical distances and relatively low population), couldn't possibly survive without some form of subsidy, so lack of substantial support from our biggest potential supporter was always a problem.

There is, however, a larger problem contributing to *Broadside*'s demise, one that I don't think has been given much serious consideration. The government's supposed commitment to funding "doubly disadvantaged" groups (Black women, immigrant women, visible minority women—though clearly *not* lesbian women) is a reflection of a social movement affecting all feminist groups in Canada. The most crucial aspect of feminism in the past few years has been the efforts to incorporate anti-racist perspectives into feminist practice and analysis. White women have been forced to deal with the issues raised, forced to face the fact that it may no longer be the role of White women to frame the debate and direct the struggle. With the growth of global feminism in the past decade, White feminists are no longer the majority (if they ever were).

Not only has the Broadside collective until very recently been an all-White one, it was formed in an environment of White feminist perspectives. It's not that women of colour don't share a concern for issues of violence against women, pornography or nuclear arms, it's that *Broadside* couldn't help but operate from a lopsided view of things, even in the latter years when we were more conscious and open to understanding feminism's diversity. I think perhaps it's time for us to let go of our hold, and to pass on the responsibility for reflecting and shaping our political struggle to others.

This is our last issue of *Broadside*. When planning its contents, we started with the idea of a retrospective: ten years in the life of feminism in Canada. But this is a false category, based solely on the fact that *Broadside* published for 10 years and is now folding. Feminism isn't folding. Things just keep happening, things we want to write about now. Things that have happened so recently—like the Dodd and Daigle abortion injunction cases—we'd like more time (or another issue of *Broadside*) to comment on them.

Some of the articles, nevertheless, do look back over the years. Joyce Mason's article on film specifically addresses *Broadside*'s coverage of films since our first issue in 1979. Our feature on feminist theatre provides a visual exploration of the changing form and content of the genre in more general terms. Ruth Pierson reflects on changes in her reading tastes from pre- and protofeminist days to the present. Susan G. Cole considers changes in the way we have dealt with the connection between sex and violence in the past decade, and Connie Clement chronicles changes in women's health provision. Marjorie Cohen discusses changes in feminist approaches to the economy, particularly with respect to NAC. Located more in the present, Lorraine Greaves *et al.* give a critique of NAC's "process" and how it affects the participation of its members. Susan Crean describes the appropriation of the language of equality by the right wing, particularly fathers' rights, groups. And Eve Zaremba's "Movement Comment" specifically directs us to look to the future—the women's liberation movement, after all, is here to stay.

As we prepare to close up shop, I would like first of all to say that although it isn't financially feasible for us to refund subscriptions, we are negotiating with the Black Women's Collective for them to honour your sub by sending you their newspaper, *Our Lives*. We hope you will enjoy it, *and* resubscribe to it at the end of the year.

And finally, on behalf of the *Broadside* collective, I would like to thank all of you, our readers, for your continued support over the years. We couldn't have done any of it without you.

Philinda Masters

COMMENTS

THÉRÈSE CASGRAIN: A VOICE FOR WOMEN
by Kay Macpherson
Volume 3, No. 3 (December 1981/January 1982), p. 6

Thérèse Casgrain died on November 3, 1981, at her home in Montreal. She was 85. Her career as a fighter for women's rights, for the vote, for Family Allowances to be sent to the woman of a household, for native women and for human rights has been well documented and recorded. Her often repeated statement, "I want peace and I've been fighting for it all my life," was her well-known theme song.

Her connection with the Voice of Women is seldom mentioned in the accolades. Since I was one of the women outside Québec who saw a good deal of her during those years, I would like to recall some of those occasions.

Thérèse took over as President of Voice of Women in September 1962, when Helen Tucker moved on to organize a Women's International Committee for International Co-operation Year. Thérèse had organized La Voix des Femmes, the Québec branch of VOW, so when she became National President, the office moved to Montréal. Soon after, the Women's Peace Train to Ottawa was organized. Seven hundred Québec women were joined by a bus load from Ontario, and together we all walked up Parliament Hill carrying with us a laundry basket filled with telegrams from all over the country demanding "NO NUCLEAR WEAPONS IN CANADA." We were addressing the Diefenbaker government and was undecided about Canada acquiring nuclear weapons. An English-speaking cabinet minister was sent in to hear from the women, who were insulted, and said so quite forcefully until a French-speaking minister was hastily substituted. A sequel to this incident was a conversation between an English-speaking Québec member and Solange Chaput-Rolland, the writer, on the train returning to Montréal. Solange was volubly hurt and resentful and the English woman who spoke sympathetically to her in perfect French was the author Gwethalyn

Graham. Their subsequent friendship and collaboration created the book "Dear Enemies," and that was one of the forerunners of the Royal Commission on Bilingualism and Biculturalism. The Bi Bi Commission was given its nickname by Ghislaine Laurendeau, wife of the Co-Chairman and a VOW Vice-President and close friend of Thérèse Casgrain.

Thérèse was unable to resist the call to stand as a candidate in the federal election of 1963. Pearson had declared he was going to accept the Bomarc missiles. Thérèse stepped down as VOW President—we were very sensitive about being non-partisan in those days—and I was left "acting" in her place. After her defeat, with the VOW annual meeting coming up, she was undecided whether to stand again for President. I was thought to be *very* radical at the time (I was married to a Marxist professor) and Helen Tucker even considered coming back to save the day, though in the end I stayed as President. I remember sitting between these two previous presidents of VOW, each wearing an enormous and colourful hat, and being totally eclipsed by the one's grandeur and presence and by the other's flamboyance. In those days I was the equivalent of a blushing violet.

During the Casgrain reign in VOW we travelled to Montreal for Council meetings, often held in Thérèse's home. One was held on the day President Kennedy was shot. At another we received letters from women in Vietnam describing atrocities and the hardships they were facing. (In 1963 we had to find out where Vietnam was.) Casgrain was an enchanting mixture of granddame and peacenik. She enjoyed shocking her children who thought their mother's activities were often very embarassing. Solange Chaput-Rolland, who was one of her protégés, recalled that when she dropped in for a cup of tea she might find Prime Minister Nehru, or Madame Vanier, the Governor General's wife, or a prominent politician having a quiet chat. Or perhaps Thérèse was giving advice to one of her grandchildren. I remember that when their number reached 13, she had a bracelet with charms on it for each of them. This was the perfect conversation piece in meeting women all over the world. Thérèse might not know a word of the woman's language but after a minute or so there would be smiles, nodding of heads, finger counting, showing of snapshots and firm friendships cemented.

Thérèse arrived in Paris late in 1964 having attended a women's conference in Israel. I had been at a conference organized by Helen Tucker in the UNESCO building. She had a broken ankle at the time but ath didn't stop her. One of my cherished memories is of Helen Tucker in what looked like a witch's hat and black cloak, sitting in a wheelchair going up in the foodlift of the Air France jet loading in Dorval airport.

Thérèse and I joined a group of women from NATO countries who, as a follow-up to their meeting in The Hague six months earlier, were protesting the proposed NATO Multi-Lateral Nuclear Force (whereby each NATO country was going to be able to press the nuclear button). We arranged with the authorities that we would present a statement from the NATO women to the Secretary General of NATO and we agreed to send only one woman from each country (one English- and one French-speaking from Canada) so that we did not appear to be a demonstration. The French police were very nervous. There were other peace groups protesting NATO's actions and the streets around the NATO building were filled with police cruisers and baton-brandishing gendarmes. We walked quietly in twos and threes up to the building and after some parleying were told that only one woman could enter. This wasn't good enough. We wanted a minimum of two, preferably more. There were women present from the US, France, Belgium, Britain, Germany and the Scandinavian countries. While we were talking to the guards an enormous uniformed monster reminiscent of Hermann Goering stumped out, swept us all up in a gesture, and ordered that we be arrested.

We were hustled into a police paddy wagon and I shall never forget the delighted look on Thérèse's face as she was rudely pushed up the steps. There was a wonderful cartoon later in Montréal's *Le Devoir*, "Thérèse Casgrain à Paris," where she is stepping daintily into the paddy wagon brandishing a peace sign. We were driven half way across Paris and taken to what later turned out to be a police barracks or training college. There, a group of (I think) police recruits were ordered to search and record these dangerous criminals. The two French women in the group had by this time been hustled off to some unknown fate other than their own. We were the foreign agitators. So our handbags were searched for dangerous weapons.

They took my scissors and pocket mirror and when I asked why, the official vividly demonstrated how I could break the mirror in two and cut my throat with it. That idea had never occurred to me. All this was much too exciting and we were already plotting, first, how much of a nuisance we could make of ourselves and then, more important, what we could do with the press. Besides Thérèse, there were two or three women who were experts at getting publicity for their cause.

We were finally escorted under heavy guard to a large cell with wire netting for walls. Thérèse dubbed it a salad shaker. There was a bench round the sides, so we sat down and planned strategy. The Belgian woman had an appointment with her Ambassador which she raised the roof about missing. One by one we asked to visit the washroom—a primitive place if ever I saw one—and this meant an individual escort across two courtyards, with doors to be locked and unlocked police time to be wasted. Then to our delight we discovered that one of our women was pregnant. How could those brutal police treat a "femme enceinte" in such a callous way, we asked. It was very cold in our unheated salad bowl.

Paris in December was anything but tropical. Thérèse put her long and elegant gloves over her feet to keep them warm. One of the British women discovered the searchers had overlooked her small flask of scotch, so we all had a thimbleful to cheer us. I even tried the heat of a cigarette to warm myself (and then took five years to stop smoking again).

Finally, after about five hours during which our demands to see our ambassadors never ceased, we were visited by an important-looking group of officials. They read us a severe lecture and explained in threatening tones that we would be released if we promised never to demonstrate or march, nor to do several other things on pain of never being permitted to enter France again—or was it instant deportation; I forget. (The next time I was in a demonstration in Paris was about five years later. I wasn't deported.)

Off we went to make the most of our experience with the press and our embassies. Voice of Women and its "two distinguished representatives" (I liked that) were on the front page of *The Globe and Mail* and the Québec papers for three days. Official notes were sent. (Our Canadian Ambassador in Paris told Thérèse, who of course had known him since childhood, that she really must warn him when she was planning more of these escapades, so that he could protect her!) More important, when all the fun and games were out of the way, the real reason for our protest did get through. We were opposing this highly dangerous escalation of nuclear force by NATO. (It sounds familiar, doesn't it?) Months later, NATO dropped its plan for the MLF. We will take credit for some of that, although it was probably due to all kinds of other reasons.

On our return Thérèse was fêted. The Premier of Québec, meeting her by chance in the main dining room of the Windsor Hotel in Montréal, rushed up and embraced her. "Let me kiss my jailbird," he exclaimed. My treatment was rather different in Toronto. I faced a mini-inquisition of Voices for my experience in Paris. "Drinking in a Paris jail! Was that fit behaviour for the President of the Voice of Women? And who were you associating with? Did you know all the women? Were there any *communists* in the group? Who were they? What will our members think?" The McCarthy era was still affecting Canadian attitudes, and not least affected were many of our more timid and inexperienced women. We lost quite a few of our local members but, as Solange Chaput-Rolland said, "When the wind blows hard, some of the leaves fall off the tree." On the other hand, the response from VOW members across the country was tremendously supportive, and they showed it in their telegrams and letters to Thérèse and me.

There were many other occasions when the delight of being with Thérèse and our admiration for her were cherished by all of us who knew her. We'll miss her, but what an example she set!

AND NOW FOR A REALLY BIG SHOE...

by Sarah Sheard

Volume 4, No. 5 (March 1983), p. 14

> Light she was as any fairy
> And her shoes were number nine
> Herring boxes without topses
> Sandais were for Clementine.
> —*traditional*

Shoes should not be any tougher to buy than, say, records, or books. But if you are a woman whose feet are larger than the manufacturers' norm, forget it.

My feet are not deformed or out of proportion. Just size 11. In romantic poems, women's legs terminate in delicate hooves, dainty trotters that fit the palm of a lover's hand. Lady's slippers make good champagne glasses.

I outgrew that poetry and broke the sex foot-barrier when I turned thirteen. I remember the very day. The salesperson at Eaton's girlswear measured me, shook her head and pointed towards boyswear. And the guy in boyswear took one look down and banished me to mens wear, whereupon my mortified girlfriends shucked me at the escalator. Sic transit self-esteem.

Anyway, I walked into high school wearing men's Converse hi-cut sneakers (white) with the red and blue fireballs on the ankles and later switched to Greb Kodiaks that the groovy wore half-laced.

Comparisons are odious but wasn't that what high school was about? I found myself mentally removing the shoes from other women's feet. Measuring their development against mine during the gym showers. I encouraged them to talk provocatively about their shoe sprees. The details excited me strangely. They teased me, let me hold their stockinged feet in my hand, hissed words like "pump" and "slingback" at me as I wrote exams. Ahh, the delicious agony of my first fetish.

I clumped off to university in Frye snubnosed cowboy boots and now that it was the seventies, I got away with wearing them to formal events, funerals, etc. But the blisters. Those boots never wore in—although they did wear out.

Illustration by General Idea's Jorge Zontal.

Now it was 1982 and I was desperate for a new look. One that didn't weigh so much. I wanted a pair of glove-soft Robin Hood fetish boots that crumpled around the calf.

So I started at Bloor and Spadina and worked my way through the stores, all the way over to Yonge. I pretended I didn't really need a pair of boots. By Yonge and Wellesley, I'd shrunk my spiel down to a pithy, descriptive paragraph, saving the punchline for the end. It was only when I held a dream boot in my hand that I would ask for it in size 11. By the time I reached Yonge and Dundas, I'd bought four pairs of socks and was actually wondering if I could sew leather soles onto them instead and save myself further humiliation.

I called my mum.

"Pull yourself together," she said. "There's a store called Tallcrest. It's in an arcade and you find it down a stairwell on the northeast corner of Bay and Adelaide.

"That's the side the sun rises on, right?" She knew I was flustered. "It has lots of modern styles, dear. Check it out."

My hope rekindled, I hopped the subway. Found the stairwell, although I've walked past it dozens of times and never seen it. It appeared this time, like magic that works only when you deserve it. That stairwell led to a subterranean catacomb that other people with "my problem" shared. If Tallcrest didn't deliver, I doomed myself to custom-made orthopedic footwear—very, very expensive. It's listed, together with prosthetic devices, in the yellow pages.

The Tallcrest sign glowed like a friendly aquarium at the end of a passageway of glass and mirrors. It turned out to be a very tiny store for us long people. The precarious display of footwear propped up on glass pegs made me claustrophobic. If I touched one, I envisioned the entire display cascading to the floor on top of me. I reached past a pair of statuesque browsers and plucked a sensible loafer off the bottom peg. It was incredible. Holding it in my hand, I realised how deluded I'd been by the scale. Out of context with its mates, this shoe was, in reality, almost an arm's-length. It looked like it could talk on a child's TV show. I put the shoe back. It was time to take a chair.

There were other women sitting with their shoes off on either side. It was like a waiting room where we'd all come to see the doctor for the same unmentionable problem. A nurse—I mean a saleswoman—emerged from the stockroom with a clipboard. She whispered something about stock to the woman opposite me and her face fell. I glanced down at her "problem area" and actually blushed. The saleswoman murmured to a few other women whose faces all crumpled. There were simply not enough shoes to go around. We were like women in the Soviet Union, queuing up in vain to buy the one style of footgear they manufacture. The kind that fits either foot. My neighbour caught the saleswoman's sleeve and implored: Wasn't there anything in a snowboot, size thirteen?

Wow.

The saleswoman disappeared.

A moment later she returned, carrying a box the size of a child's coffin. My neighbour sighed audibly when she saw it. She pulled out the snowboots, zipped them up and clumped into the middle of the room while the rest of us watched her and watched each other watching her.

In another corner, a teenaged girl, a Mariel Hemingway type, was strapping on her maiden pair of high heels. She was fifteen maybe. When she rose to walk to the mirror, she needed to support herself on either side with her mother and her grandmother, both of whom resembled Mariel Hemingway in stages of life she has yet to reach.

I watched that Douglas fir of a teenager study herself with dismay in the full-length mirror, clinging for balance and wailing with twisted lip that she was never gonna be able to dance in these, no way, and why did she have to wear heels, she already towered over her partner and ohhh, the bittersweet anguish of her predicament. She would have looked great running barefoot up mountains and straddling rivers, dancing barefoot to the end of her days.

Both her mother and her grandmother interposed their bodies

protectively between the girl and the mirror as though to forestall the self-consciousness that Amazons unavoidably acquire. Watching that trio I sent out a tiny rallying call to women caught in awkward zones everywhere. To women squeezing and tugging, slouching and staggering across the planet. To women secluding themselves in private despair-towers because they'd burst the manufacturers' norm-barrier.

And if all the Clementines in this world lined their feet up heel to toe, they'd girdle the globe three times around. And if those heels and toes commenced stamping and drumming, the globe would be compressed to a hard little ball. And the tattoo, carrying to the farthest reaches of the galaxy, might just fall on sympathetic, inter-galactic cobblers looking for fresh markets upwind.

To serve us right.

Sarah Sheard works for Coach House Press in Toronto.

DOWN, NOT OUT

by Lisa Freedman and Susan Ursel
Volume 4, No. 10 (August/September 1983), p. 3

THE RAID

On Tuesday, July 5, 1983 at approximately 11:30 am, carloads full of uniformed and plain clothes police arrived and the raid on Toronto's Morgentaler Clinic was underway.

Before the raid that day, two undercover police began to set the stage. A man and woman approached the clinic as a couple fran-tically searching for abortion services. Concerned about their confidentiality and their peace of mind, a few supporters outside the clinic asked insistent reporters not to photograph the couple or ask them questions. They discreetly let the two pass through the already growing crowd of media. No one realized they were police.

Andrea Knight, a pro-choice supporter, later commented: "I felt angry and used because of all our attempts to be as supportive as possible. I felt used and betrayed by her (the policewoman)... because of the support I tried to give her and what she did with it." Ironically the first concern of many on the outside was for the "woman patient" they thought had been caught in the raid.

Once the couple were inside the clinic, the police began to arrive. Uniformed police and members of the Morality Squad swarmed up the front and back stairs of the building. Anyone in the way was roughly shoved aside. It was clear they had planned this raid down to the last melodramatic detail and they weren't going to let anyone upstage them. They were completely flustered when folded cardboard cartons being carried into the clinic kept slipping out of their hands. Their irritation clearly showed at this unexpected hitch in the production.

At this point shoving began between the police and spectators. A major confrontation was avoided though. At that moment the clinic staff, who had stayed in the clinic to give reassurance to patients, appeared in the doorway. They waved to the crowd and raised their hands in the symbol of victory. Supporters immediately moved back to allow them through the crowd, but the police watched passively as the three women were hounded and harassed by the media. It fell to two supporters to escort the women away from the reporters, who were apparently intent on adding another trauma to these women's day.

Where did all of this support come from? Tight organization, dedication and level heads helped make sure the support materialized when and where it was needed. Under the watchful eye of the police, people used the phones in the Toronto Women's Bookstore to activate other phone networks. The message was simple: "This is it. They're here." Those phoning for support were the eye of the storm. Calmly they set aside their anger at the bluster of events occurring around them, and got the word out.

By mid-afternoon the police had left, carrying off clinic files and equipment. One doctor was arrested and two others had warrants issued for their arrest. Supporters were left with an office, a phone and a passionate belief that the clinic must remain open. After fielding phone calls requesting advice and offering support they closed the office at the regular time of 6 pm. And opened it again the next morning at 8:30 sharp.

At the turn of the century the powers that be used brutal force feedings, threats of violence and beatings to intimidate and discourage women who fought for universal suffrage. Today the tactics are slightly more subtle but all the same are intended to intimidate and thwart our efforts to realize justice.

Police in Winnipeg have given the term "stormtrooper" a new lease on life in Canada. Brutal and degrading invasions of women patients' privacy have characterized the raids on the clinics in both of these cities. While the attorneys-general in these two provinces moralistically intone that the law must be upheld, far more basic rights than those enshrined in man-made law are being violated.

Feelings about the Toronto raid operate on two levels for those who were outside the clinic offering their support. At one level they are angry at the tactics of the police, and question the legality of their actions. But at a deeper level the clinic has become a symbol in this city. It stands for the constant struggle women are engaging in simply to realize the basic right to self-autonomy and control of one's life. It stands for the determination of women against all the odds and their will to win justice.

How does an academic question like "Would you be willing to go to jail to defend your rights?" become a personal and political fight? Andrea Knight was there the day of the raid and helped efficiently marshall support outside the building on Harbord Street. She probably speaks for many who were there during the raid and for more who heard about it later on the news or from their friends.

"I got involved because I thought it was an important struggle for women. I thought we could win an important victory for women across the country. It's not just a philosophical question. I feel I'm on the front lines of the struggle. These women (who are coming to the clinic) need help... I would go to jail for this. I'm not sure I would have before, but I would now. When I heard the police boots it was a reality as it has never been before."

We often talk of our rights as if they were some kind of abstraction, interesting points for debate but not something we feel are very tangible. The actions of the Toronto and Winnipeg police and the attorneys-general have helped women all over Canada bridge that conceptual gap. It is we who are being threatened, it is we who must defend ourselves and our sisters and it is most assuredly some of us who have and will continue to lay down our lives in this cause. For helping to make the battle lines so very clear we can genuinely thank those men in blue and their bosses who cower behind the facade of "law and order."

Lisa Freedman and Susan Ursel are two Toronto feminists still struggling to understand the logic of the legal system.

STANDARDS OF SISTERHOOD
by Catharine A. MacKinnon
Volume 7, No. 3 (December 1985/January 1986), p. 6

The spectacle of women who identify as feminists siding with pornographers affects not only one's expectations but probably also one's standards of sisterhood. Still, Varda Burstyn's appearance in pornography (*Forum*, September 1985) struck me as more collaborationist than unsisterly. It belongs where personal disloyalty, even on the basis of sex, becomes political complicity. As much because of some of her faintly critical views of some pornography, the content of her interview gives the pornographers what they have been wanting (and, of course, getting) ever since the civil rights approach to pornography was born: feminist-identified support for their bottom line, which is: the pornography stays.

Women, as any feminist knows, do not matter much, and feminists matter even less. So why have women like Burstyn suddenly become valuable to the pornographers? The answer is the same for her as for any woman who matters to misogynists: she is useful to them. Women who identify as feminists have been useful to pornographers as long as there has been a feminist movement against pornography, which has been escalating since 1970. The tradition of such use comprises the precedents Burstyn cites to justify herself. What made Burstyn specifically useful at this time is the civil rights approach to pornography, conceived and fielded by Andrea Dworkin and me, with others. We actually managed to threaten them—women—with feminism. So they could use (not need, use) one like her supporting them—a woman—with feminism. As they put it in their introduction to Burstyn's interview, "Females with raised consciousness can co-exist with pornography." Meaning, according to *Forum*, Varda Burstyn can live with a slave traffic in women, a system of use and torture and subordination of women for fun and profit. *Forum* tolerates her in their magazine so long as she tolerates *Forum* in her feminism.

Any criticisms of pornography that Burstyn made in the interview itself only give additional weight—her weight such as it is—to this institution of woman hating, because she opposes effective action against it. I say her weight such as it is, because women count here, to repeat myself, to the degree they are useful to pornographers: high among women, low on any other terms. Women who thus become useful to the pornographers probably count more now than they ever have in their lives—or, given the disastrous effect of pornography on women's social value, more than they ever will again, if they win. Too, it is difficult to figure out how anyone who so obviously cares so passionately about being thought well of—I am referring to her extensive, I believe unsolicited, self-defence in *Broadside* (October, 1985)—can tolerate the catastrophic impact pornography has on how women are thought of. Maybe the hitch is the part about how women means her, too.

It thus makes sense that her apologia for her interview (*Broadside*, October 1985) served as a foil for her attack on, and distortion of, the events and politics and analysis of feminist attempts in the United States to pass ordinances to give women civil rights against pornographers. Before getting into the specifics, forget for a minute that the magazine in which the interview appeared is itself part of a practice of violating women's civil rights. Notice only that here we have a socialist being interviewed about an industry in which a tiny number of people (about 15) make a huge amount of money from the outright coercion and precluded options of a huge number of people who make a tiny amount of money: typically, economically desperate people who are discarded when they are used up, which is soon. But so long as the few are men and the many are women, and the commodity is sex, and especially when it is done through words and pictures, the only time this socialist utters the word "exploitation" is to describe a critique of these conditions. Thus, Andrea Dworkin "exploits" rape when she talks about how pornography is based on force. Here we have a self-styled feminist in a feminist newspaper, writing about an industry that lives off sex inequality, and the only time freedom comes up is in affirming that *she* appeared in pornography of her own free will. Whenever we describe the reality of pornography for women, the other side reacts as if we are being emotionally manipulative. I do take it as a good sign that they react against these accounts, but I wish they would have as strong a response to their reality as they do to hearing about it.

As to the Right. The Reagan administration is committed to opposing sex equality. As an example, two Reagan-appointed judges, one adopting the American Civil Liberties Union's politics of the status quo, and one vindicating the neo-conservatives' "free market" Social Darwinism, have opposed sex equality by finding our ordinance unconstitutional. Both said that, constitutionally, harm to women is not as important as preserving the pornography that does that harm. Do you suppose that our opponents will reassess their position, once they face who their allies are?

I would also think that the politics of the liberals—you know, those people who keep supporting the Nazis and the Klan—might be relevant to this assessment of alliances. Not to mention that the so-called "anti-censorship feminists" are in active cooperation with the pornographers; in some cases in the US they are pornographers themselves. Not even siding with organized crime seems to give rise to agonizing over "terrifying alliance of these forces with certain women in the feminist movement."

Then there is the fact that everybody is being lied to through a press that is determined to defeat us by tarring us with the only brush that, at the same time, makes us real to them: alliances with men. So far, we have received no support—meaning no legitimacy, votes, audiences, money, access—from the organized Right. Only one conservative individual, a woman, has worked actively with us, along with hundreds of progressives. Indianapolis chose her to work with the bill, but I would work with her over a lot of liberals still. Some conservatives have voted for our law, some haven't, in about the same proportions as the liberals. In the press, only the conservative opposition, not the liberal support. If we ever do get support from the Right, we will have the media to thank for convincing them that they are on our side.

As to those facts the press's powers of self-fulfilling prophesy have yet to alter, Burstyn (as is typical of attacks on us) simply gets them wrong. Examples: Andrea Dworkin participated in planning and executing *a demonstration against* the cabinet minister who spoke at the Toronto conference she addressed. It was even reported in *The Globe and Mail*, with photograph. Andrea Dworkin did not sue *Hustler* "for calling her a lesbian" but for doing dirt to lesbians and to her good name and for attempting to intimidate and silence her in her exercise of her First Amendment rights by making her and her mother into pornography. The *New York Times* had the accurate information but printed the factual falsehood that has been widely circulated and would not print a correction. Surely leftists know that the established press is unreliable on the activities of radicals?

The saturation of women's sexual experience with forced compromise, as a matter of political analysis, either is a feature of male supremacy or it is not. I do not see how *saying* that it is raises an ethical issue. It strikes me that saying that it is may raise conflicts felt as ethical for those who recognize the truth in this critique but feel loyalty to this system nonetheless. Which really does raise an ethical issue, the one about speaking the truth no matter what it costs.

I suppose I should be glad that Varda Burstyn is open to hearing about the consequences of her debut in pornography as a basis for re-assessing it. What if her interview, like similar acts of similar women in the US, is quoted to defend the pornographers in court, to justify keeping horribly abused women from getting any relief? What if it is used to support forcing anti-pornography feminists from jobs, revoking book contracts, evictions from homes, cited as legitimization for hostility and harassment and shunning? What if it contributes to a climate in which it becomes more permissible to target anti-pornography feminists in pornography? I am curious hew she sees her accountability working, since she will never pay for what she did like we will. Nothing short of retraction will make much difference in a world that she has made more dangerous for us and safer for these pimps. She is part of their pointing at all women, feminists specifically, anti-pornography feminists in particular, Andrea Dworkin and me as individuals, and saying: get her, it's all right with us. Although, again, because she is a woman, nothing she does on their side matters all that much. It's just the difference between being stabbed in the front and being stabbed in the back.

All this space on whether Burstyn did a good thing might have been devoted to an assessment of whether the civil rights approach to pornography would be useful in Canada. It seems to me, to put it tentatively, that existing laws and boards of censors in Canada tend to be as beside the point and dangerous as obscenity laws in the US. With the collapse of the customs restrictions, Canada is on the pornographers' (i.e., Americans') list for invasion this winter. Once they are finished, Canadians may not have another chance. In a place like Canada, with the state already so actively involved in this area, seemingly to little good effect, it seems to me that putting power for redress of concrete harms in the hands of victims, meaning particularly women and children as our law would do, has a lot to recommend it.

Forum also asked me for an interview. I told them that, upon consideration, while I appreciated their assurance that my text would be printed as is (a noncensorship I am seldom granted but rather have to extract), I did not want to appear voluntarily in a context that would legitimize the rest of what they do. I acknowledged that while I might reach an important audience, I thought the context would undermine me, more than anything I could say would undermine it. Then, too, I didn't want men masturbating to the women and reading me. I didn't want to be part of anything that other women pay for. I didn't want to give the pornographers anything that other feminists would pay for. Although their use of me would have been different from their use of Burstyn, use is use. And women are women, making the politics of noncollaboration here the same as the politics of our ordinance: women first.

Varda Burstyn chose to be where she felt she belonged. Who am I to say she was wrong?

Catharine MacKinnon is co-author with Andrea Dworkin, of the "Minneapolis" Ordinance, and is professor of law at the University of Minnesota.

THE WHITE IMPERIALIST GAZE

by Mariana Valverde

Volume 7, No. 9 (July 1986), pp. 3–4

Feminist analyses of pornography (and of mass culture in general) are generally carried out from the premise that gender difference is the most important or even the only category to be examined. I have spent quite a bit of time reading porn magazines and analyzing them, in the expectation that knowing how gender (and gendered sex) is constructed in this form of mass culture would reveal important things about women's oppression.

The analysis of representations of gender in porn remains an important component of the intellectual activity of the women's movement. However, a sustained analysis of one particular kind of representation tends to blind us to the perhaps more banal misogyny of other forms of culture (as many feminist writers such as Lisa Steele and Varda Burstyn, have pointed out). Even more politically, our collective ongoing analysis of *gender* as a major category of cultural analysis has perhaps put other important aspects of popular culture in the background. Women are after all not oppressed only on the basis of gender: women of colour, for instance, are equally oppressed by racism and ethnocentrism. It is only white, middle-class women who are enabled, by their relative privilege, to concentrate solely on gender.

What does this have to do with pornography? Certain problems arise as soon as one seriously asks the following questions: is the distorted representation of gender difference necessarily the main problem in porn? And, even if this is the case, is porn necessarily the most oppressive cultural form for all women? Are women of colour—who are after all the majority of the world's women—not equally oppressed by racist forms of culture? Is it not rather artificial (and ethnocentric) to say that racism in our culture oppresses women of colour *as* women of colour and not as women and hence feminists need not pay more than token attention to it?

Thus far, feminist analyses of porn—which have with very few exceptions been carried out by white, middle-class feminist writers of European descent—have more or less assumed that porn is the worst cultural enemy of women in general, and furthermore that the main problem with porn is its portrayal of gendered sex from an unrealistic and masculinist perspective. But it is necessary to challenge these two assumptions. And to critique these assumptions involves a lot more than simply noting the fact that women of colour are subject to particular forms of stereotyping in porn. To add an appendix on racial stereotyping to our "general" analysis of porn is simply to "add" a token footnote about how the "general" notion of patriarchal oppression (derived from white women's experience) needs a couple of small additions so that it will "fit" the experience of women of colour. (Or, more accurately, so that women of colour will fit into "our" analysis).

If there is something that I and a lot of other white feminists have learned from the current debates on racism, it is that one cannot go around trying to "incorporate" women of colour into a notion of patriarchy developed by white, middle-class American feminists in the 70s. To begin by assuming that patriarchy is always, necessarily, *the* overriding principle, and that racism is a derivative or secondary form of oppression, is racist.

What would it be like to seriously rethink the pornography debate in the light of an anti-racist perspective? The answer began to dawn on me as I watched a TV newscast which described a space mission as "just like Columbus discovering America." How in the world can people still talk about Columbus "discovering" America, when they know damn well that there were all kinds of *people* already living in the continent when he descended on the hapless inhabitants of what is now the Dominican Republic with his message of imperial conquest? I fretted and fumed. But then a thought struck me: it is not that people don't know that there were and are indigenous people on this continent. Rather, indigenous people are acknowledged as existing, but as existing only as *objects* for the white imperialist gaze. The Carib Indians existed only in order to be seen, objectified, and conquered by the Spaniards. The Iroquois and Cree and Ojibway existed only as potential objects of "discovery." The possessing gaze of the "conquerors" turned the Indian peoples into quasi-objects—the white imperialist gaze is the ideological precondition of the wholesale exploitation and geno-cide of indigenous peoples.

The white imperialist gaze constructs subject peoples in a way that is strikingly similar to the construction of the feminine gender by pornography. Yes, women do exist in porn, and they even exist as having sexual desires: but their bodies exist in order to be possessed, and their desires are portrayed as dark, evil desires that justify the use of force against them. The male gaze has to construct female of desire as dangerous and evil in order to legitimize both outright hatred and benevolent male despotism: in turn, the white imperialist gaze has to construct subject peoples as "savages," in order to legitimize both genocide and paternalism.

Women, and men, of colour are portrayed as "naturally" subordinate in just about every piece of mass-produced American-style culture that one can name. Westerns are as offensive to Native people as porn is to women, and it thus follows that Native women might put a higher priority on fighting racist images than on fighting pornography. World War II movies depicting the Japanese as evil creatures in search of ever more refined tortures serve to legitimize the atomic bombs dropped by the US on Japan, and are thus as bad or worse than any "Snuff" movie. And these forms of mass culture do not only legitimize past conquests and destructions: they continue to justify and glorify American imperialism and racism. American images of Arabs, for instance, portray them as "naturally" "fanatical," as born terrorists in the thrall of an irrational tyrannical religion: and so Reagan can invoke the Christian God when dropping his preacher-blessed terrorist bombs on Libya.

Mass culture à la Hollywood glamorizes *all* the main relations of domination. For instance, *Dallas* and *Dynasty* eroticize class domination by focussing on the sex lives of oil magnates and getting the TV-watching working class to see wealthy sex as the only culturally significant sex. The Hispanic population of Dallas exists only as a picturesque backdrop to Sue Ellen's escapades into the slums, and the workers who produce the Ewing millions are simply invisible.

War and spy movies about evil "Orientals" might not at first seem related to sex; but there is often a clear sexual overtone to the stories, especially when they involve, as they often do, torture and violence. When the white American hero is captured by the Chinese or the Indians or the Japanese or the Arabs or the Africans, when he is tied up and threatened with being skinned alive, there is a certain erotic charge. (Especially since these scene usually depict the half-naked, muscular hero in Adonis-type poses). The captors are portrayed as ugly, short, squinty-eyed sadists engaged in the gratification of their "natural" passion for evil. Hence, when the hero finally gets help from the CIA and murders all his captors in one final orgasmic rescue scene, the audience is supposed to breathe a sigh of relief that everything can now return to "normal"—i.e., the white male can return to his post at the Pentagon.

Within the framework of mass culture, it is "normal" for the people of colour to get killed in the end, because their desires are constructed as abnormal, as involving the sullying of white American manhood, and sometimes womanhood. The imperialist desires of the US are thus *projected* onto the very people who are its victims, just as in pornography masculine desire is often projected onto the supposedly perverted "sex bitch" who is "asking for it."

We can see then that there are interesting structural similarities between misogynist and racist forms of mass culture. However, it would be a superficial analysis to conclude from this (as Andrea Dworkin does in her book *Pornography*) that sexual antagonism between men is the cause of racism. Rather, erotically tinged images are used to glamorize racism as a social, economic and psychological system. To say that racism is derived from patriarchy is to assume that a feminist revolution would automatically abolish racism. But we know from current movement debates that one's radicalization as a feminist in no way guarantees the overcoming of racism. A separate educational process is needed to overcome racism among feminists, precisely because racism is, though closely intertwined with patriarchal relations, not simply derivative.

It seems to me ethnocentric to concentrate only on criticizing cultural products that exalt misogyny, without ever saying anything about cultural products that justify and even eroticize racism and imperialism. Surely women of colour are not oppressed just through being "stereotyped" in pornography: they are equally if not more oppressed by being portrayed (along with men of colour) as irrational, half-human creatures in white-male adventure stories and war movies.

Ethnocentrism in the anti-porn movement can serve to compound the racism of the mass media, insofar as it creates the impression that misogyny is the only, or at least the main, problem with the media. White women who protest against sexism in the media by saying, "But they wouldn't allow blacks to be portrayed all tied up... They wouldn't allow Jews to be portrayed being raped by Nazis," are perpetuating the myth that racism is something which happens far away in South Africa but not here. They should watch a few adventure movies or Tarzan re-makes, or read a few paperback Westerns, before lightly assuming that racism is no longer allowed in the North American mass media. In any case, misogyny does not exist separately from racism, and although pornography happens to emphasize one more than the other, most forms of mass culture use both at the same time.

We also have to stop assuming that patriarchy is always, *a priori*, the most important structure of domination. For white North American feminists with interesting jobs, patriarchy is indeed the only significant form of oppression in their lives; but to conclude that patriarchy is the essential factor in all women's lives is a form of feminist cultural imperialism. When Winnie Mandela says that racism is the most important factor in her life, I think it behooves us not only to take her at her word (which many white feminists do not) but also to reflect on how her statement ought to move us to change our theoretical framework.

The notion of patriarchy developed by white American radical feminists in the 70s is far too absolutist, and it presupposes a universal "women's experience" that does not exist. The socialist feminist approach is somewhat more flexible because it already posits two main forms of oppression, not just one Original Sin. However, some socialist feminists, whose minds are already boggled by the attempt to integrate patriarchy and capitalism at the theoretical level, have tried to minimize racism by reducing it to an offshoot of capitalism. It is true that racism only reached its genocidal heights as European capitalism and imperialism developed; however, racism, like sexism, is analytically distinct from class relations and must be granted the same degree of autonomy from both capitalism and patriarchy that these two sets of relations have from each other.

I do not want, however, to posit three grand solid systems labelled "patriarchy" "capitalism," and "racism," and then proceed in typically academic fashion to try to define exactly where in these structures everyone is located. I doubt whether anything is to be gained, at this point in our collective thought process, by the use of such abstract and yet weighty concepts. Rather, I think we need to do more concrete analyses of concrete situations—to use Lenin's words—without pre-supposing from the start the primacy of any one form of oppression. This article is an attempt at sketching out one such concrete analysis, by seeing how an anti-racist perspective might require changing the basic terms of the feminist pornography debate. Once we have figured out how racism, sexism, class exploitation and imperialism interact in many different concrete instances, we might then be in a position to make some theoretical generalizations.

(Thanks to Linda Gardner, Cynthia Wright and Carolyn Egan for their ideas and support, and to the International Women's Day Committee as a whole.—M.V.)

Mariana Valverde is the author of Sex, Power and Pleasure. *An earlier version of this article was printed in the International Women's Day Committee Newsletter, May 1986.*

Broadside A FEMINIST REVIEW

Volume 5, number 5   March 1984 $1.5

RISE UP — INTERNATIONAL WOMEN'S DAY

FEATURES:

POLITICAL PORTRAIT:
Barbara Deming is an American feminist, civil rights and peace activist, whose philosophy of non-violence has been the common thread of her life, in her actions and writings. Long-time friend Mary Meigs draws a portait of Deming. Page 8.

Meigs and Deming

THE GODDESS IS COMING!
In the second of a 5-part cartoon strip called 'Judgement Day' by artist Beth Walden, the Goddess continues her return journey to Earth. Don't miss the unfolding story. Page 12.

INSIDE BROADSIDE

NEWS

ACTION FOLLOW-UP: The follow-up committee on the Action Daycare proposal for International Women's Day, and beyond, presents its strategy for action—a working document for which they invite discussion and revision. Page 4.

POST-SOCIALISM: At a socialist feminist forum the topic of discussion was the poor record of traditional socialism and its lack of recognition of women's oppression. The real agenda was the role of men. Philinda Masters reports. Page 6.

WHO'S REAL? Canada's R.E.A.L. Women (Realistic Active Equal for Life) claim to have 10,000 supporters, the real women of Canada, whose main concern is the stability of the family. Although anti-feminist, they couldn't exist without 20 years of work by REAL feminists. Pat Daley reports. Page 6.

MOVEMENT MATTERS:
Read about a Canadian women's mailing list, a women's studies and publishing conference, a survival law manual for women, a daycare hotline, a drop-in centre for transient women, Women and Words, the fate of VSW, and more. Movement Matters, pages 6 and 7.

COMMENT

MEDIA & PORNOGRAPHY:
The porn issue is everywhere, even in the groves of academe, where it has gained "credibility." Susan G. Cole comments on the unexpected feminist presence at a male-dominated Media Violence and Pornography conference in Toronto. Lisa Freedman also reports on the problems of media misrepresentation of the pornography/obscenity debate. Page 5.

☐ ☐ ☐

OUTSIDE BROADSIDE:
Don't miss this month's calendar of Toronto women's events, for March 1984. Page 15.

ARTS

CLOUD CUCKOOLAND:
Nobody's who they should in *Cloud Nine*, Caryl Churchill's play about sex stereotyping in Victo¬ian colonial Africa and in the present. What can ycu expe from a play in which the daughter is played by a dol and the former father wear big frilly pink dress? Reviewed by Amanda Hale Page 10.

ANTAGONY: Even thougl Theatre Plus's version of *Antigone* is set in a present-day third world country, it' still a classical Greek traged Reviewed by Patricia O'Lea Page 11.

BOOKS IN REVIEW: *Voic from the Shadows* by Gwyr Matthews, reviewed by Chri Lawrence; *A Gathering Instinct* by Betsy Warland a *The Larger Life* by Libby Scheier, reviewed by Alexa DeWiel; *In Search of Our Mothers' Gardens* by Alice Walker, reviewed by Anne Cameron; and *Harems and Other Horrors* by Anne Inn Dagg, reviewed by Jud.th ' hnson.

CHAPTER 2

Movement Matters: News and Purviews

What is news? Who decides? Can you write about news if you're one of the people who helped make the subject newsworthy? Can you be objective if what you're writing about is happening to you? Doesn't your bias disqualify you from writing? Or does objectivity, that hallmark of conventional journalism, actually get in the way of the search for truth? These are the questions that feminist magazines, including *Broadside*, were asking as soon as they were established.

Many of the news articles that *Broadside* published could never have appeared in mainstream publications precisely because the writer herself was experiencing the injustice. Consider how so-called objectivity would have thwarted feminist coverage of violence against women. According to findings from renowned researcher Diana Russell, the percentage of women who will experience some form of sexual abuse—harassment, violence, sexual assault—in our lifetimes is an astounding 94 per cent. Most women, whatever their political stripe, are survivors. How can we leave the exposé of this systemic abuse to the 6 per cent who have never experienced it, who don't know what it feels like? We certainly couldn't leave the job to male writers who, at the time of *Broadside*'s launch, gave very little attention to any women's issues. Women named sexual assault, wife assault, and child sexual assault, then initiated actions to deal with it—including writing about it.

Some articles here are about developments for which the writers themselves are directly responsible. Vicki Van Wagner, a trailblazing midwife, contributed a piece, reprinted here, about midwifery and its place—or lack thereof—in the health system. Her activism alongside her sister midwives helped transform healthcare systems' attitudes toward their practice, giving women more choice in childbirth.

What is news? The women's movement, that's what. Every issue of *Broadside* included the section called Movement Matters that highlighted the issues that were on feminist minds and reported on feminist political action. Articles in other sections of the newspaper covered important conferences—such as Women and Words and the annual general meetings of the National Action Committee on the Status of Women—legal rulings on feminist issues, and the release of reports on key issues, such as Rosalie Abella's report on Equality in Employment.

We also kept track of other feminist publications, marking the launch of the magazine that became *Herizons*—which is still going strong in Manitoba—and the feminist book fair, which helped get women's books into the more than one hundred women's bookstores operating across North America at the time.

Broadside never shied away from debate. Where many considered coverage of our controversies and arguments the equivalent of airing feminism's dirty laundry, we knew that *Broadside* had to remain a forum for conflicting ideas. In this chapter, for example, Debi Brock, one of Canada's foremost advocates for sex workers' rights, argues that prostitutes need protection. Another article, this one on an organization for former sex workers, argues that prostitution is a form of sexual abuse and should be eradicated.

When it came to issues that continue to be relevant, *Broadside* was often first out of the gate. In Volume 1, No. 1, issued in October 1979, tapping the work of tireless researcher Fran Hosken, *Broadside* published an article uncovering the persistence of genital mutilation in fundamentalist communities, mostly in Africa. Women are still victims of this violence and within the last two years they have sought—and failed to get—asylum in the United States lest they be returned to their home countries and be forced to undergo this tribal practice.

In other instances, however, circumstances have changed so profoundly that some of our news reports are no longer relevant.

Susan G. Cole's report on how hard it was to advertise tampons when, so beset were media outlets by female pollution ideologies, it was forbidden by the advertising standards of the time to articulate what they were for. Check out the stunningly explicit ads for these products that are on view on prime time TV today.

With regard to *Broadside*'s lesbian content, we always felt that we were in a lose-lose situation. Many readers despaired that we had too much content about gay and lesbian liberation, politics, and arts, that we might "alienate" potential budding feminists. But, given that the Broadside collective was almost entirely lesbian, others argued that there was way too little. (See Jane Rule's comment on lesbian invisibility in the women's movement in Chapter 4, "Interviews"). We ran a number of lesbian-themed articles, including Yvette Perrault's take on police and anti-lesbianism, a feature on lesbian writer Nicole Brossard, and Lorna Weir's piece on a 1980 lesbian march with the thrilling headline "Coming Together in a Hot Gym." You'd have to survey all ten volumes of *Broadside* to make your own determination.

You will see in this chapter, and in our centre spreads in the next, the *Broadside* contributors who were some of Canada's already accomplished writers, including Joanne Kates and Margaret Atwood. We also gave voice to writers who would later become published authors. Some of the *Broadside* articles in this chapter—the ones on gender in sports and the dubious value of the Olympics—are by Helen Lenskyj, who went on to write seven books in her field. Reading these articles, you can see why we take a great deal of pride in the fact that, in its ten years of publication, *Broadside* put writers and issues in flight in ways that changed the political landscape.

Susan G. Cole

RITUALIZED MUTILATION

by Susan G. Cole

Volume 1, No. 1 (October 1979), p. 4

Last February, physicians, midwives and other health professionals gathered in Khartoum, Soudan for the World Health Organization (WHO) Seminar on Traditional Practices Affecting the Health of Women. The presentations of the participants confirmed that the external genitalia, including the clitoris of over 30 million female children and women are cut off and mutilated, often in drastic operations that result in permanent health damage: hemorrhage, which may be fatal, infections including tetanus, terrible scarring which prevents normal childbirth and even infertility may result. The operations, often performed on very young children, also result in life-long fridigity, painful intercourse, menstrual problems, fistulas (rupture of the vaginal walls), incontinence and a number of permanent disabilities.

The operation most frequently practiced is clitorectomy or excision — the cutting out, without anaesthetic, of most or all of the external genitalia of female children, from newborn babies to the age of puberty.

The most, dangerous operation, infibulation, or "Pharoanic Circumcision," is practiced in Sudan, Somalia and along the Red Sea coast, as well as in Mali, West Africa. It means that after the exterior genital organs of the child are removed, the vagina is closed by scarification or sewing. The legs of the child are tied together for several weeks until the wound is healed, closing the vagina except for a small opening for elimination created by a splinter of wood. Thus virginity, which is considered important by Moslem men, can be proven before the brideprice is paid.

We live with a post-Holocaust consciousness. Vietnam's refugees are lovingly photographed on the front pages of our dailies, the torture of a handful of American POW's at the hands of the North Vietnamese sparks the kind of outrage that will mobilize thousands. Whether it is to Idi Amin's chamber of horrors or to the Ayatollah's Draconian rule, world's humanists respond and from the gut. But the atrocities against women described at the World Health

Conference have been met with a conspiracy of silence that is only just beginning to break down.

Health professionals whose goal it is to end the sexual mutilation of women in Africa have encountered obstacles on nearly every front. They have assumed that a world-wide response from women would exert enough pressure, particularly on international agencies like the United Nations, to force governments and health professionals to take action.

The reaction has been slow in coming. It is almost as if the sexual politics are so explosive women find it hard to assimilate, and act on, the outrage.

In Africa, the excision of female children is performed to make them faithful to one man, especially in societies where polygamy is practised. In Moslem societies, virginity is a critical factor because the bride must be a virgin for the male head of the family to collect the maximum brideprice. To establish paternity unequivocally the males make sure the females are tightly "closed." Re-infibulation is also practised in Sudan and Somalia. After a woman has children and is divorced she is resewn so that the next man who buys her sexual services (by making the brideprice) is certain that any children she has are his. This kind of control is absolutely effective: sexual intercourse is so painful that the re-infibulated woman is hardly tempted to engage in sexual activity.

Apologists for the sexual mutilation of women in Africa argue that those of whatever sex who sanction the operations are not in the least blameworthy, that instead those who want to stop the operations and break the conspiracy of silence are a threat to African culture, and guilty of racist interference.

Fran Hosken, author of the definitive work on genital mutilation (*The Hosken Report*, published by WIN News, 1979) spent years trying to trigger a response from the World Health Organization and only recently had some success. She was consistently confronted with the criticism that genital operations or "operations based on customs" are a cultural matter. Stay out. Tampering with African culture is verboten, particularly in a climate of sensitivity to the emerging black African nations.

Hosken and her colleagues have been persistent, and finally at this year's WHO seminar they were convincing enough to walk away with ratified recommendations, designed to end the sexual mutilation of African women. But they had to be vigilant. Originally the recommendations formulated by a special committee before the conference were worded in such a way as to permit the modernization of traditional genital operations by introducing them into the health care field and even into the hospitals. All the male physicians argued that this was defensible and good medical practice because the action would "prevent infections and worse harm". This is the kind of logic that would argue that gang rape at the hands of a troup of boy scouts is more palatable than random rape because at least it's organized.

Dr. Bertha Johnson of Nigeria saw through the ruse and responded swiftly, pointing out that "defenders" of African culture cannot have it both ways: performing traditional operations in western-equipped hospitals (and making large sums of money in the process) is hardly non-interference with African culture. Eventually the seminar did not sanction the introduction of female castration into the modern health care system, where, it is important to note, excision and infibulation would have received international financial support. Instead the recommendations were rephrased and are unequivocal:

Adoption of a clear national policy for the abolishment of female circumcision.

Establishment of national commissions to co-ordinate and follow up the activities of the bodies involved; including, where appropriate, the enactment of legislation prohibiting female circumcision.

Intensification of general education of the public including health education at all levels, with special emphasis on the dangers and undesirability of female circumcision.

Intensification of national programmes for traditional birth attendants, midwives, healers and other practitioners of traditional medicine, showing the harmful effects of female circumcision, with a view to enlisting their support along general efforts to abolish the practice.

Ms. Hosken sees this as a victory and writes that WHO, in spite of its earlier intransigence, should be commended for having finally broken the code of silence. But recommendations are not useful unless they are implemented. The agency which should be most directly involved in bringing about WHO's proposals is UNICEF and Ms. Hosken's experiences with this target group have not been altogether promising.

Immediately following the Khartoum conference, Hosken went to see the UNICEF officer in Somalia. She reported to him the recommendations and asked about infibulation which is almost universally practiced in Somalia. The officer, who has seen three quarters of his 2 year tour of duty knew nothing of the operations. Would he take action on the recommendations? No, not unless the government requested the programme. No matter that the UN charter clearly states that "in the performance of their tasks, the UN staff shall not seek to receive instructions from any government". No matter that Somalia *has* already organized a national commission against Pharoanic circumcision which included the Ministers of Health and Education.

The implementation of the recommendations depends first on their becoming public knowledge. *The Hosken Report*, written just as Hosken was setting out for Khartoum is a complete and often devastating account of sexual mutilation. The May 1979 issue of the WHO publication *World Health* contains a full discussion by Dr A.H. Tabor of the operations, the health damage and the Khartoum Seminar. Even as the information seeps into the public sector, Hosken's run-in with an ill-informed uninterested UNICEF officer makes it clear that pressure will have to come from concerned woman before international agencies will commit themselves to action. Hosken suggests that letters to Mr. H.L. Larouisse at UNICEF headquarters in New York (866 UN Plaza, New York, NY, 10017) are useful. The Canadian Executive Director is Harry Black (443 Mount Pleasant Rd., 3rd Floor, Toronto M4S 2L8.)

Of course the most eloquent statement of support for the recommendations is the withdrawal of financial support from UNICEF and any other agency that refuses to come to grips with the issue. CIDA, the Canadian International Development Agency, which funds programmes in Africa, has been alarmingly silent and should be confronted. In this the International Year of the Child, it is particularly appropriate for women to contact the Women's International Network which has been set up to facilitate the WHO recommendations and to organize support for women in Africa working for change. More information is available from WIN News, 187 Grant Street, Lexington, Massachusetts 02173, USA.

"The failure of an agency to recognize the recommendations," writes Hosken, "means it is supporting genital mutilation. And that must be challenged because it is a political decision." As for women who are just beginning to integrate the horrifying facts, collective queasiness is simply not an adequate response.

REBEL MUSIC: ROCK AGAINST RACISM
by Susan Sturman
Volume 1, No. 3 (December 1979), p. 12

Earlier this fall, after the police slaying of Albert Johnson, a group of concerned women and men met together to found a Toronto chapter of the British-based Rock Against Racism movement. Susan Sturman takes a look at the history of RAR and its more recent offshoot, Rock Against Sexism, and discusses their implications for women.

For those of us whose political education began in the late 60s, rock music seemed a necessary adjunct to rebellion—against parental authority, archaic sexual mores, the war in Vietnam. Then came co-optation and neo-conservatism, the 70s, and just as young politicos were being bought off, rock musicians were becoming more concerned with amassing their personal fortunes than with any social consciousness. Rock music embraced a reactionary individualistic philosophy, and male disillusion increasingly found an outlet in mindless misogyny, cock rock in its glory. Nobody flinched when the Stones decided to combine racism and sexism in their notorious "Brown Sugar." And of course, anyone who objected to all this macho posturing was "a queer."

This situation was especially true in Britain, where crippling recession had begun to push political tempers toward the right. The fascist National Front was gaining support for its campaign of racial purity and repatriation of non-white immigrants. By the summer of 1976 unemployment had reached one and a half million. During that "long, hot summer," the National Front marched in the streets provoking race riots, four Asian immigrants were brutally killed, and lesbians and gays were attacked and harassed by gangs of young NF supporters. Rock star Eric Clapton (who had only a few years earlier supported friend George Harrison's Concert for Bangladesh) demonstrated public support for right-winger Enoch Powell's racist repatriation scheme.

A group of rock fans and musicians were appalled by the racist and sexist backlash that swept the country, and were especially indignant that white male rock stars like Clapton, who owed so much to the influence of black musicians, could suggest that black people had no right to live among them. Punk and reggae music were emerging from the streets as part of a grass-roots challenge to the rising reaction, and out of this coincidence of events, Rock Against Racism was born.

RAR took as its platform an opposition to discrimination and violence against immigrants, racial minorities, women and gays, recognizing the political potential of rock music as a means to fight intolerance and oppression. The support of popular groups like the Tom Robinson Band, The Clash, and Elvis Costello helped RAR draw more rock fans to their philosophies, and RAR chapters have grown up throughout Britain and in the United States. Recently, an RAR group has started in Toronto (see box).

RAR in Britain has a fairly wide base; its political leanings are basically anarchist. Through its diverse musical affiliations it has managed to attract the support of various mass movements; the participation of the Tom Robinson Band has encouraged a strong gay liberation and feminist following: reggae, political music in itself, has wide appeal among the West Indian immigrant population. Punk, the perfect anarchic music, is largely the product of working class youth. This mass support has made RAR the darling of the Left.

Unfortunately, as with the Left, much of RAR's pronouncements on sexism have been lip-service. There have been more than a few instances where bands playing RAR concerts performed material that is blatantly offensive to women. Although RAR's platform opposed sexism, few of the male bands involved have been seriously willing to examine and change their own sexist attitudes (sound familiar?), and even fewer are prepared to challenge the rock industry on sexist grounds. Fascism and racism have taken priority as more "important" (read "convenient") issues. Some of the women involved in RAR grew tired of the constant struggle to educate the men within the movement, and, a year ago, an autonomous women's campaign, Rock Against Sexism, was founded.

Feminists have often rejected rock as inherently male and sexist. Rock *has* traditionally been made by men and used primarily to express their feelings about sexual relationships. Many feminist musicians have turned away from rock in favour of folk, jazz, funk or other less "macho" musical forms, and still regard rock with distaste. Those of us who still like rock music have often been forced to be "in the closet"; we find ourselves in the schizophrenic position of loving the music while hating its content. The music has energy and enthusiasm, and an ability to *move* people that has always been, potentially subversive. The problem with rock is not with the music itself, but with the sexist attitudes of those who make the music and run the industry.

The women of RAS view the combination of feminism and rock as a powerful force for change, and this is reflected in their five basic aims: "1) to fight sexism in rock music, and to use rock music to fight sexism in the world at large, 2) to challenge the stereotype images of women and men and promote a more positive image of women in rock, 3) to attack the exploitation of women in advertising, in the press and on the stage, 4) to encourage women musicians by giving them more opportunities to play, and 5) to assert the right of everyone to determine their own sexuality."

Rock Against Sexism appears to be catching on. Many local chapters of the movement have started throughout England, and their concerts have drawn increasing numbers. Their philosophy is basically populist, and it has been successful; the appeal of punk and reggae has been no accident in England. "You've got to make sexism into something which isn't just what 'nit-picking' feminists go on about," says Angele, of the women's band Spoilsports. The women in RAS see the campaign as "a way of introducing the ideas of the women's movement to a lot of people, especially teenagers, who wouldn't otherwise hear these points of view expressed. RAS gigs should help to blur the damaging and sometimes artificial distinctions between 'feminists' and 'non-feminists'" (Lucy Toothpaste, in *Spare Rib*, April 1979).

The women see their music as a good way of breaking down barriers; they hope to provide a comfortable atmosphere for women at RAS concerts (which are sometimes women-only, sometimes mixed), and to promote a new relationship between the performers and the audience. To reinforce this positive propaganda, RAS also distributes posters and leaflets on sexism. They understand that many of those attending may have had little or no exposure to the ideas of feminism, but hope that through the concerts they may begin to make connections.

In addition to the concerts, RAS also holds regular music workshops for women; there are practical workshops on various instruments for experienced and beginning women musicians, theory workshops, and also workshops on sound engineering. The women have also been publishing a bulletin to announce RAS concerts and to stimulate dialogue on music and sexism.

Feminists have long recognized the political potential of popular culture, but they have seldom exploited it. Given the increasing interest in women in rock taken by the mainstream media (*The Globe and Mail* and the *Star* have both recently featured articles on the subject), Rock Against Sexism may be an idea whose time has come. The question is: would RAS have the same kind of mass appeal here as in Britain? Or, for that matter, would RAR? So far, Rock Against Racism has met with only limited success in the United States, especially when compared with the response that the anti-nuclear coalition MUSE (Musicians United for Safe Energy) has received. Part of the problem is that RAR in the U.S.A. is heavily identified with the revolutionary Left (the Revolutionary Communist Party in particular), and although they love the masses, the masses do not necessarily love them. Teenagers and workers in North America have not undergone the same kind of politicization as their British counterparts. RAS, which has not yet crossed the Atlantic, might connect in some way with the "women's music" movement, but that would limit its appeal to a fairly small audience. And, unfortunately, within that movement, there is still somewhat of an "official" prejudice against rock music. However, more women's bands are springing up in punk and New Wave centres like New

York and Toronto, and perhaps they will provide the impetus for an RAS movement here. Toronto seems well disposed to RAR, as people become more aware (through the efforts of Toronto's police force, among others) of the anti-immigrant, anti-black, anti-gay and anti-woman backlash present in the city. As more women's bands emerge here, an autonomous body like RAS may follow.

Are you ready for some *real* rebel music?

FPC: GROWING PAINS
by Sheila McIntyre
Volume 1, No. 9 (July/August 1980), pp. 7 and 17

In February 1979, a group of Toronto feminists began meeting to debate the best route toward real political change for women in Canada. Ultimately they concluded that women's best interests would be served by the establishment of a formally constituted political party rather than a political caucus or yet another feminist lobby group. On June 10, 1979 the first public meeting of the Feminist Party of Canada—Parti Féministe du Canada (FPC—PFC) was held in Toronto. Its founders outlined why they believed the Party was needed, detailed its goals and constituency and signed up members and volunteers for committees in the anticipation of a founding convention then proposed for the summer or fall of 1980.

To commemorate that first public meeting last June and to account for a year of activity, the Party held a first anniversary celebration this year in Toronto on Sunday, June 8. Approximately 300 women and a sprinkling of children and men spent the afternoon listening to speeches by Party members, liberally punctuated by poetry, music and dance by women.

Something of the promise of this party was symbolized in the opening of the celebrations. Margaret Atkinson performed a "War Dance" which she dedicated to Lizzie Tomlinson, the six-year-old recently raped and murdered in Toronto. The dance depicted the process of a woman channelling anger into action, and self-effacing feminine charm into bold self-assertion.

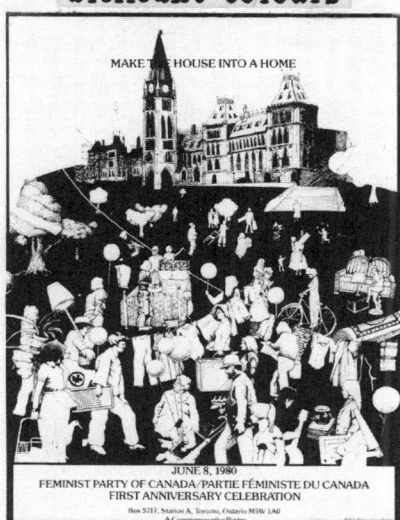

The Feminist Party of Canada advertises its four-colour poster.

Next, following readings of feminist poetry in both French and English, FPC—PFC member Patricia Hughes summarized the philosophy of the party and its activities to date.

The Feminist Party, Hughes explained, is in the process of developing strategies which will go beyond lobbying for reforms within the existing political structure and towards fundamental change in the way society is organized. Its concerns will be reproductive and creative in the broadest sense: it will be based on non-violence; dedicated to the protection of the environment; economic production based on community benefit rather than individual profit; active in lobbying for progressive, adequate child care, safe contraception, equal pay and the protection of minority rights. Above all, it will be a Party as committed to the quality of the process by which change is achieved as the achievement of change itself. Feminist principles will be honoured before pragmatism.

While the process of establishing policies and programs continues, the FPC—PFC will follow the pattern of the past year in responding to specific political issues on an ad hoc basis. In Toronto, for instance, party members have represented feminist concerns on several fronts: members challenged candidates for the recent federal election on issues of concern to women; pressured City Hall to refuse to send delegates to conferences in U.S. states which have not yet ratified the Equal Rights Amendment (such a by-law has been passed, though watered down); presented a brief at the CRTC hearings on sexism in the media; protested Metro Toronto's decision to invest in elaborate technology to register pregnant women on a computer system identifying high, medium, and low risk mothers (see *Broadside*, Volume one, Numbers 3 and 8); and marched under the FPC-PFC banner at International Women's Day and anti-nuclear demonstrations. The Party has also opened a Toronto office, registered members in every process and begun the groundwork to run a candidate in the forthcoming municipal elections.

Hughes closed her remarks by urging the audience to act on the understanding that women's low socio-economic status has political roots. Our oppression has nothing to do with our emotional or psychological makeup, but with the political system governing our lives. The only way to improve our status is through political change, change instigated, directed and implemented by a feminist party.

The second speaker, Mary O'Brien, was charged with defining the "creative bureaucracy" by which the Party intends to govern itself. As O'Brien focused on the process of decision-making, she implicitly addressed those members and those outsiders who criticize the fact that the FPC-PFC has not yet formulated an official plank or set a date for its founding convention.

Traditional bureaucracy, O'Brien maintains, is the "efficient public face of power." The creative bureaucracy favoured by the FPC-PFC, however, is based on a division of energy and on trust, not power. Instead of a hierarchical structure of prominent leaders and an invisible executive committee making all policy decisions, the FPC-PFC has chosen a vertical structure of autonomous chapters and committees that report to the Strategy Committee, each with equal authority and responsibility. Instead of the efficiency of centralized power far removed from the majority of voters, the FPC-PFC is prepared to risk a less efficient organization which will integrate the concerns of all its members and be sensitive to individual differences, regional autonomy and the eclectic needs and interests of women. This route, sometimes confusing, always time-consuming and absolutely dependent on an actively committed transnational membership, will result in a truly representative and egalitarian democracy.

Sculptor Maryon Kantaroff had the last word and, unfortunately, didn't take full advantage of her rhetorical position. She recounted current evolutionary theory on the natural origins of sex roles and the division of labour by sex to argue the time is right for women to take history into their own hands. The gist of evolutionary theory is that homo sapiens' standing upright instead of on four legs shortened the gestation period of human infants, thereby binding women longer to child rearing. The vulnerability of women and infants while men were off hunting also bound women into co-operative communities, the earliest "networks," Kantaroff's punch-line was a version of the dancing dog theory: it's not the skill of a dancing dog one so admires as the fact of its dancing at all. Highlighting some of women's creative contributions through history—the development of weaving, pottery, agriculture, animal husbandry, and later the women artists who produced despite the social sanctions against such expression—Kantaroff claimed that the beauty of women's history is not that we made these contributions despite natural and social laws limiting our survival, but that we survived at all. Now, she claimed, we have the numbers, the need, and above all the highly evolved intelligence to shape history rather than be shaped by it.

The question, alas, is how to take history into our hands, how, in fact, to make the fundamental changes on which the future survival of our species depends. The June 1979 FPC-PFC meeting didn't really address the sobering issue of nuts and bolts practical matters: where do we get the money, the expertise, the human resources to have the clout and political savvy of, say, the gun lobby effectively blocking licensing of hand guns? The gap between the heady vision of a political party run by feminists to bring about what O'Brien termed the politics of the good earth, and the practical problems of governing without leaders, without a fixed party plank and without the wealth native to the powerful was reflected by a difference in the climate of the meeting last June and the one this June. In general, though entertaining and informative, the June 8 celebration lacked the passionate mix of hope and defiance that infected us last year.

It didn't help that there were no decriers in evidence this year to galvanize and provoke the audience into a "we'll show 'em" spirit. Last year's meeting featured speaker Laura Sabia and several members of the audience suggested the FPC-PFC didn't stand a chance: women could never organize themselves well enough to launch a viable political party; existing political parties were showing signs of responding to women's needs; women would be alienated by the word "feminist" in the party's title. So insulting and patronizing were these claims that the need for a feminist party was patently demonstrated.

This year we lack a tangible enemy to rally us into opposition. Further, we have no leaders to follow or tidy little campaign planks to generate specific responses. The really hard work has begun, difficult questions are being posed, the inefficient but necessary process of collective democracy is in motion. Most members are rank amateurs in this era of high-tech and slick politicking. We don't just have a massive social and economic system against us, we have our own internal procedural principles slowing us down. It's no surprise the audience left on June 8, not in a state of euphoria like last year, but subdued, exhausted by the thought of the frustrating groundwork still to be done.

The moral of the story is that if we want a political party to represent us, we'll have to do more than scorn the Chrétiens who would redefine rape laws to "prove" the victim didn't consent, more than decry the Labour ministers who admit that equal pay is too expensive for our economy, more than criticize the Toronto alder*men* who fear that boycotting anti-ERA states might lose Toronto some revenue. We'll have to work on FPC-PFC committees, start local chapters outside Toronto, circulate copies of the petition requiring 10,000 signatures to grant the party official political status, and if we can't afford the time to do the heavy lifting of organizing, will have to donate funds instead. Decide what contribution you can make and send in your $5 membership fee: FPC-PFC, Box 5717, Station A, Toronto M5W 1AO.

CONSTITUTIONAL CONFERENCE: VALENTINE'S DAY REVENGE

by Jane Hastings and Judith Lawrence
Volume 2, No. 5 (March 1981), p. 4

When the Advisory Council on the Status of Women executive decided in January to postpone the women's constitutional conference scheduled for February 13–14, Doris Anderson asked how this postponement would be explained to the women of Canada. Someone suggested cynically that the women of Canada had been lied to before and could be lied to again. But telling a lie is one thing; getting it believed is another. Canadian women were not to be bamboozled nor deprived of a chance to make themselves heard en masse on the subject of their displeasure over the constitutional proposals.

1,300 women from every region of Canada converged on Ottawa on February 14 to make one final attempt to be heard by the government as it moved toward the end of its discussions on patriation. The ad hoc women's conference, superbly organized by the "Cow Café Committee" in Toronto and its Ottawa counterpart (see accompanying article by Kay Macpherson) embarked at 9 am on a day of panel presentations, group discussions, and plenaries to produce recommendations to be delivered to Parliament the following week. By six pm it was apparent that too much work remained to be done to stop at the appointed time, so the assembly voted to cancel the evening's social events and return after a dinner break for more work. So intent on work were these women that at 9 pm, someone getting a drink of ice water for the translators reported only one woman to be found in the bar set up in a nearby room.

The intense commitment and dedication to hard work apparent among these women indicated the extent to which they realized the importance of the issues before them. Canadian women have had an opportunity unique in Western countries in the 20th century to participate in defining the terms under which they are to participate in their political and legal system. Although the Constitution consists of the BNA Act and various other statutes enacted over the years, it does not presently contain a bill of rights.

It has become a crucial women's issue to obtain a bill of rights acknowledging the equality of women in Canadian society. The Ad Hoc Conference debated long and hard on the issue of whether or not the Constitution should be "matriated" with just an amending formula and no bill of rights (the PC position) or with the bill of rights currently under discussion. (Liberal/NDP position) Early Saturday afternoon the Conference voted to table the matriation motion under discussion and go on to deal with specific clauses because consensus could not be reached and the discussion was taking a turn for the partisan.

Conference participants were keenly aware of the many vested interests in seeing the Ad Hoc Conference co-opted by the Tories and showed determination to keep the proceedings non-partisan and to stick strictly to women's issues. The discussion of the clauses finished after the dinner break and resulted in a set of proposed amendments to the Charter of Rights and Freedoms, all passed with the consensus of the group, (see box).

Apparently most women had discussed matriation over dinner, so that the issue was raised from the table after the amendments were passed and the following compromise on entrenchment was given unanimous endorsement: "Be it resolved that this Conference endorse in principle the concept of an entrenched Charter of Rights as per the recommendation passed February 14, 1981, and that unless the charter reflects the amendments made here today that it not be included in the submission to the British Government in order to provide time to incorporate these amendments." Put simply, we're for entrenchment only if the Charter contains our amendments—otherwise not.

Work ended around 10:30 pm with a strong feeling that "we've all won." In a press conference the following day, male reporters harassed organizer Linda Ryan Nye about whether the conference represented a victory for the Tories. She adamantly refused to be bullied into saying anything other than that the conference expressed the demands of a considerable spectrum of Canadian women concerning their constitution. Certainly, "the parties" were in evidence: both MPs Flora MacDonald and Pauline Jewett made brief welcoming speeches at the opening of the conference, and it was well-publicized that the NDP furnished coffee and that the meeting rooms in the West Block of Parliament (where the original conference was to have taken place) were obtained through the efforts of Flora MacDonald.

But significantly, the major effort to sidetrack discussion of the Charter clauses into a partisan argument on matriation was an ill-timed outburst by Maureen McTeer which was vociferously rejected by the entire three rooms full of participants. The women were determined to keep to the topic at hand and carry forward the work of debating and voting on the resolutions. MacDonald and Jewett were present off and on throughout the day and all through the evening session, both maintaining a quiet presence and blending with the group, as did MP Pat Carney.

The major thrust of the proceedings was the strong, universal concern for the women's issues at stake. The participants—not "delegates" necessarily, since many women were not representative of any group—reflected a huge variety of Canadian women. All provinces and one of the territories were represented, although Québec had only three women present; many Francophones came from the Atlantic Provinces; the age range extended from very young (including a couple of infants) to a goodly number of women with snowy hair and canes; there were women in jeans and plaid shirts, in slacks and sweaters, in elegantly tailored suits and dresses. The coatracks were revealing: a scattering of fur coats but no mink), a lot of quilted coats and jackets, and a lot of duffle coats. Although many women paid their own way, many others requested and received travel funds, and special trains and buses brought them at economy rates. The Ottawa committee arranged billeting and childcare and provided for inexpensive lunches. Clearly a wide range of economic positions existed among the participants. Native women constituted a strong presence, although their presentation requesting a supportive resolution was set aside because it asked for support of their plea for independent nationhood rather than for anything to do with issues of specific concern to native women themselves.

Although the Québec representation was minimal, the Francophone presence was strong. The Conference received gratifying support from the translators; in return for the postponement of the original fall conference as a move to support the translators' strike, they donated their services free even though the ad hoc planning committees had budgeted for their services. And they returned after dinner to work the extra, unscheduled session, also without charge. Many Francophone women spoke at the microphones, and a panel presentation by a Francophone lawyer received careful attention from the roomful of Anglophone women in a closed-circuit TV room where there was no translation. Hall conversations frequently occurred in assorted mixtures of French and English. So the language atmosphere was positive; the lack of Québec presence was clearly political rather than linguistic.

Marion Dewar, Mayor of Ottawa, made the City Hall and all its excellent facilities available for the Sunday session on the Status of the Canadian Advisory Council on the Status of Women. Another full day of hard debate produced nine resolutions pertaining to the assessment and reorganization of the CACSW with a view to making it non-partisan and truly representative of Canadian women and their concerns (see box). Shirley Carr of the Canadian Labour Congress, an organization which represents a million unionized working women, participated extensively in this debate and told of the efforts of women from the labour movement to get just one representative on this Council. Again and again, she reported, the government asked for names to be submitted as potential Council members. Labour organizations had recommended highly qualified women with excellent credentials but these candidates had been passed over for political appointees with no background or interest in women's issues. It also pointed out that not one Native or Inuit woman had ever sat on the Council—unlike in some provincial status of women advisory councils, where, as in Saskatchewan for instance, Native women have been included from the outset.

Doris Anderson's speech at the Sunday session received a standing ovation. She made many positive comments about the Advisory Council staff, whom she praised and complimented on the excellence of their research work. She noted that these women are still at work, producing further papers on topics such as the economic and educational problems of Canadian women. As in the Saturday sessions, the debate surrounding the CACSW was constructive and non-partisan. Women from the various provinces told how their provincial status of women councils were organized, how they worked, and how they reported, and with what results. The final nine resolutions set forth a program for reform of the CACSW and the restoration of its credibility.

So where did it all go after Sunday? Oddly enough, a number of women who were active in the Ad Hoc Constitutional Conference were to see Axworthy the next day at his Monday conference with representatives of women's organizations. One was Deborah Acheson, a lawyer from Victoria, B.C., invited by Axworthy as a representative of her profession. In an interview on CBC-AM radio's morning program from Vancouver, she reported that Axworthy stated his refusal to resign and took the rest of the recommendations under advisement. According to Kay Macpherson, representing NAC at this meeting, a number of the invited representatives supported the government and backed the three vice-presidents for whose resignation the Ad Hoc Conference had called. In "The House" on TV Monday night, MPs Pauline Jewett and Flora MacDonald took the Conference's recommendations to Parliament, calling for the resignation of Axworthy and reform of the CACSW. Trudeau carefully avoided a direct response on the subject and talked generally about the constitution. As *Broadside* goes to press, the prospects of the government's taking seriously the work of the Constitutional

Conference are gloomy. But the great victory for all Canadian women took place on Valentine's Day when 1300 women showed their determination to be reckoned with one way or another. The Conference was one way…

I'M IN THE MOOD FOR SEXUAL REVOLUTION

by Joanne Kates

Volume 2, No. 7 (May 1981), p. 9

Erotic desire is the most delightful of all the forces that drive human beings. Making love is the most intimate thing that two people can do together, it can be sweet and strong and slow. It can engage two minds and bodies in complete congress. Wonderful sex engages the heart and the soul as well as the body and takes them on a magic carpet ride to places that cannot be reached by any other method. You know you've had it from the immense feeling of well-being, like waves on a hot beach. None of this erotic transport is possible when you wear your mask to bed, when you leave your heart and mind outside the bedroom because it's against the rules to show who you really are. Sex is hot, anonymity is cool, and when you mix them, what you get is lukewarm.

Welcome to the (hetero)Sexual Revolution! We know it's here because we read about it in the paper (not this paper). In his 1980 bestseller *Thy Neighbour's Wife* Gay Talese said: "This nation… is being gradually overtaken by a silent revolution of the senses, a departure from conventionality. And even within the middle class, where I'm concentrating my research, there is now an ever-increasing tolerance for sexual expression…." Talese spent nine lascivious years researching his book on sex. With a six-figure advance from Doubleday, he traversed America and Europe buying sex directly, in massage parlours (that was his favourite) and indirectly, through his (male) author's access to private orgy retreats in California. He got all the sex he wanted while his wife stayed home and raised their two daughters, and the story he wrote is very much determined by the way he did his research.

Talese is an extreme example of the pundits who have been touting the Sexual Revolution, but there is no qualitative difference between him and his less privileged brothers. From the men who bring us the daily cheesecake photos in the Toronto *Sun*, to *Playboy* to Gay Talese, the message is the same: Hurrah fellas, jump on! It's the Sexual Revolution. Women have been "liberated" to flop on our backs at the slightest provocation, rotate our pelvises perfectly for any man who asks, and act as if we enjoy it.

Before the late sixties and the so-called Sexual Revolution, the pressure was on women to be chaste and virginal, and now the pressure is on women to put out. It's a simple reversal of pressure, and women who do not give in to the pressure to put out are labelled frigid or uptight, and they are scorned. Catch-22 is that in spite of the nominal Sexual Revolution, the double standard is alive and well in heterosexual relations. Women who say no to casual sex are called cold and they get rejected, but women who say yes to casual sex get rejected afterwards for being too easy. As one man I interviewed said: "Sure I'd go to bed with almost anybody I met in a singles bar, but I wouldn't ask for her number in the morning. I don't want to go out with anybody who's that easy. If she was that easy with me, she'd probably be that easy with other guys too." The good girl/bad girl stereotype lives on: The "bad girl" gets a reputation as an easy lay and she's despised; the "good girl" is the one they marry and then if they're successful (à la Gay Talese) they leave her at home with the kids and go out and play around with the "bad girls."

This is not to imply that casual sex is bad and the only good sex is that which occurs inside the confines of a long term and committed relationship. That is not true. Sex between friends who are also lovers has all the potential to be splendid, but most casual heterosexual encounters probably don't occur between friends. Why: Because only equals can be friends, and the relations of power between men and women are so skewed that it's hard for a man to be any more to us that what the French writer Colette called "dear enemy." Sex and power are inextricably linked; if one person has power over another, it's impossible to keep that power relation out of the bedroom. The source of that male power over women lies in all the social relations between us. By and large they are the bosses and we are the employees; they are the doctors, we are the nurses and the patients. In the realm of production the wage gap between men and women in Canada is growing, and unemployment for women is substantially higher than unemployment for men.

In the realm of personal life too, women are subordinate to men: in the family, father earns the most money (and power) and tradition says father knows best. Men tend to rule the domestic roost, and this is proven by the fact that most women still have to work a double day of labour: first in the office or the factory and then at home. In the bedroom that power differential still translates into women's silences about our sexuality. The sexual arrangements between men and women are no different from any other arrangements: man proposes, woman waits and hopes that something to her taste will come along. If she protests, she's likely to be rewarded with accusations of being a ball-breaker.

In the area of sexuality, the relations of power between men and women are particularly acute, exacerbated by men's fear of female sexuality, which they imagine is so dangerously powerful that it will variously swallow them up, cut off their penis with a blunt instrument or with the teeth they imagine to be hiding in the vagina. The fear of female sexuality leads men to punish women whenever our sexuality is showing. How do they do that? The vitriolic reviews of Judy Chicago's art exhibit *The Dinner Party* for its images of vaginas; the attacks on our right to abortions; male managers' choices to leave birth control technology where it is and let women be physically damaged by contraceptives like the Pill and the IUD; firing pregnant women, the only people in society who bear the visible evidence of their sexual activity; firing lesbians and taking away their children; clitoridectomy (surgical removal of the clitoris) in some cultures.

In this ersatz Sexual Revolution, women are still not permitted to be sexual in our own right. We are permitted to have more frequent sexual encounters that we were in the 50s, but we get punished for doing it too much. We are still trained to use sex as a necessary tool with which to snare a man. We've been schooled from girlhood in the feminine art of how to look and act in order to tempt men, in the interests of getting them to meet us at the altar. In doing so, all a woman's real sexual power must be relinquished. Sexual power is the power to determine a sexual situation in co-operation with your companion, it is the power to make love fully, to engage yourself at all levels, to get what you need in order to be fully present, and women are not generally allowed to do that with men, particularly not if they have to use their sex as a tool to get something else. Furthermore, she has to relinquish her sexual desire, because it gets in the way of sexual teasing. She has to look sexy, smell sexy, dance sexy and talk sexy, but at certain carefully calculated moments she also has to turn off and play hard to get in order to keep him wanting more. Because sexual desire is no mechanical impulse, it cannot be turned on and off like a tap. You can fake the desire, but it goes into hiding. Think back to all the women you've seen whose sexuality is being publicly used: hookers on the street; *Playboy* centrefolds; strippers; movie stars wearing décolleté on the cover of People magazine; the women dancing half nude in the movie *All That Jazz*. Do they look sexually aroused?

The Hite Report asked 1664 women if they ever fake orgasms, and 1,093 of them answered yes. Why? Because the rules of the Sexual Revolution dictate that we're supposed to have orgasm after orgasm, that if we were really *women*, we'd be having multiple orgasms. The New Woman (a media creation and the female counterpart of the Playboy Man) is supposed to come like crazy, and if she doesn't, she must crack the fragile male ego by letting him know that he didn't do what she needed him to do. The majority of women in *The Hite Report* said that casual lovers did not usually touch their clitoris. Masters and Johnson's definitive study, *Human Sexual Response*, proved that most women need direct clitoral stimulation in order to have orgasms; they're not getting it in casual sex with men.

What is strange and terrifying is the fact that so many men are blissfully unaware that the women they go to bed with are not having orgasms. I interviewed about 25 single men and asked them if their lovers were having orgasms. They all said yes. I then asked whether these orgasms were the result of direct clitoral stimulation or just intercourse, and the majority answered it was just intercourse. They all said they performed so well it made women come.

This view is shared by the majority of the 4,000 men surveyed in *Beyond the Male Myth*, a 1977 US sexual survey book: "Our study shows that nearly one third of men brought their partners to orgasm *through intercourse* nearly every time, and more than half succeeded

60 per cent of the time." The authors, lacking electrodes and a laboratory, relied on the men's reports of what was happening in their bedrooms. They got the same answers I got because the men did not want to admit, either to themselves or to anyone else, that they had failed in the main task of the modern male stud. Their self-deception is of course facilitated by the utter lack of communication between women and men.

The vicious circle is that women are afraid they'll get rejected by men if they don't stroke the male ego by seeming to erupt like Mount Vesuvius from his ministrations, so they fake orgasms. The men then have a good excuse not to bother figuring out that it's not working, so they continue to bang away like a piston on a Chevrolet. She then gets more disappointed, and her hopelessness about ever having a satisfying sexual encounter is intensified and she is therefore even less likely to take the risk of stating what she really wants.

The alienating encounters of the Sexual Revolution are more socially useful than they appear at first glance. In much the same way as alcohol and drugs, they function as a pressure release valve for the woes of the repressive social system. The encounters look so free, but in fact they are anything but free.

Herbert Marcuse, the radical German philosopher, married psychoanalysis, which is the study of individuals, to the study of social life in capitalism; he used psychoanalysis to analyze exactly how the system gets under our skins so that we play along with it. Marcuse had a particular interest in sexual repression, and in the modern mores that masquerades as sexual freedom but in reality results in more repression of what's alive and erotic in human beings. He theorized that there are two kinds of repression: Basic and surplus.

Basic repression is the repression that Freud identified in the training that all children go through in order to become "civilized." It includes learning to repress urges to defecate on the living room floor and write on the walls and chew on electric wires; these are the socially necessary repressions in virtually any political system, and children are taught to sublimate those anti-social desires into activities like finger-painting and useful work. Those are the kinds of repressions and sublimations that society needs in order that we may live together in relative harmony. But Freud failed to understand a whole other layer of repression, the surplus repression which is not necessary for human beings to become human, but which is necessary to train us to fit into the system of domination in which we live.

Surplus repression is the repression of the power and the vitality and the sensuality present in all children that would make them too rebellious to be useful if it persisted. It is surplus repression that keeps women acquiescing in our oppression. We have been trained through surplus repression to agree to be dominated by men, to let them keep the power. Men too have been diminished by surplus repression. When children are taught to be quietly obedient in school and not argue with the teacher, that's surplus repression. Their high spirits and their power are being repressed so they'll learn to be quiet and obedient workers. When little children are caught "playing doctor" and are punished for it, that's surplus repression: their sexual curiosity is being repressed in order to teach them that their bodies are not to be freely enjoyed, so they will settle down in chaste, monogamous marriages and go to work every morning and raise quiet children, instead of having sexual adventures that keep them out of the family and up half the night. Basic repression makes us human; surplus repression makes us obedient.

TOO SOON TO JUDGE
by Val Edwards
Volume 3, No. 6 (April 1982), p. 6

When *Broadside* asked me to write on Bertha Wilson's appointment to the Supreme Court of Canada, I accepted; but I soon became aggravated by a sense of regret for accepting the assignment. I knew nothing about Madame Justice Bertha Wilson.

Well, not quite nothing. In first year law school, my professor in contracts introduced the class to one of Wilson's decisions. He stood at the front, of the class waving the case about in the air. "Idiotic!" he ranted. "Stupid! crazy! insane!" The students all chortled and clucked as they highlighted the impugned paragraphs with screeching yellow magic markers.

When news of Wilson's appointment trickled through the law

office where I work, there were no clucks or chortles. The event was noted with some small interest, but there was no excitement, positive or negative. I wondered how my old contracts professor had taken the news, and could imagine him gleefully rubbing his chalky hands together at the prospect of scoring even bigger points with the peanut gallery. In any event, the appointment came as a surprise to no one.

In order to write about her, I spent a week digging out Wilson's decisions and calling every lawyer I knew for an opinion. There is a clear consensus among lawyers that Wilson is a bright, studious and competent judge. Some consider her one of the outstanding judges on the Ontario Court of Appeal. And what about her politics, I asked? Is she a liberal? Is she a feminist? Few of the people I spoke to understood the relevance of this line of inquiry, and even fewer had answers.

It is extraordinarily difficult to assess a judge politically. Of course, there are exceptions. For example, we all knew where His Honour Judge McEwan stood a few years ago when he refused to accept the evidence of a witness because she was middle-aged and probably in menopause. But by and large judges cloak themselves in the intricacies of the law. They are technicians, not policymakers. Even where a judge is known to hold certain political views, his decisions rarely reflect them.

Let me give you an illustration. Bertha Wilson's one claim to fame among feminists is her dissenting judgement in the Debbie Bazso case. The Ontario Rural Softball Association (ORSA) refused to let Debbie play in the league. The girl's family sued on the grounds that her rights under the Ontario Human Rights Code had been violated. The Ontario Court of Appeal ruled in a 2–1 decision that the baseball league could not discriminate on the basis of sex.

What most feminists do not know is that Wilson also delivered the majority judgement in the Gail Cummings case, which was decided at the same time as Bazso (August 30, 1979). The Court of Appeal unanimously held that the Ontario Minor Hockey Association (OMHA) could exclude girls from the league.

Why did Wilson swing both ways on the same issue? Both cases focused on the interpretation of the Human Rights Code. The relevant section reads: "No person...shall discriminate against any person or class of persons with respect to the accommodation, services or facilities available in any place to which the public is customarily admitted…" In the Bazso case the only issue was whether the word "public" referred to the physical space or the type of service offered. Wilson felt that it referred to the space, and since ballparks are normally open to the public, the softball association could not exclude girls.

In the Cummings case, however, there was an extra twist. The OMHA was unincorporated, unlike the ORSA. Did the OMHA constitute a "person" within the meaning of the Code? The law in this area in quite clear. Corporations are legal persons; unincorporated groups are not. From the layman's perspective, the reasoning and result are bizarre — what difference is there really between the two leagues? From a legal perspective, the discrepancy in Wilson's decision makes perfect sense.

The American experience with the judiciary is very different from ours. It is much easier to discern a judge's political colours in the United States, partly because many-judges are elected to their positions. More importantly, however, the American Constitution invites judges to make, rather than just interpret the law. Many more American judges are willing to make innovative decisions based on broad considerations of public policy than Canadian or British ones.

The Charter of Rights should open things up a little in Canada. The character and composition of the Supreme Court in the next ten years will determine whether Canadian judges will follow the American example. Wilson's appointment could not have come at a more critical time because there is *some* evidence that she may assume a leading role in interpreting the Canadian Constitution along liberal policy lines.

Potentially, the Charter of Rights' most significant impact will be in the area of criminal law. The *Toronto Star* recently cited criminal law as one of Wilson's weak spots. The article claimed that she concurs in criminal decisions rather than writes her own judgements. Not so, says lawyer Brian Greenspan, who argues as many criminal appeals as anyone in Ontario. "Wilson is a compassionate, relatively defence-minded judge" who is not afraid to take on the heavyweights on the Court of Appeal — Justice Dubin and Justice Martin — in criminal decisions. Wilson is much more likely than they are to find that a trial judge's error has resulted in a miscarriage of justice to the accused. Without such a finding, an accused will not receive a new trial no matter how many errors the trial judge made.

Wilson's dissenting judgement in the Bezaire lesbian mother custody case is another indication of her potential for doing "good works" on the Supreme Court. Mr. Justice Arnup for the majority stated: "In my view, homosexuality, either as a tendency, a proclivity, or a practical way of life, is not in itself alone a ground for refusal of custody." In other words, homosexuality is just one of many negative factors which a court should consider in granting custody. Contrast Wilson's approach: "I would like to add…that in my view homosexuality is a neutral and not a negative factor as far as parenting skills are concerned. To the extent the learned trial judge proceeded in a different view I would respectfully disagree with him" (October 6, 1980).

Since law plays a relatively minor role in custody cases, there is a lot of leeway for judges to demonstrate social and political values. I doubt that Wilson was motivated by sympathy for the gay and feminist movements. Her roots in the legal community are quite conservative—she was a senior partner at Osler Hoskin & Harcourt, a high-powered Bay Street law firm specializing in corporate/commercial law. However, she is a woman with liberal Christian values who is active in community work with the Clark Institute and with the United Church of Canada's committee on the status of women. Where two judges opted for an exceptionally narrow interpretation of the Human Rights Code in the Bazso case, Wilson took the liberal route, stating that her brothers on the court were defeating the very purpose of the Code.

Wilson is in a position to tip the Supreme Court of Canada to the left at a time when all eyes will be watching how the court responds to the Charter of Rights. Prior to Wilson's appointment, the Supreme Court consisted of roughly 4 liberals and 4 conservatives, with Mr. Justice MacKintyre of British Columbia swinging to the right or left. Wilson replaces Roland Martland, one of the most conservative members of the bench. MacKintyre's vote is now less critical—the liberals form a majority without him—at least in theory.

We will soon know whether or not Wilson wishes to lead the court in a liberal interpretation of the Charter and, more importantly, whether she will be able to do so. When the nine judges meet in chambers to discuss the cases before them, Wilson will be called to give the first opinion as the court's most junior member. She has a reputation for being quiet and softspoken during court sittings. Unlike many of her counterparts who try to dominate lawyers during argument, Wilson has never honed her advocacy skills through practising civil or criminal litigation. However, sometimes judges with the biggest mouths are incapable of appreciating novel or subtle legal arguments. Wilson's primary asset is her legal acumen: her credibility as technician will stand her in good stead on a court that, for now, may not be able to handle anything more.

Val Edwards is currently articling at a Bay Street law firm.

ZEROING IN ON ZIONISM
by Lilith Finkler
Volume 4, No. 1 (October 1982), pp. 4 and 10

The following article by Lilith Finkler represents one view of many, and we hope that as issues rise for discussion, such as the role of Jews in the women's movement, Jewish women's invisibility in North American and European cultures, Zionism and anti-Semitism, Broadside readers will contribute their opinions. Finkler's article, to set it in context, was written in June 1982, before the invasion of Lebanon, and therefore does not deal with the most recent charges. "The issues, however, remain the same," says Finkler.

In many recent feminist and lesbian-feminist publications, anti-Zionism and anti-Semitism have been inextricably linked. *Lilith, Ms, Lesbian Lives,* and *Nice Jewish Girls,* a recent lesbian anthology, all contain articles that support this political connection.[1]

An American group called Feminists against Anti-Semitism said in a statement published in *Lilith*: "Today, when explicit anti-Semitism is no longer acceptable, it has surfaced as a virulent anti-Zionism which rejects the right of the Jewish state to exist.

Zionism is the national liberation movement of the Jewish people. Criticism of Israeli governmental policy is not anti-Semitism, but villifying Jews who support Zionism is anti-Semitism."[2]

This remark and some of the articles referred to above are a direct response to the events of the 1981 International Women's Conference sponsored by the United Nations in Copenhagen.

Representatives of the PLO apparently managed to make many of the workshops into vehicles for consciousness-raising and stacked meetings so as to control the speakers' list. From their reports, it is obvious that many North American women suffered emotional battle scars which included profound alienation from non-Jewish feminists. It would not be hard, given their experience, to conclude that all those who were opposed to Zionism as a political movement were also opposed to them as Jews.

However, one conference does not a movement make: the reality of Copenhagen is merely the reflection of much anger and frustration experienced by those whose legitimate claim to Palestine is constantly being ignored.

It is obvious from their writings that these Jewish women, radicalized in other spheres, have yet to understand the complicated Zionist terminology and Israel's history.

To be anti-Semitic is to attribute specific character traits to Jews or to be hostile to them as a religious or social minority.

To be anti-Zionist is to oppose the existence of the State of Israel.

To believe that those who oppose Israel as a physical reality are against the Jews as a group reflects a myriad of other misconceptions.

First, one must presume that the survival of the State of Israel will ensure the survival of the Jewish race. Nothing could be further from the truth. Israel, as a nation, has interests which often conflict with those of Jews in the Diaspora.

Argentina, a safe harbour for Nazi war so. criminals and with a government well known for its virulent anti-Semitism, received valuable weaponry from Israel, most recently during the war over the Falkland Islands. Is Evelyn Torton Beck, editor of *Nice Jewish Girls*, aware that Jacobo Timmerman, the very man she quotes in her article in that book, languished in an Argentinian prison while Israel provided his jailers?[3] Ethiopian *falashas* being massacred by co-patriots of various political persuasions have continuously been denied entry into Israel. Speaker of the Knesset in 1952, Israel Yishayahu, actually suggested publicly that the *falashas* solve their problems by converting to Christianity![4] Needless to say, discussing these black Jews might have put the Israeli government in an uncomfortable position with its special friend and ally, Haile Selassie.

Yehuda Dominitz, head of the Jewish Agency's Department of Immigration and Absorption, stated: "Taking a *falasha* out of his village is like taking a fish out of water.... I am not in favour of *falasha* Aliyah."[5] This in spite of the fact that his Jewish brethren now sit in refugee camps awaiting salvation.[6]

Perhaps most revealing of the nature of political Zionism is the role of its leaders during World War II. They responded to cries for help with calculated logic.

Nathan Schwalb, then a representative of the Jewish Agency in Switzerland, when approached by a a rescue committee of Czech Jews for a sum of money to halt transports to Auschwitz, replied in a letter that serves as a testament to Zionist interests: "...they (the rescue group) must always remember that...after all, the Allies will be victorious. After the victory, they will once again divide up the world between the nations as they did at the end of the First War. Then, they opened the way for us for the first step, and now, as the war ends, we must do everything so that Eretz Yisroel should become a Jewish state.... We must be aware that all the nations of the Allies are spilling much blood, and if we do not bring sacrifices with what will we achieve the right to sit at the table when they make the distribution of nations and territories after the war? And so, it would be foolish and impertinent on our side to ask the nations whose blood is being spilled for permission to send money into the land of their enemies in order to protect our own blood."[7]

It was a philosophy of " selective immigration," expressed by Chaim Weizman at the Zionist Congress in London in 1937. "The hopes of Europe's six million Jews are centred on emigration. I was asked: 'Can you bring six million Jews to Palestine?' I replied, 'No, from the depths of the tragedy, I want to save two million young people.... The old ones will pass. They will bear their fate or they will not. They are dust, moral and economic dust in a cruel world. ...Only the branch of the young shall survive.... They have to accept it."[8] It was a case of Zionism using anti-Semitism, not as its raison d'être, but rather as an emotional and political backdrop for its activities.

Another presumption commonly held is that if one denounces the State of Israel, one is also denying the Jews the right to national self-determination. That is not necessarily so. Instead of uprooting other people to provide for our own, why not form "Jewish space" wherever we now live?

Surely we can look to the women's movement for inspiration! We form "women only" space, women's centres, women's land, and we have created a network of women's self-help services. Why not form "Jewish only" cities in areas where we now live? This would not be a reversion to a ghetto life-style since any Jew could choose to live among her co-religionists or not. We could create our own government based on Jewish values, as opposed to those of our neighbours. We would feel safer and more secure in our own environment and would have displaced no one in the process.

Some feminists, in an attempt to justify Israel's racist policies, have drawn a parallel between lesbian separatism and Zionism: "I am saddened and angered by feminists who never call a separatist coffeehouse or women's centre sexist, but who are quick to call the Jewish law of return racist" (Phyllis Chesler).[9] Chesler fails to grasp the conflicting nature of these two ideologies.

Lesbian separatism is a peaceful form of self-definition and autonomy. It can indeed by applied to the Jewish way of life. Sarah Feinstein, in her article "It Has to do with Apples," describes how her grandmother, Rivke, aligned herself only with other Jews, and how she chose to continue that feeling of separateness as a lesbian.[10]

Feinstein saw separatism as a question of where a lesbian puts her energy, as opposed to a desire to throw all men out so she can have more place for herself. Zionism attempts to create a Jewish-only space by removing the indigenous population, the Palestinians. The law of return which permits Jews to become citizens of Israel immediately also prohibits four million Palestinians from returning to their own land.

Between 1948 and 1967, 385 Arab villages were wiped off the map.[11] The land acquired through mass uprootings was first held under the jurisdiction of the Jewish National Fund and later distributed to settlers to form kibbutzim and moshavim. Consider the village of Umm al-Fahm, which had a population of 5,000 in 1948, as well as 140,000 dunams of land. In 1978, it had a population of 20,000 but only 15,000 dunams of land, most of it unfit for agricultural use. The best land had been confiscated. Ironically, today on this same area there are a moshav and two "socialist" kibbutzim![12] The argument that Jews can take over and create their own space because of our oppression elsewhere does not hold water.

Another argument used to defend Israel in feminist circles is that it is "progressive." Referring to the Copenhagen Conference last year, Letty Cottin Pogrebin wrote in *Ms*: "Under national instructions, they (female representatives of the Arab world) used their once in a lifetime vote to condemn Israel, the only democracy in the Middle East and the only state that grants suffrage to all women."

One has only to read the wealth of material published on the situation of women in Israel to know that it was and is today as oppressive as any other country in the Middle East. It is a weak "my-patriarchy-is-better- than-your-patriarchy" argument.[14]

If one wishes to analyse critically a society's values (or even a subsection of a society for that matter), one must examine not only how women are treated, but how other elements, such as classes and ethnic minorities, are regarded as well.

Natives in their own land, the Palestinians are limited to the most menial work at the lowest pay, denied access to the areas in which they once lived by a series of "pass" laws, prohibited from expressing national pride by a censor board which monitors their cultural activities, and prevented from holding public office.[15]

Any individual protesting this most undemocratic regime is hauled off to prison as an "administrative detainee" under the 1945 Emergency Regulation Act. Felicia Langer, an Israeli lawyer, has worked extensively with Palestinian prisoners and documents numerous such cases in her book, *With My Own Eyes*.[16]

Israeli feminists, most of whom acknowledge government repression, have tried to make alliances with Palestinian women. Their attempts have been less than successful. During a workshop on Feminism as a Unifying Force at the National Feminist Conference in Jerusalem in June 1981, the participants remained undecided as to whether the fight for Palestinian national liberation should remain separate from the fight for women's rights.[17] This indecision clearly indicates the different priorities of the two groups.

One Palestinian, Leila Khaled, born in Nazareth, recounted an incident which further illustrates the gulf in understanding: "I went to visit Marcia in Haifa at the women's centre and we talked. She asked me at one point: 'Leila, why don't Palestinian women ever come to the battered women's shelter?' So I answered, 'Marcia, the problem of the Palestinian women is not that she is beaten by her husband, but that both of them are being beaten by the Israelis.'"[18]

Although the validity of this statement is readily acknowledged by Jewish feminists, they still maintain that the state itself has a right to exist: "I believe that it is important for Jewish women to support Israel in addition to working towards important political, economic, and social change."[19]

By supporting Zionism, or a Jewish state in Palestine (as opposed to some other arrangement), these "radical" feminists are refusing either through ignorance or denial to recognize that the State of Israel was founded on the graves of yet another people.

Contrary to popular belief, Israel was not created in 1948 but rather during the 1880-1939 colonialization period. The cooperative settlements and towns built over this 60-year period formed a cohesive substructure upon which the Zionists later were able to develop a national base. The land bought during this time was from rich effendis, or landowners, who resided not in Palestine but in other large centres of the Middle East. They charged exorbitant prices for their feudal holdings because they were aware of the Zionists' intense desire to buy them.

Once a piece of land came under Zionist control, all the Palestinian peasants who had worked the same land for as long as thirteen generations were kicked off and forced into the cities to search for employment. At the same time, the Histadrut, a Jewish-only trade union, was being formed and managed to limit the number of Palestinians working in urban areas.

It is no wonder that in their transition from rural subsistence farming to urban unemployment a great deal of resentment arose. There were numerous riots and eventually an armed uprising in 1935–6 to protest this gradual but pervasive takeover.[20] But this was just the beginning. Until 1948, only 6 per cent of the land was under Zionist control.

During the "War of Independence," the Jewish Defence Forces

proceeded to force the Palestinians off their land in a reign of terror very similar to a course they are now on in Lebanon. A long-standing member of the Knesset, Yical Allon, admits: "We saw a need to clean the inner Galilee and to create a Jewish territorial succession in the entire area of upper Galilee.... We therefore looked for means which did not force us into employing force in order to cause the tens of thousands of sulky Arabs who remained in Galilee to flee....

"We tried to use a tactic which took advantage of the impression created by the fall of Safed and the Arab defeat in the area which was cleaned by Operation Mateteh (Operation Broom!), a tactic which worked miraculously well.

"I gathered all the Jewish *mukhtars* who had contacts in different villages and asked them to whisper in the ears of some Arabs that a great Jewish reinforcement had arrived in Galilee and that it was going to burn all the villages of Huleh. They were to suggest to these Arabs as friends to escape while there was still time."[21]

The Zionists, in fact, used other more violent methods to persuade the natives to flee. Although the massacre of Deir Yassin is well known, there were many other mass murders carried out by the regular forces of the Hagganah, Nasr-al-din, Ain-al-zeitouneh, al-Bi'na, al-Bassa, Safsaf, and Hula in Lebanon.[22]

Jewish feminists who support the State of Israel support not only what they term "Jewish liberation" but also the uprooting and destruction of the Palestinian people.

To be anti-Zionist is not the same as being anti-Semitic.

FOOTNOTES

[1] Evelyn Torton Beck, editor, *Nice Jewish Girls* Persephone Press 1982; *Common Lives, Lesbian Lives* (Spring 1982) 42-6; Letty Pogrebin, "Anti-Semitism in the Women's Movement," *Ms* (June 1982); Regina Schreiber, "Copenhagen: One Year Later," *Lilith* 8 (Fall 1981)

[2] *Lilith*, p. 10

[3] *Nice Jewish Girls*, p. 193

[4] Coleman Romalis, "Rights and Wrongs: The Endangered Falashas," *The Canadian Forum* (April 1982). See also *The Lost Jews* by Louis Rappaport.

[5] Ibid., p. 37

[6] Ibid., p. 38

[7] Reb Moshe Shonfield and Neturei Karta, *The Holocaust Victims Accuse* (1977), p. 27.

[8] Ibid., p. 25

[9] *Ms*, p. 65

[10] Sarah Feinstein, "It Has to do with Apples," *Lesbian Inciter* (July 1981)

[11] Israel Shahak, chairman of the Israeli League for Human and Civil Rights, Shahak Report (Tel Aviv 1973). This document contains the names of each of the 385 villages destroyed and indicates their original locations.

[12] Edward Said, *The Question of Palestine* (Vintage Books 1980), p. 248

[13] *Ms*, p. 49

[14] Rachel Katznelson Shazar, *The Plough Woman*; Ada Maimon, *Women Build a Land*; Lesley Hazelton, *Israeli Women*; Natalie Rein, *Daughters of Rachel*. See also *Broadside* (April 1982) and Tzena U'rena (Israeli women's centre)

[15] *Our Roots Are Still Alive*, *The Shahak Papers*, Fawaz Turki, *The Disinherited*, Leila Khaled, *My People Shall Live*

[16] Felicia Langer, *With My Own Eyes* (London 1975)

[17] *Venus* (Hebrew magazine) (Fall 1981), p.

[18] Marcia Freedman, a leading Israeli feminist. See also *Nice Jewish Girls*, p. 211

[19] *Nice Jewish Girls*, p. 211

[20] Rosemary Sayish, *Palestinians: From Peasants to Revolutionaries* (Zed Press 1979), pp. 39–46

[21] Yigal Allon, *The Book of the Palmach*, vol. 2, p. 286, cited in *Palestinians: From Peasants to Revolutionaries*, p. 77

[22] *Ibid.*, p. 75

Lilith Finkler is a Jewish radical feminist and non-Zionist. She spent six months of 1981 in Israel.

MOVEMENT MATTERS

International Women's Day pull-out
poster, designed by Susan Sturman, 1979.

Dorothy Smith and her OISE
colleagues organized an alternative
all-women's march for an early
International Women's Day.

International Women's Day march, winding through Queen's Park, 1985.

Take Back the Night demonstrations demanded safe public space for women.

Arson attack against the Morgentaler abortion clinic that destroyed the Toronto Women's Bookstore in the same building.

Feminists attempted to shut down the deeply misogynist University of Toronto engineering newspaper, *Toike Oike*. The paper survives but its overt misogyny does not.

Canadian Women's Movement Archive
collective members sort through their
holdings. The Archive is now housed at
the University of Ottawa.

Subscribe to Broadside... And Win!

"Dove"

A sterling silver pendant/sculpture by Maryon Kantaroff
(Dimensions: 2" x 3")

The Dove, a sculpture by Maryon Kantaroff, was donated as the prize in a *Broadside* subscription drive.

RENEW HIS INTEREST IN CARPENTRY.

Who says feminists have no sense of humour?

REBIRTH OF MIDWIFERY

by Vicki Van Wagner

Volume 5, No. 3 (December 1983/January 1984), p. 11

Midwives have been persecuted, controlled and driven underground many times in history. In the 14th- and 15th-century European witch hunts and later in New England, during the consolidation of the medical monopoly over women's health care in the late 19th and early 20th centuries, and in western countries today, midwives seemed to patriarchal institutions a dangerous key to female autonomy.

Midwives have traditionally preserved and passed on knowledge about birth control, abortion and childbirth. They symbolize female control of reproduction, and, historically, are often painted as leaders in a conspiracy of women against male order and civilization.

Single mothers, working mothers in traditional families, lesbian mothers—all kinds of women, of every class and race and age—give birth and raise children. How women do this, and how they bring their children into the world, carries social messages which reinforce the status quo of the culture they live in. In our culture misogyny and violence against women is both obvious—rape, pornography— and hidden. The misogyny and violence of modern obstetrics has been well documented, by Ehrenreich and English, Rich, Anns and Katz-Rothman (see resource list), to name only a few, but is not obvious to most women. Not only does obstetrical care carry negative social messages to women, it is not in fact the safest care. Don't misunderstand, obstetrical skill and technology can be vitally important in some circumstances and must be available when necessary, but not routinely used for reasons other than the health of the mother and baby.

Hospitalization, forceps, caesarean section, epidural and general anesthesia and episiotomy can be helpful and/or life-saving when their use and the need for them is understood and chosen by mothers. Sheila Kitzinger has eloquently pointed out that the reason these procedures are overused is not medical. The rationale for their routine use has never been scientifically documented. Many others have argued that fear and awe of female reproductive processes and sexuality, menstrual blood and birth in particular, have deep roots in patriarchy. Modern obstetrics is an attempt to be in control of these experiences. Most women believe that without their male rescuer, their babies or themselves would have been in danger. This is usually just not true. Modern obstetrics creates most of the emergencies it then 'saves' us from.

Just picture the difference in the symbolic meaning, in the social message, of a woman giving birth flat on a delivery table, drugged, her baby removed with instruments, taken from her by the male expert above her; and a woman upright, actively pushing, working with the pain and power of her body processes, reaching down to catch her own child, assisted by the women around her.

Labour is difficult, usually painful and emotionally trying. Most women in labour, often late in first stage or transition, feel that they cannot possibly make it through, that this is the hardest and most horrible thing they have ever done. This time of labour is a dark night of the soul, and women deserve the most tender, supportive care to help them through it. Most women, allowed to continue and push their babies out into the world, experience a rush of joy and a sense of pride and power. When this does not happen women frequently feel, and not always consciously, robbed, and often raped, by the care they get. And yet typical of our conditioning, most women turn this in on themselves. They "needed" the forceps delivery which tore and damaged their bodies, because they were not right somehow: their pelvis was not big enough, or their labour did not happen quickly enough to fit the medical deadline. And some women take this inadequacy as a strange proof of their femininity; they needed help. Women do need a great deal of help in labour, but what kind of help we give them, what kind of help women choose, tells us a lot about our attitude towards women.

When a woman chooses a midwife as her primary caregiver, she is making a decision in complete opposition to female conditioning and conditioning we all have about the "experts." Instead of choosing God-the-Father-Obstetrician, she chooses a woman very much like herself, a caretaker who will relate to her as an equal, instead of as a child-patient. She decides that what she needs to help her through her labour is not male authority, but someone who will inspire self-confidence and help her make her own decisions. It is an act of demystifying the medical profession, of trust in the female body and the process of birth, of trust in herself to be an active decision maker, of trust in other women to have the skill and knowledge to care for her.

To me, being a midwife means respecting and nurturing women, giving them back control over a process which can either strengthen and inspire them or reinforce female submission and male dominance. Women in labour are beautiful in their courage and endurance, a symbol of female strength.

It has been easy to see the need for control of reproduction in terms of *when* we give birth: the right to choose whether and when we will have children. *How* we give birth, indeed *how* we prevent pregnancy is just as important. In the words of Adrienne Rich, in *Of Woman Born*: "To change the experience of childbirth means to change women's relationship to fear and powerlessness, to our bodies, to our children; it has far reaching psychic and political implications."

NO SPORTING CHANCE
by Helen Lenskyj
Volume 5, No. 4 (February 1984), p. 4

The Ontario Human Rights Code guarantees equal treatment with respect to goods, services and facilities, regardless of sex. Right? Wrong!

In 1981, when the code was revised, a specific exemption (Section 19(2)) was made with respect to membership in athletic organizations. Participation in athletic activities and access to the services and facilities of recreational clubs. This had the effect of giving *carte blanche* to the male-dominated sporting establishment to continue the practice of excluding girls and women from sporting activities to which they were demanding access. When the exemption took effect in 1982, there were more than twenty unresolved cases of sex discrimination in sport filed with the Ontario Human Rights Commission.

In the face of this embarrassment, the Ontario Ministry of Labour set up a task force in April, 1982, headed by Toronto lawyer and former Argo player John Sopinka, to investigate whether the rules and policies of government and other agencies determining participation in sport are fair in terms of according both sexes equal treatment. Supporters of women's sport hoped that the task force would recommend the repeal of section 19(2), or, alternatively, that it would propose adequate funding for the development of separate-but-equal programs for girls and women. When Volume I of the report, entitled *Can I Play*, was released last November, reaction ranged from disappointment to outrage. This volume, reporting on the first phase of the inquiry, deals with amateur athletics in the community, a level of activity in which gentle government persuasion—for example, with-holding financial assistance to sports governing bodies and municipalities which discriminate against females—would prove particularly effective. Sopinka, however, opted for the "Strasbourg goose" argument: You can't stuff sexual equality down the throats of reluctant coaches. After all, these dedicated folks, mostly men, volunteer their time and energy to coach boys teams and many would quit if forced to include girls.

This blackmail tactic, usually accompanied by emotional outbursts on the magic of male bonding in the locker room, has worked in the past, and Sopinka's report virtually ensures that it will continue to work. In fact, it is difficult not to dismiss *Can I Play* as an endorsement of the status quo when one reads statements like the following: *Separation of competition (by sex) is deeply rooted in the psyche of our society (p. 90).*

Perhaps the same may be said for other forms of sexism, or racism, or ageism, but it does not follow that "deeply rooted" wrongs cannot be righted. Integrated competition is one of several possible solutions to the problem of discrimination against female athletes; Sopinka's appeal to some undefined social "psyche" to dismiss integration is not an adequate substitute for reasoned discussion of all the options. *Integration would require that girls be admitted to boys teams and vice-versa…therefore complete integration would have to be written down to integration one-way only (p. 94).* Or, more succinctly, an affirmative action program would need to be established, permitting talented female athletes to join male teams in order to have equal access to the level of competition for which they are qualified. Male players, however, would not be admitted to female teams.

This arrangement would improve the situation for the top female players, while ensuring that male players did not swamp the female team. Since most team sports, as presently constituted, emphasize speed, strength and endurance, top male players (after puberty) have an advantage over top female players. Therefore, a temporary solution which permits one-way movement, while the gap between the sexes persists, seems a fair one. Moreover, this kind of rule is not unknown in sport: weight categories which operate in combat sports, for example, permit movement up to a higher level (of weight/difficulty) but do not allow movement down. No, says Sopinka. "Equality in only one direction is a concept that is foreign to human rights legislation (p. 95)." The fact that affirmative action programs operate elsewhere in the community is ignored. *(In integrated teams) forms of physical contact offend against public decency. I mention rugby as an example where contact with the genital area is inevitable in some of the sport manoeuvres (pp. 92–3).*

It is significant, of course, that this genital contact is desexualized when players are male, but becomes charged with sexual overtones when women and men, or women and women, compete together. Curiously, body contact between female mud wrestlers seems to titillate, rather than offend, male spectators (and there is no doubt that T V exercise shows perform the same function.) In view of this trend, it could be argued that body contact (male/female and female/female) in the sport context might have a positive outcome: contact, whether it be touching or tackling, need not have sexual connotations, and men's power to distort it in this way limits women's access to the full range of sporting activities.

A unique problem of the female athlete relates to breasts (from Appendix 6, on female physiology). When the day comes when a female physiologist writes, "A unique problem of the male athlete relates to the penis," we will know that the revolution is at hand. A problem-oriented approach to sports gynecology currently pervades both medical and popular literature. And Sopinka's report is no exception. The concept of "female biology" is used to justify various limitations to be applied, regardless of ability, to all female athletes. As Harvard scientist, Dr. Ruth Hubbard argued so convincingly in the 1983 Bronowski Memorial Lecture at the University of Toronto, human biology cannot be explained solely in terms of gender: social practices, environment, diet, etc. are more, or as likely to be, responsible for differences between individuals, across the sexes and across cultures. On the breast issue, for example, it is both inaccurate and ludicrous to suggest that the alleged problem is experienced in the same way by the pre-pubescent gymnast, the 100 lb marathoner and the 150 lb soccer player, simply because they are all females.

Despite the glaring inadequacies of *Can I Play*, some of its recommendations, if implemented, might improve the situation for girls and women in sport. Sopinka proposed an amendment to section 19(2) of the Human Rights Code providing for the appointment of an equality coordinator, whose job it would be to "exercise a broad discrimination in determining whether equality was denied" to an athlete. The "ultimate sanction" of the equality coordinator in relation to sport governing bodies would be the withholding of public funds. The proposed amendment also sets out the steps available to these organizations if charged with denying equality of opportunity to either sex. Failure to provide either integrated or separate but "comparable" teams in the same or "equivalent" sports, equal training opportunities and equal allocation of public funds or facilities, and failure to include members (an unspecified number) of one sex on the board of directors of an organization, all constitute denial of equality of opportunity. Among the responsibilities of the equality coordinator would be the tasks of determining what is "a comparable level of competition" and an "equivalent sport."

It appears likely, however, that the Ontario ministers concerned, Reuben Baetz of Tourism and Recreation and Russell Ramsay, Minister of Labour, will not implement this recommendation without public pressure. Therefore, it is important to make you views known by writing to them, at Queen's Park, urging that they establish the equality coordinator's position and take steps to repeal the discriminatory section of the Human Rights Code.

Helen Lenskyj is currently writing a book on women and sport.

REAL WOMEN?
by Pat Daley
Volume 5, No. 5 (March 1984), p. 6

One of their steering committee members is named "Femmie." One of their aims is "to promote, secure and defend legislation which upholds the Judeo-Christian view of traditional marriage and the family." They are R.E.A.L. Women, "realistic, equal, active for life," and they're "out for action," according to President Grace Petrasek.

At a February press conference announcing the organization's existence, Petrasek said 10,000 women have joined since they got together last October "to express the beliefs of the majority of women throughout the country."

If their aims are indeed "realistic," the majority of Canadian women recognize woman's role as educator and nurturer of the family in the home, recognize woman's unique contribution to society through her volunteer work in the community, support policies for women whose primary concern is the care and well being of their families, and support the right to life of all innocent individuals from conception to death.

"We have touched a nerve across the nation," Petrasek said. She may be right, especially if one considers the nerves of the three to four million women represented by the member organizations of the National Action Committee on the Status of Women (NAC).

"Their (NAC and Status of Women Council's) views on many crucial issues undermine the family and are not those of the *real* women of Canada," according to the Thornhill-based organization's brochure.

Petrasek said R.E.A.L. women have no interest in affiliation with NAC and would not work with feminists against pornography, for instance. They plan to affiliate with other organizations but Petrasek would not say with whom.

She did admit, however, that R.E.A.L. Women are looking into co-operating with organizations like the Alberta Federation of Women United for Families. (R.E.A.L. Women claims to have 1,000 chapters in Alberta). AFWUF was formed in November 1982 at a conference featuring American anti-ERA activist Phyllis Schlafly. It would appear that Schlafly is also the inspiration for R.E.A.L. Women.

"We know her and know her work," Petrasek said, adding, however, that there is no connection with Schlafly. Even so, they have adopted her definition of the family—two or more people living together, related by blood, marriage or adoption—and share her mistrust of the media.

In fact, R.E.A.L. Women's program could have come straight from Schlafly's speech to AFWUF: *opposition* to choice on abortion, no-fault divorce, affirmative action, equal pay for work of equal value, universal day care; *support* for criminalization of prostitution, increased family allowances, a separate mother's benefit, homemakers' pensions, financial recognition for caring for elderly parents in the home, and government-funded parenting courses among other things.

The one thing R.E.A.L. Women have not adopted is Schlafly's radical rhetoric. Rather than denounce feminists out of hand, they acknowledge the progress that has been made in the areas of homemakers' pensions and services for battered women.

But their attempt at soft-selling doesn't wash with NAC President Doris Anderson. "They're undermining all the work women have been doing for the last 20 years and at the same time enjoying all the work the feminist movement has accomplished," she says, pointing out that it has taken a long time to reach the point where homemakers' pensions are a possibility, and "the work wasn't done by those women."

Many of the women active in R.E.A.L. Women come from the anti-choice movement, but Petrasek said they wanted an organization that could address broader issues. For Anderson, this base raises the question of whether the organization can attract other women.

"My own feeling is there is a broader base of a lot of women who are dissatisfied," she says. "I don't think they'll be deluded."

Although there are 10,000 members, presumably each paying the $5 membership fee, Petrasek says R.E.A.L. Women has no funds. They will be applying for government funding for their lobbying efforts and their efforts to "safeguard the family, the basis of our society."

Also printed in the Toronto Clarion, *February 1984.*

THE ABELLA REPORT: AT THE FEET OF PRIVILEGE
by Sarah Elliot
Volume 6, No. 5 (March 1985), p. 3

The law, in its majestic equality, forbids the rich as well as the poor to sleep under bridges, to beg in the streets, and to steal bread.

Such is the promising epigram which introduces Judge Rosalie Abella's Royal Commission Report on Equality in Employment. Focussing on women, native people, visible minorities and disabled persons (altogether 60% of our population), the Commission received 274 written submissions, held 137 meetings and consulted with 160 other individuals. The final distillation was 117 specific recommendations.

All in all, very little of the data in the report is new. This is not necessarily a criticism; discrimination has been around so long it's becoming difficult to be innovative about it. The litany of wrongs and inequities is well documented. Why else the pervasive sense of *déjà vu* as the statistics are trotted out once again? Women earn 63% of the male wage. Native women make 71.7% of that (or 40% of the male wage). Fifty per cent of disabled persons who want to work are unemployed. Domestic workers—largely immigrant and non-white—are excluded from employment and human rights legislation.

The data is known and the implications, as promulgated by Judge Abella, are equally familiar, though still powerful. Whether discrimination is intentional (Abella is much kinder than need be here) it is systemic. Voluntary measures to eradicate this discrimination have been magnificently ineffective and only one option is left:

> The choice for government is between imposing and hoping for equality in employment, between ensuring the right to freedom from discrimination and its mere articulation. In a society committed to equality, the choice is self-evident.

More importantly, the report pinpointed education as the locus for changing current societal perceptions. If disabled persons receive segregated schooling; if white males are perceived as the authority figures, and if only they implement policies; if girls, native people and visible minorities are streamlined into vocational and clerical training, discrimination in employment will not and cannot change.

If language training does not exist in an accessible, practical fashion then non-English immigrants will have that work disadvantage perpetuated. A current language program prerequisite demands that language training be necessary to obtain a job. However, language for many immigrant women does not prevent obtaining jobs in ghettoized, low paying occupations. Language, Abella concludes, is as basic a need as shelter or food.

By far the most moving and eloquently articulated section of the report deals with the issue of childcare. The current impoverished and apathetic attitude toward childcare stems from well-known preconceptions about the mother's "duty" and a lack of respect for children. Using the metaphor of the handicapped, the report notes that, "Childcare is the ramp that provides equal access to the workforce for mothers."

In 1981, women had 963,000 pre-school age children; there were 123,962 childcare spaces. The average cost of childcare in Canada is $2,500–$3,500 per year; women earn, on average, $10,500. Low income subsidized childcare segregates children on a socio-economic basis and discourages mothers from taking promotions which will render them ineligible for the program. (How many promotions cover $3,500 per child per year?)

Childcare workers earn approximately $10,000 a year, kindergarten and elementary schoolteachers earn twice that. Abella concludes

> Our society purports to value children but is not willing to pay adequately people, usually women, for looking after them. If mothers stay home, they are unpaid. When they join the labour force, they are underpaid. And when parental substitutes are hired, these alternative care-givers are likewise underpaid.

Judge Abella sees universal childcare as a necessity, a notion which will be resisted just as public education was in the 19th century. It places a responsibility on everyone, it forces us to reshape the still prevalent image of families as "man and wife" into one of autonomous individuals with equal rights and responsibilities where women would not be "deemed as economic satellites of their partners."

The last, and probably weakest, section of the report specifies how mandatory enforcement of employment equity should be implemented. Abella recommends that all federal agencies have employment equity programs and that contract compliance (all businesses trading with the government) be imposed by legislation. Quotas are not recommended (though not dismissed as some reporting would have it) and many data collecting processes are urged. A major finding of the report revealed that while companies have statistics on women, none of the eleven Crown Corporations surveyed had information on the other three groups: numbers, income or job placements. (Perhaps they think there can be no discrimination where there is no documentation.)

Before evaluating the merits of the Abella Report itself, there are preliminary issues to be answered. What is the general purpose of this Royal Commission Report and other government-sponsored works of the same ilk? If it is to transform paper into process, then no one would begrudge the report's recapitulation of known facts. But what happens to such reports and their reform-minded recommendations? If they were implemented, then this 1984 report would not echo much of what already exists in the 1970 Report on the Status of Women. Perhaps their purpose is solely one of pomp and circumstance. They direct our attention to the glorious parade of good will, while distracting us from their ultimate disappearance into some special government black hole, chewed up and spewed into the ozone by white, male politicians whose bastion of privilege they threaten.

Let us be practical. A government comprised almost exclusively of white males commissions a report which finds that 60% of the population is discriminated against in favour of white males. The report concludes by urging this privileged sector to legislate and enforce employment equity. The report also notes, over and over, that the four groups have wearied of begging, they are tired of being the supplicants at the feet of privilege. Yet the report proposes an enforcement agency (modeled on the Human Rights Commission) which would stand as another external structure to which these groups would go—to ask for equity. The theoretical advantage is that such an agency would be one of eventual self-destructing paternalism unlike the self-perpetuating paternalism now operative in society. But in either event, the perceived powerlessness of the groups themselves persists. The government is asked to institute an agency to bring about change, the government is requested to mandate legislation to revolutionize societal, educational and cultural inequities. The white, male government will bring about systemic change to destroy its own long standing system of privilege for the purpose of integrating visible minorities, the disabled, native persons and women equally into all strata of society. Does anyone believe this?

Sarah Elliot is a somewhat civil servant.

THE FRASER REPORT:
SEX AND THE SPECIAL OFFENCE COMMITTEE
by Debi Brock

Volume 7, No. 3 (December 1985/January 1986), pp. 8 and 9

The Fraser Report's recommendations on prostitution are the outcome of a longstanding battle—between feminists and civil libertarians on one hand, and citizens' groups, city officials and police in areas affected by street solicitation on the other—to determine the rights of prostitutes to conduct their business on Canadian streets.

A liberal government in decline, pressured by these competing forces to take legislative action on prostitution through its decriminalization (by the former grouping) or further criminalization (by the latter), responded with the appointment of a committee in June, 1983, headed by Vancouver lawyer Paul Fraser. This politically astute move provided the federal government with the appearance of taking action on the controversial issues of prostitution and pornography, while getting these issues off the political agenda in the upcoming federal election campaign.

In November, 1983, the four woman/three man committee released an issues paper to set the terrain for the debate which discussed, among other things, considerations respecting the role that the law should play in the legislation of morality, the allocation of 'rights' in a democratic society, alternative legal and social strategies for dealing with prostitution, and outlining some of the legislative history of prostitution in Canada.

Its terms of reference were:

1) to consider the problems of access to pornography, its effects, and what is considered to be pornographic in Canada;

2) to consider prostitution in Canada with particular reference to loitering and street soliciting for prostitution, the operation of bawdy houses, living off the avails of prostitution, the exploitation of prostitutes and the law relating to these matters;

3) to ascertain public views on ways and means to deal with

these problems by inviting written submissions from concerned groups and citizens and by conducting public meetings in major centres across the country;

4) to consider, without travelling outside Canada, the experience and attempts to deal with these problems in other countries including the US, EEC and selected Commonwealth countries such as Australia and New Zealand; and

5) to consider alternatives, report its findings and recommend solutions to the problems associated with pornography and prostitution in Canada, as soon as possible, but not later than December 31, 1984.

The issues paper set out a number of questions which the committee considered critical to addressing its terms of reference, for example, by querying the relation between prostitution and organized crime, venereal disease, violence, and the deterioration of neighbourhoods. To supplement the public submissions it received, the Department of Justice commissioned a number of studies on prostitution for the committee's consideration. In preparing its final report, the committee also drew upon the findings of the Special Committee on Sexual Offences Against Children and Youths (the Badgley committee), whose findings were released in the fall of 1984, and which dealt with juvenile prostitution at some length.

On a manifest level, therefore, the Fraser Report is a response to competing interest groups which coexist in a 'democratic' pluralist society, and an attempt to arrive at a public consensus on the issue of prostitution. The report also operates on another level, however. A central effect of the report is to expand the power of the ruling apparatus' in the articulation and disposition of the realm of the sexual. This apparatus, which includes levels of government, the courts, police, psychiatry and social work, and so on, (the sites of government, administration and management, as well as professional organizations) is increasing its power of inspection over the private and public lives of us all, through such documentary processes. That it may be seen to have our 'consent' makes this process particularly pernicious.

The Fraser committee comprised conscientious and devoted liberals attempting to come to terms with their responsibility to ensure that the law does not interfere with individual liberty, unless the activities of the individual may cause direct harm to others. It is in relation to the liberal concept of harm that the committee structured its recommendations, as it attempted to determine how "the public" believes this harm principle should be operative in relation to prostitution.

The committee, while recognizing the absence of consensus on prostitution in Canada, attempted to balance out the interests of the competing pro- and anti-criminalization forces in a way which would satisfy both sides as much as they were able, and ended up satisfying no one.

While the committee clearly supports social rather than legal initiatives in developing effective responses to the problem of prostitution, and therefore recommends that the role of the law be minimized as much as possible, it also asserts that those persons living in areas affected by street solicitation experience real harms and interference with personal rights as a result of the activity. It attempts to reach a compromise solution suitable to both pro- and anti-criminalization forces when it recommends that:

> the prostitution-related activities of both prostitutes and customers should be removed from the criminal code, except insofar as they contravene non-prostitution related code provisions, and do not create a definable nuisance or nuisances.

The committee proposes the repeal of section 195.1—soliciting for the purpose of prostitution—and a shift of street solicitation to a more general nuisance category through a revision of section 171 of the code, rather than singling it out for special consideration as currently exists in legislation. However, it expands the category of "public place" (which in current interpretations of existing legislation does not, for example, include the interior of a motor vehicle) to encompass:

> any place to which the public has access as of right or invitation, express or implied, doorways and hallways of buildings adjacent to public places and to vehicles situated in public places.

Moreover, its suggested definition of public nuisance activity, which includes disorderly conduct, indecent exhibition, littering, soliciting and so on, is so broad that it can be used to prosecute virtually every street prostitute and prospective client. This may occur regardless of actual conduct, since the only evidence required is the word of a police officer. Given the expansion of the definition of "public place," the legislation could potentially be used not only against prostitutes working on the streets, but in a wide variety of circumstances and settings; for example, against those engaging in same sex activity like kissing in public view, like their cars and doorways.

Therefore, despite their insistence on the need for social rather than legal initiatives in dealing with street solicitation, the committee has proposed an expanded and quite punitive means of social control. However, it attempts to balance out its strategy for further criminalization of public sex for sale through a rigid differentiation between acceptable forms of private and public sexual conduct in allowing for a liberalization of bawdy-house provisions.

The committee argues, with respect to bawdy houses, that it be permissible for two persons over eighteen years of age to use their residence for the purpose of prostitution, and that licensed and regulated prostitution establishments (the committee considers the term "common bawdy house" archaic, and recommends its elimination from the criminal code) be permitted to operate according to schemes established by the relevant province or territory. The operation of any other form of prostitution establishment would remain a criminal offence.

On the surface, this measure is a progressive one, since it attempts to make more favourable options available to prostitutes than the unstable and often dangerous practice of street solicitation. It could allow prostitutes more autonomy in determining the hours and conditions of their working environment than available at present to those who work for "escort services" or massage parlours by reducing the need to depend on predatory third parties who provide these pseudo-legitimate business fronts in exchange for a portion of the prostitute's income.

A further bonus of this formula is that bawdy house legislation could no longer be used for the harassment of gays in the bars and bath houses, since it specifies that the new legislation would apply to places resorted to for the purposes of prostitution and drops the inclusion of places resorted to for the purpose of "acts of indecency," as current legislation specifies.

The committee makes this recommendation because it asserts that "it is our belief that it is preferable for prostitution to take place in private rather than in public." Feminists may be quick to agree with this argument, because it supports reduction in the visible sexual commoditization of women—visibility which reinforces and helps to reproduce prevailing perceptions of women's social "utility" (i.e., woman = cunt). However, this recommendation also reproduces a central feature of the pro-criminalization position, by providing a formula through which prostitution can be shifted around to provide for greater invisibility of the activity. In doing so, it provides a formula for the more effective reproduction of patriarchy (and where young male hustlers are concerned, heterosexual hegemony) since, while prostitution would carry on, its existence would be obscured. In rigidly differentiating between acceptable forms of private and public sexual behaviour, the committee creates an insidious alliance with the forces of conservatism, which would prefer the evidence of its own power obscured, while both displays of sexuality and women themselves are confined to the private realm.

While the recommendations on soliciting and bawdy houses would eliminate some of the most blatant sexism and heterosexism from prostitution legislation, they merely shift patriarchal application of the law, keeping key ideologies like the code of private/public and, indeed, patriarchy itself in place.

Canadian law has traditionally left women an easy prey of male family members in the private realm of the home—where physical, mental and sexual abuse occur routinely—while at times being overly protectionist where women and girls (at least those of chaste character) were considered liable to fall victim to public forms of vice. At the turn of the century this protectionism, which sprang from reports of a "white slave trade" ostensibly occurring in Canada, led to the considerable expansion of procuring legislation in order to protect "innocent or foolish girlhood" from ruination at the hands of the traffickers in human flesh.

In contemporary Canada, this legislation does little to prevent the commercial exploitation of women by pimps, yet it has the potential to interfere with the self determination of prostitutes. For example, current living-on-avails legislation, which applies to those "habitually in the company of prostitutes," can be used to deny a prostitute the right to establish consensual domestic arrangements with a male lover or friend, since it can be construed (particularly if he is unemployed or lacks legitimate means of employment) that he is living on her earnings.

The Fraser committee's recommendations would go on some distance in correcting the protectionist bent of the law, by limiting procuring and living-on-avails statutes to those who use coercion or threatening behaviour to achieve their aims in the exploitation of prostitutes. However, while this is a more sensitive treatment of prostitute/pimp relations in legislation, a difficulty remains in the determination of violence and coercion, particularly where it is psychological in character. The most specific methods of dealing with substantiation that the committee can propose are that special police units be established to investigate suspected cases, and that the corroboration of a prostitute's testimony by another witness no longer be necessary.

While most of the Fraser committee's recommendations are organized around a distinction between acceptable forms of private and public sexual behaviour, a secondary feature is the distinction it draws up between acceptable forms of adult and youth sex-related conduct. While the committee believes that young people should be accorded the same rights as adults expecting equality, responsibility and dignity, it asserts that family and the state must impose limitations on their liberty in order to protect them from harms resulting from youth inexperience.

The committee considers "youths" to be those under eighteen years of age, in accordance with the criteria established by the Young Offenders Act. It is in agreement with the Badgley committee's perception of prostitution involving young people as a form of sexual abuse, and that this age demarcation between the "vulnerability" of youth and "autonomy" and "responsibility" of adulthood therefore warrants separate legislation pertaining to the customers and pimps of young people. A customer who "engages in, or attempts or offers to engage in, sexual activity for money or for other consideration of a reward" would be liable to a charge, whether he knew that the prostitute was under eighteen or not.

Proposed legislation for procuring and living-on-avails could be broader in scope than those recommended in cases involving adults, including not only coercion and threats, but "encouragement" and "persuasion." Finally, people under eighteen would not be permitted to work in prostitution establishments.

The only major break the Fraser committee makes from the stringent reccomendations advanced in the Badgley report is their decision not to promote the criminalization of the activities of young people themselves. While the Badgley commitment would have it an offence to offer, provide, or agree to offer provide sexual services, in order to gain a legal foothold for retention and "treatment" of young prostitutes, the Fraser committee maintains that there is no evidence to support the idea that such measures will necessarily lead to effective treatment. They would, however, be subject to the same promised nuisance provisions as adult prostitutes, meaning that they would be subject to stringent policing on the streets, and they would have no indoor options available to them. Young people would therefore be the hardest hit by the solicitation recommendation.

The Fraser committee's recommendations on prostitution involving young people is so heavily imbued with information from the Badgley report, using the same data and opinions, that often even the same wording in the text, that, with the exception of its discussion around the above mentioned break, we may as well ignore this section of the report and read the real thing. While it may appear appropriate for the Fraser committee to defer to the more intensive study of the subject provided in the Badgley report (the latter devotes more than pages to the study of prostitution involving young persons), in doing so the Fraser committee falls prey to the same errors and omissions of the earlier report. It cannot, for example inform us why young people enter into prostitution, beyond the vague suggestion that they have experienced "unhappy home lives," nor who the customers are and what motivates them to seek out the services of young prostitutes. It does not venture to consider why existing social services are so inadequate in treating youths, either before or after they have entered the life, since most of them had been filtered through a system of courts, foster homes and detention centres. And most importantly, it reproduces the Badgley report's failure to examine why it is virtually always men who are the customers of prostitutes, and why most prostitutes are female. Without no understanding of the patriarchal relations which prevail in our society, there can be no understanding of prostitution. For a conservative, moral-protection oriented committee like Badgley *et. al.* to ignore this point is to be expected; for the liberal Fraser committee, which professes to be sympathetic to the feminist point of view, it is indefensible.

A few key features of the Fraser report are central to the way in which it organizes our perceptions of prostitution: first, the way it sets the stage of what is to be known about prostitution; second, its relation to feminism; and finally, the structuring of the report around the code of private/public.

From the inception of the committee, the limits of what was to be known about prostitution in Canada was determined through a proscribed mandate. The committee's investigation was designed to improve the scope of the law as an instrument of social control through an examination of the Criminal Code's definitional version of what prostitution is about—"street solicitation," "bawdy-houses," "procuring," etc.—terms which express the "organizational properties of the law." In light of the passage of the Charter of Rights, the Fraser committee plays an additional important role here, in providing a critique of the constitutionality of prostitution legislation.

Through a narrowing of the scope of the committee to the ambit of the law (as it is now interpreted), the committee addresses prostitution as a problem of public order, thereby disguising the moral basis of prostitution legislation and its own *raison d'être* as a strategy for sexual regulation. This further shields it from the necessity of confronting the ideologies which motivate the pro-criminalization forces as much as a concern for the material conditions of their neighbourhoods. These individuals, organizations and official representatives want to preserve not only the quality of their own neighbourhoods, but their class and gender interests. It should be no surprise that prostitution is most controversial where it takes place on the streets of high income neighbourhoods, and the biggest fight against street solicitation has taken place in BC, where the forces of conservatism have dismantled social service programs, revoked BC's Bill of Rights, and caused precisely the sort of social deterioration that leads women and the young into prostitution in the first place.

Narrowing the terrain of visibility means that social strategies for dealing with prostitution become a secondary feature of the report, despite the committee's belief that social rather than legal initiatives are most required. It directs our attention to the need to overcome sexism, as well as develop healthy sexual attitudes, yet because the committee places its focus on prostitutes themselves, rather than the men who are their pimps and clients, it cannot address the reality that prostitution is about men's sexuality, not women's. For the female participants, prostitution is an economic, not a sexual relation. The committee therefore cannot adequately address sexism and sexuality, and moreover, serves to reproduce the focus and therefore the blame on prostitutes themselves.

A further narrowing occurred through the committee's focus on street solicitation, which is only one aspect of what prostitution may entail. To be fair, it is street solicitation rather than prostitution itself which has been constructed as the problem in Canada today, because of the visibility of the activity. The problem, as it has been defined, is therefore not prostitution per se, but public displays of sexuality. As an illustration of this point, the Bureau of Municipal Research estimates that street prostitution constitutes only about 20% of all prostitution occurring in Toronto, and this number drops to about 5% in the winter months. At the same time, however, escort services and other indoor methods of business are permitted to flourish. The 1985 Toronto Yellow Pages advertises 143 escort services alone, which are far from discreet about the nature of the services provided.

The focus on street solicitation as the source of the problem of prostitution was directed within public presentations before the Fraser committee. Only those reports presented by the de-criminalization forces attempted to go beyond this narrow focus and address who the prostitutes are and why they are offering their sexual services in the first place. A notable absence of prostitutes on the Fraser committee aided this process of obfuscation, a committee which, ironically, comprised people whose legal and professional skills were considered most advantageous to doing justice to the issue.

The focus on street solicitation and, therefore, the question of visibility, exposes the theoretical and material basis of the committee's strategy of regulation, which entails a strengthening of the distinction between acceptable forms of private and public sexual conduct, while advancing a particular view of feminism and its discontents.

What is our relation to the ruling apparatus as feminists? The report certainly appears to take up and stand in agreement with a feminist viewpoint: it is even willing to recognize a multiplicity of feminist viewpoints in its introductory category in the subsequent pages. The brand of feminism which the report puts forward is tempered by a heavy dose of liberalism, so that we find no mention of terms like "patriarchy," or "female subordination" and feminist concerns are reduced to problems stemming from "society" and "female disadvantage." This is the language in which the ruling apparatus takes up, diverts, contains and neutralizes grassroot feminist activism. It is also what feminists have, or should, come to expect when we are, necessarily, forced to fight the ruling apparatus.

What we do not want, nor often recognize, is the shift of power, authority and control over what we consider feminist issues away from grassroot feminist activism, and their transformation into depersonalized and centralized administrative routines, as abstract, de-feminized methods of social regulation.

What feminism is within the context of this report is an interest group, whose concerns must be addressed in a pluralist, "democratic" society, and whose demands must be balanced against competing social forces. This approach only superficially addresses feminist concerns, since the ruling apparatus has a vested interest in maintaining structures of dominance. Through a successful mediation of the demands of opposing forces, the ruling apparatus can provide the appearance of democracy at work (the appointment of the Fraser committee is one such method), while at the same time continuing its primary role in the maintenance and reproduction of patriarchal and class interests.

A tension therefore exists for feminists as we assess our position vis-à-vis the ruling apparatus. We want the judicial system to protect women from domestic and sexual degradation, while at the same time we demand that it keep its "laws off our bodies" through the decriminalization of abortion and prostitution. We often expect the law to solve, or at least make some inroads into the resolution of, our problems (as in the fight for sexual assault legislation) when the law is really a part of the problem, rather than the solution. We may be able to alter existing legislation, as is clearly happening with the Fraser committee's recommendation on soliciting, without fundamentally challenging the patriarchal relations which remain structurally embedded in the foundations of the law. This is because the law, as Annette Kuhn expresses it in her article "Public versus Private: the case of indecency versus obscenity," is:

> the privileged site of expression of the code public/private, in that it constantly constructs distinctions between public and private as bases for its peculiarly authoritative discourse of regulation.

While the law is largely used to regulate the public domain, the ruling apparatus, which creates law, may shift the definitional boundaries of public and private, as is evident in the Fraser committee's recommendation to expand the definition of "public place" in order to increase police powers of arrest.

As the boundaries between private and public are manipulated, this process reveals the Fraser report's core tendency: it is about the power of disposition over sexual conduct. The report represents a further disguise of the moral basis of the law, through its organization of prostitution as a nuisance if conducted in public and a matter between consenting adults in private. This moral basis is exposed, however, in the code of public/private. As Stuart Hall commented on Britain's Wolfenden Report of the 1950s (whose pronouncements on acceptable forms of private and public sexual behaviour have influenced sexual legislation in Western industrialized nations ever since), documents like these, which are grounded in the code of private/public, construct a double taxonomy of moral regulation, whose core tendency is "increased regulation coupled with selective privatization through contract or consent, both in a new disposition."

This kind of strategy produces contradictory gains and losses. There is more interference by the ruling apparatus in public sex, through a more punitive and repressive means of control than existed in the recent past. However, contractual arrangements between individuals in private through the reform of bawdy-house legislation is approved at the same time. As the Fraser committee states, a firm demarcation of public and private sex on the part of the law corrects the "uncertain" legal status of prostitutes, since as legislation is presently interpreted and enforced, prostitutes may find these laws sometimes being enforced in public places like the streets, and sometimes in private places like massage parlours.

The Wolfenden strategy is clearly influential upon the Fraser Report; the committee in fact specifies that its recommendations and suggestions are based upon the Wolfenden committee's view that the function of criminal law is not to intrude upon the private lives of citizens, but to preserve "public order and decency" by protecting citizens from offence and injury, and the safeguarding against corruption and exploitation of the vulnerable, for example, those who are weak in mind and/or body, and/or dependent physically, economically or officially.

Feminists have come to define the divisions between private and public as the same as that between female and male. But this distinction goes beyond gender; sexuality, in so far as it can be separated from gender (for example, same sex sexual preference), is also organized in this way through categories like "indecency" and "obscenity" within the context of the law. Moreover, the position of women in legal discourse is constantly sliding between public and private according to the civil rights we are allocated, our perceived ability to consent, or our need for protection.

˙This term, devised by Dorothy Smith, better expresses the complexities of the prevailing organization of power relations than does references to 'the state,' which tends to be conflated as a uniform and monolithic formation.

FORCES OF OPPOSITION

by Karen Dubinsky

Volume 8, No. 6 (April 1987), pp. 5 and 6

It's unlikely that you've missed hearing about that curiously titled R.E.A.L. Women of Canada (RW). It is also unlikely that you have read or heard much about them from a critical, feminist perspective. The Canadian women's movement has been extremely slow to react to this challenge. It is time we began. Fast.

The anti-feminism represented by the RW has to be seen in the context of an increasingly conservative political climate in North America. It's wrong to separate the "economically right wing" (those who attack unions, or social service spending) from the "socially right wing" (those who oppose abortion, or gay and lesbian rights). They represent the same phenomenon, they spring from the same impulses and, increasingly, they are the same people. We need look no further for an example of this than the "Coalition for Family Values" which recently organized to oppose Bill 7 in Ontario. This group brought together fundamentalist churches, anti-abortion and anti-feminist groups, as well as the "traditional" right wing, the National Citizens' Coalition.

Another point about the RW is quite simple, but in at least some feminist circles, controversial. So called pro-family groups are fundamentally opposed to feminist ideas and the practice—indeed, the existence—of the women's movement. Simply put, *they exist* to *oppose feminism*.

Having said this, it should be clear that I think the women's movement must fight back. RW cannot be ignored, treated as "part of the spectrum" of feminism, or wished away. They, and more importantly, the image of feminism they are trying to exploit, must be challenged.

In order to do that, we must keep two elements in mind. We have to understand anti-feminist women as political actors *in their own right*. There's a tendency in the women's movement to see RW as "dupes of patriarchy" or, as a popular feminist cliché puts it, "men in skirts." That's wrong. It's insulting to those involved, and it denies them any responsibility for their actions. These people are not stupid. It's indeed difficult for us to understand how our movement for the liberation of women could be opposed by some women—it seems absurd. Yet it is possible to understand why anti-feminism exists without being patronizing.

To understand all this, we have to allow ourselves—the women's movement—to be self critical. What is it about feminism that some women are threatened by, or opposed to? In a bizarre way, RW provides the women's movement with a necessary shaking up to see where we have been going wrong.

HISTORY OF R.E.A.L. WOMEN

The formation of RW was announced February 1, 1984, at a press conference in Toronto. Quite audaciously, they announced their membership as 10,000 at this time—no mean feat for an organization which had scarcely published its first newsletter. This attempt to fudge their membership figures began a controversy about the size of their constituency which continues to this day. Despite a steady increase in reported membership, the organization has constantly evaded questions about membership lists and procedures, as well as sources of funding. Working backward from their 1986 membership income ($28,000), their membership figures are more like 2,800—a far cry from the 45,000 they currently claim.

Several other recurring themes were announced at their public unveiling. Grace Petrasek, their first president, announced RW's opposition to most feminist issues: i.e., abortion, easier divorce, universal day care, equal pay and affirmative action; and to feminism itself. She vowed that the organization would "fight back on every single issue the radical feminists make with which we do not agree."

RW also set the tone for one of their most emotional and stirring themes: their defence of the family. RW's major premise was and is that the family is the "cornerstone of Canadian society" and, as Petrasek articulated at the press conference, "The prime responsibility of a woman is her family."

Through the rest of 1984, RW spent time recruiting, writing position papers and submitting briefs to government. Perhaps their best remembered action of that year was their attempt to cancel, then disrupt, the televised debate on women's issues held by the three party leaders during the federal election, on the by now familiar grounds that the NAC panelists were "unrepresentative" of most Canadian women.

The organization celebrated its first anniversary by holding its first convention. Two hundred "delegates" attended — though I use the word advisedly, as there was no attempt at representativity, democracy, policy making process or structure at the gathering. Their focus remained an overt attack on feminism. Participants were told, for example, that NAC was a "danger to this free country" because it "breaks up marriages and destroys family life."

Invigorated, perhaps, by their convention, the organization took bolder steps in its self-declared war on the women's movement. In Ottawa, organizers of International Women's Week 1985 were faced with the dilemma of RW's request to celebrate this internationally recognized day of feminist solidarity with an anti-abortion workshop. (IWW said no, and was ridiculed by the press.) Later in the year the group made its second well publicized request for funds from the federal Secretary of State Women's Program.

It has been in the last twelve to sixteen months, however, that the organization has begun to receive the kind of legitimacy from the government and the press that they have been seeking. They held two lobbies of Federal MP's last year, one of which was attended by 40 Tories and 9 Liberals. Their "gift" of homemade muffins (sprinkled with pink icing) earned them national headlines, and no doubt endeared them to not a few politicians. Their support in the House has extended from the lunatic fringes of the Tory backbench into the Cabinet, notably in the person of Health and Welfare Minister Jake Epp.

A look at their leadership is revealing. (A membership profile would also be most interesting, but given their secrecy, impossible.) Five of the seven women who initiated the organization have university or professional degrees. Their provincial representatives in 1985 included a pharmacist, two businesswomen, a social worker and a teacher. Lynne Scime, their recently elected president, is also a social worker. Most are also married to professionals, thus they lead comfortable middle class lives. Most of these women quit their jobs to raise their children, yet virtually all are also veteran political and community activists — primarily in the anti-abortion movement. In light of what RW has to say about "selfish and upwardly mobile feminists," it is indeed ironic to see such an active and accomplished group of women at the helm.

IDEOLOGY POLICY

We can get the flavour of anti-feminist ideology from the policy statements of RW. In many ways the organization is getting politically smarter. They are far more careful in their public and policy statements than they were at the beginning. Petrasek's unequivocal statement at their first press conference that a woman's prime responsibility is her family has been replaced in a recent brief with more flexible and reasonable comments, such as: "To support homemaking as an option is not to say that we believe every woman should be in the home. We believe every woman should have the option to remain in the home if she so choose. Neither motherhood or a masters degree is for everyone."

I would argue, however, that this doesn't represent a major ideological shift in the organization, but is rather a skillful bit of public relations. RW remains committed to a fundamentally anti-feminist program. To really get a sense of what the world would look like if RW were in charge, read Margaret Atwood's novel *The Handmaid's Tale*.

To see this, we have to start where they start, with the notion that the family is the cornerstone of society, and women's place is within it. Their opposition to most feminist issues springs from this beginning.

Universal daycare is opposed, for example, because they believe children should be raised by their mothers. They confidently cite the work of psychologists published in the 1950s to argue that "without an early foundation of love and trust, the victims of maternal deprivation might be gravely damaged for life, pathologically suspicious and detached."

Easier access to divorce is opposed as "trendy legislation" which lets couples off the hook too simply. "There is nothing new about unhappy marriages," they argue. "What is new is the unwillingness of a married couple to work through the problems that are inevitable." Even male violence is not seen by some as sufficient grounds for marital break up. In one of their more horrifying statements, one of their leaders has insisted that "too often a woman is sexually attracted to a man and rushes into marriage within six months. If she had waited a couple of years, she would have realized that he was the type to beat her up." A program of tax deductible marriage and pre-marriage counselling is put forward as a "solution"—to prevent unhappy marriages and to bolster shaky ones.

Their strident opposition to human rights protection for gays and lesbians shows that this is one issue they have difficulty even pretending to be liberal about. They participated in the Coalition for Family Values which engaged in a vicious campaign against Bill 7. Their own literature is similarly hysterical. They claim that gay rights legislation gives "special privileges" to a group which has chosen an "offensive lifestyle"—and with this logic argue that groups of alcoholics or gamblers might claim similar protection. The gay rights movement exists, they claim, to redefine the family, to promote homosexual marriage, and to seduce the young. "The homosexual seeks sex in the young age group. As he ages, when he begins to lose his attractiveness, he resorts to buying sex from young boys...Homosexuality involves acts such as oral sex, anal intercourse, sado-masochism, bestiality and other perversions." Not surprisingly then, RW believes that "homosexuality is one of the gravest threats to society in the last two decades of the twentieth century."

FUNDING CONTROVERSY

As soon as it became clear in 1985 that RW's funding application to the Secretary of State was opposed by the women's movement and by some members of government, they went on the attack. Their newsletters began to read like scandal sheets. The Women's Program was "riddled with radical feminist extremists," they claimed. Certain recipients of federal funds were targeted, such as the publications *Herizons* and *Kinesis* ("lesbian papers" to our intrepid inquisitors) and NFB's Women's Studio (another hotbed of "radical feminism"). Federal politicians also came under the gun, including such notorious subversives as Judy Erola and Flora McDonald. RW supporters were urged to complain that federal funds are being used to "promote lesbianism in Canada."

Clearly, lesbian baiting is a favourite trick. Most recently, Ottawa IWW's funding from Sec. State has been stalled thanks to RW's complaint that approximately five of over 200 IWW events have a lesbian focus. RW also uses the funding issue to denounce what they call "professional feminists" or "feminist selfishness." RW has a particular vision of feminists as young, white, upwardly mobile career oriented women who simply don't give a damn about men or children. The women's movement must counter this vision in our struggle against anti-feminism.

RW cast the funding debate in all or nothing terms. They have stated on several occasions that they don't care if they are denied funding, so long as the government shuts off the tap to every other women's group as well. The funding issue is the clearest example of RW's attempt to set themselves up as the alternative to the women's movement, or, as they have begun to call themselves, the "new women's movement."

In fact, it's possible RW applied for funds for precisely this reason—they were as interested in damaging the women's movement and engaging in a virtual lesbian witchhunt as they were in actually getting some money. As Gwen Landolt, one of their leaders, said when they were denied funding: "Without equal funding, we can't enter the national debate with the radical feminists."

IMPACT OF ANTI-FEMINISM

There is an increasing legitimacy of anti-feminist ideas within government and the press. It's true that support for RW has extended beyond the realm of Tory dinosaurs who oppose every idea generated after the seventeenth century. It's also true that it's more and more common to see RW commenting in the press on stories which contain a "women's focus." These are troublesome and annoying instances, but they hardly represent an avalanche of anti-feminist sentiment, and we shouldn't push this legitimacy argument too far. What is more important, and more insidious, is the way in which the existence of groups like RW can and have been used by the state to either actively oppose feminist demands, or to justify inaction.

An example of the first can be found in Ottawa. Last year a right wing city council, which clearly had no desire to assist the women's movement, used RW as a cover to justify their reduction of funds to the local women's centre. This kind of thing is likely to happen elsewhere.

Using an overdrawn opposition as an excuse for inaction has long been a favourite delaying tactic of government. The federal government has refused for years to change restrictive abortion laws, on the basis of a so-called "polarized political climate"—this despite the fact that polls consistently report a huge pro-choice majority.

Anti-feminist rhetoric is indeed creeping back in to circles where it was once considered unfashionable—or at least indiscreet. How else are we to understand the wistful recommendation of the Forget Commission on Unemployment Insurance, that if women would simply go back home, the unemployment problem would be solved.

We should also be concerned about the impact of a potential anti-feminist cold war within government bureaucracies—especially those concerned with the status of women. Most feminists never believed that the state would fund or organize our revolution for us. Yet we all recognize the importance of feminist research and policy analysis within government agencies. Press reports quote several unnamed feminists in government complaining that more and more of their time is taken up justifying actions or decisions someone higher up is afraid RW will get angry about. My own discussions with feminists in government reveal similar frustrations. One's imagination can truly run wild here. We should remind ourselves that only 30 or 40 years ago Canadians were jailed and deported for their association with another great incarnation of evil, Communism. Left wing activity (however defined) is still seen as sufficient cause for the harassment of federal civil servants.

ANALYSIS—WHAT IS THE NEW RIGHT?

The first point that most feminist accounts of the rise of the new right stress is that it is *about* feminism and sexuality. What is important and new about the new right is two elements: they have discovered what feminists for generations have been arguing—that issues related to the family, sexuality and reproduction are political at their root; and they have succeeded in combining two conservative impulses, so called economic and social conservatism. What brings these two impulses together and gives new right ideology its coherence is its defence of the patriarchal family and its promotion of a particular notion of privacy. As feminist theorist Rosalind Petchesky argues: "Historically, the concept of privacy has included not only free enterprise and property rights, but also the rights of the white male property owner to control his wife and his wife's body, his child and his child's body, his slave and his slave's body. It is an ideology which is patriarchal and racist, as well as capitalist." Defence of the family involves the re-establishment of the family—not the state—as the provider of social welfare. It also involves the re-entry of women into the home where we become defined as subordinate reproductive beings.

Why do *women* so enthusiastically support this vision? Unlike Andrea Dworkin, I don't believe women "consent" to patriarchy solely because they are terrorized by male violence. The hegemony or popularity of patriarchal ideas lie in their ideological appeal—they simply fit, or make sense of the world for large numbers of people. It's only when these presumed natural, commonsense ideas start breaking down that the whole structure begins to shake, and an attempt may be made to reassert dominant ideas in a particularly virulent manner. This is what we are witnessing with the rise of the new right, and the culprit in this case is feminism.

This is the sense in which the new right is not only a response to feminism, but a measure of our success as well. But our success is only partial. Feminism, in combination with great changes in the economic and social structure in recent decades, has certainly freed many women from some traditional domestic roles, but such freedom has often proved rather illusory. For many it has meant entry into the low paid monotonous world of the female wage ghetto. It has meant an increase in female headed single parent families. And, as Dworkin points out, "sexual freedom" can also be rather bogus. "Sexual liberation," as it unfolds in a still patriarchal and capitalist society, can have the effect of "freeing" women from one of the few sources of security we have had—a stable and responsible male breadwinner. As Petchesky has pointed out, "Anti-feminism has attained a mass following and a measure of political power because it is in fact a response to real material conditions and deep-lying fears—a response that is utterly reactionary but nevertheless true."

Thus, when NAC recently announced that they were "taking the gloves off" in their fight with RW, what was missing—at least in the press reports—was an analysis of what *creates* anti-feminism. As a friend of mine asked, "Why isn't NAC saying that if the state had acted on women's movement demands regarding women and poverty, childcare, pensions, and workplace equality, RW wouldn't have a leg to stand on?"

We must also look at the women's movement and examine our failures. I believe that in many ways the rise of RW is intimately connected with the rise of liberal feminism. Barbara Eherenreich has argued that what she terms "lifestyle feminism" has allowed fewer women to identify with the women's movement. "Outside the middle classes, lifestyle feminism can be actively repellent. If feminism is for women who are slender, intelligent and upwardly mobile, and you are over 40, perhaps overweight and locked in to a dead end job or marriage, then you are more likely to see feminism as a put down, rather than a sisterly call to arms.

Feminism as career strategy is clearly the image of feminism RW runs with. They pitch their message to older women, women with large families, women who do not work outside the home, or women with less than professional jobs. They tell these women that it's the fault of feminists, not the state or business, that their work isn't valued properly. Feminists have often responded to RW by angrily reminding them that *of course* the women's movement has long championed the cause of all women, whatever economic or social choices they have made. I know that, you know that, the point is why don't the women attracted to RW know that?

Anti-feminism forces us to ask some difficult questions about ourselves. I used to think that liberal feminism could be tolerated. Now I wonder if they do more harm than good. I used to find feminist culture (i.e., young, educated, urban women spending most of their lives in long and intensely personal political meetings) sustaining. Now I find it alienating. I wonder how the women's movement can balance its claims to work for the liberation of all women, without ignoring or wishing away very real divisions among women based on class, race, age and politics. Paying attention to what RW is saying is depressing, and clearly induces pessimism. But unless we are willing to challenge the perception of feminism which they are trying to exploit, we run the risk of losing the little ground we have gained.

And that's *really* depressing.

Karen Dubinsky has recently given workshops on RW in Ottawa and Kingston. This article is an updated version of a paper published by the Canadian Research Institute for the Advancement of Women (CRIAW). All quotations from R.E.A.L. Women come from either their own literature (newsletters, policy statements and briefs) or from press reports.

IT'S ONLY SEXUAL TERRORISM...

by Melanie Randall

Volume 8, No. 9 (July 1987), pp. 5 and 14

Sexual attacks on women appear to have escalated in Toronto this past year. In fact, it is only the media attention to a number of vicious stranger rapes and assaults, particularly but not exclusively those in the Riverdale and Scarborough areas, which has made salient what women working the area already know: sexual terrorism is a constant and real part of women's everyday lives. Some of us get attacked and raped on the streets. But for every sexual assault perpetrated by a man who is a stranger, there are perhaps ten or more sexual, assaults against women perpetrated by men who are known to them, as husbands, landlords, bosses, co-workers, doctors, lovers, dates, friends. We can never be reminded enough that those rapes which women are brave enough to report to the police represent only the tiniest tip of the iceberg.

Last summer in at least three separate communities in the city—Riverdale, the Annex, and the Church-Wellesley neighbourhood—women organized to raise awareness about violence against women and to devise an empowering response to it for the women concerned. Again this year, women in the Riverdale area, as well as throughout the rest of Toronto, have been angry and concerned about the recent spate of stranger rapes in their communities these past months. Some of the most recent attacks have been particularly brutal; weapons were used in many of them. One woman had a fractured I skull; another woman was so viciously beaten about the head that she had to undergo brain surgery.

Women from the Riverdale Women's Action Committee, working with women in WAVAW (Women Against Violence Against Women) and the Toronto Rape Crisis Centre, organized three related actions to raise community awareness and to act against the acute fear of rape and violence which women in the community are experiencing and expressing. Two thousand flyers were distributed to homes in the neighbourhood notifying residents of the rapes in Riverdale, including composite sketches of two of the suspected rapists and the locations of the most recent attacks, all of which had occurred at knifepoint. The flyers also announced the "Walkabout," held on Saturday June 6, and the community meeting planned for the following week.

More than two hundred women, some from across Canada visiting Toronto for the Canadian Association of Sexual Assault Centres conference, marched through the streets during the Riverdale Walkabout, holding candles and carrying signs calling for an end to rape. The march stopped at the ten places where women have been sexually assaulted on the street during the past year. At each location a woman's silhouette was spray-painted on the sidewalk with the words "Woman assaulted here" stencilled inside the figure, an eerie and graphic reminder of the violent sexual attacks.

At the same time we have seen the Toronto police respond with the by now familiar and fatigued myths about women and rape. In *The Globe and Mail* (May 25, 1987) a police officer was quoted as saying that women's summer clothing was linked to an increase in sexual assaults. When a woman phoned Public Complaints to point out the sexism and victim-blaming in this type of comment, the officer she spoke to said, "No, we're not blaming women for rape. We're just saying they're the cause of it." The glaring contradiction in these statements aside, this officer is quite explicit in his identification of what the problem about rape is. Women are the problem. That so many men assault and rape women would appear to be normal and taken for granted in this world view. And men's proclivity for sexual violence and aggression against women is uncritically accepted.

Not only are the police revealing their profoundly sexist and woman-blaming attitudes regarding sexual violence through their public comments, they have once again revealed their trivialization of and ineptitude regarding incidents of sexual harassment and violence towards women through their actions. On the night of the Riverdale Walkabout a man antagonized women and disrupted the march by exposing himself and masturbating publicly. When several women flagged down a passing police car, the first officer to the scene responded by chuckling. The police then further enraged the crowd of women, who had circled the man to stop him from fleeing, by refusing to lay a charge. Infuriated, the entire march stopped and began chanting "Cops, do your jobs," and "Men protecting men." In a neighbourhood where the issue of violence against women is so salient at present, it is shocking that the police were so quick to dismiss this act of hostility as harmless and irrelevant. We do not need to be reminded that recently in Scarborough, a man suspected in a recent rape case was later also seen exposing himself to women several streets over. We also know that even though the police have been quoted as saying that "It's only indecent exposure," some of those very few men who are convicted of rape and sexual assault have previous convictions which include such "harmless" offences as indecent exposure.

We need to ask ourselves what is going on when a group of women peacefully marches through the streets and some man feels compelled to respond by making a hostile and confrontational sexual gesture to them. More specifically still, what is the connection between this man's aggression and hostility towards women and the exhibition of his erect penis? Later on in the march another group of young men harassed women by shouting out "Suck this big one, lesbians." Aside from their misapprehension that calling women lesbians is insulting, these men clearly know that their penises are used to threaten and harm women. This seems to be the point that is missed when people trivialize what is going on with a man's "indecent exposure." Though it is not the most violent of acts in the continuum of men's intrusive and abusive sexual violations of women it is, nevertheless, intended to be an act of hostility and intimidation. And if a woman experiences a man exposing his penis as hostile and threatening, it is.

In this particular case, the police are saying that the onus is on those women who witnessed the man's exposure and masturbation to lay charges because, without being witnesses themselves, there was "nothing they could do." This, of course, used to be and is often still their response to wife assault. But the police officers at the scene clearly saw that the man had exposed himself and are obligated to lay charges against him for causing a public disturbance and making an "indecent exhibition" (under sections 169 or 171 of the Criminal Code). At the police station later that night, women gathered to protest this flagrant example of police inaction, and were told that the man in question "could have had his zipper broken, or could have been relieving himself." The officer who had been at the scene continued to insist that the police were not legally able to lay charges.

But after consultation with several criminal lawyers, women in

WAVAW and the Riverdale Women's Action Committee learned that the police, deliberately it would seem, had completely misrepresented the law. We were consistently advised that the police were indeed empowered to lay charges, and are able to do so whenever there are "reasonable and probable grounds to believe that an offence took place." What they are saying to us, then, is that the testimony of the many women at the scene, taken together with the fact that the police themselves saw the man with his pants open, does not constitute "reasonable and probable grounds" to charge this man. Furthermore, the police department's failure to take action against this criminal offence and act of hostility towards women shows us that they do not consider sexual harassment of women to be a serious problem.

Charges against the man who exposed himself in Riverdale have since been laid by one of the women on the march. In response to public pressure and media attention the police offered, not to lay charges themselves of course, but to "escort" her when she went to the Justice of the Peace. She declined their offer. On the morning she went to lay charges, two police officers decided to pay a surprise visit to her place of work, where they harassed a receptionist and the woman's boss as to her whereabouts. Incensed by this invasion of privacy, a Toronto rape crisis worker called later that day on behalf of the woman who had laid the charges and asked whether it was customary to go to an assaulted woman's place of work and advise her co-workers of the situation. A Staff Sergeant responded: "Look, this is only indecent assault and you women are the ones that are flogging this whole thing."

By insisting that the women who were "offended" take time off work to go to a Justice of the Peace to make a complaint in the first place, the police have chosen, once again, to make men's sexual harassment of women an individual woman's problem, instead of treating the issue as one which affects the community as a whole. Furthermore, the men who are police officers are themselves guilty of negligence for their refusal to lay charges, and of harassment for their intrusion into this woman's place of work. Clearly the police do not "serve and protect" women in this city.

There is, of course, an inherent contradiction in feminists expecting, and working towards, improved police service, as we know from our experience with various institutions and agencies of the state. The police, in Toronto as elsewhere, represent an extremely male-dominated, hierarchical, conservative and, more often than not, oppressive force. As such, any political work around the police is fraught with serious, perhaps insurmountable, inconsistencies and problems. We can hardly expect the men who so very often typify the misogynist attitudes and practices of a patriarchal society to serve in any useful way when women are sexually assaulted and harassed. At the same time, however, when women do choose to report a sexual violation we are inevitably up against the institutions of a male dominant society, specifically the police and the criminal justice system. It is imperative, therefore, that we work to eliminate the "second assault" which women go through when seeking redress through the criminal justice system or demanding safety from continued violence. With specific reference to the police, this means, among other things, that a woman's claim that a sexual assault has been committed against her will not be "unfounded" by the police; this means that women will not be interrogated at length by many different officers about their past sexual history; this means that the police must no longer tell women at community meetings that they should not fight back in sexual assaults and should "let the guy have his two minutes pleasure"; this means that women who report rape will not wait for months on end to do identifications; this means that police must stop blaming women for men's behaviour and must lay charges in all cases of sexual assault, wife assault, and indecent exposure. And this would be only a beginning.

In this way, then, we must insist that the police, like other institutions through which women at times must work, respond to women's demands. Specifically, this means that we must insist that the police and the courts treat men's acts of sexual violence, exploitation and harassment in a manner which is accountable and responsive not only to the women who have been directly harmed, but to *all* women. Otherwise, we abandon those women who choose o have no choice but to work within the system t the sexist attitudes and practices which continue to construct and reinforce our subordination throughout society as a whole.

As the recent organizing in Toronto demonstrates, women are determined to continue to organize and combat men's sexual intrusion violations and often brutal assaults which are so pervasive. Increasingly, women who have not previously considered themselves to be "feminist" or "politicized" are angered by and are acting against the huge issue of our sexual vulnerability to men's violent and harassing behaviour. And the "second assault" to which we are subjected at the hands of the police and the courts continues to be exposed and combatted by women who refuse to live in a world of sexual violence and inequality.

Melanie Randall is a member of Women Against Violence Against Women in Toronto and an editor at Resources for Feminist Research.

ENOUGH IS ENOUGH: NATIVE WOMEN'S RIGHTS
Volume 9, No. 2 (November 1987), p. 4

Enough is Enough: Aboriginal Women Speak Out, *edited by Janet Silman and published this fall by The Women's Press, is the story of the women of the Tobique Reserve in New Brunswick, told in their own voices, and their fight for Native women's rights. Excerpted here are introductions to the various chapters of the women's lives.*

In June 1985 the Canadian Parliament passed a bill which ended over one hundred years of legislated sexual discrimination against Native Indian women. The passage of legislation to amend the Indian Act marked the culmination of a long campaign by Native women to regain their full Indian status, rights and identity. An extraordinary group of women from Tobique Reserve in New Brunswick have been in the forefront of that struggle. The Tobique women actually began to form as an "entity" in the mid-1970s, not initially to change the Indian Act, but to improve local conditions for women and children. Countless surveys and government reports have documented the formidable problems faced by Native women in Canada. For example, a federal study done in 1979 concluded that:

Indian women likely rank among the most severely disadvantaged in Canadian society. They are worse off economically than both Indian men and Canadian women and although they live longer than Indian men, their life expectancy does not approach that of Canadian women generally.

Furthermore, "About a third of the Indian deaths (irrespective of sex) are reported as being due to 'accidents, poisoning and violence' in comparison to about ten percent for the total population."

There are approximately six hundred reserves in Canada. The reservation system is as old as Canada itself, "Lands reserved for the Indians" being defined in the Constitution Act of 1869. Since 1876 reserves have been governed by the Indian Act, a comprehensive piece of federal legislation which holds Indian land in trust by the Crown and regulates virtually every aspect of reserve life, including band politics. For example, the chief and band council are elected every two years, regardless of whatever traditional patterns may have existed. It also defines who is legally Indian.

An Indian self-government movement has gained in momentum in the past decade, seeking to gain greater decision-making powers for aboriginal people who see themselves as First Nations. However, legislative change has been approached with caution because, although the Indian Act has constrained aboriginal people, it also has defined their special status. This is one reason why Indian women seeking to eliminate sexual discrimination from the Indian Act met with resistance from some sectors of their own community. Prior to 1985, the last time the Indian Act was amended was in 1951, and even in 1951 the main aspects of the 1876 legislation remained unchanged. A 1983 federal report on self-government stated that:

> The new Indian Act did not differ in many respects from previous legislation, ie., protection of *Indian lands* from alienation and *Indian property* from depredation, provision for a form of *local government*, methods of ending Indian status, were preserved intact.

Indian reserves are "home" for over 200,000 aboriginal people in Canada. The social conditions for many bands are appalling, and even for those, such as Tobique, where conditions recently have improved somewhat, the scars may be less visible, but the wounds of over a hundred years of government regulation are still fresh.

Unemployment, suicide, school drop-out rates, health problems and housing shortages are at epidemic levels on most reserves, Tobique being no exception. While Native women long have endured the grim reality which underlies these statistics, in the mid-1970s the Tobique women decided they no longer were going to accept their situation without a struggle. Over the years more and more women were being thrown out of their homes by husbands. While the men then moved their girlfriends—often white—into the family home, the Indian women and children had to move into condemned houses or in with relatives who already were overcrowded. Since the Indian Act gave men sole ownership of property through *certificates of possession*, women had no housing rights or recourse to help through the law. Finally in 1977 when yet another woman was evicted from her home, two women, Eva Saulis and Glenna Perley, started to gather women together to protest against the situation...

Because the chief and band council would not listen to the women's grievances, what began on August 30th, 1977, as a demonstration, turned into an occupation of the band office which lasted for nearly four months. The women's occupation was marked by episodes of violence and a polarization of the entire reserve into "supporters of the women" and "supporters of the band administration."

The band office occupation received almost daily media coverage, and the Tobique women rapidly learned the value of publicizing their story. Also, as they sought (and received little) assistance from government officials, the multi-layered Indian Affairs bureaucracy came into sharper focus, and with it, that piece of legislation which governs virtually every aspect of reservation life: the Indian Act. Women were given various reasons for not receiving assistance, but the most unequivocal "no" was to those women who had lost their Indian status by "marrying out"; in other words, by marrying men who did not have Indian status.

The Indian Act not only governs the life of 350,000 Native Indians in Canada, it also has defined *who* is, and is not, legally an "Indian." From 1869 until 1985 the determination of Indian *status* was determined by a patrilineal system; that is, by a person's relationship to "a male person who is a direct descendent in the male line of a male person." When she married a non-status man, an Indian woman born with status lost it, unable to regain it even if she subsequently was divorced or widowed. Along with her status, the woman lost her band membership and with it, her property, inheritance, residency, burial, medical, educational and voting rights on the reserve. In direct contrast, and Indian man bestowed his status upon his white wife and their children, and could bestow it by adoption upon any other children. Consequently every Indian woman was dependent upon a man—first her father and then her husband—for her identity, rights and status under the Indian Act.

Maliseets were traditionally matrilineal, tracing ancestry through the woman. However, Indian tradition was irrelevant to the architects of the Indian Act, and regardless of traditional values and practices, the Act uniformly imposed the nineteenth century patrilineal European view of women as essentially the property of men. As on many other reserves, Tobique women were unaware of the far-reaching implications of "marrying out" until they later sought to move back to the reserve. A number of women who were either divorced or widowed from white husbands returned to Tobique in the mid-1970s. As women began to exchange stories and work more closely for better housing conditions, "the non-status issue" came to light as a specific instance of sexual discrimination. During the 1977 occupation, Tobique women decided to work towards raising the awareness of the Canadian public regarding Native women's problems by taking a case against Canada to the United Nations.

Actually, as early as the 1950s, Mary Two-Axe Early of Caugnawaga, Quebec spoke out against "Section 12(1)(b)" the section of the Indian Act which stripped women of their rights if they married non-status men. In the early 1970s, Native women began to organize across Canada, 12(1)(b) being one of the issues they raised. In 1973 the Supreme Court of Canada heard the cases of Jeannette Lavell and Yvonne Bedard against Section 12(1)(b), and ruled in a five to four decision that the Indian Act was *exempt* from the Canadian Bill of Rights.

This 1973 ruling allowed the Act to remain in force, and left Native women with no avenue to challenge 12(1)(b) in Canada. Indian women who supported Lavell and Bedard were attacked by Indian leaders and labelled "white-washed women's libbers" who were undermining their Indian heritage. Organizations such as the National Indian Brotherhood mounted a lobbying campaign against Lavell and Bedard. Their argument was that the Indian Act must be kept intact for use as a bargaining lever with the federal government, and any tampering—such as amending 12(1)(b)—would play into the government's "1969 White Paper" plan of doing away with special Indian status. Although this argument was convoluted and not without holes, it continued to be employed well into the 1980s. It was used against the Tobique women when they entered the scene in 1977 by taking the case of Sandra Lovelace to the United Nations.

The reason the United Nations accepted the case as a legitimate complaint against Canada, was that, since the Supreme Court ruling against Lavell and Bedard in 1973, Native women had no legal recourse left in Canada. The final decision of the U.N. Human Rights Committee was not made until 1981, and in the meantime, the Tobique women planned and implemented another major strategy to attract Canadian attention to the problems of Native women. In July of 1979 they held a one hundred mile Native Women's Walk from Oka Reserve near Montreal to Parliament Hill in Ottawa. The women and children's walk attracted tremendous national press coverage. Upon arrival in Ottawa they staged a large rally on Parliament Hill and met with the prime minister and several cabinet ministers.

In 1981 the U.N. Human Rights Committee ruled in Sandra Lovelace's favour, finding Canada in breach of the International Covenant on Civil and Political Rights. The final ruling put additional pressure on the federal government to amend the Indian Act by "embarrassing" Canada—tarnishing the country's image—in the international community. Although the lobbying campaign to amend 12(1)(b) seemed on the verge of victory, four more years of concerted lobbying actually were necessary. During those subsequent years, Tobique women became seasoned lobbyists with an issue that had become "a political football."

AGAINST HER WILL:
JUDGES' BIASES #1

by T. Brettel Dawson

Volume 10, No. 1 (October 1988), p. 3

At the beginning of August, a Supreme Court judge in British Columbia finally got it right. He rejected the argument that a fetus is a child subject to apprehension by Family and Child Services (FCS). Of course he was a bit late. The fetus had been apprehended by Family and Child Services in May when the mother had refused to undergo a recommended cesarean. The apprehension was confirmed by a provincial court judge soon after. By virtue of the apprehension, FCS had the power to consent to any medical treatment needed by the fetus, including the cesarean. When two cars full of police and social workers (a.k.a. the Emergency Response Team), squealed to a halt at the hospital doors and poured inside, the mother is reported to have changed her mind and agreed to the cesarean before being told she had to have it. The provincial court judge later referred to this as "consent without coercion or threat."

However, Mr. Justice MacDonell of the Supreme Court of British Columbia disagreed with the whole approach. He appears to have listened to feminist submissions made by the Women's Legal Education and Action Fund (LEAF), that "the effect of authorizing an apprehension prebirth of necessity means controlling the body of the mother to complete and effectuate a custody order." Such serious and far-reaching "powers to interfere with the rights of women… must be done by specific legislation and anything less will not do," he reasoned. His conclusion was that no such power existed. This was the case of Baby R.

That should be the end of the matter in Canada: a fetus is not a child for the purposes of child welfare legislation; a pregnant woman cannot be controlled as to her lifestyle or choices during pregnancy; and she cannot be forced to undergo medical treatment against her will for the express purpose of protecting the fetus within her. However there are indications that the matter isn't quite resolved yet.

In Ontario last year, a protection order was granted to the Belleville Children's Aid Society in relation to a fetus, when the mother refused "to seek, maintain or accept any form of medical assistance" regarded by the judge as "clearly necessary for the delivery of the child." The woman was homeless and shelterless. On one occasion in March, when almost at term, she slept in an underground garage. To enforce the apprehension of the fetus, Judge Kirkland ordered the woman committed for psychiatric assessment under the Mental Health Act. The side-effects, of course, were to confine her to hospital during labour and delivery and to open her up to medical treatment against her will.

More recently, on August 3 1988 in Toronto, Andrea McKenzie pleaded guilty to charges of communicating for the purposes of prostitution and failing to appear in court, and was sentenced to 60 consecutive days in prison. This was a heavier than normal sentence and the judge rejected the woman's request that she serve her term during weekends. This is an option often entertained by judges. (Readers may recall the soccer coach allowed to serve his sentence for sexual assault over weekends.) Further, the woman had a four year old child to care for. The judge in question, Provincial Court Judge Hogg, has a reputation for being "fair" then what had provoked such rigour on his part? The answer is found in this interchange recorded in the court transcript:

Prosecutor: ...I think she appears to be pregnant

Accused: Yeah, I'm eight and half months pregnant. I'm 22 years old.

Judge: Eight and a half months pregnant, and you're out working the streets. Isn't that lovely? Isn't that lovely?

Accused: That's why I said I didn't have any intention (to continue). I'm looking for other jobs through unemployment...

Judge: Where do you live?

Accused: (address given to a location in Regent Park).

Judge: What a great place to be giving birth to a child—well known hangout for cocaine dealers, drug dealers and everything else. Isn't that lovely?

Accused: Well, that's where my mom lives, and…

Judge: Yeah, that's where your mother lives, sure. I'll think about it over recess…This is an absolute atrocity.

Having thought about it, the judge's solution was to take the woman into custody and to order her to remain in a hospital ward until the child was born. He sputtered: "I cannot comprehend what would drive a woman to act in this manner, and the only way to protect this child is to have this child born in custody, and hopefully things will be done about it." Not only was MacKenzie to be detained for the duration, but there is some insinuation that the child should be taken from her on birth. This approach is far from "lovely"!

The issue of whether a fetus can be regarded as a child in need of care and protection before birth and for the purposes of ensuring safe and healthy birth is both basic and complex. It is as basic as women's right to personal and reproductive self-determination; as basic as our right to "life, liberty and security and freedom of the person," or to not "be arbitrarily detained or imprisoned" (Charter of Rights and Freedoms, s.7 and s.9). It is also as basic as our right to be trusted and supported in our decisions and dilemmas around reproduction. It is as basic as our right to privacy and bodily integrity. To Sandra Rogers, a law professor in Ottawa:

> Judicial orders of protection of a fetus prior to birth…constitute an unacceptable and un-enforceable interference with maternal self-determination by the imposition of supervision orders or orders for detention and behaviour modification…(this) would be jarringly inconsistent with the present commitment to sex equality."
>
> —"Fetal Rights and Maternal Rights: Is there a Conflict?" *Canadian Journal of Women and the Law* (1986) 1:2, 456.)

Think about it. In the Belleville case, the integrity of the pregnant woman, already compromised by poverty, transience and possible psychiatric illness, was completely disregarded by the judge. The decisions about medical care and delivery should have remained hers to make, and the conditions in which she could make them—shelter, medication, stability and safety—should have been provided. The committal order may have been appropriate but the protection order was not. Further, if the woman's capacity to make those decisions was not impaired, the law should not have intervened at all. A woman has a right to be pregnant and to live on the street. These are problems on the wide scale of women's economic and social vulnerability, of full shelters and overcrowded hospitals; but they are problems which are played out in individual women's lives.

In Andrea McKenzie's case, the decision is sexist, classist and according to Valerie Scott, it "displayed the typical institutional bias against the business of prostitution." Darlene Lawson of the Elizabeth Fry Society adds that the case is one more indication of the unacceptable view advanced by those responsible for developing state sanctions that women are the problem and that society and children need to be protected from our choices. The reasoning took no account of Andrea McKenzie's economic circumstances, her support systems or whether she was forced to stay on the streets by economics or coercion. There was no evidence that she was a bad or unfit mother in any way. There was no evidence that the fetus was at risk and no evidence that the mother was chemically dependent. There was no consideration that the sentence itself created a terrible environment in which to be born or to give birth: after some days confined to hospital McKenzie gave birth and was almost immediately transferred to a halfway house where she spent several more days required to do chores and follow house rules.

Instead of evidence, the judge relied on offensive assumptions unchallenged by reality. This woman lived in the "wrong" part of town, did the "wrong" kind of part-time work and *ipso facto* became an atrocity of irresponsibility to an outraged judge. He had the right to sentence her for her breaches of the present *Criminal Code*, but not for her breaches of his paternal morality. Similarly, in the Baby R case, the social workers and the provincial court judge were prepared to go even so far as to put the scalpel to the mother's skin. Thus, we have women committed, detained and coerced.

What we don't have is sufficient recognition of the necessarily interconnected relationship of the fetus and the woman. Pro-choice advocates should know of course, that the common law has never recognized legal existence or rights in a fetus. Only upon birth, upon complete extrusion from the body of the mother has "legal personality" begun. Even this will be re-examined by the Supreme Court of Canada this fall in the Borowski appeal claiming constitutional protection for fetuses. But the approach, although it has often worked for women to date, is flawed.

The law seems prepared to prioritize one set of interests (those ascribed to the fetus) over another set of interests *as if those interests were completely separate*. The law thinks in measured units and in right/wrong equations. But this just doesn't make sense when one being is literally within the other. Madam Justice Wilson of the Supreme Court of Canada acknowledged this in her decision in the *Morgentaler* case. The conditions of women's lives, of our existing relationships with others, and of our relationship with this potential being within us, are interwoven in our decision making. The problem is not that the fetus and the woman are independent, but that they are connected. The question is one of responsibility—how can I care for myself, and for this potential being? What is the responsible decision?

If a woman's capacity to make those decisions is impaired, the response must be to do what can be done to restore it, rather than rushing in like knights in white armour, and then riding away from the vanquished with self-satisfaction and a bloody sword. The "compassion" of the Crusaders has long been rejected. This kind of legal intervention is similarly misdirected.

However, the issue is also complex and fraught with dilemma. Feminists struggle against abuse of children. Given that children born with addictions received from their mothers *in utero* suffer real pain in withdrawal, does rejecting the approach in these cases amount to accepting abuse of potential children? Should children born to mothers with a history of prior abuse of children, or of taking harmful substances while pregnant, be removed upon birth with the case essentially being "pre-judged"? The cases have involved fetuses nearly at term and, in the case of Baby R, with one foot visible. Does the State, through the law, have a responsibility to protect potential life at this late stage? Has the fetus really become a child at that point? Where would that point be drawn; at say, next month, or if Joe Borowski became Minister of Justice? What if we are horrified (in our comfortable abstraction) that apparently a woman could fail to nurture a child she has decided to bear? How can we define or discharge our responsibilities in such situations?

These are not easy questions. The decisions required are difficult, and they are not always made responsibly. The process is complicated and even compromised by the fact that, in our society, women are often faced with economic and power inequalities which negate effective decision-making. However it seems essential to me that we don't let the state step in to make the "right" decision. In the current context, that would lead to negating the equality and capacity of women. Coercive intervention by the state to ensure that women make decisions of which it approves will do nothing to empower women. Until the legal system can take account of the experience of women, it will inevitably act in a way which negates that experience. Accordingly, granting a fetus a right to be born and giving that right precedence over the freedom of the pregnant woman creates more problems than it could possibly solve.

The decision of Mr. Justice MacDonnell in the Supreme Court of British Columbia is to be welcomed for all these reasons. Admittedly, it is based on legal reasoning, limiting "legal rights or existence" to birth. Yet it also indicates that feminist advocacy by LEAF is having a positive effect in shaping the thinking of the law. Standing removed in time from the passions and confusion of the moment, he has also calmly restated that the powers of the state are limited by the rights of women.

SUBMITTING TO THE JUDGE:
JUDGES' BIASES #2

by T. Brettel Dawson

Volume 10, No. 2 (November 1988), p. 4

I teach a law course on the subject of women and the legal process. A theme in the course is that the way in which judges see situations involving women often differs completely from the way the women concerned experienced it and described it. The problem is that the judge's view becomes "truth" and the woman's experience becomes invisible. This is a fundamental issue but it can also be a little abstract. However, this semester, with the help of two women, I have been able to make this issue more concrete and I think it is important enough to write about.

The first woman, whom I'll call Beth, called me over the summer. She had laid sexual assault charges against her common-law spouse in a seemingly open and shut case, only to see him acquitted. She told me her story and showed me a copy of the court transcript in which she had told the judge of her experience. She also showed me a copy of the judge's decision. It read like a different case. The second woman was a visiting scholar from the U.K., Carol Smart. She has examined transcripts in many sexual assault cases and has several ideas about what is going on.

In 1983, the *Criminal Code* of Canada was amended to permit women to lay charges of sexual assault against their husbands. Of course, Beth could have laid charges even without the amendment as she was not married. However, it was hoped that the amendment would signal the end of the male-defined view that intimate relations implied consent to sexual contact. Even so, Beth was caught by the tentacles of life which cling to the old view.

Her story, supported by the intake records at a women's shelter, the court transcripts and photographs, was as follows. She had been living with her common-law spouse, whom I'll call Michael, for about four years. His children from an earlier relationship lived with them. The relationship had been going sour. On several occasions, they had separated for short periods, during which both saw other people. In the days leading up to the assault, they had been arguing. She described him as possessive. He threatened her, was verbally abusive to her in public, and listened at the door of a friend of Beth's, when she was discussing moving out. During periods of separation, he spied on her with binoculars. She decided to leave.

Beth went back to the common residence to tell Michael. He seemed to take it civilly and, as it was now late, they went to bed. Beth thought it would be okay. She slept without a nightgown— telling the judge that on another occasion when she had worn one after an argument, Michael had ripped it off her and throttled her saying that he "ought to kill her." Things, however, weren't okay. He forced her to have oral sex, causing her to choke and vomit. Then he demanded intercourse against her will—she described herself at this point as extremely upset—and said she saw no point in fighting with him. In the morning, instead of going to work, Michael turned off the alarm and began the process again. She was pinned down and distraught. She bit his penis. She was very clear about what happened next. Michael called his children into the room, told them to call the police over what she had done to him and, when they had left, he punched her twice in the face with a closed fist.

This is how the judge saw it. He described the relationship as "stormy and tempestuous" and commented that the parties were intimate with each other and very fond of each other. He noted that they were of the same weight and age, seemingly regarding this as negating any implication of coercion or domination. He lingered over the sexual relationship, detailing his conclusion that the parties had lots of sex, including oral sex. Ultimately he referred to the situation as a "rather sordid" affair. He found that they had reconciled before going to bed and that Beth coming to bed nude was a "sign that sex was contemplated." Indeed, he commented that as she had only gone to bed with a nightgown on two or three occasions, this indicated that sex was very frequent in the relation-ship. He commented that Beth hadn't "made much noise" during the alleged assaults. He concluded that the sexual contact on the night was "basically voluntary" and although neither had been much interested, "they had done it anyway." One wonders what reality this judge lived in.

It gets worse. With respect to the oral sex of the morning, the judge constructed the events as follows. When Beth wasn't "all that interested," the judge found that Michael had suggested that she pretend it was one of her old boyfriends, to which she had responded by biting him. Michael, according to this judge, then instantaneously backhanded her with an open hand—for which he was now sorry. Only after this "backhand" were the children or the police called. Having viewed the situation this way, the sex was consensual and the punch was provoked. Result: Michael was acquitted of both assault and sexual assault.

So this is the first point: the judge's 'truth' differed fundamentally from Beth's account of her experience. The judge's truth counted and Beth's truth was discounted and reinterpreted to bear witness against her. The judge, just like Michael, had the power to impose his own reality. That is enough to make me shake my head in disbelief and dismay. But another question needs to be asked: where does this male reality come from and what does it involve? This is where Carol Smart shed some light when she discussed the case in my class.

The first point she made is that the law had divided up sexual activity into consensual and non-consensual, which is conveniently black and white. However, submission gives the judge a problem, as it doesn't seem to clearly indicate non-consent. Accordingly, submission to unwanted sexual conduct is slapped down on the side of consent. This obviously doesn't help women claiming to have been sexually violated—particularly not women in coercive intimate relations. The second point Carol made was that the law sexualized women's bodies to the extent that women can be and are reduced to body parts. In a sexual assault trial, women are forced to talk about their bodies in a context in which they can be sexualized and negated. Carol noted that the judge had done it in this case when he had lingered over how often sex took place and in his description of her sleeping nude—long a state of women undressed for physical appraisal and the object of gaze, women as embodying sex. Of even greater explanatory power was her third point: that, a sexual assault trial is often reduced to a pornographic vignette in which the woman who has been assaulted and the events surrounding the assault and the relationship are constructed to follow the script of standard fare pornography. Thus, the judge may well have been approaching this case with a pornographic view of the world—and especially of women. No wonder Beth's experience was not seen in this situation.

As well, it makes it enormously difficult for any woman to disassociate herself from this constructed image. It is also difficult for a judge (or for that matter a jury) not to have a reasonable doubt about whether a sexual assault took place if this is the lens through which they see the world. This reminds me of a quote from feminist philosopher Marilyn Frye:

> Reality is that which is. The English word "real" stems from a word which meant "regal, of or pertaining to the king...." Reality is that which pertains to the one in power, is that over which he has power, is his domain. The ideal king reigns over everything as far as the eye can see. What he cannot see is not real. To be real is to be visible to the king. (*The Politics of Reality*, 1983, p 155.)

So those are the issues. Now what is to be done about them?

Broadside
A FEMINIST REVIEW

Volume 5, number 6   **April 1984**   **$1.5**

Work by artist Lynne Fernie, displayed at the Desire Show of the Alter Eros Festival.

Desire: an out-of-body experience

by Amanda Hale

There is a phenomenon called synchronic in which an idea takes hold of cert elements of the populace, spreads by osmo and generally results in some kind of cultu shift. Looking back after the event, one c trace the threads of such a development, bu is nevertheless a magical and mysterious pr cess, manifesting a kind of evolutionary evitability in its free-form lack of tangi connections. The current activity around concept of female eros is such a phenomen and it has grown out of the concern o strong feminist movement with the dam done to women and children by pornograp Pornography is the extreme perversion of pure spirit of the erotic, hence the hand-hand campaign to fight pornography a reclaim eros. The Alter Eros festival currer taking place in Toronto is a manifestation this female force of determined explorati It is a quest, via painting, sculpture, thea poetry, music and photography, to recla and assert our sexuality.

The first of three visual arts shows to op was Desire, organized by Women's Persp

DESIRE, page

INSIDE BROADSIDE

FEATURES

EROS REVISITED: Three women explore their notions of Eros in an effort to rediscover and redefine their own female sexuality. *Broadside* presents Dorothy Hénaut, Joanne Kates and Mariana Valverde. Page 8.

THE GODDESS IS COMING! Don't miss Part 3 of the cartoon series "Judgement Day" by Beth Walden. Page 12

COMMENT

CENSORY PERCEPTION: Susan G. Cole takes exception to Gordon Lawson's short film "The Censor" shown at the *Broadside/Fuse* benefit film night. Though the audience applauded, the film, says Cole, shows the same old myths about female sexuality that pornographers use. Page 7.

VERSION QUÉBEC: Women writers from Québec explore the uses and misuses of language at a panel in February. Though their message is exciting, comments Sarah Sheard, it won't be heard by many. Page 6.

NEWS

LITTON ON TRIAL? 29 women were arrested at Litton Systems in Toronto while performing a citizen's arrest of the company president on charges of fraud, murder and possession of a dangerous weapon. The women were charged with trespassing, and the February trial proceedings are reported on by Janice Williamson. Page 4.

EROS FESTIVAL ALTERED: *Broadside* publishes a statement from the Alter Eros Festival Coalition, on the organizing difficulties of the festival. Page 6.

DUAL PURPOSE: Mary O'Brien, author of *The Politics of Reproduction*, spoke at U of T about the dualism of male-stream philosophy – man *vs* woman, man *vs* nature – which comes from the sense of separation men experience in the process of reproduction. Philinda Masters reports. Page 6.

ARTS

ELEVEN OBSESSIONS: The play *Talking With* by "Jane Martin" is a series of dramatic monologues on women's lives: from a baton twirler to a snake charmer to a housewife who dwells in the Land of Oz. The characters, though thought-provoking at first, are without depth or context. Page 12.

□ □ □

OUTSIDE BROADSIDE: Don't miss this month's calendar of Toronto women's events, for April 1984. Page 15.

□ □ □

FESTIVAL & FERNIE: Amanda Hale reports on the various components of the Alter Eros Festival, and interviews artist Lynne Fernie on images and misrepresentations of women in art. Page 10.

HOOKERS ON DAVIE: Jani Cole and Holly Dale's new fil about a pimp-free street in Vancouver points up the sex-role stereotyping in our society reviewed by Donna Gollan. Page 13.

BIOLOGICALLY DETERMINED SCIENCE: The anthology *Biological Woman* criticizes and documents the effects of sexis science, and analyzes the interaction between science, sexism and social practice. Reviewed by Judith Johnston Page 13.

CHAPTER 3

Features: Debates & Debacles

The anchor for each issue of *Broadside* was the centre spread, the in-depth analysis and commentary from experts on issues that, in many cases, were just developing. We're especially proud of these pieces because many of them helped put these issues on the national agenda.

That isn't to say that no one was discussing them before we wrote about them. These questions got their first traction on the grassroots political level and in women's services where workers on the front lines witnessed the reality of women's lives. It was rape crisis workers who led the struggle to develop new laws on sexual assault. Feminist lawyers, furious at the failure of Canada's budding Charter of Rights and Freedom, sent drafters back to the drawing board when they failed to recognize and name women's equality. Women Against Violence Against Women's activism against pornography caught the attention of the federal government, which went on to amend obscenity laws to take women's experience into account.

Activists raised the issues and *Broadside* gave them a voice. Central to *Broadside*'s values was the idea that it was activists who could best express the rights they were fighting on the ground, so our best pieces—some of which are in this section—came from writers who were inside the movements they described.

Some features, like the one on Quebec sovereignty and another on the need for free-standing abortion clinics, came from whole collectives. No one knew these issues better than these writers did. We'd go so far as to say that had *Broadside* not existed or had we pursued the conventional journalistic value of objectivity that made our writers ineligible to write in mainstream outlets, many essential legal changes—those around sexual assault, pornography, abortion, and family law, to name a few—might never have been made.

Many *Broadside* writers who developed these centre spreads went on to become recognized experts in their fields. As mentioned in the introduction, Sheila McIntyre wrote her first piece on the charter of rights "Unchartered Territory" as a student and then became a recognized expert in creating equity in educational and legal institutions. Nancy Jackman, now the Hon. Nancy Ruth, who wrote about the Canadian Advisory Council on the Status of Women and the charter, sat in the Canadian Senate for many years. Anti-pornography activist Susan G. Cole published two books on pornography and violence. Cultural commentator Susan Crean, whose piece on Judy Chicago's installation *The Dinner Party* is included here, has published seven books, including her biography of Emily Carr, *The Laughing One*, Governor General's Award finalist. Lawyer Susan Ursel can, among other achievements, be credited for working on the famous *Jane Doe v Metropolitan Toronto Commissioners of Police* case that challenged the police for using women as bait to catch a sexual predator. Many of *Broadside*'s contributors went on to win awards and honours in their future careers, including several members of the Order of Canada, the Person's Award, and many law society awards.

Broadside articles sometimes articulated questions that had not fully surfaced in the public realm. A piece in Volume 1 about Vietnamese boat people and their difficulties in adjusting, post-trauma, to a new life in Canada—the first of its kind—shows deep empathy, something many critics of current immigration policy could use. An article shedding light on the distressingly high rate of child sexual abuse in families was such an early commentary that the subject was still referred to as incest, a term we now reject as too sexualized. The testimony in this spread from the survivor is particularly devastating. And Nestlé's exploitation of poor women by pushing baby formula on new mothers to the detriment of their health and the health of their babies was flying under the radar when Beverly Biderman wrote her exposé—the boycott was just developing.

As with the opinion pieces in the previous chapters, the features published here speak to the vitality of feminist debate in the 1980s. Lilith Finkler's contribution critical of Zionism caused a firestorm and the debate still rages. And again, the issues of pornography and sexuality, fiercely contested, are prominent in this part of the book. We include full-length features, excellently argued, from both sides.

The first piece in this chapter, rightfully, is a feature that articulates why *Broadside* was so badly needed. Editor Philinda Masters and collective member Eve Zaremba write eloquently on the failure of mainstream media to address women's experience. Considering how few women were on editorial boards, it comes as no surprise that our real lives were so invisible. The women's sections of the dailies—other than occasional forays into etiquette and relationship advice—regularly dealt with what housewives were expected to be doing in the home: cooking, sewing, and childrearing. While we were aware that these are crucial activities—it's not true that feminists disparaged homemakers—we also knew that it was time to consider women's experience in the workplace, to take on all forms of violence against women, and to shed light on the female artists that the arts pages were ignoring.

Enjoy this ground-breaking work—and check back to our collection of letters to see the impact it had on our readers.

Susan G. Cole

MAINLY BECAUSE OF THE MEDIA

by Philinda Masters and Eve Zaremba

Introductory Issue (May 1979), pp. 10 and 11

Most of us only know what we get from the press, radio, and TV. Mainstream media are our main contact with reality outside our individual lives. Virtually without exception these media have fed us a lot of bullshit on most important subjects. The female half of the population has suffered more than most from this. Media crimes against women and against good journalism have been many. Crimes of commission and omission, language and emphasis, ignorance and arrogance.

The messages are confused and contradictory. The female half of the population is not worth taking seriously. Women's issues—i.e. daycare, job ghettos, abortion, etc.—are dull and tedious. Special interest stuff. The Women's Movement is dead/it's won; it's dangerously radical/it's a Tupperware party; it's funny/it's dreary; it's Lesbian/it's lazy middle-class wives who don't want to do the dishes.

So who's to blame?

Is it nasty capitalist bosses sitting around plotting against women? Or the working reporters, journalists, members of the Newspaper Guild? It isn't necessary to postulate a conscious plot on the part of everyone concerned. In our society few things work that simply. For instance a complex and self-reinforcing mechanism operates at the level of "women's issues"—such as daycare, abortion, social service cut-backs, job ghettos, wage differentials and so on. For a journalist, whether male or female, "women's issues" is the pits. It's the lowest on the paper's totem pole. Carries no prestige, leads nowhere, is perceived as irrelevant, dullsville. The Women's Section and its clone, The Family Section, is a vehicle for advertising. Articles and stories are only there to keep the ads from running into each other.

Everyone connected with a newspaper knows this from day one. It's not where journalism's heavies hang out.

There is nothing to be gained for an individual reporter or columnist by taking women's issues seriously, doing any real digging, making connections, learning and passing on this information to readers. On the contrary, a snide comment or irrelevant quote is more likely to attract favorable attention or at least a smile from bosses and peers. How can this help but produce stories that are in fact dull, irrelevant or downright hostile, confirming what everyone knew to start with?

Real policy is made well above the level of the working reporters. It's not necessary to spell this policy out to them. Journalists soon become fine-tuned to the political expectations of the newspaper and even personal bias of the publisher and editors. Bright young feminists entering the business soon learn self-censorship or get out of journalism. To get on, even merely to keep a job, journalists learn not to make waves. Taking women seriously, injecting some hard headed analysis into any "women's story," would amount to making waves in most newsrooms in Canada.

Newspaper publishers and editors are captives of their own assumptions. They operate in a world of conventional professional journalistic wisdom. After the ritual "objectivity," comes "newsworthiness." What is newsworthy? Simple. Events, not issues, make "hard news." Powerful people create "events," women are at best satellites of powerful men, thus women as women do not generate "news." Simple indeed.

The Women's Movement has received abysmal coverage in the last ten years. Its death has been celebrated by the mainstream press since at least the end of 1975, International Women's Year. It's the longest ongoing wake in history. Somehow newspapers and magazines of various political colours have found it necessary to reaffirm the non-existence of the Movement at more or less regular intervals. This is hardly required where the subject has in fact expired. Since it has never bothered to find out much about the very lively real thing, the mainstream press does a very neat trick. It first creates an ersatz model of the Women's Movement, then destroys it. To the uninitiated this looks very convincing.

The line of least resistance is to treat anything to do with women under the rubric of the Fabulous Four—Food, Family, Furnishing and Fashion. Women's Liberation news, if acknowledged at all, can be equated with the Society news and consigned to the Women's/Family Section, thus magically ceasing to be news at all and becoming a "life-style" feature. Meanwhile on the news pages, reporters, columnists and editorial writers feel free to ascribe to women and especially to feminists any damn thing they like.

This approach creates problems that newspaper editors do not know how to cope with. It's hard for even the most obtuse to ignore the fact that something is happening out there—women are making unseemly waves, the world is changing. Yet without the help of big "newsworthy" events—how would they like bombs, maybe?—which fit into their professional view of what is important, how can they report on it? There seem to be consequences without observable causes. There are manifestations of some nebulous female entity, an entity without a central focus, leadership, structure, membership lists, addresses or phone number. Conventional male journalism cannot deal with such a situation. So the issue remains and efforts to get around it are pitiful indeed.

Conventional journalistic method requires identifiable sources. So who are the spokeswomen for the Women's Movement? Routine sources of information are usually women with institutional status. Lacking any understanding of, and not caring about, the phenomena they are trying to cover, reporters and their editors often assume comfortably that these women are "representative," "legitimate" spokeswomen for the Movement. It's an understatement to say that this can be highly misleading and that all but the most indifferent editors must know this or at least sense it. On occasion a woman is found who can be counted on to come up with an off the cuff, quotable quote. It's easy to make them sound "weird" and inconsequential, thus handily avoiding dealing with reality.

But the Women's Movement persists in defying all efforts of omission and commission to discredit it and make it disappear. The activist militant minority is hard to pin down and identify but it's very obviously around. Effects of the last ten years have now permeated far into the fabric of society and into the consciousness of regular down-home, non-militant women. It doesn't matter that many may be too intimidated by ridicule and hostility to identify as feminists. With no overt contact with any concrete manifestation of radical feminism they can still be very subversive indeed. The virus is rampant.

At this moment in history it should be clear to all, to friends as well as enemies, that women are a factor in our society, that the Women's Movement is alive, well and affecting all aspects of it. The press needs to break out of conventional thinking about women and what constitutes "newsworthiness" and "objectivity." It had better start taking women seriously as a major news beat. At least on par with labour, business and government, not to mention crime and auto accidents. In the news and editorial pages, using skilled, knowledgeable and unintimidated journalists. Not because of any sudden conversion to feminism or because the press gives a damn for the status, role and humanity of women. Just to retain some vestiges of credibility.

Eve Zaremba

MS. PRINT

Introductory Issue (May 1979), pp. 10 and 11

Probably most journalists would suffer unruffled the accusation that they were sexist, patriarchal, unconcerned with women's issues, etc. But most would be affected by the accusation of bad journalism. And that's what the media's coverage of women amounts to. Not just bad journalism, but unprofessional.

Imagine a small town outside Toronto where half the population of 2300, that's 1,150 people, were suddenly afflicted with a strange virus which kept them in bed for months on end. A young reporter sent to cover the story would be expected to find out what the virus was, what were its symptoms, what cures were available, what the townsfolk thought about it, how it affected their daily lives, their economy, their children.

Suppose in the course of investigation the reporter found out there was a cure but no-one was using it and reasons for this were inadequate. That would be news. Suppose, too, the reporter discovered *all* those afflicted to be women. (If the reporter were a woman she might at this point begin to fear contagion—unless she felt herself protected by the seal of, say, *The Globe and Mail*). At any rate the reporter would, you would think, rush back to headquarters and produce a comprehensive, in-depth analysis of the horrid situation for the front page.

Not to carry the analogy too far, women are *not* given that kind of treatment by reporters. In real life, the story would be treated in a ho-hum way and put on the woman's page next to an article on the latest fashions from Paris. The women would probably be blamed for catching the virus anyway. Either that, or the story would be given front page coverage, but the fact of it being women afflicted would be obscured: "1,100 people catch deadly virus."

You get the idea. How many times have you read on the front page about Canada's poor, Canada's unemployed? And how many times have you read that these "people" are mainly women?

Consider the fact that one of the greatest social movements of the past decade has been the women's movement. Then look at the media coverage. The fact that the events and trends, by any standards, are newsworthy is overlooked in the media's need to protect the status quo. 20,000 people demonstrating in Rome is news, but not if it's 20,000 women. A general strike is news, but not if it's a strike of women.

A recent *Weekend Magazine* poll indicated that only 42% of Canadian women consider themselves feminists. *Only?* Most of the accompanying article then discussed the pros and cons of using Ms., Mrs. or Miss. That's their idea of the women's movement. Incidentally, *The Globe and Mail Style Guide* states that not to use Miss or Mrs. in front of a woman's name is "abhorrent, even in sports coverage." Abhorrent?

When issues of concern to women, especially those representing women's attempts to organize, are presented in the news they are done so in the shoddiest of ways. When recently a group of women met in Toronto to discuss the formation of a political party—a political party, not a jogging club—the news coverage was positively superficial. Readers were informed the time is not ripe for such a party, and treated to a quote from Laura Sabia: "We're here because everything else has failed."

This is serious. First of all, who says everything else has failed? That's a favourite shibboleth of the press. Secondly, any journalist worth their salt would probe the matter a little more deeply. It's called doing research. Obvious questions arise: What is this amazing phenomenon, the women's movement? and is it properly represented by Laura Sabia? The fact is that Laura Sabia is not the women's movement, the spectrum is far broader; and the movement itself is alive and kicking all over the world, including Canada. But you'd never know it.

When superficial treatment doesn't work, there's always plain, old-fashioned sneering. A *Globe and Mail* story covering a public forum on women and unemployment is a case in point. How's this for a lead sentence: "Hell hath no fury like an out-of-work woman?"

The story had no by-line, which means either the reporter didn't want credit (or criticism) or the editor sent a cub reporter who hadn't done much thinking (that's how it read) or the story wasn't considered important. In any case, the first several paragraphs were devoted to describing the women's behaviour as "usually reserved for boot-camp inspection," and their critical comments as "barnyard epithets." After telling us the audience was "hostile," the reporter finally got down to saying what the meeting was about. But the damage had been done. That kind of reporting one would expect to find in second-rate student newspapers, not *the* national newspaper of Canada.

Then there's that sleight-of-hand called "emphasis," or is it out-and-out bias? It's most noticeable when one looks at what kind of "women's" stories make the front page, and what don't. When Mrs. Rideout charged her husband with rape the story was imbedded in the back pages; when they became reconciled as husband and wife it hit the front page; when she filed for divorce it was relegated to the back. Front page space with large headline was allotted to a story on the difference between men's and women's brains. It was a time-worn but supposedly subtle justification for women's inferiority. This is the stuff that sells papers, but can it be considered good, sound journalism?

Speaking of emphasis, the *Toronto Star* has a chatty column called "About Town." One of the items in said column was a list of rapes that had occurred, presumably about town.

Now consider the irony that one reason for the refusal of ad space to homosexual groups, baths, etc. is that the newspaper in question is a "family" paper. The same newspaper will give plenty of space to sexploitation flicks, complete with sexy pics. A "family" paper? All the while, women's sections are being called "family" sections. There's some confused logic here, which should give you some idea as to how the shoddy journalistic treatment of women is allowed to happen.

So, gentlemen, we understand your position, your valiant efforts to maintain the status quo. But as the great ship of mainstream journalism sinks slowly in the west, you will go down with it. We, and the children, will be rowing away in lifeboats.

Philinda Masters

CONSTITUTIONAL CONFERENCE 2: WOMEN MAKE IT HAPPEN
by Kay Macpherson
Volume 2, No. 5 (March 1981), p. 5

"Hi! Would you be able to come to a meeting at lunch time tomorrow?" I was asked over the phone. "We're so mad about that women's Constitutional Conference being called off that we want to do something about it. It's at the Cow Café on John Street. Upstairs at 12:30. See you."

A noisy meeting was in progress when I arrived. "It's shocking," said Laura Sabia. "We get pushed around all the time." "Well," said Linda, "Some of us think we should have a conference anyway. Never mind whether the government supports us. We'll organize it ourselves." "Terrific," chorused the rest of us. "D'you think Flora and Pauline would help us get the same room in the House that the Advisory Council had booked?" "Great idea. Let's ask them. Let's ask Doris what she thinks."

So telephoners were dispatched while the rest continued eating and plotting in the downtown Toronto restaurant, gloating over what the opposition had been saying in Parliament about Lloyd Axworthy and the easily swayed Executive of the Advisory Council. "Flora MacDonald thinks it's a terrific idea and she's going to talk to Pauline Jewett to see what they Can do. Now let's try Doris Anderson." "Why not?" said Doris's gravelly voice over the phone. "Sounds like a great idea to me."

The media took it up in a big way. Interviews and reports were scattered through the press and on television. Linda Ryan Nye was interviewed, Laura Sabia made pronouncements. One stalwart woman called from Ottawa: "Pat Hacker says she'll do everything she can on the spot." But then she proceeded to call together a committee for organizing accommodation, billets, translation, media, and support from everyone ranging from Mayor Marion Dewar (who provided the Ottawa City Hall for one day's meeting), to Maureen McTeer, who offered Stornaway, the Opposition residence, for a reception.

Meantime, back in Toronto, Dawn MacDonald, editor of *City Woman*, launched the Butterfly campaign. "Wear a Butterfly on Valentine's Day," "Butterflies spreading their wings, emerging, flying up." The YWCA took on the job of distributing and selling buttons. Media people across the country were alerted, interviews given, and registration started to pour in. A monster mailing was accomplished by an efficient and raucous team of stickers and lickers who kept getting more brilliant ideas as the evening wore on. In the middle of it all four of us listened to the CBC's "The Fifth Estate" over the telephone, chortling over the discomfiture of Axworthy when confronted with his talk of embarrassing the government.

Michelle Lansberg wrote columns. So did Laura Sabia. Margaret Mironowitz came to the next week's Cow Café meeting and reported progress. Doris Anderson came to town and was consulted about agenda and women for resources and speakers. NAC was having a party and so 150 women heard all about the plans and started spreading the word.

We decided that the meeting would be all day on the Saturday and spill over into Sunday, since we could use the Ottawa City Hall. At that time we would talk about the Advisory Council and make suggestions for improving it, if in fact its existence is valid. By this time Axworthy had announced that he was inviting "major women's national organizations" to meet with him to discuss how to improve the Advisory Council the day after the weekend of the conference he had called off! This ended up being helpful to us since it provided travel money for some of the women to come to our conference before going on to advise the Minister.

Saturday, it was agreed, was to be devoted to serious

consideration of all aspects of the Constitution which might affect women. It was not to be "government bashing" but constructive consideration of the needs of women, what the government had proposed, what those proposals lacked and what we would recommend.

Moira Armour had an offer to make a film and started negotiations with the NFB, and women photographers offered their services. One woman offered to match individual contributions up to $1,000, and in no time had to reach for her cheque book. The Chairwomen of New Brunswick, Saskatchewan and Newfoundland Advisory Councils immediately offered to come and to help. Others followed as the news got around. Women called from Vancouver, Labrador, Northern Ontario, Halifax and Winnipeg to say they were coming. The profits of Ma Bell and the other phone companies must have soared from the urgent business transacted by long distance: there was little time for mail after the first notice had been sent.

Organizers tried to get support from all three political parties. The two opposition parties offered us coffee, reception and accommodation in the House. Only individual Liberals helped, not the official Party, which was a pity. We didn't want to be partisan. The object was to discuss Canada's Constitution — not what the different party points of view were, but what women wanted.

At the third Cow Café meeting, two men were sitting at a nearby table. It was impossible for them not to hear what was going on. They finally came over to us as they finished eating. "I heard what you were saying, especially about media coverage," one of them said. "I happen to be a TV reporter from CTV and we've got our equipment right here. Could we do an interview?" Could they! Seldom do such opportunities fall into one's lap.

Three days before the Conference press coverage was like an answer to our prayers: Canada AM on Friday, Betty Kennedy on CFRB, Morningside with Elizabeth Gray, CFTO women covering the conference from Toronto. As Doris Anderson said, "If we'd held the Conference as the Council had planned, no one would have taken any notice. Now they've got the whole press covering it." Full glare of publicity? Who's going to be embarrassed this time?

And so ends the first installment of the saga of the Do-it-Yourself Instant Constitutional Conference of Women.

RECOMMENDATIONS ON THE CANADIAN ADVISORY COUNCIL ON THE STATUS OF WOMEN

Recommended:

1) that there is a valid role for a publicly funded advisory council on the status of women

2) that a review to determine this role of the CACW be conducted to report to Parliament by July 1, 1981

3) that the members of this review group be themselves nominated by women's groups outside government

4) that the review group be empowered to establish its own terms of reference and that in so doing, it should consider questions such as:

   - review methodology (i.e. acceptance of briefs, presentations, and/or research)
   - the role and responsibility of the Minister responsible for the status of women
   - the role and responsibility of the status, mandate, independence, style, focus, access to information, structure, staffing, remuneration, accountability, budget, operating methods, relations with women's groups, appointment process, etc.,

5) that the CACSW as restructured be embodied in a Statute, and not by an Order in Council

6) that the CACSW report to Parliament directly, and not to a Minister

7) that all appointees to CACSW be women of expertise and authority with a record of commitment to women's concerns and include representatives of all economic and ethnic groups, unions, professions, native and immigrant women

8) that in order to restore the credibility of CACSW, the three incumbent vice-presidents be required to resign

9) that Lloyd Axworthy be required to resign his portfolio as Minister responsible for the Status of Women

THE DINNER PARTY: INDIGESTION FOR THE ESTABLISHMENT

by Susan Crean

Volume 3, No. 10 (September 1982), p. 8

Judy Chicago's Dinner Party has been and gone. In Toronto and Montréal the turnout was extraordinary: 75,000 at the musée d'art contemporaine, more than usually come in a year, and 50,000 at the Art Gallery of Ontario whose Volunteer Committee brought in the show as a fundraiser. Although it had to cut back on the numbers admitted because people took so long filing through the exhibit, the Committee still grossed about $200,000 and cleared $65,000 for its art purchase fund.

There is much about the circumstances of the Dinner Party's appearance in Toronto worth criticizing, starting with the fact that a $4 admission was charged (there was no charge in Montréal) and ending with the Gallery's failure to relate the show to the work of local women artists by organizing a companion exhibition of their work (as was done by Montréal's curator Louise Letocha). It was left to the community to make the connections, which the Woman's Cultural Building collective did by organizing a panel session to discuss the issues raised by the Dinner Party (a transcript will be published in the next issue of *Fireweed*) and by leafletting the crowds waiting to get in to see the show. The collective points out that "the Dinner Party is not the culmination of women's or feminist art in Toronto—it is only one step…If high profile institutions such as the AGO are not responsive (to women's cultural work in the city), this doesn't mean these efforts have to remain invisible."

No one actually protested the coming of the Dinner Party, though the thought may have crossed several minds. When the show came to New York several years ago, a group of artists staged a mock dinner party called *Maria Manhattans Box Lunch* and invited 39 guests "of dubious distinction," including Rosie Ruiz, Patty Hearst, Tricia Nixon, Betty Crocker, Lot's Wife, Lassie, Minnie Mouse, and Judy Chicago. Across the top of the Box Lunch brochure (in imitation of the Chicago catalogue's inscription) ran this legend: "In the beginning I was just another self-centred artist. And then I beheld a vision. And the sign said, 'Look, Maria, already you're in your thirties. You're a good artist, but recognition-wise you're on the other side of the tracks. Capitalize on a movement! Jump on a bandwagon! And Lo, I conceived of the Box Lunch." A fairly devastating indictment both of the Dinner Party's middle class pretentions (this is not a show for working class people; while Chicago says she wants to reach non-art people, her catalogues still cost $20 a piece) and of the large element of hypocrisy in the hype surrounding the event.

Perhaps a phenomenon like the Dinner Party is bound to bring out the cynical in people. Yet it is true that Chicago and her work display some very disturbing anomalies. Almost before it opened in San Francisco in 1979, the Dinner Party had become a cause *célèbre*. Very shortly after, two museums (in Seattle and Rochester) cancelled their bookings, so the Dinner Party had to be moth-balled. Eventually it was booked into Houston, Boston and the Brooklyn Museum where it continued to draw record-breaking crowds. Then came the savaging by the New York critics, especially the attack of the *New York Times'* Hilton Kramer who called it a vulgar monument to women's sex organs and a tasteless example of kitsch. Here was a myth ripe for the making: feminist art dumped on by male establishment.

In fact, the reports of Chicago's assassination were exaggerated. Her single largest benefactor was the National Endowment of the Arts (for $41,000) which is the US equivalent of the Canada Council. And the Dinner Party was not without influential defenders. Lucy Lippard wrote a long article for *Art in America* (not exactly *Mother Jones*) explaining that the art world found Chicago incomprehensible (that is, it defied categorization) but took her work as a challenge to its values and responded by dismissing her. Now it may be hard to imagine what, in this age of permissiveness, could possibly offend the American art world's sensibilities. Artists have wrapped sections of California highway in canvas, and painted the desert blue without anyone questioning their integrity as artists.

But what the canon of American art requires is that art be primarily about Art, which is to say, aesthetics and formalist experimentation: If there is too much content, or the message is too loud, it is considered propaganda not art. Chicago's second violation was taking traditional women's crafts (needlework and china painting) and elevating them to inappropriate heights. Says Lippard:

"Inside the art world, art and life always seem to be in competition. Whenever life gets a hold on art it is called 'bad' or 'low'—a phenomenon challenged by the Dinner Party."

The reaction of the high priests of 'high art' was predictable, which is why I find it curious that Chicago was shocked and surprised instead of being thrilled that her aim at the art world's assumptions was dead on. She could have measured her success by the vehemence of her detractors. Moreover, there were many highly favourable reviews (including all the Canadian ones) and a vast and enthusiastic audience.

Once the rose coloured glasses are removed I find that the exhibit is fraught with contradictions. As a symbol of the lost and buried history of women, the history it recounts is buried in Chicago's elaborate iconography, and the significance of the 39 guests is lost on most of us unless we have the time (and money for the catalogues) to swat up before going. Another two bucks will buy Chicago's taped tour in which she introduces a few of her guests and lards us with more information which though interesting, doesn't help her story along. Most of us leave knowing as little about Artemisia Gentileschi, Hatshepsut, and Natalie Barney as when we arrived.

The point is not to criticize Chicago for her choice of guests; nor for attempting to take in all of western civilization in her sweep of history. Obviously, she was bound to be limited by what historians have bothered to record about women's contributions, and naturally she would inject her own cultural standards. So, for example, nine of the 13 guests on the third side of the triangular table are American, and all but Sacajawea and Sojourner Truth are white, middle class artists and social reformers. The point is, however, that Chicago's politics are not particularly radical. Her visualization of feminism, rhetoric aside, fits right in with the trendy notions of "liberated" upper class matrons.

In the same way, her talk about redefining the relationship between art and society comes with a mixed message, for she makes all the moves of someone who is playing for status and recognition with the establishment, and has even said she wants to be accepted by the art community: "I'm not attacking the art world, I'm making art." The real problem with the Dinner Party is the gap between

what Chicago says it is and what it really is. Its most daring feature
is the challenge to the art world, not its feminist politics.

Susan Crean is author of Who's Afraid of Canadian Culture, *and is
on the editorial board of* This Magazine.

JOURNEY THROUGH UNCHARTERED TERRITORY
by Sheila McIntyre
Volume 4, No. 5 (March 1983), pp. 8 and 9

A year ago, the infamous Axworthy sequence˙ launched a nation-
wide campaign by women to demand crucial amendments in the
sexual equality guarantees in the Charter of Rights and Freedoms.
There was a fairy tale quality to that eleventh hour victory because
what is now the "supreme law of the land" was rewritten, not by
high-powered legal experts, politicians or courts, but despite them.
Undoubtedly, we would not have succeeded without the legal expertise of a small but awesomely dedicated core of feminist lawyers and
academics; but they in turn could not have succeeded without a core
of lay activists and the grassroots backing of thousands of women in
every province who trusted their own judgment and that of legally
trained feminists rather than the insubstantial pronouncements of
those high-powered experts who would have sold women out.

What few women realize is that exactly the same experts who
would have sold us out are now empowered to implement the
Charter, both by rewriting existing laws which abridge our rights,
and by interpreting the language of the Charter to define our rights.
They did not champion the equality of the sexes when they drafted
the Charter, when they debated it, when they made amendments
in the first round of redrafting, or when the Canadian Advisory
Council on the Status of Women exposed the Charter's shortcom-
ings and proposed secure equality protections. There is absolutely
no reason to believe that in the less public arena of the courts or civil
service, these lawmakers will promote egalitarian principles on their
own initiative. Last year's victory does suggest that they will live up

to the promises of the Charter if forced. Accordingly, women must take the initiative immediately to exert such force.

In order to understand what initiatives are most urgent, it is important for us to understand how legislatures, the courts and the Charter fit together. Legislatures pass laws; courts interpret and enforce them. Until the Charter was entrenched, government-made laws, however unwise, unfair or unconscionable, prevailed over the common law (judge-made law). The Bill of Rights was supposed to guarantee that certain fundamental freedoms would prevail over conflicting federal statutes (it did not apply to provincial laws), but the courts were consistently reluctant to interpret Acts of Parliament that judges deemed to reflect the will of the voting majority. In effect, the courts, when confronted with a conflict between rights and federal laws, balanced majority will against abstract rights and, with rare exceptions, deferred to the "wisdom" of the legislature and the will of the majority.

The Charter, in principle, is intended to eliminate such a utilitarian (the greatest happiness of the greatest number, etc.) balancing process, primarily because there is no provincial or federal law on an equal plane with the Constitution, the supreme law of the land. Individuals and minorities now have a constitutional guarantee against the state that prohibits majority-sanctioned abridgments of their rights. If any government does enact laws which violate individual rights, the court now has both the power and responsibility to declare offending portions void and of no effect.

This is the theory. However, there are several catches. Foremost is Section 1 of the Charter which subjects our fundamental freedoms and rights to "such reasonable limits prescribed by law as can be demonstrably justified in a free and democratic society." There are a host of technical legal debates about this phrase, no less than political implications, and just what the courts are persuaded to find "reasonable" will be critical in deciding whether our new rights are more than rhetorical. Some of the earliest Charter cases provide cause for despair: "Canada is free and democratic, therefore this infringement is demonstrably reasonable…" or "the reasonableness of this law is self-evident, therefore it is demonstrably justified…" Insofar as the courts have been historically reluctant to strike down legislation, and Section 1 gives them the perfect excuse to evade their new responsibilities, we need to lobby strongly and persistently that s.1 should be invoked only very rarely in extraordinary circumstances, and should *never* be invoked to limit racial or sexual equality.

Worse, women and minorities have much to fear whenever the courts are called on to interpret what is "reasonable." In law, this is considered an "objective" test, commonly referred to as the "ordinary, reasonable man" test—i.e., what the ordinary reasonable man would think, do, believe, if asked. Far, far, too often, this "objective" standard, when analysed closely, is what the ordinary, white, middle class male does, thinks, believes. This has had appalling results when, for instance, the amount of force used by a woman in her own self-defence is judged by the reasonable man test; or the violence triggered by a racial slur is weighed against the level of provocation likely to be experienced by the ordinary man; or the offensiveness of pornography is tested objectively against "contemporary community standards." Women cannot afford to have sexual equality subjected to a reasonable limits test defined by the elite males in the courtroom or the ordinary man in the street.

Another catch to the theory is that using the courts to assert one's rights is expensive, slow and risky. Having a law overturned may be small compensation for actual discrimination. And, where the facts of the case are unusual or of narrow application, even a victory may be of little general benefit to others in the same minority or discriminated-against group.

The final catch is that the equality provision of the Charter (s.15) does not even come into effect until April 1985 in order that provincial legislatures have time to amend those of their statutes which currently violate the Charter. But how assiduously are the various governments scrutinizing their laws, and how perceptively do they identify and define discrimination? Given the courts' historical deference to the wisdom of legislators, if politicians find little to amend, the court may use the "reasonable limits" test to find very little to strike down. And in turn, lawyers, whether out of traditional legal mindsets, or conservatism, or their own lack of familiarity with discrimination, may tailor their arguments around the stance taken by legislators and courts instead of arguing for our rights in absolute terms.

Because legislatures are mindful of the public will, and courts are mindful of legislative will, the shaping of the Charter over the next few years will be an intensely political process, potentially far more responsive to public pressure than constitutional law will be again in history. Women cannot complacently sit back and hope for the best (not the least because lobbying legal experts has already begun, and early indications from Crown Attorney offices show they would like to see the Charter interpreted very narrowly to maintain the status quo). It cannot be overemphasized that in legal battles, one does not want to be on the defensive fighting to reverse precedents once they've gone against women, or arguing *after* legislation has been redrafted and published that the pros should go back to the drawing board. That the Charter could be a potent tool for promoting sexual equality is proved by the intensity of the battle in the United States for and against the ERA. In s.15 and 28, we now have an ERA equivalent. However, women still face the risk that these equality protections will be narrowly interpreted or "reasonably" limited if we do not educate legislators and legal professionals before they have first crack at our rights. The only question is how do we educate them?

To begin with, without underestimating their power, we must stop belittling our own in the belief that we lack the skills to fight successfully. One of the popular myths (even among feminists) that allows lawyers and judges to command exorbitant fees and prestige, and that leads otherwise independent minds to defer to seemingly absurd jucidial pronouncements, is that legal "professionals"—whether they are lawyers, politicians, legislative drafters or judges—have acquired intellectual tools and technical expertise beyond the reach of ordinary laypeople. So when the ordinary layperson reads the language of the Charter and finds such phrases as "equal protection" or "life, liberty and security of the person," she assumes that although she does not know their "legal" meaning, the professionals do.

This is simply not true in the case of the Charter. Certainly there are hundreds of cases where such phrases have been interpreted by the courts, and there are preferred lines of reasoning. However, the Charter, and especially the equality provisions, present the courts with powers and legal language totally unprecedented in Canadian law. The judges will therefore have to look elsewhere for the authority (i.e., legal precedents) to back their conclusions. The most obvious sources are not too helpful. England, the source of our common law, has no constitution; the US has no ERA and its equal protection judgments on sex discrimination are in an unsettled, transitional state. Furthermore the US has no affirmative action provision as we do. Arguably, women and minorities understand discrimination better, can identify it more readily, and are better equipped to propose appropriate legal remedies.

It becomes obvious, then, that we had better assert and share our expertise. And fast. Otherwise, when 1985 comes and discriminatory laws are still on the statute books, legislators can simply dare us to sue for our rights. And if we haven't already briefed the courts, then despite their unpredictability when deprived of legal precedents, one thing is predictable. They will resort to traditional legal devices and patterns of thought to lay down guidelines of interpretation, tests of reasonableness, procedures for weighing conflicting rights, and rules to generate uniformity. And as soon as they can. They will not want to reverse themselves too soon (then it will be clear they don't know what they are doing), so they will avoid rulings likely to be reversed. The stance taken by the legislators and the courts in the next three to five years will set the pattern for all that follows.

Women's efforts must focus on three key areas: lobbying politicians to amend existing laws; preparing articles and briefs for the use of lawyers and the courts which argue persuasively how the Charter ought to be read and why; and building a legal defence fund so that key cases reach the courts early and are well argued. All of these tasks fall as logically to laywomen as to legally trained feminists. In fact, because minority women, working class women, disabled women and rural women are so under-represented amongst feminist professionals, I would argue the Charter initiatives cannot and should not be entrusted solely to women "experts." Indeed those women professionals already working on the Charter want lay input. Perhaps, more to the point, these will be political battles and we need all the bodies we can muster.

The most urgent focus of action must be Section 15, which guarantees to every individual equality before and under the law, equal protection and benefit of the law, and prohibits discrimination on *any* ground. Although this clause goes on to enumerate certain grounds of prohibited discrimination—"race, national or ethnic

origin, colour, religion, sex, age, mental or physical disability"—
these specified grounds are not exclusive. In theory, discrimination
based, for instance, on sexual preference or marital status is also
prohibited by s.15 and is vulnerable to a Charter challenge.

Anyone who has fallen victim to an existing law which is discriminatory on any ground has the credentials to lobby her legislature
to change it; to show why it is discriminatory and how it should be
amended. Similarly any special interest group—whether a union, a
battered women's hostel or an immigrant community centre—can
direct its expertise to preparing briefs or lobbying politicians to
change offensive laws. The beauty of it is that if we act before 1985,
reforms may be effected on government time and money and no individual will have to bear the onerous costs of suing under the Charter.

According to insiders who have observed some of the work
being done to clean up the statute books, many of those assigned to
this task have no idea what discrimination really is, how it works, or
how to draft language to prevent it. Nor do they agree on the nature
or extent of amendment necessary.

Generally speaking, there are three types of discriminatory
legislation which should be the focus of our lobbying. The first is
the most likely to be identified by government staff, provided they
are seriously intending to rewrite their laws: laws discriminatory on
their face. For instance, in Ontario, a married couple cannot give
their child the wife's surname, but may only use the husband's name
or a hyphenated conjunction of the maternal and paternal surnames,
provided the husband's comes last. Such laws should either be to
deleted or amended.

The second type is a law which appears egalitarian on its face,
but leads to inequality when implemented because it ignores wom-
en's inequality in society. Under Ontario's family law, for example,
each spouse has a duty to support her/himself and her/his partner,
according to need and ability. However, there is no provision
instructing the court to calculate a woman's ability to support herself
(and her need for spousal support) in the context of the differential
earning power of women and men. Such a principle should be written into the law.

Finally, there are laws which are neutral on their face but which
have been interpreted in a sexist fashion by the courts. Federal

divorce law and Ontario family law allow courts to alter their original support awards when the circumstances of one of the parties change significantly. If Mrs A is awarded $500 a month support upon her divorce from Mr A, and later begins to live with Mr B, the court is likely to grant a request by Mr A to have his support payments terminated. The usual argument is that now Mr B has the duty of supporting Mrs A. Fine. Except Mr A can also seek a reduction, and often wins it, if he remarries. His plea will be that he cannot afford to support two women. Sometimes this is true, although his new wife knew his financial liabilities when she married him. The problem is that the court will not consider the second wife's income or acknowledge her spousal duty to support Mr A, when calculating Mr A's new domestic budget and his ability to maintain his support obligations. The court sometimes argues that the new wife should not be asked to subsidize the old wife. Yet Mr B is not deemed to be subsidizing Mr A. Basically the courts continue to see women as dependents, not as partners, in an economic union. Even if Mrs A2 is loaded, even if Mr A is not strapped for money given his new wife's contribution to domestic expenses, the original Mrs A may lose her only means of support because of the court's "gallantry" towards the new wife.

All three types of discriminatory laws must be erased or amended if equality rights are to be written into our statutes by 1985. In my view, only the most obvious type will be perceived and rectified unless we lobby and educate our governments effectively.

On the assumption that our efforts in legislative lobbying will not be wholly successful, we must also build a body of research on how the Charter ought to be interpreted and applied. This research needs to be in the form of both scholarly and popular writing, published in straight legal journals, circulated to legislatures and visible to the press. There are dozens of topics which need discussion and resolution. Should pregnant women be barred from certain worksites because of risk to the fetus? If so, is this discrimination? Is the regulation or censorship of pornography a reasonably justified infringement of freedom of speech? Do the Charter's protections of native rights permit the loss of native status of Indian women if they marry non-Indians? Are there any circumstances in which it is reasonable to discriminate on the basis of sex? What remedies are most appropriate rectify sex discrimination which has been entrenched by law for so long that simply voiding the law cannot compensate women adequately? Are affirmative action programs which institute a quota system likely to be found discriminatory despite Section 15? More generally, what judgments do we wish to adopt from US equal protection jurisprudence and which do we want to criticize? On what basis do we wish to balance conflicting fundamental rights: for instance, freedom of the press and prohibitions against sexist discrimination in advertising?

Some of the more technical legal arguments must be left to people with some legal training, arguments such as how broadly the Charter applies to government actions (does it bar hiring discrimination by employers funded by government?), whether the provinces can opt out of the sexual equality provision in Section 28, and whether a citizen can challenge a law before her rights have been abridged (for instance, can we sue if City Hall gives advance notice it will ban marching on International Women's Day?). However, we could greatly extend the research available if teachers of law, history, politics, and Women's Studies assigned Charter-related research as essay assignments; if students choose to write papers and theses on civil liberties issues; if interested women form study groups to focus on topics that concern them. Law librarians (usually women) may be eager to join such groups and share their skills, or, at least, will help laypeople find their way to necessary materials. Human Rights Commissions often have staff members willing to give answers to lay questions. Law students are usually looking for ways to put theory into practical form and may welcome an invitation to help such study groups. All of this research can also feed into political lobbying wherever it suggests the need for pre-1985 statutory reforms.

Finally, women's groups had better start organizing now to build a legal defence fund and to establish the principles by which legal aid will be allocated. Few victims of discrimination can afford to launch a lawsuit. Yet some legal battles may be more crucial to establishing key precedents than others. As well, we need to decide who should be our spokeswomen if the Supreme Court invites interveners to present briefs in cases of national importance (the Borowski abortion challenge, pornography cases, affirmative action cases).

It is almost impossible to emphasize how urgent this activity is. Or how critical the involvement of women at the grassroots level will be to its success. There is no woman who lacks the ability or self-interest to take on at least one of these tasks. For women who believe that legal reform will be one of the keys to the promotion of sexual equality, there will be no forum as vital in the next few decades as Charter litigation. Because both governments and the courts are cautiously feeling their way, our input will never be so timely or so open to reception again. Governments are (finally) sensitive to the potential clout of the "women's" vote so we must exploit our momentum to hold them to their constitutional promises.

˙ Lloyd Axworthy, then Minister of State responsible for the status of women, cancelled a conference on women and the Constitution, causing an uproar and the subsequent resignation in protest of Advisory Council president Doris Anderson.

Sheila McIntyre is a Toronto freelance writer, and currently a law student at the University of Toronto.

FEMINIST PRESS: FRONT PAGE CHALLENGE
by Philinda Masters
Volume 4, No. 8 (June 1983), pp. 8 and 9

In Canada, there are currently [1983] about 20 feminist newspapers, magazines and quarterlies, about four feminist publishers (two in Québec), feminist bookstores in most large cities and any number of newsletters coming out of women's centres and women's organizations. Together we are members of the feminist press, an amorphous collection of committed ideologues who tend the fires of the women's movement. In this article I will explore mainly the feminist periodicals, their roles in the movement, the rewards and pitfalls of producing them and the everyday reality of feminist publishing, relying heavily on my experience at Broadside, which is what I know best.

INTRODUCTION: A HEN'S LIFE

Producing a monthly feminist newspaper, as we do here at *Broadside*, reminds me of the life of a hen: we take the germ of an idea, get it out, fertilize it, incubate it and at the end of the process we start all over again. It is a process of one part creativity and nine parts hard work in a never-ending cycle. And, unlike real hens, we feminist egg-layers have to market the fruits of our own labour. After all that gestating, we have to get up off our bed of straw and *sell*. What we need is some kind of feminist egg marketing board, to protect our interests and to develop and ensure our market.

To twist the egg analogy further, there's the matter of chicken and egg, cause and effect: to what extent does the feminist press affect the women's movement in Canada, and to what extent do we reflect it? What is our importance to other feminist endeavours and to the world at large?

No one denies the importance of eggs. We all know their role in our lives—how else could we get western sandwiches or chicken tetrazzini? But what role does the feminist press play? Why do some of us go through the egg-laying process month after month, against

The front-page image illustrated our centrefold on the challenges facing the feminist press.

often hefty odds? What are our goals and rewards? What's in it for us, and what's in it for you?

Having now hinted at the philosophical, political and practical ramifications of the feminist press, it's time to follow the example of the TV egg ads and "get cracking."

AN OBSTACLE COURSE: THE NITTY-GRITTY

In April I was a panelist at an Alternative Press conference at York University. In a prior meeting to discuss how we would approach the subject of the feminist press, several of us came up with three or four topics: the political context, funding, obstacles, goals, etc. I decided, in a pessimistic moment, that everything pertaining to the feminist press could be discussed under the heading: Obstacles.

Of course the main obstacle is money, or lack thereof. But there are related obstacles: access to funding, limited resources (material as well as financial), volunteer or low-paid labour, limited time and energy. Et cetera with a capital E.

Every so often someone calls up the *Broadside* office and accuses us of inefficiency because we didn't expedite some matter or other as quickly as the caller expected. I usually explain that we are not *The Globe and Mail*, we don't have the resources of the mainstream press: only one paid staff, not hundreds (or even tens) of employees, no computer to track down errant subscriptions in seconds, no news-team with a *Broadside* car to rush out to the latest movement event. We, like all other feminist publications, are a shoestring operation. We just scrape by as best we can. The caller is usually mollified.

Similarly, at a seminar a year or so ago, the editor of a slick Toronto magazine was discussing the ramifications of good editing. At one point, referring to factual accuracy in news reporting, she said: "If you're not absolutely sure of your facts, just go down the hall to your checker and get them to verify the information." Well, it may come as a surprise, but most of us don't have a hall, let alone a checker. This is not to say that we don't strive for accuracy, just that we don't have several editorial assistants lounging around our office complex waiting on our every whim.

So, we don't have enough money, we don't have enough people, we don't have enough time. Why are our resources so slim? According to the prevailing economic value system, if a business (which is what a feminist press is, after all) provides people with what they want, it will succeed, it will turn a profit. So if a business is having trouble, the people don't want its product. That's the logic. Does that mean that if feminist presses are having trouble surviving, nobody wants us? The trouble with the logic is that it's based on a myth. That's *not* the way things operate. It's not a reasonable way of defining the problem.

Although there *are* other obstacles littering the feminist press's path to success (see below), the main one, I repeat, is money. Most publications, feminist, alternative, even mainstream (yes, even *The Globe and Mail*), have trouble surviving economically. A publication's revenue (what pays the rent and the printer) comes chiefly from a combination of subscriptions, advertising and government subsidies (known in our circle as grants). And one source of income tends to depend on the health of the others. The most successful publications in the mainstream are those with either a guaranteed readership—generally trade magazines targetting a specific industry like Maclean-Hunter's *Bus and Truck*—or those with a very high percentage of advertising, often 75% (like Maclean-Hunter's *Bus and Truck*. The subscription and ad money just keeps rolling in. Since these publications are seen as a good risk, they have no trouble securing other kinds of financial backing.

Most of us, though, are in a different ball park. Unlike trade magazines, general interest or political publications can't *buy* our readership with gimmicks or freebies, and then sell our product to advertisers on the basis of that high circulation. Our readership is limited (are there more truck dealers than feminists?) and therefore our ad revenue is curtailed, advertisers needing as large an audience as possible. Without large PR budgets to expand our readership, and without the womanpower to secure advertising clients (those who might *want* to advertise in our pages), our financial bases remain meagre.

As to securing government grants, feminist publications are in a dicey position. In appealing to government agencies, whose interests very likely do not coincide with those of the women's movement, hiding your radical feminism, your lesbian content, your anti-patriarchal views is no easy task when that's what you're all about. Most government funding is directed towards one-shot promotion projects, which isn't useful if what you need are short-term operating funds, or to special theme issues, which isn't useful if you're a general interest newspaper. Other funding agencies support the Arts, with an apolitical A. In other words, money for the feminist press ain't easy to come by. And, as we all know, looking for that money, and satisfying the requirements of the granting agencies is a full-time job in itself.

Putting money matters aside (if possible), there are other problems feminist publications face. In a report on the feminist press a few years ago, Sharon Batt (then editor of *Branching Out* and board member of the Canadian Periodical Publishers' Association) figured that the circulation ceiling for feminist publications in Canada was a mere 2500. Apart from Montreal's *La vie en rose* which sells 10,000 to a highly political Québécoise readership, most of us haven't yet topped the 2000 mark, even those of us who've been around for a number of years. Well-meaning critics suggest that our focus is too narrow, we're preaching to the converted (obviously a small number), or simply that women haven't the money to support us. It is probably the single, most urgent question plaguing us all. And if anyone has The Answer, I'd like to know it. The feminist press can't please everybody, but we need to please more than 2000 each if we're going to succeed.

One more obstacle, before I move on to other matters, one which is not specific to the press, feminist or otherwise, is the geography of our country. Most feminist publications (apart from local newsletters) attempt to have at the very least a national profile. We do not wish to be merely house organs for our local, city movement. But that presents problems. Face-to-face encounters with our sister journalists across the country, and with potential subscribers and contributors, is almost non-existent. On-the-scene reporting is pretty well impossible. At *Broadside*, we don't even have a long distance phone budget. We're like the early pioneers before the CPR went through. Getting money, for instance, for women to travel to the Women and Words Conference in Vancouver this summer is a major struggle for the conference organizers and a severe strain on the budgets of individual women and publications. Without easy communication, we are missing out on a major support network, and our publications suffer for it.

HOW TO RUN THE BUSINESS AND STAY PURE: PHILOSOPHICAL CONSIDERATIONS

As feminists, we have a stake in remaining PC (that's politically correct, not Progressive Conservative). In other words, we are involved in political work and we try to remain true to our politics. The attempt produces certain symptoms: our non-hierarchical structure, our approach to professionalism, how we deal with our contributors, our relationship to other feminist publications. The attempt to live our politics also results in a good deal of soul-searching as we try to deal with the contradictions of purity vs. poverty, of efficiency vs. exactitude, of co-operation vs. competition.

Early feminist publications were marked by two things: their publishers didn't believe in layout, or in editing. The papers were often sloppy and hard to read. This was partly the result of lack of money, partly because the producers were in the early stages of developing skills: they couldn't afford classy publications and they didn't know much about layout or editing. But it was also a stance: slick, professional papers were *male*, and elitist; to edit copy was to exert control over one's sisters. This was not all silly narrow-mindedness. Women were finding new ways to do things, slick publications were often empty and regressive, editing has been used as a tool of control, particularly over women. But in making one point, they missed another: feminist publications are a means of communication and to succeed as such they must be readable. The reader has to want to read an article, her eye must be drawn into it, hence the layout, and the message to be communicated must be clear and coherent, hence at least a modicum of editing. The rules of straight lines, grammar and syntax have their uses. This may seem like an odd point to belabour, but it's a point hard-won in feminist publishing.

Another tricky point is the use of the word "editor." Many feminist publications eschew the title still. Since we operate non-hierarchically, that is collectively, we have no time for bosses or leaders. But some of us have editors, even an editor (as at *Broadside*). The title does not denote a position of prestige or authority, but rather a function. The real editorial authority, the position that in the mainstream would be called Executive Editor or Editor-in-Chief, is vested in the collective. It is the collective that makes policy decisions, it's the editor who carries out the day-to-day co-ordinating work.

Speaking of work, there are differing opinions as to the place of volunteer labour in feminist periodicals. The reality is that, left to our own devices, we couldn't afford very many reasonably paid workers. Some publications refuse to operate with volunteer labour and would prefer to go under. Others would continue at all costs, publishing out/of their own basements, in the middle of the night, with no phone. In the best of all possible worlds we would all be highly paid, but as it is we have to limp along, making peace with our political values.

Some publications, those affiliated with Status of Women groups or university departments, have at least their basic expenses covered. Although this may appear to be a luxury to some of us, the question is debatable. *Network* in Saskatchewan ceased publication in March because its mother organization, the Saskatchewan Action Committee on the Status of Women, turned down a grant from the Secretary of State on the grounds that there were too many strings attached. University-affiliated journals are subject to the political whims and budgetary restraints of the particular administration. So whether we are dependant on organizational subsidy or government grants, we are always vulnerable.

And, we are often put in the position of competing with each other for tidbits. Whether we are trying to increase the number of our subscribers within a limited community, whether we are trying to convince advertisers to spend their dollars advertising in our pages, whether we are trying to squeeze money out of government programs with relatively little money to juggle, we are, in fact, in competition. The amazing thing is that the *feeling* in the community of feminist publishers is one of co-operation, not competition. We feel we are complementary to one another; we in fact work amicably together (when time permits).

But the question remains: would we be better off pooling our resources into one big Canadian publication and so get all the subscription, advertising and government monies in one place? If there are 2,500 feminist subscribers out there, and ten publications (an adjusted figure, accounting for reader overlap), does that mean there are only 2,500 feminists reading all of us, or 25,000 feminists each reading only one of us? If there are 25,000, then there's room for all of us, competition is a moot point and we're better off with a lot of little publications all specializing in our particular area, all attempting to expand our circulation.

WHAT'S MY LINE?: THE ROLE OF THE FEMINIST PRESS

When a feminist publication sets up shop, it very quickly comes to be seen as an institution in its community. This may be more true for newspapers than for other types of press, because newspapers purport to deal more directly with women's lives (as opposed to literary quarterlies or scholarly journals). Whatever the reason, the publications become identified with authority, and then a number of things happen: we are imbued with exaggerated powers, saddled with unrealistic expectations of perfection, or eyed with distrust. Sometimes all three. It's hard to convince people we're just simple folks trying to do our bit for a better world. We are also presumed to have a stance, a "line" on everything: what does *Broadside* think; what does *Kinesis* say? But most of the feminist periodicals in Canada do not have a rigidly adhered to line, other than an often vaguely articulated commitment to feminism. Most of us see ourselves as a forum for women in the movement, a place for dialogue, not as disseminators of any official position.

People often ask: feminist periodicals who their audience is, exactly, who they're trying to reach, who they do reach. This is a difficult question to answer. *Broadside*, for example, has never done a demographic survey, though we suspect our readers are mainly of the high education/low income/political activist category (not a large segment of any population). The question often translates as: are you trying to convert the masses (housewives in the burbs), female business executives, high school women, etc. (and if not, why not)? The answer to that is that we're not trying to convert anyone; we're not publishing a newspaper for "them"; it's for "us" because it *is* us. A feminist newspaper is a place to air our concerns, discuss our experiences, explore the issues that matter to us. In doing so, we develop skills at articulating our position, and at a point in the movement when developing a critical feminist analysis is a priority, the ability to articulate is crucial.

The feminist press is also a focus for the many diverse activities across the country. It gives us a feeling of links, between cities and between struggles. It helps create momentum for these struggles.

It is not a passive press sitting on the sidelines reflecting news and events, partly because feminist journalists and writers are often politically involved in other work, and partly because the feminist press is part of the action. It provides food for thought, recipes for action, information to prevent otherwise isolated groups from forever re-inventing the wheel. And it gives us a sense that there are a lot of us (25,000?) in this thing together.

An FBI report leaked to a feminist media conference in Washington, DC, two years ago stated that the women's movement in the US was held together by its network of feminist periodicals, presses and bookstores. Of course you can't believe everything the FBI says, but it might be right about this. Imagine life stores, women's appointment calendars from Women's Press. How would you catch up on what's happening? Who would you write your letters about the latest movement controversy to? Where would you publish your (otherwise unpopular) feminist research? How would you find out the real story, after reading the *Sun* or the *Globe*? What would you read while relaxing in the bath after a long day's work? What would you do?

You'd probably get a group of women together and start putting out a feminist newspaper. The feminist press will always be with us, through thick and more likely thin, because we need it. Period.

CONFRONTING PORNOGRAPHY:
BOUND, GAGGED AND SILENCED

by Susan G. Cole

Volume 4, No. 10 (August/September 1983), pp. 6 and 7

The following article is a reprint of an article originally published in Volume 3, No. 2 of Broadside, *nearly two years ago. Since its publication we have had many requests from interested readers for copies and we now have exhausted our supply. We have decided to reprint the piece with some minor alterations and an update on changes in the Criminal Code with regard to obscenity. As a result of writing the article, Susan G. Cole began doing extensive research on pornography in Canada and is now writing a book on the subject.*

THE PORNOGRAPHIC IMAGE

Most of us pretend it isn't there. Every newsstand is jammed with it. In the back of almost every variety store entire displays are devoted to it. Partly because it's the worst of our culture, and partly because we can't believe that the fear and loathing of women can be so strong, we try to shut it out.

The pornographic image. Woman in a state of ecstasy, the plaything of her male master; woman grovelling for more abuse; woman strapped in leather, straining to get loose; woman still hungry for the next lash. Who is she? How much longer, even as we avert our gaze, can we pretend that she isn't affecting us?

Essentially we tend to exclude the pornographic image from among those that really matter because the image is perceived to be a fringe phenomenon, part of the underside of our culture. But the profit figures associated with the pornography industry, greater than those of the film and record industries combined, suggest that this is big business and not a series of fly-by-night operations designed to cater to the transient and the furtive.

And the industry is far from underground. The makers of the National Film Board's "Not a Love Story," a film about pornography, travelled to the peep shows, the live shows and the trench-coated set to uncover horrifying images of women. But the most grotesque portrait was not to be found in the bowels of our culture. It was there on the cover of *Hustler* magazine—a woman's body churning through a meat grinder—available on every newsstand in the US.

We are expected to accept that the male aroused to orgasm by the sight of a woman being brutalized is a relatively benign phenomenon, that we should leave the poor fellow alone in his fantasy world. And who are we anyway to deign to exercise the kind of thought control that would judge anyone's fantasies? Fantasies after all, are an inalienable right. This would be a very useful question were it true that the male fantasizer is repulsed by his tendencies, filled with self-loathing because he needs to conjure up the image of a mangled female body for a sexual object that he is, at least in healthy quarters, supposed to love.

But *he* isn't conjuring up the hideous images. The pornographer does it for him. And the men in the films and photographs who shove bamboo up women's vaginas are not depicted as crazed weirdos. Quite the contrary, they are lionized, imbued with strange powers, role models, if you will, for the fantasizer. Whereas it could be true that a random male, may, if left to his own devices and fantasies, develop a sense that his proclivities are peculiar, that something is not quite right, the pornographic image presented in mass quantity serves the function it would in any mass medium. It legitimizes the consumer's disease. Far from bringing the consumer to terms with who he really is, the pornographer absolves him of his guilt.

Of course fantasies are an inalienable right, provided that they remain fantasies. The rise in the rape rate and the incidence of violence against women in the home provides a convincing argument against the notion that pornography is a safety valve that keeps men off the street and without any need to *act* violently. We are told nevertheless that the pornographic image is harmless and that under no circumstances is it ever translated back to real women in the real world.

The image itself is not a great deal different from the one that graces countless billboards or the movie and television screens. That "something about an Aqua Velva man" is the same awesome power the male has over the female in girlie magazines. The pornographer is no rebel. He reinforces images already prevalent in our culture. He is the absolver of the sexually dysfunctional male's guilt as he informs his consumer that the desire to violate women is not only acceptable but has its own rewards. With the possible exception of the advertising executive, he is our culture's most effective propagandist, designing as he does this vicious hate campaign. His success depends upon our silence.

BREAKING THE SILENCE

It is not always easy to break the silence. But as unpleasant as it is to accept, we have to face the fact that any opposition to the free dissemination of pornography is an unpopular stance: that resistance to the point of view is emotional and can evoke incomprehensible anger; that the tactics used to diffuse our arguments will be very, very dirty; and that any measure will be used to coerce us back into the cocoon of silence.

But what do we say? What do we do? We are uncomfortable with the unattractive option of censorship and with the fact that any desire to dismantle the pornography industry is shared with interests, the moral majority in particular, with whom we really prefer to believe we have nothing in common. Our hands are tied by liberals who balk at the notion of denying anyone freedom of anything and by artists who believe that their creative vision will be cramped by constraints imposed on them by an external body. For the most part, one can find a sympathetic ear to the notion that pornography is not good for women. But it is difficult to argue forcibly for solutions to the problem that don't raise the hackles of even the most progressive and well-meaning listener.

It would probably be useful if we were to stay away from the word censorship and replace it with the more acceptable "regulation." Regulation is actually a more accurate term for what should be done with the pornography industry and speaks more eloquently to the fact that only an infinitesimal amount of pornography could possibly fall under the rubric of art, which we are least likely to want to restrain. The rest is not art, it is *product*, and there is nary a product on the market that is not regulated in some way or which does not have standards to which the product must comply. So, when we say that the product must not celebrate violence against women and suggest that the censor administer that guideline, we are seeking to regulate in the same way as we say that white bread can contain only so much preservative or that hot dogs can contain only so much cereal.

This is admittedly a piece of fancy verbal footwork but it helps to place the pornography industry in its proper context. It is an industry and as such deserves no more special treatment than any other industry. There is no convincing reason why the pornography industry deserves a hands off policy, one which is accorded to no other capitalist venture.

The main drawback to stern regulation is the degree which the guidelines may prevent the artist from exploring potential for erotic art. But for our purposes, the prop guideline in question provides no threat to anyone who w to depict graphically any sexual acts. Even the depiction of violence would be acceptable, as long as the perpetrator of violence is not portrayed as a hero. It is curious that a individualist has enough confidence in humankind to grant of us the right to say anything about anything, confident the right would not be abused, and at the same time refuse believe that an individual knows the difference between glorification of violence and its depiction pure and simple.

The progressive-minded is worried most that regulation be used against political dissidents and anyone else who sports alternative points of view. As a member of *Broadside* certainly not a mainstream newspaper, I am keenly aware of such dangers. But I'm hard pressed to imagine that *Broadside* would be threatened by a clear guideline proscribing celebration of violence against women in film. The assumption of the fearful progressive is that if we let the at violence then the banning of everything erotic will closely behind; give the state an inch and it will take a mile bear in mind that the state has seen fit to regulate what out of the Inco smoke stack without preventing us from cuing in our own backyards.

The issue of freedom continues, nevertheless, to be near and dear to the hearts of committed liberals, in spite of the fact that there does not exist a single social policy that does not t extent curtail individual freedom. The basic tenet of our contract is compromise, that we cede our rights in order in this world together. Yet instead of asking the pornographer to cede his right to exploit and propagandize, we grant to cold-blooded entrepreneurs the right to ply their trade even if in so doing we deny ourselves the right to walk the streets free from the fear of violence.

This last is a critical point that challenges one of society's most accepted assumptions, that freedom is our most precious value. But is it? Freedom of speech always *sounds* splendid, and in the abstract is worthwhile to be sure, but in reality it is precious only if it is afforded to everyone. The pornographer tells his customer that women have no right to speak, only the right to get fucked, and so the pornographer works to deny *us* the freedom of speech. And the experience of feminists attempting to avail themselves of a public forum in order to discuss exactly this is turning democracy's much-vaunted free market of ideas into something of a joke. An even more radical formulation is to say that as long as there is no real equality, freedom of speech is useful only to those who already have power.

Many will argue that if power is to be vested in any body, the last to be given more clout is the Censor Board. But regulation does not have to take place only at the hands of the censor. The members of the film industry might consider some form of censure of popular directors whose specialty is the glorification of violence against women. Filmmakers might do well to throw out of their associations and academies those filmmakers who abuse their craft and eschew art for exploitation.

The courts could be used more effectively if the Criminal Code, particularly section 159 which deals with obscenity, were taken a little more seriously. Obscenity has to be defined more clearly so that any photograph or film that makes brutality directed against a female heroic is *de facto* obscene. Sub-section 7 of the section on obscenity makes it an offence to depict pictorially any crime. This section has the potential to allow charges to be brought against anyone who distributes material in which the assault of women is made titillating. Assault is, after all, a crime. But either of these approaches has its problems. While it could discourage pornographers from their most gross excesses, it could also clog the courts with case after case, conceivably grinding our already moribund justice system to a halt.

If the notion of regulation either by the courts, by the "artists'" peers or by the censor cannot be made palatable to the public, then perhaps we should allow the pornography industry to run amok and then tax it to death, both at the consumer's and manufacturer's ends. The goal would be to take some of the profits out of the industry and back into the hands of those battling the industry's influence. It would be a new kind of Reconstruction program.

Add a hefty tax to the price of a girlie magazine and possibly consumption would fall off. If the appetite for pornography is so voracious that the consumer is still willing to shell out his money, then a tax on the pornographer's income might defray profits so considerably and add so much to his paperwork that he might choose to leave the business.

Such a solution places pornography in the same category as alcohol and tobacco—another vice for the state to exploit—but this time with a twist. The tax monies derived from the industry could be earmarked for the services that exist to mitigate the effects of violence against women. At least rape crisis centres, the shelters for battered women, and counselling services would have a greater means to undo the damage.

ARE WE ANTI-SEX OR SEXUALLY BERSERK?

Protestors would encounter less resistance if the image were of a Jew being led to the chambers while a swastika-adorned German jacked off, or if the pornographic image were of a Black being lynched to the sexual delight of a white hangman. The outrage of the Jew, the fury of the Black would be understood by cultural critics. In fact, our legislators have been so moved as to devise hate literature laws that ban the dissemination of material that advocates the genocide of any group, but only on the basis of religion, creed or colour, not on the basis of their sex. Hence, only women are without protection.

Why that is the case has to do with the mysteries of sex and eros, subjects that lend themselves only to analyses of the most abstract variety. We can speculate that the desperate need the consumer of pornography has for the pornographic image is connected to his need for total control and domination. He may be able to render women dependent on him—for money, for status, for information, for survival—but the last frontier is the one between the sheets, and while he may have a female sexual dependent, one whom by law he can force to have sexual relations, he can never master her the way the pornographic image tells him he can.

In the light of his failure to master her he must be convinced that she is totally depraved, and that if he can't bring her in line some-one else can. And so her erotic energy becomes transformed into something pornographic. Hence the image is what it is—women capitulating to a sexual frenzy brought on by the manipulations of a masterful male. It is an image of women possessed, at once by her uncontrollable sexual urges and by the men who can exploit them.

The very existence of the myriad photographs and films of women as victims give to the men who peer at them a sense of security. Just the fact that women pose for them is proof of our depravity. That women who work in the industry do so mostly because of a lack of economic options is no matter. That the only other option available to many women in the trade is prostitution, one they perceive to involve many more risks, is of course not going to cross the consumer's mind. According to the man getting off, if the women submit to the humiliation of being photographed, then the message in the actual contents of the photograph must be true.

The pornographer's strategy is to harp on the symbols already woven into our cultural fabric—particularly the dual symbol of woman as either whore or virgin. She is either destructively depraved or completely innocent until, with the invasion of one of her orifices, she finds her true self—sexually berserk. Of late, the consumer of pornography can get the best of the virgin and the whore. Women are as corrupt as ever, enjoying especially masochistic experiences that find her branded with hot irons or gang-raped. Less and less, though, is she portrayed as the coy virgin. That role now falls increasingly on the shoulders of children.

As the pornography industry continues to burgeon, especially in the areas of kiddy porn and violence, more and more concerned observers are thinking that the most positive steps can be taken in the area of sex education, so that the pall of terror and disgust that hangs over the sexual arena can be dispelled. A crucial subject for study is the pornographic image, because it reinforces the power and control that the obsessive consumer of the image can never have. His quest for domination is doomed not because there is such a thing as a lesbian, or because historically men have been less than artful in their sexual relations with women, but rather because sexual energy was never meant to be manipulated or used or taken away—from anyone by anybody. Our erotic energy is our own, to share when we please, and for our own sake.

But the pornographer continues to rage against the power we want to keep. In the face of the barrage, we are expected to settle for the dubious assumptions of pornography's various apologists.

We are asked to believe that men have the right to get sexual pleasure from the image of victimized women, and that the pornographic image never affects real women in the real world. We are asked to believe that the pornographer is a potential artist and that his vision can brook no constraint. We are asked to believe that the smallest amount of protection in the form of regulation of the industry works against us. We are asked to believe that if we protest against the pornographer's propaganda we are either crazy or sexually dysfunctional.

We are asked to remain silent.

It is all too much to ask.

OBSCENITY LAW UPDATE

Federal Justice Minister Mark MacGuigan has recently proposed changes to the obscenity sections of the Criminal Code. If Parliament agrees, Section 159 will no longer define obscenity as the "undue exploitation of sex or sex and violence," but instead will make illegal the distribution of materials containing the "undue exploitation of sex, violence, crime, horror or cruelty and the degradation of the person in a context of sex or violence."

There is both good and bad news to these developments. The good news is that Mr. MacGuigan has been listening. Indeed, MacGuigan has accepted, in principle, specific ideas that women brought to him. The Criminal Code, we argued, focused on sex and ignored violence, making it illegal to depict a woman sucking a penis but perfectly legitimate to portray her sucking a gun. This, we reasoned, meant that obscenity legislation catered to a bankrupt morality and left women without protection from what we perceived as a massive libel—images that consistently showed us as the willing victims of violence—and a hate propaganda campaign designed to perpetuate the maxim, both sexual and social, that men belong on the top and women on the bottom.

Some feminists brought new definition of obscenity to the Minister's attention. Helen Longino, for example, urged that obscenity be defined as "verbal or pictorial material which represents or describes sexual behaviour that is degrading or abusive to one or more participants so as to *endorse* the degradation." Others, like Jillian Riddington, tried to refine the definition, asking that obscenity include depictions where "an imbalance of power is obvious or implied by immature age or by contextual aspects of the presentation." In the end, MacGuigan's proposals look like a variation on feminist themes, referring both to degradation and to context.

The good news is not only that MacGuigan has been listening but that he was *compelled* to listen by the sudden shattering of the silence surrounding pornography.

In fact, the feds have moved with breakneck speed to mollify the unlikely coalition of women, including those anarchists in the Women's Fire Brigade who blew up three Red Hot Video outlets in BC last fall, those protesters who froze in the wintry streets to vent their anger at Playboy's programming on Canadian Pay Television, and those persistent lobbyers who cajoled, badgered and threatened the Minister until he made some concrete proposals. Naysayers who insist that the government is impervious to women's rage should learn from this one: Women can have real clout in the political arena.

Fearful politicos who worry that the feds will simply use the new legislation to harass free-thinking individuals and publications must recognize that MacGuigan and the Liberals originally wanted nothing to do with making changes in the Criminal Code. They have always mouthed the familiar platitudes about freedom and privacy when it comes to sexuality and its peripheral issues. Remember how swiftly Frances Fox was reinstated after fiddling with abortion forms in an Ottawa hospital? His forged signature was a "private" matter. Child porn legislation went by the boards because the government worried about the "private" right of legitimate photographers to take snapshots of nude kids. And Pierre Trudeau said it himself more than ten years ago, something about the state having no business in the bedrooms of the nation. This is a government perfectly content to tread on political toes of political dissidents. But collectively, the Liberals have made a point of being groovy in the sex department and of articulating their unhappiness about putting constraints on people's private behaviour.

As for the provincial Tories, people who are convinced that the Attorney General needs these changes in the Criminal Code to find a way to persecute *The Body Politic*, for example, underestimate the extent to which Mr. McMurtry can manipulate the justice system. If he didn't harass the *BP* using obscenity legislation as his instrument, you can bet he'd find another, zoning by-laws for example, or any other means he could dream up. With that in mind, we cannot very well recommend striking every article of the Criminal Code that has ever been abused by everyone from the lowly cop on the beat to the high and mighty in the Attorney General's office. Otherwise we'd be left with a pathetic shred of document that would leave no substance to our social contract. If we are concerned about the machinations of McMurtry's henchmen, the answer is not to dismantle the Criminal Code or to oppose plans to toughen it up, but rather to turf the Conservatives out of office and to replace them with a government that is not obsessed with bullying the gay community.

The bad news about MacGuigan's proposals is that we are still saddled with the antiquated articles that make the undue exploitation of sex obscene. Regardless of one's personal tastes and one's views or analysis of the pin-up and its impact on our culture, the Criminal Code's reference to sex is outdated and has no value in a social context. In practice, the undue exploitation of sex means only one thing—penetration; explicit sex; in other words, the real thing.

Besides, the article concerned with the undue exploitation of sex emerged from the conventional debate on pornography, the one that was taking place before women were deemed "relevant" to the issue. In the old days, "freedom loving" pornographers battled it out with repressive members of the decency contingent (male representatives of the Church usually) for the right of the (male) user of pornography to get off on whatever images gave him pleasure. The argument was about men's right to sexual freedom. In the end, the apparent proponents of repression won out and our laws prohibiting the undue exploitation of sex are the result.

These are the laws which imply that porn something to do with sexual freedom. These are the laws which were developed without the slightest attention to women, who have since then brought a fresh perspective to the porn issue. Instead of focussing on how the user exercises his freedom, we are analysing the way in which women are enslaved by images celebrating our sexual coercion. Finally, the fixation on sex has created laws that will prevent women from developing an alternative sexual imagery which will allow us to reclaim our right to define our own sexuality.

The Justice Minister, though, wants to have it both ways. He wants to retain the old laws that threaten sexual exploration. And he wants to tack onto them new proposals that view pornography from an entirely different vantage point than the one which informed the original obscenity legislation in Criminal Code. What we really need is the elimination of the entire existing body of jurisprudence on obscenity and the chance to start, again in the area of obscenity using MacGuigan's new proposals as guidelines.

Unfortunately, MacGuigan hopes he can satisfy feminists with anti-violence legislation and placate the decency contingent by retaining the old anti-sex legislation at the same time. The Minister probably thinks feminists are Bible thumpers in drag. He's wrong. If he keeps listening, maybe he'll find that out too.

SEXUALITY AND ITS DISCONTENTS
by Susan G. Cole
Volume 6, No. 6 (April 1985), pp. 8 and 9

In sex, what works, what brings mutual pleasure should be the criterion of "good." The problematic issue is consent, not whether my desire is better than yours.

—Esther Newton, Shirley Walton,
"The Misunderstanding," *Pleasure and Danger*.

With a few exceptions here and there, most women I know would like to have more and better sex, and they wish it would last longer. Many women are relieved that feminism has finally got around to talking sex. I mean talking good sex.

Good sex, not the frightening kind that Ti-Grace Atkinson was writing about in her radical essay "The Institution of Sexual Intercourse." Atkinson argued that since sexual intercourse was good only for male pleasure (the myth of the vaginal orgasm had just been exposed) and for getting women pregnant, the "act" itself was patriarchal to the core.

Good sex, not the protestations of celibates who claim that it is easier not to bother and that sex gets in the way of political action.

Good sex, not the kind we hear about again and again, where sex gets defined as women's sexual abuse.

Good sex, the kind that feels good, the kind that empowers women, the kind that redefines sexuality in our own terms. Now really, who could be against that?

After Atkinson, celibacy and the litany of sexual abuses that are real for women, feminist theorists would like to take sex back. The catalogue of feminist literature on the subject has been beefed up considerably over the past several years by the publication of a number of books focussing on sexuality and related issues (see bibliography). The British anthology *Sex and Love*, reflects a wide range of opinions, but two American books, *Powers of Desire* (especially the section on current controversies) and the more recent *Pleasure and Danger*, sustain the argument that it is crucial for feminists to stop harping on our potential for victimization in the sexual arena, and necessary for us to get to the good part—the good sex, the kind where women become sexual subjects not sexual objects, where female desire is fulfilled.

Read Ellen Willis's "Feminism, Moralism and Pornography," read Judith Walkowitz's "Male Vice and Female Virtue" both in *Powers of Desire*. Add to that Ellen DuBois's "Seeking Ecstasy on the Battlefield: Pleasure and Danger in Nineteenth-Century Thought" in Pleasure and Danger and the pattern begins to appear. These writers insist that, historically, feminism has scared women away from sex, that feminism has characterized women as the bearers of a moral standard in such a way as to make the right wing proud, and that feminism has created a theoretical framework in which there is no safe sex. We are left with a liberation that can only come from sexual purity. To writers reared in the 60s and in a culture that gives enormous rewards for sexual appeal, the nineteenth-century feminists—and those Willis would call their imitators in the second wave—are no fun at all.

Having vilified feminists in the first wave for associating freedom with sexual abstinence, the second wave backlash, evidenced in these books and in the quote that begins this article, argues that sexual liberation equals sexual activity, period. Women have had no authentic sexual voice, you can hear the "let's do it" women say. How can we know what we want unless we "explore more"?

Women have been allowed no sexuality. Expression is everything. Imbedded in this view is the notion that sex is proto-social, that is, untrammelled by patriarchal concerns of power and powerlessness, and that by engaging in sexual activity we can reclaim it, we can change it. Female orgasms will make us free. In a hypersexualized culture where personal identity is so wrapped up in sexuality, where even the women's movement has its own sex symbols, this sex-positive feminism sounds very appealing.

But we accept the view uncritically at our peril. To embrace it is to underestimate the extent to which sexuality is a social construct not so easily undone by female orgasms per se.

II

To simply celebrate whatever gives us sexual pleasure seems to me both problematic and too easy; we need to analyze how it is that certain things turn us on, how sexuality has been constructed under patriarchy to produce pleasure in the dominant/submissive forms, before we advocate these modes.
    —E. Ann Kaplan, "Is the Gaze Male?" in *Powers of Desire*

Like Kaplan, I think it is important for feminists to identify a patriarchal sexual ideology that is held together by three strands. The first is the practice of forced heterosexuality, a phenomenon addressed by Adrienne Rich in "Compulsory Heterosexuality and Lesbian Existence" (reprinted in *Powers of Desire*). Feminists have begun to unpack the cultural and sexual baggage with which this particular ideological strain has saddled us, and that struggle in the second wave, with the high profile of lesbian activists, has produced a lively debate that recognizes the Lavender contingent as a vital, perhaps central force in a sexually conscious movement.

The second ideological strand perpetuates the women-as-submissive/men-as-dominant configuration within the heterosexual paradigm. Pornography's practice of eroticizing sexual subordination is particularly useful in the promulgation of dominant/submissive male/female gender categories Pornography is just one of the cultural institutions committed to this second strain. There is a great deal else done to make our own demise sexually arousing to women and to make our conquest at their hands sexually arousing to men: for example some of the more excessive and sexually explicit rock videos the dynamics of Harlequin Romances; or the signifiers; fashion magazines.

What is crucial about the way sexual ideology works is that it does not operate on the "idea" level. It works in our bodies. Just as a great number of women think that heterosexuality their "natural" choice and not relentlessly promoted by a culture that needs it badly, many men and women really "feel" aroused by domination and surrender. This is not an argument for feminist essentialism and the acceptance of men and female qualities as natural. If women were born to submit and men to dominate, why do the products of culture have to keep reminding us about it?

The fact that men get to act in the world, and women get nurture them in their pursuits, gets acted out in sexual terms men act and women receive—sexually. Men take and women are taken. The reason why penetration by men has so seldom been construed as engulfing by women is because the term is entirely inconsistent with our culture's sexual ideology. Even the most enlightened and progressive women and men get off on pornography's sexual subordination. This does not make these people sick, it makes them well-socialized products of culture determined to make sexuality the most powerful for keeping us in our rightful places.

Feminists have argued closely that pornography lies. I think we have to accept that the lie of pornography, and its imitate in the mass media, is becoming the truth about life.

I do not think that feminists have come to grips with the second strand of patriarchal sexual ideology, at least not enough to change it. Given the definition of sexuality under patriarchal-construction, the best we've been able to do in the feminist struggle has been to fiddle ever so slightly with a few roles, give lesbians a chance to be "tops" as well "bottoms," without challenging the hierarchical construct the first place. Actually, the very best evidence we have that sexuality is socially constructed and not biologically determined is the fact that not only have some lesbians resisted the ideology of forced heterosexuality, but have resisted the male/dominant female/ submissive role demands by changing places at will.

The third strand of patriarchal sexual ideology is that power and sex are inextricably bound, that sex without aggression and violence and tension and conflict is non-existent, or boring at best. Judging by material in the new feminist texts, this third strand is not only not rejected in the thinking, but is actively embraced by feminists who would rather have power-laden sex than no sex at all. Although the evidence for this abounds in both *Powers of Desire* and *Pleasure and Danger*, the capitulation to the third strand is plainly put by Esther Newton and Shirley Walton in 'The Misunderstanding" *(Pleasure and Danger)*, where they explain their failure to consummate their friendship by the fact that they were incompatible: they were both tops. They don't bother to analyze how this came to be. In fact, they refuse to deal with it at all and submerge the entire question of power into a scenario where nature wants it that way. "Power and sexual desire," they write "are *deeply, perhaps intrinsically, connected* (italics mine) in ways we do not fully understand and can't abolish." Some feminists are so solidly in the grip of sex-can-only-equal-power ideology that when I suggested alternative to the dynamic—i.e., a serious feminist initiative to eroticize equality in both our cultural product and in our personal sexual practice—a feminist writing for the vehemently sex-positive gay newsmagazine *The Body Politic* reported that I had advocated celibacy.

Newton and Walton deliver the female-orgasm-equals-radical change motif. When they say, "What works is what's good," they mean that what works is what *feels* good. But what feels good is constructed from something other than a feminist framework, like thousands of years of sexual oppression and the perpetuation of a sexual ideology that is certain to women down. Why do so-called "pro-sex" feminists not care about this, or ignore it, or misinterpret it, or interpret it in a desperate attempt to avoid the anti-sex prude label?

Muriel Dimen, in her article "Politically Correct, Politically Incorrect?" *(Pleasure and Danger)*, tried to be conciliatory, but ended up saying that sex and political correctness are incompatible. "Sexual intimacy," she writes, "is resistant to rules of political correctness, or rather when it succumbs to rules, passion disappears." But Dimen has not only missed the point, as turned it around. Feminists do not set the rules, patriarchy does. The very source of our passion is rooted in patriarchal interests. For some reason, Dimen worries more feminists telling her what to do than the extent to which bona fide sexual ideology has already laid down the rules for. Given the absence of close analysis in these discussions, the rate some feminists are espousing the view that more the answer, I'm beginning to think that even though I bout the quality of sexual life, I'll concede to them the sex label, the way feminists have had to concede the pro-sex label to the right wing even though we know we care a great more about the quality of life issues. If pro-sex means the celebration of sex, the doing of it, at all costs, I'd rather be, well, pro-choice.

III

Erotic chauvinism cannot be redeemed by tarting it up in Marxist drag, sophisticated constructionist theory or retropsychobabble.
—Gayle Rubin "Talking Sex," *Pleasure and Danger.*

Just as agreeing not to mention danger requires that one's sexual autobiography be recast, agreeing not to speak about pleasure requires a similar dishonest alchemy, the transmutation of sexuality into unmitigated danger and unremitting victimization.
—Carole Vance, "Pleasure and Danger: Towards Politics of Sexuality," *Pleasure and Danger.*

The tendency of some feminists to regard women purely as victims rather than sexual subjects, and to define the movement's goal as controlling male sexuality rather than demanding women's freedom to lead active sexual lives, reinforces women's oppression and plays into the hands of the new right. It is a dead end, a politics of despair. Feminism is a vision of active freedom of fulfilled desires, or it is nothing.
—Ellen Willis, *Diary of a Conference on Sexuality*, (out of print).

Sex is not the problem, sexism is.
—Lisa Steele, "A Capital Idea," *Women Against Censorship.*

These quotations are taken from among the most eloquent proponents of a new feminist perspective on sexuality. To what extent do they take on the issue of patriarchal sexual ideology? Not much, from what I can see. Gayle Rubin, whose article "Talking Sex" is really the centrepiece of *Pleasure and Danger* (and who unfortunately repudiates the truly brilliant "Traffic in Women" which she wrote in 1973), does an exhaustive analysis of the way in which legal proscription against sexual behaviour has caused unspeakable trauma for people who have done nothing to warrant such persecution. Her critique of legal sanction is extremely useful. Rubin has always been a force to reckon with in this debate. But her main point is that erotic chauvinism is reprehensible: "Variation is a fundamental property of life…yet sexuality is supposed to conform to a single standard." But Rubin picks on the wrong standard. She worries about the persecution of S/M practitioners and "cross generational" sexual activists, calling them the true dissidents, when in fact they express one of the fundamental elements in patriarchal ideology—the desire to dominate.

In her introduction to *Pleasure and Danger*, Carole S. Vance complains that feminists have transmuted sexuality into unmitigated damage, once again placing the blame on feminists for theorizing about how sexuality works. Ellen Willis also wants to be a sexual subject, a sexual actor and not a victim, as if we could wish away an ideology that is deeply entrenched. Why do these women resist the idea that sexuality is gendered to the ground? I think they resist the view because they *are* eager for sexual freedom and they do not believe that they can get it as long as they think of themselves as victims. To say that women are not victims in sex becomes the means for them to feel empowered in the sexual arena. While I sympathize with their desires, I don't think putting on blinkers is the answer. To say that women are not victims in sex is to trivialize everything we know about rape, incest and wife assault. I do not think we can afford to do that lest we retreat into the silence that has kept women victimized for so long.

The desire for orgasm is not worth that. This is not to say that we shouldn't have sex. It means we have to continue to question how and why we get our pleasure; we have to question the role of sexual intercourse in a sexist culture; we have to question the social meaning of fellatio; we have to question the ways in which conflict, aggression and hierarchy get us hot. We should be able to do so without anyone thinking we are saying women should stop participating in any of these activities. (This tendency to sniff out "censors" and "judgments" in the feminist debate permeates Gayle Rubin's article, for example. She seems to think that just talking about these things means the same thing as applying legal sanction.)

What's fascinating about the new developments is that women like Carole Vance and Ellen Willis are anti-censorship feminists with strong views about the action of state and legal mechanisms. Both of these women would be prepared to argue meticulously that patriarchal structures exist to maintain the status of the powerful over the powerless. The question here is this: Why is sexuality so different? Why can we agree that cultural and political life have been organized over centuries to protect the status quo—with a few reforms allowed—while sexuality has not? Why does the left wing, for that matter, automatically become victim-oriented when analyzing the state, but refuse to question the way in which sexuality can be used against us? If the forces of political dominance have been so careful to appropriate every other avenue of human expression and change, and given what we know about sexuality's potential for empowerment, why and how could we imagine that the forces of political power would have left sexuality out?

The new sex-positive feminism seems to assume that the operative sexual ideology of patriarchy, if one exists, has been repression and not oppression. I am not impressed with this view. I look around in this culture and I do not see a great deal of repression. I see a hypersexualized society less concerned with having no sex, than with having the right kind of sex—men on top, women on the bottom; a society in which, for example, American men spend fifty million dollars a day on prostitution. These men spend the money to have sex, not to avoid it. This is a culture in which men's sexual access to women is guaranteed by a pornography industry that remains for all practical purposes protected, or by health workers who in the wake of wife assault, tell the victims to go home and be more feminine, or by law enforcement officers who think wife assault is "just sex," or that marital rape is a man's right; a culture where adolescent women purchase T-shirts with a heavy metal rock band's logo featuring women in chains on their hands and knees, and advertise their inevitable readiness to participate in sex that will sit quite nicely with patriarchal constructs; and finally, where one out of four women will have her first sexual experience before the age of sixteen with a member of her family or someone close to it, in a context of force and inequality. Likely no one will find out, and she will learn that sexuality is essentially a source of her own victimization. Cultural products aren't the only things that keep us in line. Real experience works just as well.

Lisa Steele's "Capital Idea" in *Women Against Censorship* is a thorough analysis of how mass media sex stereotyping keeps the prevailing sexual ideology unthreatened. But I disagree with the comment that "sex is not the problem, sexism is," even though it is a formulation feminists, especially anti-porn feminists, have espoused since the critique was first developed. Sex is a problem for a lot of women. Ann Landers found that out (see *Broadside*, February 1985) and I think *that* is the significance of her survey. She discovered that 72% of women preferred cuddles to the act.

I mentioned this poll to a woman who would no doubt appreciate the "sex-positive" label. Her response was swift: "I'm in the other 28%." The implication is, "What's wrong with the other 72%? Maybe if they weren't so repressed they would get into it more." But the women who responded to Ann Landers's poll did not say they preferred cuddles because the Bible told them that fornication was a sin; they did not complain about jism and come and how it made them gag. Their problem was not that sex was "yucky." Their problem was they felt used and used up, as if the act were the exercise of power over them and not something which gave them pleasure. These women are resisting. What's amazing, given the intensity with which they are encouraged to like it the way it is, is that there were so many of them who were willing to say that they didn't. They deserve our support, not our contempt.

What most of us want to believe is that sexuality is unremittingly positive. We want to believe this because sex gives us pleasure, regardless of whether it has been constructed by political ideology and its cultural agents. Sometimes women can be heard arguing that they like to be sexual objects. What they mean is that they like to have sex, that they cannot imagine anything else but objectification through sexual response. The last time I heard a woman say this, she was cheered by an audience who agreed that she shouldn't have to give up sex. She and her audience's insistence that sexual objectification was worth maintaining, lest none of us ever has sex again, locks out change. Objectification, conflict and danger in the sexual arena are not inevitable for women.

We do not have to give up on sexual pleasure, but we cannot afford to be afraid to examine where it comes from and how we get it. In the lead article in *Women Against Censorship*, Varda Burstyn warns that we have to be careful about the strategies we develop, "to mend and reweave the delicate fabric of sexual life." Sexual life does need mending and reweaving, and with an entirely new set of threads and strands. The feminist struggle is not against sexuality, it is the struggle for change in the sexual arena.

BIBLIOGRAPHY

Varda Burstyn, ed., *Women Against Censorship*, Douglas and McIntyre, Toronto and Vancouver, 1985

Sue Cartledge and Joanna Ryan, eds., *Sex and Love: New Thoughts on Old Contradictions*, The Women's Press, London, 1983

Anne Snitow, Christin Stansell and Sharon Thompson, eds., *The Powers of Desire: The Politics of Sexuality*, Monthly Review Press, New York, 1983

Carole S. Vance, ed., *Pleasure and Danger: Exploring Female Sexuality*, Routledge and Kegan Paul, Boston, London, Melbourne and Henley, 1985

BEYOND IMAGES:
HOOKERS AND FEMINISTS

by Debi Brock

Volume 7, No. 6 (April 1986), pp. 8 and 9

At a recent Toronto conference on the politics of pornography and prostitution, there was in evidence what could loosely be defined as two camps of opinion among prostitutes and ex-prostitutes. One was at least sympathetic to feminism (most notably, Margo St. James of Call Off Your Old Tired Ethics—COYOTE), while the other, more vocal grouping (mainly Canadian Organization for the Rights of Prostitutes—CORP, particularly its irrepressible spokesperson, Peggy Miller) was not. A third grouping comprised feminist, non-prostitute women, who are active in hookers' rights campaigns (i.e., Downtown Hookers Action and Alliance for the Safety of Prostitutes—ASP).

In addressing the tensions amongst the various groupings, I begin from my own experience. I was around the prostitution business for nine years, from about 1975 to 1983, a proximity which was "accidental" in that a close friend ended up making her living this way. Because I had spent my teenage years in a rural, economically depressed area, I knew more girls who moved to Toronto to work in massage parlours than I knew females and males combined who went on to university. I say this not only to authorize myself to speak, but also, I hope, not to appear patronizing towards prostitutes, an attitude which feminists all too frequently are guilty of conveying.

In order to clear the ground of many of the myths and distortions which surround prostitutes, it's important to say who I think they "are." Women who are prostitutes have generally been dealt more shit in their lives than anyone should have to tolerate, both prior to and after entering the business. Most have come from poor families, and some were sexually abused when young. But as feminists have argued, the rate of sexual abuse among all females is very high, and only a small number of abused (or for that matter, poor) women end up working as prostitutes. There is something more going on here, I think, a lot of which is circumstantial. For instance, a woman is broke, sick of doing menial jobs for insultingly low wages, and meets someone in the business who presents it as a lucrative option, given the constraints women face in the labour market. There may be some moral qualms to get over at first, but after all, every woman recognizes at some point that she is most valued for her sexuality, and isn't our function as a commodity flashed at us from every billboard? Prostitutes actually represent a pretty broad range of people and life experiences, and if they have been sexually abused or come from poor families, well, that is what it is often like to grow up female in a patriarchal, capitalist society.

My friend, whom I'll call Anne, and her business partner were fairly motivated women, making a conscious effort to get ahead the best way that they knew how. From working the streets and in massage parlours and escort services owned and operated by men, they eventually set up their own escort service. Many of the other women I met through Anne who worked in the parlours, as well as those who worked for Anne's escort service, were not so motivated. Some of the latter, in particular, looked upon the job as occasional work, a way to get some quick money when the rent was due or when they wanted to go out partying. Temporary or occasional work for an escort service was certainly preferable to the streets. Others treated the job as a full-time occupation, but were satisfied if they did one or two customers a day. Some of the women are quite bright, others are not. Some enjoy challenging themselves with new ideas and realizing their creative potential, while others live in small worlds. I won't go so far as to say that they are just like other women, however, because they are all too aware of the stigma attached to their jobs and this sets up a perception of difference, of ones who stand apart.

The hookers who attended the Toronto conference last November showed us that far from being the abject figures hookers are often portrayed as, their numbers include women who are bright and politicized. (These women won't necessarily disagree with the descriptions I have given so far, it is a little further on that the trouble starts.) They did, however, attempt to present prostitution in as positive (and therefore one-sided) a light as possible, for political/ strategic reasons. The hookers' rights advocates are different from many of the women in the business (right now, anyway) in that they are formally organizing; they take the extra step from complacency to action. I don't think that most prostitutes regard organizing as important enough to engage in at this point—if they think of it at all—because most women, particularly the young ones, regard the job as only temporary, on the road to somewhere else. The women still in the business, who attended the conference, clearly regarded it as a long-term career: they were asserting their identities as prostitutes as a positive choice. As with the formation of the feminist, gay and black power movements, the assertion of a positive identity is the first step in political organizing. It is necessary not only for the sake of women who are prostitutes, but for all women, as an interim measure on the road to self-determination. Even middle class homemakers are usually only one man away from welfare, and every woman is a potential prostitute. Prostitutes, more than any other women, recognize this quite clearly.

However, part of this assertion of a positive identity by some prostitutes at the conference entailed the advancement of a "free to choose" philosophy. Prostitutes were also represented as bright, articulate entrepreneurs who enjoy both their jobs and a high standard of living, and prostitution was promoted as natural and inevitable, and therefore beyond criticism. One woman made this clear when she stated that prostitution was not about patriarchy or matriarchy but human nature. These women appeared to represent a large constituency, and on one occasion Peggy Miller actually claimed to speak for all prostitutes. With no disrespect intended to Peggy, she cannot claim to speak for all prostitutes any more than I can claim to speak for all feminists.

I had never, before the conference, heard a hooker say she enjoyed her job. Loved the money, yes. But with respect to their customers, there was only an occasional display of compassion for a regular who was faring badly, while most of the time they were relegated to the status of "pig," or considered "not bad shits, for shit." How can you enjoy your job if you say of your customers, as Anne did, that, "Sometimes I wish there were condoms that covered their entire bodies." However, some of the women at the conference would have us believe that prostitutes are the equivalents of sex therapists and social workers, and that they derive sexual pleasure from their jobs. Perhaps *some* do, *sometimes*. I know that when feminists investigate women's sexuality we tend to concentrate on the negative and coercive aspects of sexuality (sex as danger) rather than determining what women get out of it (sex for pleasure and/

or profit). There is a tendency to deny that women can experience sexual fulfillment in a patriarchal culture. But as one woman in the audience pointed out in an understated way, if you are having sex several times a day with different men, you are not going to enjoy yourself with every customer. These men are, after all, chosen for their ability to pay rather than perform. As Anne's partner, Donna, told me,

> you tell them, "Lie on your back and let me pamper you." And what you really mean is, "Lie on your back; don't you fucking touch me, and let me do my job my way so that I can get to have the least amount of contact with you. You just sit. Play dead."

Asserting that hookers enjoy sex with their customers reinforces how patriarchal culture presents these women: as nymphomaniacs looking for an outlet. Customers are therefore not culpable, but mere recipients of the women's lust. It asks us to believe what hookers would have their customers believe, that he has gotten the woman off, since it enhances the customer's sexual pleasure, and a happy customer is a repeat customer.

What the defenders of prostitution were also conveying at the conference was a picture of prostitution under "ideal" conditions: in a clean bed, with a well kept and wealthy man with whom one can relax and fulfill one's sexual fantasies, while drinking Dom Perignon, perhaps in an exotic location. This fantasy bears about as much relation to the reality of most prostitution as my life does to the Ewings' on the TV series, *Dallas*. It may be easy and clean and fast. It could also, for example, take place in a car, or a customer's dirty apartment, with a man who at best objectifies and at worst is repugnant. Perhaps there are some exclusive call girls around whose engagements approximate this glamorous, class-specific stereotype, but she is not to be found on the streets, or even in the yellow pages.

Linked to this was the disconcerting presentation of prostitution as a form of anonymous sex, as liberated sex (what determines the liberated character of anonymous sex, I assume, is its separation from the context of familial relations). This would be fine if prostitutes really performed their work for pleasure, which I think it is clear they do not. Like other forms of work, prostitution, for the purveyor of the service, is an oppressive and alienating economic relation, a condition which is exacerbated further still by its clandestine character. Presenting prostitution as liberated sex is as silly as the idea that the sexual "revolution" liberated women's sexual expression in the 1960s.

Many of the hookers and ex-hookers also attempted to legitimate prostitution by promoting it as a business like any other. However, they under-emphasized the economic rationale behind prostitution (and what other rationale is there behind business?) in favour of justifying sex as liberating and pleasurable. This strategy works against their presentation of prostitution as something akin to the corner grocery store. I do not think that prostitution is as different from other forms of women's work as popular "wisdom" would have it. However, I certainly do not believe that it is a business like any other, precisely because of its history (ideological baggage which prostitutes cannot just wish away), nor would I like to see it treated as such. I wouldn't want the state to pimp women through licenses and taxes, and I think that feminists and prostitutes lobbying for decriminalization must assert this exemption as a political act, should the time come. And, most importantly, there is no place for bosses in this business: women themselves must maintain control over their own working conditions, since their work begins with their own bodies. This kind of control is of course something we would all do well to work towards.

Some hookers and former hookers attending the conference considered these assertions necessary tactics in legitimating their right to continue working. But I for one do not need to be fed this in order to defend prostitutes' right to work in a social order where, as Richard Symanski in *The Immoral Landscape: Female Prostitution in Western Societies*, asserts, "Men are willing to pay more for sexual access than for almost all forms of labour." Prostitution, when undertaken as a steady job and where the women have a degree of control over their working conditions and their income, offers the possibility of an income undreamt of in the usual female occupations like secretarial or fast-food work, however different the reality may often turn out to be.

Consider this autobiographical note: A number of years ago I was working as a chambermaid in a hotel, and if my friend Anne had come to regard men as pigs through her experiences in the business, I was beginning to think that way about almost everybody (it really is amazing what people can do to a hotel room in under 24 hours). Sometimes Anne would do an "escort" at the hotel we worked at. One day I cleaned a room after she and a customer had vacated it. She had just made $200 for a half hour's work; I made $2.30 in the same amount of time. On another day, I met Anne at 4.45 pm after working an eight hour day that included cleaning twenty bathrooms and earning $30. Anne had only been working since noon and already had $450 in her pocket (though of course not every day was this good). So who was being exploited? I knew too that all women experience their subjectivity as objects, and that I was not accorded a great deal more respect working as a chambermaid than Anne was as a hooker.

I had a lot of time to think while I was spending my days cleaning hotel rooms. I came to the conclusion that prostitutes and feminists actually have a lot in common, as former prostitute Margo St. James has been trying to tell us for some time (though for perhaps somewhat different reasons). Both prostitutes and feminists have broken the rules, and in the process revealed the character of those rules. Since we do this, we are "bad girls." Feminism is concerned with developing an identity which is not dependent on male approval, which is why men find it so threatening (even more threatening, I think, than the idea of sharing the housework). Prostitutes are not generally regarded as the property of any one man, and this provides them a peculiar autonomy, peculiar because prostitution exists to satisfy male "needs." We are unified too because all women are really whores in the patriarchal imagination, and any woman's sexuality can be treated as a commodity, or depicted and distorted for male pleasure. Even lesbian women are not free from this, as is evident by the proliferation of porn ostensibly depicting sex between women for heterosexual male consumption.

There is a certain amount of justified hostility towards men from both hookers and feminists, which comes from realizing that men, in the last analysis, have the power to determine the tune and set the price. For example, women in the business have revealed that perhaps their "choices" were not so fully theirs after all (how many women actually freely choose, as opposed to being "freely compelled," to undertake a particular form of labour?). One prostitute at the conference revealed that she had blocked out whole periods of her life. Donna once commented that if she had been a guy she would have had more options. Anne told me that she became a prostitute because she couldn't handle poverty anymore. And most notable is the anger women I have known have exhibited towards their customers and their jobs.

Reinforcing these relations, there is of course another level of authority and control exerting its influence on the lives of women—the state apparatus and its front line of repression, the police. As one hooker remarked, in a statement which contradicted most of what had been said by hookers (including herself) before, "We have heard a lot about patriarchy at this conference. We know about this. We call it "The Man." Implicit in this statement is the realization that, important as decriminalization is, it is going to take a lot more than this to make women who are prostitutes free from oppression.

These prostitutes declare that they have a *right* to work because their business is no different than any other, except that selling sex is more honest than using sex to sell. Neither position provides an adequate explanation. Their falsity lies in their exclusivity.

I think there are three interdependent ways of conceptualizing prostitutes, which accounts for both the wide range of prostitutes' experiences (for example, some have pimps, others are independent, some have to take their chances working the streets, while others work indoors in relatively safe and comfortable conditions) and the contradictions which prostitutes live in this kind of society. First, we can regard them in a very limited sense as victims; second, as survivors; and third, as empowering themselves. Prostitutes are not simply victims, but are active agents making their own history, albeit, like all of us, not under conditions of their own choice. In this way we can regard hookers as not only surviving under conditions of victimization, but also as empowering themselves to act on their own behalf, whether or not we believe that prostitution is a legitimate path for women. This remains true whether their actions are motivated by economic necessity or through a desire for material success.

The social structures of prostitution, like social class and the institutions of patriarchy and femininity, become sources of meaning and identity. While decisions based upon these structures appear to be freely made by the individual, they also serve to reproduce these social institutions on an aggregate level. However, the structures themselves exert their influence upon the individual, not in a mechanical way, but mediated by cultural relations, thereby allowing the production of alternative outcomes. Therefore, while I believe firmly that prostitution as a social institution is rooted in female subordination, I also recognize that institutions and the people who fill particular places in them are not the same thing. We must realize that working as prostitutes can be a means of women doing their best to improve their material conditions; that women may be "freely compelled" to become prostitutes. This recognition means that feminists can support prostitutes without supporting prostitution, and prostitutes can assert a positive identity without defending or obscuring patriarchal relations. I think that once we realize this, feminists can overcome. some of their ambivalence in dealing with prostitution, an ambivalence which has clearly not revealed itself in feminist efforts towards the censorship of pornography, where the involvement of sex trade workers can be more easily obscured.

As feminists explore the commoditization of sex more thoroughly, taking into account the position of sex trade workers, whether they be strippers, prostitutes or porn models, it is also hoped that *all* prostitutes will become more aware of how their condition reflects the position of women more generally. I think that prostitutes attending the pornography and prostitution conference gave feminists a much needed shaking up, and I'd like to know what new information prostitute activists took away with them. This kind of information sharing is vital if we are to fight against repressive measures like Bill C-49 and for the decriminalization of prostitution, in the context of broader social, economic and sex-related changes to bring about women's liberation. This does not mean that we must always fight together in the same organizations. We need to respect the right of sex trade workers (whether feminist or not) to organize autonomously, without feminists who are not participants in the sex trade attempting to take up and transform their agenda. We in turn can use our own organizations to defend prostitutes, demand that women gain more control over their conditions of work in the sex trade, and organize for a future where the institution of prostitution no longer exists.

(I hope these comments, partial and tentative though they may be, serve to continue the dialogue between women inside and outside the sex trade.)

Debi Brock is a student at OISE in Toronto, and a member of the International Women's Day Committee.

CHAPTER 4

Interviews & Profiles

Although the original work of artists and the protests of activists often spoke for themselves, *Broadside* could not resist the words these women said during interviews or speeches. We published conversations that allowed us to explore the artists' and activists' ideas, to ask them tough questions, or to just let them speak their minds. While many of these interviews took the form of a Q&A, some—like the ones with Gloria Steinem and singer Diana Braithwaite—are combinations of reviews and interviews. Some of our subjects, like Steinem, Rigoberta Menchú—who went on to win the Nobel Peace Prize in 1992—critic Dale Spender; science fiction writer Judith Merrill; and iconic painter Georgia O'Keeffe were world famous. The fact that they spoke to us reflects both their generosity and their appreciation for small magazines like ours—although writer Deena Rasky's pursuit of O'Keeffe suggests that persistence played the most important role in securing that interview. Other interview subjects, such as Jane Siberry, and Joyce Wieland were Canadian home-grown heroes. Some of them were not as well-known but, like the women of the Tobique First Nation struggling to secure their status, were activists and visionaries doing grassroots work that we knew could inspire our readers.

When we began looking back at our content, we were intrigued by the fact that our participants so often touched on similar themes. Both Angela Miles and poet Adrienne Rich talked about the difficulties of making feminist politics a priority while under pressure to join coalitions. We featured interviews that dealt with the challenges of dealing with erotica and censorship, including insights from visual artist Lynne Fernie, anti-pornography activist Andrea Dworkin, and artist and writer Kate Millett. Many of our interviewees, such as Spender, Nicole Brossard, Daphne Marlatt, and Betsy Warland, were preoccupied with the limits of language to express women's experience. They and others, like filmmaker Léa Pool, speak eloquently about how the best art is deeply personal.

The activists we featured, such as Charlotte Bunch, who worked to end the sex trafficking of women; Nikki Colodny, who bravely fought Canada's antiquated abortion laws by performing abortions in her free-standing clinic; and Dworkin—through a devastating speech—openly reflect on the challenges of being on the front lines.

The interview, reprinted here, with author Sylvia Fraser about *My Father's House*, her memoir of recalling sexual abuse at the hands of her father, is particularly poignant. Fraser had come under fire in an early issue of *Broadside* for her hyper-sexual novel *The Emperor's Virgin* and sent an angry though respectful response to the review (both the review and her letter appear in this book). In this interview, she generously allows that she may have missed something, that she had been out of control and that the writing of that early novel may have been a form of acting out.

We are particularly proud of the fact that many of *Broadside*'s interviews, including the ones with Dale Spender and Nicole Brossard featured here, were conducted by Eleanor Wachtel, who went on to host the CBC's flagship literary series *Writers & Company*, and became a Member of the Order of Canada in 2004 and an Officer in 2014. She and our other interviewers gave voice to subjects whose wholly original ideas and practices fuelled the women's movement, making it one of the most important social and political phenomena of the twentieth century.

Susan G. Cole

CLARE COULTER: ONE WOMAN SHOW
Interview by Deena Rasky
Introductory Issue (May 1979), p. 17, excerpt

I was on a train journey out west a couple of years ago. I was thirty four then. I was reading in *Ms.* magazine about a woman doctor who had wanted to have children. Finally she did get pregnant but she miscarried. I was reading this and I burst into tears. I thought, "That's very peculiar, Clare, because you have never shown any interest in having children or in that life at all, the life of a family. Suddenly you find yourself bursting into tears when you read that somebody miscarried, so something's going on." That alerted me to the fact that maybe I want things that I have no idea about, and I'm putting them out of my mind, because I'm very good at putting things out of my mind for years and years. And nature doesn't wait that long. So I would like to find out while I have a couple of years left in my life to have children what I really feel about it.

I'll never forget that incident on the train. The feeling that the theatre takes away from you the responsiveness you should have to nature and to the reality. That's a real fear in my life. I knew a man who said actresses aren't very attractive, they're not very sensual people at all. I thought about that quite a lot and wondered. When I'm doing performances if they're very taxing performances I know that a lot of myself as a woman, every thing that I feel in life, goes into the performances and I've come out exhausted without any-thing to give. So how could I be anything except some *thing* ready for bed, ready to crash out and wake up the next morning ready for work again. And so what normally makes a woman attractive goes into performances. And that's something I'm afraid of. And I'm sorry if that's true. On the other hand I keep thinking of all these mythological actresses from centuries ago who had great carryings-on in their lives.

Now in my family, my father never had anything to do with the children. He worked behind closed doors and when you wanted to speak to him you knocked on the door and waited to be admitted. That's how my mother wanted it. There was never any question that any of the responsibilities of the children were his business. No, they weren't. Things have changed. People share now.

But then it's odd about giving to people. When I was a baby there was a polio epidemic. I caught polio, then my sister caught polio and my mother caught polio. The two babies recovered and my mother didn't. She was paralyzed. It meant that for nine months she wasn't able to move at all from her bed. There were nurses around. Then she had to learn to walk and that took most of my childhood, getting herself back on her feet. We had maids at that time.

The interesting thing is that my mother didn't really take charge until I was past the earliest years which are supposed to be so important. A lot of the work of looking after me was done by other people. The wonderful thing about that period was that there were two influences in my life: there was the wretched person down in the kitchen that fought with me and told me that I couldn't have two bowls of soup if I wanted them and sent me up to bed and did this and that to me. Then there was that angel on the second floor. If things were really bad you could knock on the door and go in and say, "Pearl says I have to do this." Then she would say "Well now, what Pearl says is right." And then you'd suddenly be quite happy.

But it was as though there were two worlds: there was the Ultimate World. When the Real World failed you, you could go to this. And that was what Mother was to me. But someone who is always looking after her children and doesn't have maids or anything, that's an entirely different thing. I think there is so much criticism about people other than the mother looking after the children. In my experience it was wonderful. But then I must say my mother, it wasn't that she had another career, I mean she was always upstairs on the second floor. Her psyche was with us. It was never distracted. I think that's the trick. The great danger in the entertainment business is that your psyche is just whipped out from under you like a carpet.

You go to a new theatre and suddenly if you're a shy person you're meeting thousands of new people and there are all these vibes coming from everywhere. Then you come back and your friend's waiting for you or your husband or your family or whatever… people who know you. You think "Who are these people? I've just had a day somewhere else." And you don't relate.

B [Broadside]: And is that what you're particularly finding now as a result of the fame that's come your way?

C [Clare Coulter]: No, I'm trying to keep my hold on the people that are my life, want to know me and share my life with me, and not be distracted by the people who surround me in my work and so on. I want to hold on to the people that are my life because it's very easy just to become strangers.

Now if I had a husband and children that whole thing would be intensified, that struggle. I would prefer it that way I think.

B: What about the bonus of what comes back to you as performer, that approbation that you receive from the audience? You must pick up the audience response to the character that you're projecting. That must be a two-way thing; I mean, it's not total drain.

C: At first, I couldn't take the responsibility of holding these people's attention for two hours. It was just too much. I used to wake up after we opened and think: "I can't do it today. I can't, I'm not up to it. I'm gonna phone a doctor and tell him I have some difficulty." So then I had this kind of breakthrough. One night I saw Janet Amos' mother in the audience and an actor and his wife that I know that love my work. And I came out facing this audience in my usual state of fear and not feeling up to it at all. Then I said to myself, "Why shouldn't this audience, rather than being there draining you of every ounce that you've got from their critical withdrawn selves, why shouldn't they all be your Mother? With that amount of pride and pleasure in seeing you come out here to give them two hours? Why shouldn't it be just like that? Just like in the living room when you were a kid and they said 'Please dance for us.' And it was a real turnaround. I suddenly believed that 128 strangers in Toronto were all as absolutely proud as punch to see me out there and loved me as dearly. It was really a great moment.

I've felt much more secure about audiences ever since. Even now when I face the audience there are faces out there—sleeping faces, literally snoring. I don't know if it's the heat or what. Something puts them to sleep anyway, and I look at a face. I used to bounce right off it and fly to an interested face. Then I thought

"No, no wait a moment, this is a sleeping beauty here, you must wake this face…." And now I concentrate on the sleeping face to see if I can get through to their consciousness. Any face that does wake up and find my gaze on them…it must be quite a shock. As you pan the faces you can see them looking all weird. I know the people are having their own thoughts about what you're saying. Their faces are contorted in various types of concentration, either negative or positive. You, meanwhile, are drifting on your pre-ordained route of emotion no matter what you might see out there. You've got this route to travel. I travel all these weird bumps in the road of faces and just pass straight on. You pass straight on but you go over them, you see those faces, all of them.

I remember the first time I actually had to talk to the faces right beside me. It was for Paul Thompson. I thought Paul was making me go mad. I thought "Passe-Muraille's fallen to pieces and now he's trying to turn his actors mad." That wasn't what I was trained to do. I was trained to have a fourth wall up there and the whole thing was imagination that you were really talking to people. Then he was asking me to actually face these faces. Reality! He was asking me to bring imagination so close to my reality that it was making me go nutty.

See, if I were in a character right now and I had to face you, you would be looking at me and it would make me throw off my character. You're not a character, you're yourself; the audience isn't a character, they're themselves. You have this double reality and you want to come down to their level, you want to meet them and be the same. And that's quite difficult.

The first time that happened to me I was talking away to a woman and I had learned—I was so proud of myself—I had really learned to just be speaking intimately to any old face that happened to sit down in the chair and pay their five dollars…So I was talking away to this woman and she became very involved in what I was saying. At one point I was complaining about my life as the character. I was a Quebec woman complaining about my life and I said "Oh, this was when I was pregnant…." And she leaned forward and said "Ohhh…." And something inside me just *screamed*. And I yelled at the top of my voice "Not Really!! Not Really!!" I was so humiliated that she had broken through me!

B: What sort of plays do you have lined up for the future?

C: Well I just have one play by Michel Tremblay: *Damnée Manon, Sacré Sandra*. There's just two characters. And it follows a line for me of trying to release the emotions and reach areas of intensity and passion without stepping on areas not yet explored, which is quite hard. I have to choose my roles very carefully.

B: Has this play been done before in Montreal?

C: No, I don't think so. I know that it's only just translated into English.

B: Have you started work on that?

C: I've got the script, but I haven't looked at it.

B: How long will it take you to get a character down? What sort of time before you have it?

C: Three weeks is too short to rehearse anything. Three weeks is what they gave me for Emily Dickinson. But I had been at it all summer long and I had some of it "on ice." But three weeks is too short for me. Although, I don't know, it's very hard. People feel that I'm too slow.

B: Three weeks is *slow*?

C: No, but they just feel that I am a slow person and I ought to jump out faster. I don't know whether I could be pushed to do that, I don't know. But I have a sort of inside clock which will not come up with a character until a certain number. I think I'm about three weeks; a crisis happens and my character comes out in about three weeks. It's now a familiar pattern so that I don't, of course I do worry each time. Directors say to you, "Well, I'm not worried because I know what you can do." And you think "Well, just a minute. It's happened in the past but it just might not happen this time." I mean each time it *looks* like it's going to be a disaster and each time it *could* be a disaster. There's a trap in saying "Oh, but it always comes out." Because then you're avoiding the actual pain which gives birth to a character. You've got to really feel that it might not happen to give it a chance.

In the early days, because it had never happened to me before, I didn't know what was going on. The directors would all be having fits, and the phone would ring at the end of this difficult period of rehearsal and they would say "I'd like to talk with you." And then I would say "Well all right, I know I'm ruining the entire production and I'll resign, tomorrow morning I'll resign."

I would resign and that became a pattern. And then the director would say "I know you can do it." I would be very humble and accept all the sympathy and encouragement. Which was ridiculous now that I see it.

It was a natural thing that was taking place inside me. As I see it, a character is another person. You don't want to abandon the person that you are in order to become this other person. You don't want to abandon the person that you are in order to become this other person. You don't want to. You'd rather stay with the one you have. So I go through the readings and rehearsals in a terrible state of reluctance to say or do or feel or think or move in the way it's indicated. And a director who doesn't know me thinks, "She doesn't know *anything*. Is this how she's going to do it? It says 'giggle' and you can't even get a smile out of her. Is she an actress or what?"

What's actually taking place is I'm just rejecting everything that is being presented to me, the invitation to become another person. And I'm rejecting and rejecting and rejecting. What I'm really doing is getting to know the strange territory of what this person is. Then when I think I know what that strange person is, it's safe enough to venture maybe two paces forward into that other personality. And finally when it says smile, I can actually smile without it being too dangerous because I can get back to myself. I know that smile goes just that far.

B: How is it in reverse after you're finished. How does it affect you leaving that part? Does it happen very suddenly?

C: It's traumatic, absolutely traumatic. The night after we close

I'm usually out for dinner somewhere. At about eight o'clock the play starts happening in my head. The lines start, I start thinking of getting up from the table and doing what I have to do. That goes on for three or four days. At the end of the fourth day it's kind of a rickety old record of the play. Then it's left me. But at the same time, I've lost the closest person in my life; just like that it's gone, never to come again.

I have an image in my mind of when I was a kid. I used to be very tidy with my toys and I used to put all my dolls and toys in shoeboxes. I would label the shoeboxes and put them stacked up in my cupboard in my room. And in my imagination I have this stack of characters in shoeboxes.

I just lay my character out, and put it away in a box. But I'll never get it out again. You can never come back to that person. You never do.

DIALOGUES WITH WRITERS
NICOLE BROSSARD: FANTASIES AND REALITIES
by Jean Wilson
Volume 2, No. 8 (June 1981), pp. 11 and 18

Since the publication in 1965 of her first book, *Aube à la saison*, Nicole Brossard has been transforming both the form and the content of Québec literature. As well, she herself has been transformed since then by her personal growth towards a feminist consciousness and her acknowledgement and expression in her life and writing of her lesbianism.

Born in 1943, Brossard, "like a lot of people," wrote conventional love poems at first. However, when she was about 18, she began to take poetry seriously and after publication of *Aube à la saison* became one of the most influential young writers in Québec. In 1965 she co-founded *La Barre du Jour*, a literary journal whose purpose was to provide a place for young writers who were experimenting with language but had few outlets in which to publish. At that stage of literary development in Québec there were few literary journals and critics were speculating about whether there even *was* a Québec literature, just as critics were doing in English-speaking Canada. "At that time, it wasn't even called, 'une littérature québécoise,' but rather 'une littérature canadienne-française.' We said, yes, there *is* a Québec literature, and you'll see it in our writing." As well as publishing in *La Barre du Jour* Brossard and other writers also brought to public attention the work of early twentieth-century Québec poets already unknown to the new generation of poets.

In her own writing, especially after publication of *L'Echo bouge beau* in 1968, and in "a more obvious way" in *Suite logique* (1970), Nicole Brossard was actively "interfering" with traditional, bourgeois language, with what she would now call "the patriarchal mentality." Her aim was "to break clichés through language, as a consequence of which conventional attitudes and habits would also be broken."

In 1970, Brossard published her first novel, which was simply called *Un livre* and which has neither characters nor story in the usual sense. It is essentially a series of fragments of lives as observed by the person recording them, that is, the author. As she remarked in the conversation on which this article is based, Brossard had assumed previously that only poetry could express what was most important in life, namely "extreme pleasure and extreme pain." These two extremes are, of course, very difficult to describe accurately in any form. But Brossard realized that although she would never be able to describe them accurately, she was in fact not limited to poetry and would be able to write all her life because "I'd try to write about those vital things and to travel through the infinite possibilities in language. That I published my first novel in 1970 is also due to the fact that I needed more space, even though in that novel there is really no story and my characters are only pretexts for experience."

After *Un livre*, Brossard wrote two more novels and then returned to poetry with *Mécanique jongleuse* and *Masculin grammaticale* in 1974. About that time, her personal world began to change radically. She more or less simultaneously read such feminist writers as Simone de Beauvoir, Kate Millett, and Ti-Grace Atkinson; she fell in love with another woman; she became pregnant. "For me, my feminism and my lesbianism are related to those two realities—pregnancy, which united me with *all* women, and lesbianism,

Highly acclaimed Quebec poet and
novelist Nicole Brossard.

which revealed my own territory to me. As well as reading all those books and doing my own consciousness-raising, Luce Guilbault and I did the film *Some American Feminists* (NFB 1976). She and I also worked on *La Nef des sorcières*, a feminist play first performed in Montréal. And when I returned from making the film in New York I recognized that there was no feminist newspaper or magazine in Québec so I decided to start one." The result was *Les Têtes de Pioche* (Pick-Axe Heads), a monthly feminist newspaper which was published from 1976 until 1979.

Brossard began to write *L'Amer* in 1976. "It was very hard to write because it was like trying to change the meaning of all the words we (women) were using and confronting myself with reality and fiction at the same time." Because of its relevance to the experience of writing *L'Amèr* and her subsequent writings, it is useful to quote here Brossard's answer to a question asked at the May 1 dialogue: "How has your feminist consciousness affected your use of language?"

As long as we view language as a mental space by which we can express, formulate, and explore new dimensions which of our individual and collective realities, it is obvious that a feminist consciousness leaves traces in our practice of language. For me, the most important thing is that feminist consciousness creates new paths, new possibilities of being active and activist in language. When I say active, I mean producing and creating new dimensions in reality, new perspectives. When I say activist, I mean interfering with what has been taken for granted, with what is taken for granted in society and in language (both being patriarchal and sexist.)

I have always been actively concerned with words, forms and language. I could say that this is my existential trade mark. Things can happen in your body, in your skin, but as long as you cannot create a satisfactory syntactic environment for words of emotion you can be devoured by them. You can vanish in a sea of silence or disintegrate in a patriarchal society. For me to use words is not only a matter of expressing myself, but also a way to produce a new territory, a new space, a new environment for my body as skin able to transform and be transformed by language. Feminist consciousness also makes it possible for a woman to say we, and through that possibility of using the plural to concentrate more precisely on "I," or on "us" as individuals.

Feminist consciousness made me question reality and fiction. For example, when I was writing L'Amer, I felt that I had to move reality into fiction because patriarchal reality made no sense and was useless to me. I also had the impression and the certainty that my fictions were reality—they are full of meanings—and that from there I could start a theoretical work. That's why I called that book "une fiction théoretique."

I think that when we are little girls, we perceive reality clearly, as it is: patriarchal. But we are soon told that our perceptions are mistaken. What is first perception becomes impression and then is called imagination, as in "darling, you are imagining things." In other words, our certainties slowly become fiction. This is the knot that stays in our throats, sometimes all our lives. And this is the knot that feminist writers have untied in their work.

For women, so-called reality is a fiction because it is not made up of their perceptions, their sensibility, their minds, their necessities. Reality is constructed, reproduced, and transformed by a patriarchal mind, a one-track mind. Let's name some fictions: the military complex, the price of gold, the television news, pornography.

On the other hand, women's realities have been perceived as fictions. Let's name some realities: maternity, abortion, rape, prostitution, physical violence. The newspapers will tell you that there are news items and not information. So if you are writing with a feminist consciousness, you suddenly find yourself writing at the edge, at the very limits of fiction and reality. You can use delirium to travel from one to another, entering a spiral, spinning.

To answer the question more concisely, I would say that my feminist consciousness affected my use of language in the sense that it made my texts more flowing, more evident in their syntax, for example. Also one's interior beat changes and so affects the rhythm of one's writing. You concentrate differently on words' meaning. You discover the meaning of words you thought you knew before—and some words disappear from your vocabulary altogether.

I know that after writing L'Amer, which was ma descente aux enfers, to write Le Sens apparent was just like surfacing and spinning. After that book, I think that my writing became more affected by a lesbian sensibility, that from then on my body became a skin able to produce la pensée de l'émotion et l'émotion de la pensée.

Certainly *Amantes*, published in 1980, reflects a distinctly "lesbian sensibility." "It is a love poem which gets into a new dimension, of the skin, instead of the body. My hypothesis is that since my body is not original or unique—there are and have been many women's bodies—it is collective. I am united with all women. Only my skin is *me*. No one else has my skin. J'ai un corps collectif et un peau individuel. In the years to come I'll concentrate more and more on what can be learned from the skin, from the surfaces. That is an important word for me."

As is "spinning," which became so significant with *L'Amèr*. "The spiral is a form that I see in literature, especially in Gertrude Stein's and Monique Wittig's work. It's a form in which you say something and repeat yourself but in so doing advance a step. It's a very dynamic form of life that you can find from the bottom of the sea to the nebula. I've concentrated in my work on that form, which is related to lesbian sensibility. There's a lot of work to do on this subject and for me it's still an intuition, but I want to explore it. In traditional writing, everything is linear, a 'whole' line, which can be very boring. The formalists questioned this traditional line, breaking it. But it was still a line. You can remake the line by replacing the fragments. Fundamentally, traditional forms don't change. But then comes the form of the spiral and a new dynamic and a new way of relating with the world in your mental space, a new way of being."

Brossard explores in her writing how patriarchy affects women's minds and said that she is now particularly interested in analysing the import of such words as "ideas," "abstraction," and "utopia," and expressing how women themselves have been and still are perceived by men as abstractions. 'In patriarchal minds there is a lack of imagination. They find it impossible and threatening to imagine women together and not simply as symbols. If we go beyond this lack of imagination, we will formulate that new territory, or mental space, where we can be together, producing new ways of existing in a social reality. We must never forget our *anger* at the deprivation women have suffered because of patriarchal attitudes. If we relax too much, we will fall back into patriarchal values. We can do lots of important things in politics, economics, and cultural matters, but if we can't change the patriarchal imagination we'll always lag behind. For example, what drives some male critics crazy in *Amantes* is not the lesbian content but the fact that in that book they don't exist. The fact of not existing for a man is the worst thing that can happen to him. But that is just what men have insisted about women, that they don't exist. We need to legitimate our own existence."

Gradually, Brossard believes, this feminist consciousness is being circulated in Québec and changing the course of literature there. One of the main ways in which this is happening is through such literary activities as Collection Réelles, a feminist fiction and non-fiction series published by Editions Quinze. In the works, for example, are books on the history of women in Québec, one on the Québec patriarchy, and one on women involved in politics in Québec, including the "Yvettes." Like most literature from Québec, this series is not well known or distributed in the rest of Canada because of the language barrier, nor is literature in English well known in Québec. Gradually this situation is improving, owing to the efforts of such small presses as Coach House Press in Toronto, Talon Books in Vancouver, various small literary magazines such as *Room of One's Own* and *Fireweed*, and anthologies such as *Landscape* and Nicole Brossard's *The Story So Far 6*. And there is an expanding network of writers, critics, and translators exchanging information and ideas on both sides of the Québec border. A particularly important occasion on which such an exchange will occur in Toronto later this year will be a conference at York University on criticism and translation of women's writing. (See future issues of *Broadside* for details about this conference.)

But above all, for Nicole Brossard, the essential way in which she is now attempting to transform Québec literature is through her "lesbian sensibility" and it is most appropriate to end this article with her own explanation of how she thinks such a sensibility contributes to shaping contemporary literature:

Lesbian sensibility contributes to shaping contemporary literature by influencing my reading, my thought, my writing. It is needed by all lesbians, visible or not, as well as by any woman questioning "reality." It means exploration, travelling through cities and myths, through memory, through the future, and, of course, this is done through language. And that is a voyage that starts with your skin.

Lesbian sensibility can propel a woman writer in time and space in such a way that she cannot avoid creating a new mental territory with her skin, imagination, and the words that go with them. What is important for me is how reality and fiction are questioned with words and how they can excite the mind in a way that you step into what you thought was unimaginable.

For me, what is working most in lesbian sensibility is the skin. The skin provides the thought and the thought affects the whole surface of the body. It is through the skin that you catch and transmit energy. The skin is tactile memory. It protects your inferiority, your integrity. Your skin works like a synthesizer, transmuting words, emotions, and ideas. We have the imagination of our bodies, of our sex, and most of all of our skin, which synthesize time and space. Imagination is travelling through our skin, all of its surface. A woman's skin sliding on a woman's skin creates a slipperiness in the meaning of words and makes a new version of reality and fiction possible. It gives what I would call a tridimensional vision. It introduces the possibility of understanding how the patriarchal system works subliminally and therefore how it is so effective in hypnotizing women.

Lesbian sensibility shaped Gertrude Stein's Ida, *Djuna Barnes's* Nightwood, *Adrienne Rich's* Dream of a Common Language *and* On Lies, Secrets and Silence, *Mary Daly's* Gyn/Ecology, *and Michèle Causse's* Lesbiana. *It shaped Monique Wittig's work. It is shaping Jovette Marchessault's work. It is shaping my mind and my work every day. And this is contemporary literature.*

Thanks to Coach House Press for providing copies of books by Nicole Brossard translated in their Coach House Québec Translation series; to Giselle Izier for her help in arranging an interview with Nicole Brossard; and especially to Nicole Brossard herself, for an enriching afternoon of conversation and for providing her notes read at the May 1 dialogue.

SYLVIA FRASER:
SURVIVING IN HER FATHER'S HOUSE

Interview by Susan G. Cole

Volume 9, No. 3 (December 1987/January 1988), pp. 8 and 9

Sylvia Fraser has been something of an enigma on the Canadian literary scene ever since she published her first novel, Pandora. *The most mystifying aspect of her work was the sexual content of her fiction. It was violent and shocking, so much so that even when celebrating her craft, reviewers found it necessary to query the point of all the nastiness.*

Now, with the publication of My Father's House, *a novel of Fraser's self-discovery, the key parts of the puzzle have fallen into place. As Fraser tells it, four years ago she realized that she had been sexually abused by her father and only then did she even begin to understand the subtext of her own fiction and the forces that shaped her own life. She began to understand her own motivations for things that she did, relationships that she lost, and she understood that the descriptions of child rape and exploitation that she described so meticulously in her books were the words of an incest survivor trying to come out.*

The key to her survival had been her ability to keep an alter ego functioning, another personality who was the victimized child, a frightened and tormented creature. The alter ego existed only in her father's house, a place she never allowed any of her school friends to visit. Her real self suffered convulsions, interpreted by teachers and other observers as the behaviour of a recalcitrant child, and hated her father for reasons she never could understand. In her adult life she completely buried the experience of sexual assault. During her process of personal revelation, she was able to take herself back to the point at which her personality split, a point at which the child with the secret could exist and could continue to be abused without her conscious self knowing it.

Her decision to write about her experiences and to travel the country promoting the book is a brave one, as any survivor knows. It also resonates for me personally, for I had been one of those reviewers of The Emperor's Virgin *who had slammed Fraser for becoming one of what I referred to as a new breed of pornographers (see Broadside, February 1981). She was furious and wrote an angry letter to Broadside*

(March 1981) in which she denied exploiting anything or anybody. Now that she knows what she knows and has written about it, I realize that I may have been right in my heart but I was wrong on paper. I was wrong in calling Fraser a pornographer, but I was right about The Emperor's Virgin. *It was a document of female subordination: I just didn't know whose subordination was at stake. I certainly didn't know Fraser had been and would continue to write about child rape and male power because she was blocking the truth about her own life.*

She spoke to me while she was in the middle of an intense promotional campaign for My Father's House.

Broadside: You are on the road promoting a book that is more personal than anything you have ever written. Does it feel different from the media work you have done with your other releases?

Fraser: The response has been so positive. I thought I'd have to fight my way through people doubting my statements, doubting that I could remember.

The truth is, I wrote the book on the basis of my own convictions, and with my sister's support. It was only after my mother's death that I got total corroboration. I could hardly help but feel jagged about the timing of my mother's death. I had told her about the book. We had worked it out, but not entirely, and I felt jagged for having stressed out the last part of her life. After the funeral, I listened for the thousandth time about what a saint she was, how much she would be missed—and I knew she would. She was a cheerful woman, always around the Church, looking after other people. Then a man came up to me and said what a wonderful man my father was. That just tripped me right out. Nobody ever thought that about my father.

I began losing my sense of reality, thinking "How do I know this book is true?" Then another man started talking to me about what a hard time my father had given my mother and suddenly it seemed to me that I was having a real conversation. I told him, "I have a desire to tell you something" and he said, "Tell me." I told him that my father sexually abused me and he said, "I knew that, everybody in the neighbourhood knew that." I told him that I had just found out.

Broadside: I don't know if you know this or not, or whether you did any work on the issue before you started writing the book....

Fraser: ...I deliberately avoided all research....

Broadside: ...you have described what we know now is a pattern: the tantrums at an early age, the drawings you discovered in your drawer, the types of drawings that are used now for incest therapy for young children. I was especially interested in how others sexualized you and how surprised you were when that happened. You also write about a number of incidents of victimization at the hands of people other than your father, incidents in which you were paralyzed, unable to react or defend yourself. You write that somehow men could smell your fear. An ignorant person might even say you consented to these things because you didn't resist hard or fast enough.

Fraser: As a child I had a lot of sexuality about me. Our boarder Mr. Brown sensed that. He sensed that I had "victim" written all over me. Also, the split in my personality made things happen in certain ways. All my aggression was in my conscious personality and all my anger. Women are brought up to convert anger into fear and men are brought up to convert fear into anger. It's the social norm. But throughout my life I feel like I was compelled in all my decisions. Everything I did was compulsive.

There are all kinds of pictures of me as a child that show all kinds of seductive details. I was made precocious and seductive. Some power was to be gained by that, despite the price: the power in being the keeper of secrets, and being the other woman in my mother's life. I had learned that there was power in sexuality. When I was in public school, because I was this wretched thing, I turned it around and created myself as a princess. I wrote in *A Casual Affair* a fairy tale that is about as accurate a description as could possibly exist about the scullery maid who thinks she's a princess. I required all the little boys to have a crush on me. It was a requirement. It gave me status among girls even though it wasn't as important as what we girls did together.

Then I got to high school, when that extraordinary thing

happens: what girls think about you doesn't count at all. It's what all the boys think about you. I felt that for my own status and the front I was trying to keep up, I had to keep those sexual feelers going.

Broadside: But then you seemed so surprised that boys saw you that way.

Fraser: Everybody in the movies had bleach blonde or flaming red hair. There were no brown heads in those days. All I did was bleach my hair and that caused a sensation. It was the most damaging thing I could have done. There were other things too. I felt so much sexual guilt, with a reason, so I was attracting reasons to me. I had a set of emotions for something I was blocking out, so I had to create reasons for the sexual guilt. Yes, I knew I was doing it. No, I didn't know I was doing it. I was just frozen in terms of boys. I had to keep attracting them because I went through them so quickly. Only two dates and I couldn't stand to see them again. But I had to keep getting dates, so then I became more blatant. I gave off sexual signals to hide the fact that I was frigid.

There was so much hypocrisy then. The boys whistled at some girls and took out others. The thing that saved me was that I was smart. The cliché was "dumb and sexual and blonde." But I was smart. I was able to maintain a kind of power. I wanted the whole thing to crash at the same time as I was desperate to hold it together. There were so many things operating at the same time that I just lived in a state of confusion. But I really wasn't doing anything. We lived in such a restrictive society. My bust size hasn't changed as far as I know and yet everyone remembers me as having a huge bust. I didn't have a huge bust. It was an image thing.

I've been caught in an image thing all my life, partly of my own manufacture. I paid a lot of attention to appearances. That's a big part of the defence mechanism. As an adult, people would think I was wealthy because I always wore silky stuff or velvety things, but that was still the princess thing. I did it all with trailing robes, but I did it very unconsciously. My hair was blonde: princesses always have blonde hair. It really bothered me when my hair began to go dark. There were textures, furs, off the shoulders. It's all complicated. There was a "me" and a "not me." So the business of wearing the right clothes or having the right hair and a lot of makeup, that was to emphasize the "me." I also had a fear of pregnancy because it would have been a nine month rape. It would have been like having something inside me that I couldn't get out. I now believe I feared pregnancy because my memory would have been too jogged.

Broadside: In fact, you concocted many masks for yourself in order to survive: the princess in your early childhood, the cheerleader in high school, the eye-glassed philosopher in university...

Fraser: ...and then I got married, so the healing had begun. And we were being the best couple on the block. It was somewhat of a mask too, and he enjoyed it. But the reality of the feeling between us was not a mask, and so our relationship was a good one. But it was like re-parenting, though he wasn't like my father. He was more of a mother. In fact, he and my mother were born on the same day and they died precisely six months apart. The launch date for my book was set for September 15 and I thought, "Wonderful, a completely innocuous date." But then they moved it to September 22, which is my mother and ex-husband's birthday. There were a lot more coincidences, but I had to leave them out of the book because I was worried that my credibility, might suffer if I reported them all.

Broadside: It is hard for the people closest to incest survivors to go through it all with them...

Fraser: He wouldn't let me suffer enough. He would only hold me at a level of sludginess. Here is what happens. As long as you are out there struggling to survive on some level, you're fully engaged, and the problem is on hold. But at the point where I would relax and be happy, I couldn't be happy because the little ragamuffin in me, that other child, would come and say "Now it's my turn."

This is why we're so often called neurotic, because when everything is in order and we should be happy, then all those things from the past come to the one in four women [as reported in the Badgeley Report on Sexual Offenses Against Children] who have been sexually abused when they were young. There are depressions. Had I not chosen the route I did, to be a writer and to explore this, I would have spent my life having periodic depressions, being suicidal, being given Valium and being considered neurotic. But something inside me led me deeper. So whenever I had a depression, I went into it.

I did a fundraiser for the Elizabeth Fry Society and asked them what the statistics were in terms of abused women and women who are in jails and they told me it was something like 95%. That blew my mind. I've been quoting that data all over the country. I've now come to the conclusion that incest is the cornerstone of all female self-destructive behaviour. It's like discovering that one virus creates most disease.

Broadside: There are all kinds of incest victims that do not have your survival techniques and who do not become famous writers. That has to do with your gifts and the sacrifices your working class family was prepared to make for you. Can you talk about your process of self-discovery, and when you figured out that there was a victimized child struggling to get out from inside?

Fraser: It started earlier than you might think. My father really did love me. It's a funny thing to say. But at some point I knew my father loved me. It actually made me feel attractive. My home was stable. My mother was a good woman. Everything else was in order. If I had had to move around and change schools I would have been thrown a great deal. But because of the absolute predictability of the environment....

Broadside: But that would have made it harder. The fact that something horrible is going on in the midst of this ordinariness can be very crazy-making.

Fraser: But the split worked. It's called a creative neurosis. I got enough support when I went to school. Boy, was I over-motivated. I was supposed to be smart. My sister had been smart too. I developed a lot of fast social skills. I turned my situation with my father into being a princess, powerful. It was my defence. So I was able to get enough strokes from the environment. The personality I threw up that went to school was almost without fear. Anger I had a lot of, but no fear. All the fear and passivity was in the other personality.

And because the existing personality was so strong, I was able to confine that other personality to my father's house. It never left the house.

Until about four years ago, I thought that I was pretty normal. I had met someone casually with the release of *Pandora* [Fraser's novel about the astonishing and sometimes frightening adventures of an eight year old girl]. A reviewer had said that children were not innocent, that children were seductive at an early age and that women complained too much about this sort of thing. He didn't believe the incident with the breadman in which Pandora is almost attacked but gets away in time. He said all of this in such a smarmy way that my other self instantly caught onto this man and knew that he knew more than he was saying about the situation. The child inside me that knew my secret was a very psychic and intuitive child, always on the alert for ways to survive.

Then I found out that this man was a sexual abuser. So, what my other self knew and what I myself was understanding just came together. In an instant I understood all the codes in my book *Pandora*. It was like a microchip going into a computer. I was ready to remember, or it wouldn't have happened. And if it hadn't happened, something else would have. When I found out that the reviewer was a sexual abuser, I didn't experience it as just an incidence of sexual abuse from a hypocritical man. It took me right back to my book *Pandora*. Suddenly all the metaphors clicked. I felt like a bomb had gone off in my chest. As the conversation continued I just felt stranger and stranger. I got up and said, "I think my father raped me." And as I said that I just knew it was true. I walked home in a state of near euphoria, because suddenly I knew.

I had been dropping in and out of therapy, but I didn't think I had a problem. I was just curious. But I was collecting all sorts of information so that by the time I started to remember the abuse, the last thing I wanted was therapy. I wanted to preserve my own fragile memories. I knew very well that if you go to a Jungian therapist, you dream Jungian. Anyway, I knew enough not to be panicked by what was happening.

It is a huge leap, to think that your father sexually abused you, and then even worse, to face the fact that it went on long after your memories of other things begin. I went four times to a hypnotherapist and every time I went something important happened. I went to a psychic a few times. Once he asked me, "Why does your father look so sad?" and I answered, "Because he sexually abused me until I was five." And he said, "It was a heckuva a lot longer than that, wasn't it." And I didn't react. But that night I went into a state of anxiety and I understood why the images of the child inside my head was so much older than what I would have had to be to fit into my game plan of being abused until age five.

I went to a Freudian therapist too. My dreams were full of incest and they confused me because I knew that I hated my father and that I never would have wanted him to touch me. Well, the Freudian gave me a convenient way to discount what had happened because he had all that Freudian lore about the innocent father and the seductive daughter. I should say though that he got me writing, but he really retarded my deep understanding of what was happening to me.

Broadside: Are there any therapies that you think would work for you now?

Fraser: I always found it easier to believe what I spontaneously remembered. My body was damaged and my head had taken over. My body had been left behind. Doing massage at points where the tension formed brought back memories and culminated in memories I had through convulsions. I think that many incest victims are too far into their heads, so any therapies that work on the body can be useful.

Broadside: You have a lot of compassion still for your father. I was amazed that you could write at the end of your book that "there are no villains here." Through my discussions with others who have read the book I've found out that this may have been the most controversial statement you make. Personally, I feel we have to respect the ambivalences women feel in these relationships. Yet still, I found it hard to accept that after all of this, you don't see your father as a villain. Do you see him as responsible? Blameworthy?

Fraser: I see him as responsible, not blameworthy. As a fiction writer I never would have guessed this, but the irony is that I hated him until I discovered the cause. But as soon as I knew the cause for hating him, my hatred flew out the window. I couldn't have predicted that. I could only see him as pathetic. Another thing I could never have understood unless I had lived through the experience, was that when I regressed back to the point when my psyche had split in two, I actually felt that I caught that moment, and the sense of helplessness was so deep, so bottomless, that I understood why as a child it had been better to become my father's accomplice and to feel that I was in control: I was choosing to be bad. You can't live helpless. Survival demanded that I take that rescue station and identify with his power. Once you've done that, you're forever part of the crime. So as long as you work within the blame system, you're stuck, because you can't help blaming yourself too.

A lot of people who survived the concentration camps felt guilty too, because there was no way to survive except at someone else's expense. Even if it meant just being silent, you had to collaborate to survive. One of the problems with victimization, particularly with incest when it happens to someone so young and the psyche is so unformed, is that it has such a dirty connotation. I don't mean sexual dirty, I mean dirty in terms of guilt. What is happening to me now is that I have become activated on behalf of incest victims, but not projected by any personal anger at all. That's done with.

On the criminal level though, it's the man's crime. I want to make that clear.

Broadside: As you know, in the discussions of incest, mothers are often blamed for not protecting their daughters. Can you tell me how you would react to the statement that your mother was to blame for what happened to you?

Fraser: I feel that my mother was as profoundly split as I. I honestly don't know what she could have done differently. The times were such that even the word divorce—we're talking the thirties and forties—was not spoken. She'd been through the depression with a family that had all sorts of problems. They covered up so much trying to look ordinary. My mother was a fine woman, a compassionate person. She certainly was there for me when I needed her, when I told her. I had a very positive experience. If she had flown at me or attacked me, it would have been really hard. I don't think my mother was prepared to face her own victimization and how deep that was, not just by my father but by life in general. She really hadn't put together a real person for herself, in terms of an identity.

Broadside: What about your writing? I sense that your perspective on it has changed since you've worked through your personal revelations.

Fraser: I began to realize that something had been missing from my writing. At the point when I had my first memories, I was writing *Berlin Solstice*, and I suddenly understood why I was writing the book. I felt embarrassed—that's a light word—that I was writing about a period of time for which so many people paid so profoundly with their own blood and scars. Yet here I was writing about it, and I had a very compelling urge to do so. I understood the literary codes. I understood that I was writing it because my father was German and I had all these dreams of being tortured by Nazis. So I identified with all that sado-masochistic sexuality of the Nazis—the women with shaved heads, stripped naked, and all that leather. I recognized that I was writing the book to study my own victimization.

Broadside: What about *The Emperor's Virgin*?

Fraser: That was about as autobiographical a book as I've ever written.

Broadside: Did you know that at the time?

Fraser: I hadn't the slightest idea. It was written before things came together. The emperor was Daddy of course. As for the vestal virgin who was buried alive for breaking her vow of chastity, at the time I thought that came out of the fifties and that I was making a statement about women in the fifties. But when I think about the guilt the vestal virgin felt because she had enjoyed the emperor's eroticism, and Marcus, the man who was her rescuer, it was obviously a glamorized version of my father and my husband. It was a personalized metaphor, only it was so close that I sealed up without recognizing it.

You and I had an altercation about that at some point. At the time I was accused a lot of exploitation, and it didn't fit. It's extremely difficult to read reviewers who try to impute motive to you, to say you're doing this to make money or to exploit. It didn't feel that way and I had enormous frustration about that. Now I realize that I was not able to write with the depth and insight so close to that which was autobiographical and yet I felt compelled to write it. I knew it was coming from some place deep but I was wordless to explain it.

I stand by the book. I stand by all my books in a certain kind of way, but I recognize that I was running a two-legged race with one leg, because I was compelled to write out of the area on which I was most blocked. It was a tease. My other self would present the topic and then disappear just at the moment when I wanted to close in on it. What I see about *Pandora* now is that I got myself right up to the darkness and then the metaphor went over the edge. I haven't reread everything myself but I'm sure that everything is metaphorically or accurately a portrayal of my new book. *My Father's House* is like the Rosetta Stone of all my other books.

Broadside: So what happens with the next book? Do you feel any pressure?

Fraser: It'll be way off this kind of thing, if I ever write again.

Broadside: Why wouldn't you write again?

Fraser: Because my impulse to write may have been that of the healing; in which case, then I'm healed.

JOYCE WIELAND: SHE SPEAKS IN COLOURS

Interview by Deena Rasky and Barbara Halpern Martineau
Volume 2, No. 7 (May 1981), pp. 13 and 17

The question "Who is Joyce Wieland?" usually elicits responses that range from—"She used to make quilts, didn't she?" to "She made that feature film *A Far Shore* a few years ago" to "Her work is at the Spadina Subway Station."

Her press release material whimsically reminds you that her *Reason Over Passion* quilt is the only Canadian artwork to be destroyed by a living Canadian (Margaret Trudeau) in a marital squabble. Her early underground films from the 60s have been described as "sometimes recalling Manet...and getting the deep ovular splendor of a Carravaggio."

On exhibition last month at the Isaacs Gallery in Toronto, was her most recent work, over 30 coloured drawings themed "The Bloom of Matter." Upon entering the gallery, the senses were enticed by the aroma of hyacinths and the doorway was converted into an arbour of leaves and pussy willows. There were chairs in the centre of the room and a carpet-covered table with copies of her 1971 National Gallery book *True Patriot Love* alongside elaborately framed drawings. The walls had been freshly painted a pale pink. This was no ordinary exhibition.

This *Broadside* interview started by asking Joyce Wieland how she got the idea for this wonderful gallery transformation....

Joyce Wieland: I wanted it to be similar to those pictures of people in the 1880s or so. I went to the studio of Delacroix and I wanted the feeling of one of these old studios. The Grange (in Toronto) used to be like that when I was a kid. Years ago there was a big carpet and a big table where you could sit down. It really gave a focus to the room. The arrangements at the Isaacs Gallery were not exactly what I wanted but with the money and the time that's about all we could do. I just wanted to keep it like a little entrance to a garden, or maybe an exit from a garden. I had a pathway planned, but then I thought, "Well, if there's a lot of people at the opening they wouldn't be able ta observe the path."

Broadside: You have mentioned in the past that you consciously use feminine art forms, whether it's your quilts and sewing or imagery in your films, and this has forced people to take domestic art seriously. Have you found with your recent show that some people have reservations because of the so called feminine content?

Joyce Wieland: Well, not from any woman. But one guy came up to me, hemmed and hawed and said, "It's very pretty...I know I shouldn't say that, but it's very deep, too." Then this guy from the London Free Press said, "People say it's very pretty and feminine, because the colours are feminine."

Broadside: But it's not true. What's feminine about red, yellow and blue?

Wieland: I told him that those are the things everything is made of. I guess if you see those colours, they look sweet to you and if you're a guy, you're likely to pass by.

Broadside: It certainly would seem that a lot of men, and some women, would feel very threatened by the kind of sexuality in your most recent work, mainly because the women are very much in charge of their own sexuality. Usually when an image is in pastel colours, the women are passive. What sort of feedback has there been on this aspect of your show?

Wieland: Whenever I went in there a woman would come up to me and say, "You have a lot of courage to open yourself like this."

Broadside: Your work since the 1950s has dealt with sexual imagery and it's been controversial but it always has been shown at major galleries across the country. Do you think that you would have been able to show your work and have gotten a favourable response if those images had been lesbian instead of heterosexual?

Wieland: I don't know...If I had felt that way about a woman then maybe it would have been all right. You know, maybe people would have liked it. I wonder...

Broadside: On the other hand, the mainstream press has been over emphasizing the sexual aspects of your work, subtitling *The Bloom of Matter* as *The Joy of Sex*, which is hardly accurate. The cohesive elements seem to be that women are all goddesses, or soon to be, that the women are very much a part of the environment.

Wieland: I think the overall feeling was important to me in doing them. The sexuality is there the same way the trees are there. It's a feeling of being able to draw that way…with that wonderful feeling of light. It was a great feeling to put all the things I liked in my life. For the first time everything was fused in light.

Broadside: Some of the drawings would be suitable illustrations for a children's book.

Wieland: I've always wanted to illustrate children's books. In the old days you couldn't get that kind of work. I like story telling. I find I'm happiest in these little stories or vignettes because of their narrative streaks.

Broadside: The drawings you made in connection with *The Far Shore* seemed to be a prelude to this recent show. Exactly how did this work come about?

Wieland: It started by my going to the Arctic and doing a lithograph of the woman Soro Leetutu, and just getting a look at the light there. It's very clear, being able to see the primary on the edge of things. When I came back, I started doing some drawings, I don't know which were the first ones, of this woman who sometimes was a goddess and sometimes was a woman who pointed things out. In the beginning, some of the drawings were very pale. I was knocked out by the paper and what these little pencils were doing, and the kind of light I was working with. I had a big bay window facing south. That's why it's just like a little blush, a little bloom. It didn't matter to me that they were pale.

In the show you can tell which ones are the later ones because they're bursting out more, like in *The Victory of Venus*. In the earlier drawings bands of light would burst the edges, but not the figures.

Broadside: Could you tell us a bit more of what happened in the Arctic and how it came about.

Wieland: I went there because I wanted to do a lithograph. I wanted to ask a woman artist to do a drawing of me, and I would do one of her. It was very idealistic. When I got there I found they cared nothing about me, why I was there, or why I would want to do a drawing. I could not ask her. It had no significance, no meaning to her. I didn't know her, nor would I get to know her unless I spent, a couple of years up there. I simply had the translator ask if Soro Leetutu would pose for me with her baby.

Broadside: How did you choose this woman?

Wieland: I found her work among the stacks of work in the co-op. There were wonderful coloured drawings full of her humour and simplicity, but not too stylized and over-simplified.

Broadside: In your show you have included your bronze pieces from the 1971 *True Patriot Love* exhibit at the National Gallery. In a sense they do lead up to your current work since they have goddess-like qualities. The people in your drawings aren't really people because they have wings, they become animals, they aren't what they seem.

Wieland: They're getting into their environment by becoming part of it. Like *Women in Solution* with their fins.

Broadside: Even your work from the sixties had this quality.

Wieland: Especially the cartoons. The *Lapin du Nord*—the Little Rabbit of the North—had nothing on top, just this little polka-dot skirt. Her boyfriend is Tuktu, the cariboo. It's an anti-American cartoon because it has Shithouse von Whorehead, the guy with the drill who drills for all the minerals. It's really a great story. Then there's Bunny Crazy, and the first drawings of caribou, then the caribou quilt. But it seems like sometimes you think since you're doing serious art you shouldn't let these childhood things come in. This time I have them as "extras." It's almost like a movie, because you'll see that when the man is stabbing the woman on the side there's a rabbit in the foreground.

Broadside: Yet the rabbit doesn't obscure the political message of violence against women in that particular drawing. It clearly speaks of how men, after being confronted with an aggravating situation will turn around and recreate the scene violently when they're telling a woman. She can be the scapegoat.

Wieland: The drawing was about a man I knew who was in a rage, but was unconscious of his aggressive behaviour. Not that he hit me or anything. But I felt like I was being hit by something unconscious. When you're involved with that kind of person you have to get *something* out of it. When rage is unconscious, it's most dangerous because it's a free channel for negativity. At that point the man was an open channel for all negativity funnelling right through him. People don't tend to talk about that drawing.

Broadside: With that one exception, there seems to be a curious lack of any political messages. In 1974 in an interview with Debbie Magidson and Judy Wright you said, "I don't want to just harp on the politics in my art. I want a really sensitive combination of all areas of our life: Canadian independence, northern mysticism, organic farming, sex." Your political meanings are not as obvious as they were in the past.

Wieland: All those things I've worked on separately—like ecology, nationalism, or my feelings as a woman artist—but they are rarely joined. Now they just seem to melt together so that landscapes, flowers and figures all join the light together. For instance, *The Love of Trees* expresses a love of trees, water, magic pools. That's ecology. It's the poetry of nature in an essential form rather than as a statement about ecology...the magic properties of landscapes and glades and pools.

Broadside: That is where you differ from Judy Chicago, a didactic artist whose political message is foremost in her work. Laura Rabinowitz, in her article in the Woman's Art Journal, didn't mention this when she compared you with Chicago, but she does write at length about your Maritime project, which very few people know about. Could you briefly describe what it was?

Wieland: In 1970, when I was working at the Nova Scotia College of Arts, I would go around and meet women who did crafts. I found Jo McGregor's knitting and Valerie McMillan's embroidery. I had the basic design in mind for my project and I looked for the people in local fairs who wanted to try it. I'd draw the mouth for the animated mouths that were embroidered in "O Canada" and someone would send me back a sample. I traced it on a big cloth, then I'd pay her per hour and a portion of the profit. Not that many women were involved. I didn't have time to do it on a big scale.

Broadside: There is a group of women dedicated to bringing the Dinner Party to Canada. If such a group of women were to get together to make a major retrospective of your work, would it be possible to assemble?

Wieland: The Isaacs Gallery has a record of where everything is, so it could be done.

Broadside: Your recent show was open for less than one month. When the Albright Knox Gallery in Buffalo showed Sonia Delauney's work it was up for less than a month too. There should be some way of having a show that lasts.

Wieland: There should be works like mine and others in smaller museums...where people can have access to them, phone ahead or write and say "I want to see that." The big museums are useless to us. I think there should be smaller reservoirs, and more books. If they only had books, then at least people would have lovely reproductions. But in Canada you can only get that if you are a big-time photo-realist.

So few people get credit here for what they've done, whether it's men or women. They have not been given credit. There have been great innovators who are not known anywhere. It's a secret art world, bound and gagged.

Broadside: Is there anywhere you could get the funds needed to get this kind of project off the ground?

Wieland: I don't know how many thousands of dollars would be needed to do a show, but I would like to have a book done of a portfolio.

Broadside: Speaking about money and art...whatever happened to the Diviner film?

Wieland: Judy Steed worked really hard on *The Diviners* film for two years. I was there to discuss things. We had some money together. The basic problem with The Diviners was that it could come off only the way Judy dreamed of, but that would mean a co-production with Hollywood. She went down there and tried to do it. The only way to get a Canadian story across to Canada was to go really big and do a co-production. She really learned the hard way that it's a man's prerogative to make a co-production. It takes going to the meanest backrooms in Hollywood and she couldn't do it. She started losing control of the picture. She did not get to see anyone in Hollywood. The erosion starts with that.

Broadside: So does that mean that the film has been shelved altogether? What's the status?

Wieland: I think we'd hate to say it, but—shelved all together. We don't even talk about it anymore. I don't know if we still have the rights to Laurence's book.

Broadside: You've had a hard time, first with *The Far Shore* and now with *The Diviners*. It's been over five years since the public has heard about you and your work.

Wieland: After *The Far Shore* I got really depressed. I was very sick in the middle of it. My mental state was nil. I soon realized that you don't have to work all the time and I began to take it easy. So I fixed up my house and made a studio the way I wanted it. Then I went to the Arctic.

Broadside: How do you see yourself working in the future?

Wieland: I can see myself just working alone, and on a very small scale. I don't have the energy. It's impossible for me to take any stress; two or three phone calls in a day is enough. I couldn't even look at a larger project. Even if there were grade A producers available, I wouldn't look at it.

Now, to be involved in a small activity, it's not "small" at all. In a way it's shamanistic in the highest way. It can be nourishing to others, even though it's small. It's like a well, if it's good water it's a pleasure to drink from it.

CAN'T FIGHT THE RIGHT WITHOUT FEMINISM:
A POLITICAL PROFILE OF ANGELA MILES, ACTIVIST AND THEORIST

by Eve Zaremba

Volume 3, No. 3 (December 1981/January 1982), p. 5, excerpt

"I don't think (male dominated radicalism) can meet the Right on the ground that feminism has opened up and that the Right, to a certain extent, is occupying and defining at this point. That is to say, without a feminist redefinition of the struggle, what it is about, what it represents, how it must be fought, all that is possible is a defensive coalition with liberal politics. I don't think that 'liberalism' is a bad word the way a lot of people do. But it is a limited form, a defensive forum with a 'civil rights' approach. Nobody wants to deny the importance of civil rights but it is not the same level of

struggle that feminism is about and that a lot of progressive politics has claimed to be about and sees itself as. In other words, there is no alternative vision, no creative offensive response possible. There is no redefinition of questions, so no new politics can emerge. In a sense what I see in the resistance of progressives…in their refusal to see this… in their apparent contentment with retaining old forms of resistance and defensive forms of politics against the Right is to a certain extent a collaboration with the Right."

Influential activist and uncompromising academic Angela Miles.

AN INTERVIEW WITH ANNE CAMERON / "NOW WE GET SOME TRUTHS"

by Jean Wilson

Volume 3, No. 8 (June 1982), p. 12, excerpt

"History books imply that all chiefs were male. The woman whose story will be in the next book lived near Hope, BC. Once Haida warriors, the fiercest on the west coast, were coming downriver to attack this woman's village. She left it, met the raiders, said, 'We're peaceful, we don't want trouble—go home.' They did—but you'd never learn that story in history books. The whole patriarchal ideology denies that women can be shamans, healers, so Indian society as a whole has been misrepresented and women have been downgraded."

LYNNE FERNIE / DESIRE: AN OUT-OF-BODY EXPERIENCE ALTER EROS FESTIVAL

Interviewed by Amanda Hale

Volume 5, No. 6 (April 1984), p. 10, excerpt

"The visual language of our bodies is so corrupted," [Fernie] says, "that it is impossible to use the image of the female body without being misunderstood and falling prey to the voyeur. The secret and invisible nature of lesbian society has protected us from being appropriated by the mass media in quite the same way as heterosexual women. When I attempted to create a visual expression of sexuality between women, I realized that I would be providing information for the voyeur, of whichever gender."

DAPHNE MARLATT AND BETSY WARLAND / TEXT AND TISSUE: BODY LANGUAGE

Interviewed by Ellea Wright

Volume 6, No. 3 (December 1984/January 1985), p. 5, excerpt

DM: …It is important because it's two women talking to each other. When you have one woman and she's talking to the world, it's impersonal. But when you have two women in a dialogue about eroticism….

BW: …about each other, it doubles the vulnerability. I don't think I could have gone this far without that kind of mutuality, because we provoke each other to go places we have often found frightening and dangerous. To be speaking of these things or to be changing the language in this way, to be reading these poems in the Atlantic provinces, say, where you just don't know what's going to happen: it's a lot of unknown territory.

It feels good. If we were a couple and trying to keep that a closeted thing, not only in our work but in public, sometimes I imagine what it would feel like in comparison to who we are and it really terrifies me. I'd much rather name who I am, which I've done in this book. I'd much rather say it publicly to people and say together who we are than to have people say behind our backs who they think we are, in reviews like, "Oh, there's something fishy about these two books, they must be connected." I'd rather take that into my own hands and shape it.

…

DM: …We read our letters before we did the reading because much of the imagery and the concerns of the poems were first sounded in those letters to each other. We wanted to create a space that led into the poems. There's also a difference in the language level. Poetic language is highly charged and it works on many levels at once, whereas language in letters is different. It participates very much in the ordinary every day. The letters are full of clichés, and that's part of the despair when you're, in love. You wind up using the same old worn-out language.

BW: It's really nice that we as feminists, women and lesbians, are creating and evolving a new feminine culture. We don't have a choice. We have to affect the world, if we want to be around in the next ten years. We have to create this culture and get it out to the world. The presence of the female has to be much more profound. One of the things that comes up over and over again among women trying to create culture is that they are still held back by trying to do it in male ways, linear ways. They don't trust that wandering creativity, where they don't know exactly where they're going and they're stuck in paths that seem to be tangential. And they think, "Oh, I shouldn't go there because that's not the project I'm doing, or the piece I'm doing," and they go back to ABCDE. You have to risk not making sense at first. Because you won't. Because when you start producing these kinds of things and talking these ways, it won't make sense right away.

DALE SPENDER—WOMEN AND EXPERIENCE: THEORY OF RELATIVITY

Interviewed by Eleanor Wachtel
Volume 7, No. 9 (July 1986), p. 6, excerpt

EW: What happens when women write—produce literature—in a man-made language?

DS: I think there are always constraints on language. We all have specific experiences in our lives that are difficult to encode—there's very little about death or grief or bereavement. Women are not the only ones who experience this inability to express what's happening to them, but for women it is systematic and it is almost inescapable. The words don't exist; you've got to forge a new concept.

One of the greatest achievements of the women's movement is that we've pulled all our experience together, validated each other and said, "Well, that's quite all right to feel that you shouldn't want two jobs while he has only one—that's quite a legitimate thing to feel." There are still whole areas of women's lives that have no words for them. There is still no word for a sexually healthy woman. There are only two words in the English language to describe women's sexual capacity—frigidity and nymphomania. Which do you want? It isn't much of a choice. We haven't got any words in between. We haven't got any word for women's sexuality that doesn't relate to men. If I want to say, "Excuse me, but I'm a very healthy happy sexually autonomous woman," I've got to go into a lengthy description. Now, men can say they're virile or they're potent and there's no questions asked. It's so much easier for men because their experience has been validated.

...

DS: ...One of the things that really angers me about the novels of the past that have failed to be reprinted is the sense of deprivation that I feel. When I read Maria Edgeworth and Fanny Burney and Anne Radcliffe and Mary Brunton and Charlotte Lennox and Charlotte Smith and Eliza Haywood I was so angry that I'm 42 years of age and I've been reading novels for at least 25 years, so angry to think that I've been deprived of them. Jane Austen and George Eliot have been very important in my life. I've learned an enormous amount from them, and they've been, in a patriarchal society, my yardsticks, they've been my gospels, they've been things I've returned to again and again for validation and verification of women's meanings. To suddenly find that there were 30 more of them, equally important, that I'd been denied access to! It's only natural to build up an enormous resentment, which you can trace to the specific people at different times who quite deliberately eliminated those novels from our literary heritage, usually without having read them, simply on the grounds that they are by women (therefore they are romance, therefore they're not worthy of inclusion). To retain D.H. Lawrence and not call it romantic fiction—my mind boggles. If anybody wrote tawdry love stories, it's D.H. Lawrence. Why isn't that called romantic fiction and classified with Barbara Cartland? That's where I'd put it. I think they're the same genre, but because he's a man, it's in a different category. It's like when women talk politics it's called gossip, when men talk football it's called politics.

DESERT IN THE SNOW:
A CONVERSATION WITH LÉA POOL

Interviewed by Eleanor Wachtel

Volume 8, No. 2 (November 1986), p. 12, excerpt

EW: When you set out to make *La femme de l'hôtel*, did you have a sense of what you wanted to communicate?

LP: Not exactly, but there were two things. I wanted to speak about creation and love, and the link between them. That when you create something, it's very important that you are in love or you expect something from someone. It could also be the lack of love, but it's to fulfill an emptiness that you create. And this is in both my films, *La femme de l'hôtel* and *Anne Trister*. But also, I wanted to make a portrait of a woman using three women (in *La femme de l'hôtel*), three parts—one part, Estelle, is perhaps the most unconscious part of a woman; and Andrea, the filmmaker, is the active part, the creative part, the conscious part of a woman; and the actress is the body.

I used three parts because it's so difficult to make a portrait of a woman in one person; we have a lot of faces. It was an *essai* to try to do this.

KAY ARMATAGE: WORK IN FOCUS

Interview by Hewon Yang

Volume 9, No. 7 (May 1988), pp. 8 and 9, excerpt

HY: Is the future for feminist filmmakers getting better or worse?

KA: I don't see any serious improvement. There seems to be one, two at the most, films made in Canada by women directors; and that has kept a steady pace since the early eighties. And that can't be bad. If women continue to make films, we'll at least have a body of work that we can think about. Whether films have a feminist object is one question. But certainly the work in a lot of feminist film criticism has been on work produced by women—which may or may not be a feminist project. You can also dig for things that will be significant for women readers, women audiences, and certainly will be susceptible to a feminist critique or analysis. Simply a production of a body of work by women has to be part of the feminist platform. Whether or not that work speaks to, for or from, feminism is another question. Ideally, one would wish it to be so.

I've tended to think over the last couple of years that the kind of work that deals most directly with social issues is becoming more and more a province of television, rather than feature films. Television is the ideal medium for that. There's been a surprising amount of feminist work that gets to television, that has some kind of feminist resonance: sensational feature dramas about incest or wife beating. It may not be what we wish from feminist cultural production, but TV can often deal with feminist issues in a way that is accessible to a very wide range of audience: shows like Cagney and Lacey. Social-problem feature dramas, which seem more the staple of television feature drama, are all to the good. I don't see those kinds of subjects being addressed very successfully in theatrical features. Films like *Taking Care*, which was a serious, competent effort, died at the box-office. I would have predicted that it would die in that way. It seemed like a perfect vehicle for television. Even *Loyalties* seemed better suited for television than theatrical distribution. Again, it has to do with the economics of exhibition and distribution. It takes so much money to advertise a film that it all gets in the way of serious work.

…

HY: Do you have any inspiring words for the present or future generation of feminist filmmakers?

KA: From what I can see, there are a lot of women who are committed, working, determined; and it's a question of keeping on, keeping on. I don't think the future will be easy, and I don't think it's getting any easier at all; in some ways, the apparatus that you have to struggle against is getting more and monolithic—particularly in the arts.

I think, though, that there are more women interested in making films, and more women who are not dismayed at the prospects of the struggle of filmmaking. I don't think they need words of inspiration. I don't think inspiration is really the issue. I think the more important issue that we have to work hard at is support: bringing other people along, helping each other out, working with each other, making sure that other women get attention, get grants, get their films shown. All that kind of work: the networking work. The old girls' network is really important. And it's absolutely necessary because I don't think it can happen without that. I don't think we throw one woman out there and let her sink or swim.

That's really the reason I continue at the Festival of Festivals year after year. It's really important for women's work to be emphasized, to be exhibited and given a prominence.

Hewon Yang is a student in Women's Studies at U of T, currently doing a placement at Broadside.

Broadside

A FEMINIST REVIEW

August/September 1987 Volume 8, number 10 $1.7

Bergman's 'Nora' at Stratford. SEE STORY PAGE 8.

INSIDE BROADSIDE

NEWS

FUTURE ON LOAN? Single parents are now being refused student loans in Ontario, in an attempt to "protect" them from too big a debt load. A Kingston group has protested the patronizing approach which adversely affects many women. Maureen Latta reports. Page 3.

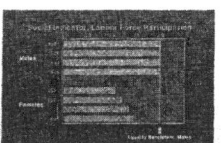

GRAPHIC EQUALIZER: The progress of women's equality is usually measured in relation to past performance, not in relation to men. An Ontario government report shows how much slower change is when an equality benchmark is used. Page 4.

ACCESS TO ASYLUM: 80% of the world's refugees are women. Many leave home and get no further than border camps. Once a new country takes them in, they are isolated and unprotected. Betty Bresko reports. Page 5.

MOVEMENT MATTERS: Read about The Woman's Common activities; about *Rites* magazine's summer benefit; about a conference on women working in the non-profit sector; about abortion rights in Ireland; and more. Pages 6 and 7.

OUTSIDE BROADSIDE: Don't miss *Broadside*'s calendar of Toronto women's events, for August and September 1987. Page 11.

ARTS

LOVE & HONOUR: Many of the Stratford Festival's plays focus on war and the concept of male honour which is one of its causes. There is also a remake of Ibsen's *A Doll's House* which poses different concepts of honour as the cause for the breakdown of Nora's marriage. Reviewed by Margaret Gail Osachoff. Page 8.

TICKET TO THE WORLD: Holly Near talks about her life as a musician, and the

connection between her music and politics: "Being a musician makes it easier to determine what one's contribution to social change is going to be." Page 9.

MADONNA OR WHORE? Many feminists will be horrified, but Susan G. Cole sees pop star Madonna as a symbol of women's power, not sex. And she compares her to tennis champion Martina Navratilova! Page 10.

Terry Jenoure at the BamBoo, Sept. 29

CHAPTER 5

The Arts: Reviews & Reports

Throughout history, art was not necessarily viewed as political and many artists considered themselves to be above the political fray. For the most part, they acceded to their patrons' demands, enjoying their status and the opportunity to flaunt their virtuosity. Were they interested in changing the world? Not so much. In fact, when art did become overtly political—through the movement for social realism, for example—the work was often criticized as too didactic and not quite beautiful enough.

Feminism helped throw a wrench in that dynamic. For one thing, we began to engage in critical analyses of the economic structures that influenced artistic creation: who paid to get it made (mainly royalty, wealthy patrons, and the church); what that patronage inevitably meant about the product (religious representation and reflections of male pursuits); and who had access to artistic training (mostly men). But more significantly, women artists began to create their own gorgeous work in the pursuit of social change.

There were three main strands to *Broadside*'s mandate when it came to the arts: to apply feminist thinking in reviews of mainstream arts and entertainment; to acknowledge and analyze the means of artistic production; and, most importantly, to shed light on female artists—most of them feminist-identified—who were not getting their due in mainstream media.

The written word, of course, has been a life force for the feminist movement and *Broadside* always featured a healthy number of book

Poster for the very vibrant third International Feminist Book Fair, Montreal, 1988.

reviews. We ran reviews of books that have become feminist classics: Mary Daly's *Gyn/Ecology*; the collection of writings by women of colour *This Bridge Called My Back*; and Carol Gilligan's *In A Different Voice*. *Broadside* also reconsidered books that had become classics before we began publishing: Kate Millett's *Sexual Politics* and Simone de Beauvoir's *Second Sex*, both of which are reviewed here. We've also included reviews of two books that sparked intense debates: *Coming To Power* and *Pleasure and Danger*.

We considered covering only Canadian writers and artists. At the time, women dominated Canada's fiction scene—we do include in this chapter a review of Margaret Atwood's *The Handmaid's Tale*— and Canadian feminist theory was a powerful force. Read Meg Luxton's *More than a Labour of Love* (under one of our best headlines ever: Who Did Marx's Laundry?) and Mary O'Brien's *The Politics of Reproduction*. But in the end, though our news and Movement Matters issues focused mostly on Canadian developments, when it came to the arts, we knew our feminism had to cross borders. Our literary coverage often introduced readers to new issues, as was the case in our important review of *Voices of the Nisei*, a book by Japanese women writers who were among the first to write about Canada's internment of Japanese living in Canada during World War II.

Theatre written, produced, and performed by women grew exponentially throughout the 1980s and we gave it ample attention. We reviewed, among other works, many productions by woman-centred Nightwood Theatre, a company that helped launch some of Canada's most distinguished playwrights, as well as shows by the fabulous Clichettes and Shawna Dempsey's memorably hilarious performance installation *Talking Vulva*.

During *Broadside*'s lifespan, feminist visual art made spectacular inroads through works from artists such as Lynne Fernie, Frances Loring and Florence Wyle, and the legendary Joyce Wieland, all of whom we revisit in this chapter. These artists were fearless, determined to shake things up. Many of them were censored because of it. Look at what happened when a creative team placed an installation featuring what looked like a used tampon in the window of Pages Bookstore. Or how our national airline reacted when Fernie displayed a giant billboard on a Toronto street with the pixelated message "Lesbians Fly Air Canada."

Because of the mammoth financial demands of its production, cinema was one of the most difficult areas of the arts for women to penetrate. But thanks in part to the National Film Board of Canada's Studio D, women made powerful documentaries (among them, *Not A Love Story* and *P4W*, also reviewed here). Crucial to the visibility of women filmmakers was the Festival of Festivals—now called the Toronto International Film Festival, or TIFF—which, under the influence of programmer Kay Armatage, screened scores of groundbreaking movies during the 1980s. *Broadside* gave an additional boost to this work through our excellent film review team, including Barbara Martineau and Donna Gollan, who reported on the festival annually. Among the most memorable of these films were Donna Dietch's *Desert Hearts*, based on Jane Rule's *Desert of the Heart*, that thrilled lesbian audiences; Agnès Varda's *Vagabond*; and Marlene Gorris's *The Silence of Christine M*, which went into wide release as *A Question of Silence*. This last film underlined the failure of the justice system to deal with sexual assault and still has a powerful resonance today.

On the music scene, Olivia Records was going strong, releasing records by feminist and lesbian artists. Among the most successful of the artists was Holly Near, who was interviewed in *Broadside*'s pages. And for the record, we covered the great Canadian dub innovator Lillian Allen long before she scored her Juno award.

While showcasing rising female talent was a priority for *Broadside*, we never lost sight of the importance of critical thinking

Dub poet and musician Lillian Allen, flanked by Arlene Mantle (left) and Rita MacNeil, performs at Our Time is Now.

about the arts in general. We reviewed Rina Fraticelli's pivotal report on women's place on theatre stages in Canada; Kate Lushington's wide-ranging essay on feminist theatre; and Susan Crean's article "Fine Arts & Patriarchy," reprinted here, that addresses the barriers that thwarted aspiring female artists.

A number of celebrated Canadian-based writers made significant contributions to our pages—a testament to the fact that feminist ideas and magazines like *Broadside* that promoted them were important to our most accomplished authors. Mary Meigs reviewed May Sarton's *At Seventy*; June Callwood reviewed the essential collection from the Women's Press *Still Ain't Satisfied*; and Margaret Atwood offered a sly review of a Harlequin Romance.

Much of what we published on the arts reflects *Broadside*'s commitment to producing alternative takes on mainstream phenomena. We couldn't ignore movies like *Norma Rae* and *Nine to Five*, which featured strong female characters. But, closer to home, how could we go the Stratford Festival in Ontario without expressing outrage at the abusive amusements of *My Fair Lady* and *The Taming of the Shrew*, reprinted here. We even published a review by Judith Quinlan of the most popular book on the planet—the Bible.

Taken all together, it's an impressive array and the reprinted articles in this chapter represent only a small fraction of *Broadside*'s coverage of the arts, which in turn could never come close to covering the explosion of women's artistic output in the 1980s.

Susan G. Cole

SIZZLERS FROM OUR SISTERS

by Susan G. Cole

Volume 2, No. 4 (February 1981), p. 15

The December 1980 issue of *Playboy* magazine features a remarkable article on the subject of sexual office politics. The article is inspired by the presence of a new phenomenon in the corporate board room—women, and according to the author, these female executives are as hungry for sexual clout as they are for corporate influence. Whereas the subtitle for the piece is "A Guide for the Eighties," it is no such thing. There is no "how to" here, because no matter what strategies the male underling may employ, he simply can't win: you see, the difference between male and female executives is that men will trade a few perks for sexual favours. Women, on the other hand, won't bargain one for the other. They want sex *and* power. *Playboy* readers are left with the terrifying news that the female aggressor, the one who knows her sexual needs and goes about getting them met, has power and is here to stay.

Where did she come from? She certainly wasn't around in the sixties when the sexual "revolution" dictated that any sexual reluctance on the part of women be construed by the rejected male as a sign that women were repressed and not "ready" for liberation. She is without doubt a post-feminist consciousness phenomenon, a product of the ideology that gave to women a sense that sex ought to be for us too, that there were many ways for us to define our own sexuality and that we could not only say no, but we could even say "Come to bed" and take some initiative.

In a way, Erica Jong has to bear some responsibility for the new sexual image of women. Her first book *Fear of Flying* sent shock waves through the literary establishment and the reading public because the heroine Isadora Wing couldn't get enough sex. The insatiable female per se isn't an original concept but she is usually the product of a male writer's imagination. Never had the craving for sex been the confession of a best-selling female author—and it was astounding. I for one found the book refreshing and Jong smart, particularly for having come to the conclusion that the elusive and now famous zipless fuck is in fact nothing but rape.

Irrespective of the novel's virtues, its author, having given us Isadora Wing, gave birth to a monster that multiplied with the help of less gifted and clever writers. Erica Jong gave way to a host of other randy female authors who wrote of their sexual adventures with painstaking and boring detail. The proliferation of sexual confessions prompted Gore Vidal to comment bitchily but astutely in his throwaway novel *Kalki* that, "In their fictions, Jewish princesses tried to become Jewish princes. The result was not erotic. They tried to describe the genitals of men in the same way that they thought men described those of women," and "Where the true shape of the scrotum was not possible to describe upon the page…the preparation of shrimp ramoulade, a lobster salad, a sumptuous casserole served on Royal Crown Derby." No doubt Vidal refers here to food critic Gael Greene's *Blue Sky No Candy*, a catalogue of sexual exploits the foreplay for which usually takes place in a restaurant over rich food. Greene's is possibly the most offensive of this new genre of books written by women who, along with their editors, think that someone cares about the quality of their orgasms.

The celebration of an author's wantonness is one thing. The fact that the rendering of random lust has become pornographic is quite another. It is no coincidence that *Playboy* is warning its readers against female sexual aggressors while female writers are writing about aggressive and violent sex with utter glee. *This* is new—pornographers, female, on the bestseller list.

I use the word pornography in the way we're accustomed to using it, defining it as an attitude toward human sexuality wherein women are exploited and reach sexual frenzy not through communication with another human being but through the mechanistic manipulation of one or more erogenous zones. Variations are essential be they on the numbers and sexes of sexual participants or on the myriad external aids the pornographer can dream up. Pornography usually blends sex with violence.

Pornographic literature is that which focuses so totally on sexual and violent events that development of character is secondary to the descriptions of characters' sexual proclivities and/or penchant for violence. Plot exists simply as a means of moving from one sexual orgy to the next. A pornographer philosophically committed to his or her task is the true sexual objectifier, so able to remove sex from any other human endeavour, that he or she becomes obsessed with the Essence of Fuck (or Brutality, or a combination of both).

Sylvia Fraser's latest novel, *The Emperor's Virgin*, careens from dismemberment to decapitation to rape to bestiality to gladiatorial orgies of violence in so breathtaking a way as to suggest that Fraser is a pioneer among the new female pornographers. So taken was Fraser with her subject matter, the rule of the tyrannical Emperor Domitian of Rome in 95 AD, that she rigorously researched the daily life and ritual of the crumbling Roman Empire. Her descriptions are as accurate as they can possibly be. All the correct numbers of people are in the arenas or in the parades and they are dressed just as they would have been in Roman times. It's still pornography. Fraser's attention to detail simply makes it well-researched pornography.

The pornographer's formula demands scene after scene depicting sex and violence of a fringe nature culminating in the ultimate fuck, usually between the only two (or more) people in the book worth rooting for. So it goes in *The Emperor's Virgin*. Penises are lopped off, horses decapitated, young boys buggered against their will and then finally the hero Maximus Marcus, the defender of what was Rome's greatness, and Cornelia, a priestess of the Temple, couple ecstatically—a welcome relief from the castration and subjugation that characterizes the book. This change of pace is what is called in the trade "redeeming social value." Even so, Fraser can't capitulate to romance and has Maximus and Cornelia going at it in the mud. Fraser's point in writing the book, one assumes, is to say that she can write about brutality as well as her brothers and has the formula down as securely as any pornographer.

But Erica Jong purports to be a feminist and so the pornographic content in her recent novel, *Fanny: Being the True History of the Adventures of Fanny Hackabout-Jones*, is all the more unsettling. *Fanny*, written in Fieldingesque style complete with capitalized nouns and archaic language usage, has a plot and some insightful feminist analysis of the lot of women in eighteenth century England, but it gets lost amidst the fucking and sucking. Like Fraser, Jong scoured libraries and archives to ensure verisimilitude. If it is any consolation, meticulous research, it seems, will be the hallmark of the new pornography. The raison d'être of the first two hundred pages of Jong's latest novel is the account of Fanny's sexual development. Remember the pornographic formula: no healthy straight ahead communicative love-related sex until the very end where Jong delivers with a rollicking foursome. But first Fanny is deflowered by her step-father, ravished by a dwarf, led into a wham bam thank you ma'am threesome (two women, one man), then a fivesome (four women, one man and a dildo). She becomes acquainted with bondage, drag queens, and so on until she has become an all around good lay. Jong's goal is to provide a treatise on prostitution, and she uses pornography to achieve it.

There is a brief respite during which Jong pays some attention to other aspects of the plot but then we are back to defecation and water sports. Jong, who is no dummy, senses that maybe there's something wrong here and writes an apology for her chronicles, protesting thus:

> For tho' I wish neither to inflame nor to disgust by writing of my Life with all its Vicissitudes, yet I *must* assume—or I would not have chosen this perilous Profession of Scribbler—that describing Vice is oft' the best guarantee of future Virtue, whilst describing Virtue is no Guarantee against the powers of Vice.
>
> Many foolish and credulous Folk believe the Opposite. They accuse the Chronicler of Vice as if he were the *Creator* of it;…Do they not understand that we Scribblers must scourge the World to bring it to its senses? Do they not understand that an Author doth not necessarily *approve* the Sins his Love of Truth causes him to chronicle?…

The lady doth protest too much methinks. Or better put: Who are you kidding, Erica?

We can certainly give Jong the benefit of the doubt and say that she doesn't approve of all these bedroom shenanigans, but whereas female pornographers don't celebrate the acts they describe as male writers often do, one gets the disturbing feeling with both Jong and Fraser that they are taking some pleasure in donning the mantle of the pornographer. In short, they are getting off. It's pretty clear that Jong wants to perpetuate her lascivious reputation. *Fear of Flying* started it. *Fanny* is bound to keep her reputation intact. Fraser's earlier novels promised something like *The Emperor's Virgin*. It remains to be seen whether she'll challenge Jong as the premier female pornographer.

There are some who may approve of the fact that women are

encroaching on otherwise male territory. There was something about that Playboy article that made me laugh and think that the female sexual terrorization of men at the office, or Playboy readers at the office, could have a temporary salutary effect. These female execs have nerve anyway. But I doubt that sexual bullying will have a long term positive impact on women.

Similarly it could be argued that Erica Jong and Sylvia Fraser are gutsy writers, taking risks and willing to explore where other female writers dared not tread. Many of us believe that there are so few female pornographers because "women don't think that way." Well, they can and do and Fraser and Jong prove it. Whether theirs is a noble pursuit is another matter entirely.

EMPEROR'S VIRGIN: FRASER'S VERSION

by Sylvia Fraser

Volume 2, No. 5 (March 1981), p. 18

I am writing in response to your article "Sizzlers from Our Sisters" (February 1981) in which Susan G. Cole discusses my novel, *The Emperor's Virgin*, along with *Fanny* by Erica Jong. I offer it in the spirit of dialogue, rather than out of any burning sense of injustice.

For the *Broadside* record: I decided to write a novel set in Imperial Rome, first century AD, because I was attracted to the true story of the vestal virgin, Cornelia, who was buried alive for breaking her vow of chastity. Like many Canadian women who came of age in the 50s, I was so blighted by society's punitive emphasis on female "purity," that today I consider virginity to be the vilest word I know—sexist, manipulative, tyrannical. The real fate of Cornelia, a woman of Rome, therefore, became, for me, a powerful personal symbol.

As the only woman with formal power in the patriarchic system of Rome, Vestal Cornelia was a precursor to the liberated career woman, but only at the price women have traditionally been forced to pay: She had to swear chastity, thus trading off her personal life for external power. During the middle ages, when heads of priories became powerful in Europe, the exacted price remained the same: chastity. In this century, that deal has gradually become more psychological than legal, civil or papal. The suffragettes were ridiculed as mannish, asexual battleaxes—i.e., no "real" woman would want the things they were demanding, and no "real" man would want them! In the fifties, a girl who yearned to be a doctor instead of a nurse, was warned she would lose her femininity, meaning her chance to marry—a personal life foresworn in favor of mucking about in the male world.

In other ways, Imperial Rome offers a fertile challenge to the modern imagination. While much like ourselves, with the same root traditions, the Romans rode their primitive instincts to unhypocritical conclusions: Instead of boxers with gloves, promoters fielded gladiators with swords. Instead of influence peddled on the sly, their politicians proudly advertised it. Instead of a pretence of equal justice for all, their lawyers based court pleadings on superior birth and rank. In many ways, to write about Rome, is to dramatize, satirize, caricature—and thus take responsibility for—ourselves.

This violence, openly espoused, is tough on squeamish modern sensibilities: How does an author make it palatable? The usual solution is to filter the gore through the sensibilities of a character who is brighter, or wittier, or more humane than the rest, so the reader can view, even enjoy, the carnage from the vantage of borrowed intellectual/moral superiority. In my view, that's a dangerous copout. Though I *did* cut down on the violence of the historical record, I did not launder it or offer readers that cosy refuge.

Another writer's problem: Sex, leaning toward the kinky and violent, was a court preoccupation—the natural result of a system which represses the softer emotions as weakness. In the first drafts of my novel, I implied sex through the time-honoured asterisk and whitespace. Again, I decided this was a copout. In the finished version, there are quite a few sexual descriptions, but they are no more numerous or intrusive than my descriptions of buildings, food and clothes, and they are detailed in the same deadpan style. That is deliberate.

An important theme of *The Emperor's Virgin* is that of evil in power: What do decent people do when the highest authority is in itself corrupt? This, of course, is the theme of Watergate, played out in blood (as the Romans were wont to do) rather than in bribery, thievery and knavery (as modern North American politicians are wont to do).

Since Susan G. Cole poses as having read my book, one might have expected her to notice some of these things. Unfortunately, she was too intent on gleefully expounding a thesis she gleaned from *Playboy*, December 1980: That women will no longer trade off sex for power, since they now want both. Which brings us to the marvellous irony of Cole's "review": That is exactly the theme spelled out in the tragedy of Vestal Cornelia, executed because she dared to want sexual feeling as well as public power, yet Cole, in the spirit of one who refuses the food so she can continue to complain about the service, sees the book as illustrating only that women, too, can be sexually aggressive. She thinks the author has written it to prove "she can write about brutality as well as her brothers," and she confides candidly to her audience that she suspects I am "getting off" on it.

Such wilful glibness takes my breath away. Does Cole believe I could write 366 pages of scenes ranging "from dismemberment to decapitation to rape to bestiality to gladiatorial orgies" without understanding that I have written a horrifying book? Does she imagine I don't know how much more marketable the book could have been if I had filtered all that unpleasantness through the consciousness of a despot rendered lovable, as Robert Graves did in *I, Claudius*? Does she think that, after twenty years as a writer, I fail to grasp that what really sells in the Canadian market is Harlequin Romance—50s style titillation without come-across? Dismemberment, decapitation, rape, *are* brutal. What makes Cole think I am too stupid to notice that? What gives her the right to assume there is only one moral conscience between us, and that she possesses it?

One last problem: Cole says, "I use the word pornography in the way we're accustomed to using it, defining it as an attitude toward human sexuality wherein women are exploited and reach sexual frenzy not through communication with another human being but through the mechanistic manipulation of one or more erogenous zones." Defining the word only in terms of women, and so broadly it seems to include masturbation, is a weird one to me.

Presumably, it reflects a feminist bias. My own overview of sex is Reichian. I believe Wilhelm Reich was right in his biological definition of sex as being the healthiest way humans deal with stress (though I hasten to state that is not *all* he/I think it is). I also accept his more controversial political thesis, that the most effective way for a government to control a population is through control of the sex drive, usually by manipulation of female sexuality. Therefore, I consider sex to be a vital theme of artistic, sociological, psychological, scientific inquiry, whether or not this intrudes upon someone else's definition of pornography. The desire of some feminists to ban sexual expression that offends their politics, or even their humanity, opens the door to a new puritanism as dangerous to women as the old stuff, since it is always women's sexual organs that are clamped, cut off, scooped out, declared sacred.

I hasten to add that Cole does not suggest, or even imply, such restrictions. My quarrel with her is in the simplistic way in which she applies labels, thus reducing the world—and especially the world of women, since that is her province—to her own perceptions. Like many otherwise intelligent writers, brought up on the heady permissions of personal journalism, Cole is in danger of considering her opinions superior to that about which she opines by virtue of her having typed them out for us. Like many well-intentioned young women, born into a time when feminism is not only possible but well-supported, she lacks a historical sense. Since the world began the day she opened her eyes, and is filtered solely through her experience of it, the sensibilities of a woman who lived 1900 years ago in Rome, or one who was born twenty years before her, are outside her easy grasp. *Playboy*, December 1980, is more likely to be where it's at.

Few novelists attempt to write about how things should be; rather they write about how they seemed to be, to certain people, at a certain time and place. I do not write un-flawed books, but neither do I write stupid or amoral ones. For some readers, my intentions in *The Emperor's Virgin* have miscarried; for others, they have not. With sisters like Susan G. Cole, who needs brothers?

Carole Conde admires the Women's Cultural Building flag.

Women's Cultural Building— Building is a verb here.

FESTIVAL OF FESTIVALS:
REELING FROM THE FESTIVAL

by Barbara Halpern Martineau

Volume 3, No. 1 (October 1981), pp. 12 and 13

*A feminist takes the standpoint of women. That is, we begin from
this place and it is the place where we are…we begin with ourselves, with our sense of what we are, our own experience.*
— Dorothy Smith, *Feminism and Marxism*, 1977

Toronto's mighty film festival struck me more than ever this year as
a microcosm of our society, based on the principles of big business,
willing therefore to accommodate anything at all, provided it serves
the ends of the festival: i.e., to attract wealthy and/or influential persons, sell tickets, increase festival prestige, harboring, therefore, an
infinity of contradictions. At the gala presentation of *Man of Iron*,
the Polish film by Andrzej Wajda which documents the struggle
for workers' rights in a "workers' state," the balcony of the Elgin
cinema was ostentatiously reserved for "VIP passes and the Press,"
solely, I gathered, so that those who Mattered could distinguish
each other from the Mass. The contradictions, as always, come in
layers—Wajda's film, strong and uncompromising in its solidarity
with the workers, is equally strong in its defense of the Catholic
Church and the institution of the nuclear family, and the character
used to make this point is a young woman film maker, who finds
happiness and fulfillment (after she has been fired from her job) in
marriage to the film's hero and in motherhood. (Hey Maria, I think
we've been shafted again!)

A story of two films:
1) On Friday, September 11, at 1:30 pm *P4W: Prison for Women*,
a 75-minute documentary by Toronto film makers Janis Cole and
Holly Dale, camera Nesya Shapiro, sound Aerlyn Weissman, shot
in the Kingston Prison for Women and produced for a total cost of
$43,000, had its "World Premiere" at the Towne Cinema. Present
in the audience were several of the women who appear in the film,
either released since then or out on day passes.

This is no ordinary "prison film" or "women's film." P4W is a dramatic, very touching portrait of five women you're not likely to forget.

—Festival program

Audience enthusiasm and rave reviews from Toronto critics led to Pan Canadian picking up the film for distribution in Cineplex theatres across Canada. *P4W* is a strong film, designed to bring the audience closer to the lives of the women, to establish first their humanity, strength, humour, and grace, and then the inhumanity of their incarceration, an inhumanity which is not immediately apparent from surface observation of their lives. They wear their own clothes, eat cafeteria-style, argue wittily and with energy about prison politics, decorate their narrow cells with cushions, dolls, photographs. Only as the women talk, tell their lives, why they are in, what being in means to each of them, only then does the true narrowness of prison life sink in. The photographs change meaning as we learn of children not seen for years, of husbands, lovers, family. The picture on the wall behind Janis is of Janis' lover, Debbie, who is there in prison with Debbie, but soon will leave, and Janis will be left to serve years and years more, for a crime she never com- mitted, that no one imagines she committed, for having been present when her husband committed a crime and then died, and she was the only one left to take the rap. Another woman makes a video tape for her daughter, and we watch first her, then her on the monitor, as the child would see her, a lined, fuzzy picture of Mummy smiling, play- ing her guitar, singing for the daughter she can't see or hug.

I talked with Holly Dale about the unexpected success of the film, asking what she hoped might come of it for the women in the Kingston pen. She is trying to get a review of Janis' parole sit- uation, and will get back to anyone who calls her at 416-964-2892, and would like to help in this attempt. She believes that a successful review would establish an important legal precedent.

The only serious shortcoming I see in *P4W* is the absence of discussion about what the Kingston pen means to women prisoners in Canada—closing that pen down, which has been frequently pro- posed, would mean that women would serve their sentences in much worse provincial facilities, isolated from other women, without any of the programs (woefully inadequate as they are) available to them in Kingston. It would be a shame if the film were to encourage that reaction in viewers.

One very heartening audience response to the film so far has been the sympathy and warmth expressed towards Janis' relationship with Debbie, probably the first time a lesbian relationship has been shown in Canadian film to be positive, nurturing, based on mutual need and caring. It is clearly a tragedy for Janis that she is losing Debbie, and the audience takes it that way. *P4W* is a strong example of the evolution of an objectifying cinema-verité into cinema-intimacy, cinema-respect, cinema-compassion.

The true subject of pornography is not sex or eros but objectification, which increasingly includes cruelty, violence against women and children…The intensification and proliferation of pornography in our time can be associated with deeply repressive patterns of political violence, such as witch burning, lynching, pogroms, fascism.
—Adrienne Rich, "Afterword," *Take Back the Night*, 1980.

"I find the use of human beings as objects pornographic," replied producer Dorothy Todd Henaut, thus throwing into question the whole idea of having movie starts, or, for that matter, movies.
—Ron Base, Toronto *Star*, Sept. 14, 1981.

Not a Love Story…it's an example of bourgeois, feminist fascism.
—Jay Scott, *Globe & Mail*, September 7, 1981.

"Male bile sullies film about porn"
—headline for Michele Landsberg's column, Toronto *Star*, September 15, 1981.

2) On Friday, September 11, at 1:30 pm *Not a Love Story: A Film About Pornography*, has its sole festival screening at the Festival cinema. A 70-minute documentary from Studio D of the National Film Board of Canada, produced by Dorothy Todd Henaut, directed by Bonnie Sherr Klein and Anne Henderson, camera Pierre Letart, sound Yves Gendron (with a crew of many more), for a budget not

publicly released, *Not a Love Story* was received enthusiastically by a packed house and panned, dumped on, bitterly attacked by the little boys who pretend to be film critics in Trona the Good.

Because the festival had cautiously asked for only one screening of *Not a Love Story* the Censor Board held them to it; the film was not re-screened, although hundreds had been turned away. It is not (at press time) known whether the Board will approve further Ontario screenings of the film, which is certainly not, contrary to the hysterical accusations of the reviewers, pro-censorship. The film in fact suffers from its lack of a clear stance with regard to censorship, but the use of porn within the film and the inclusion of several comments by feminists about the need to see and talk about what we would condemn seems to me to make the anti-censorship position of the film makers apparent, if not strongly so.

I was most impressed by the film's presentation of Susan Griffin's point, elaborated in her book *Pornography and Silence*, that pornography itself acts as a censor, silencing women, showing women bound, gagged, voiceless, impotent. This is the analysis of and response to pornography I have heard. No confusion, ban the censor board, abolish censorship, ban pornography. Pornography censors women. Pornography can be defined as the portrayal of human beings in physical subjugation for the purpose of titillation, and banned. Using such material for educational or artistic purposes, as in *Not A Love Story*, is fine. The sole criteria for prosecution would be intent—to titillate with violence is unacceptable. Any sane society, surely would see and agree with this.

We do not live in a sane society.

I wish *Not a Love Story* were a better film. I wish those women from Studio D of the National Film Board of Canada had included some Canadian feminists in their film, instead of relying entirely on Americans, wonderful as those Americans are. What a golden opportunity to validate the contributions of Canadian women to feminist thought, women such as Mary O'Brien, Dorothy Smith, Nicole Brossard, Edna Manitowabi, Rosemary Brown...And they blew it. Better still, I wished they had skipped the on-camera interviews and focussed more steadily on the porn industry and its effects, using the perceptions of feminists as a guide rather than as an element within the film. There is no suggestion within the film of possible constructive action to take; and the porn shown is mild, deceptively mild, whereas violent, sadistic pornography accounts for more than half of the market. I wish it were a better film, as it is; *Not a Love Story* should be seen widely, discussed in depth, certainly not censored.

Certainly not censored.

On October 6 *Not a Love Story* is scheduled for another Toronto screening at Town Hall, followed by a panel discussion on pornography. This is the proper context for the film—it would be an outrage if such an event were blocked by the Censor Board.

Other scheduled screenings in Canada: Montreal, October 9; Calgary, October 20; Edmonton, October 22; Saskatoon, October 26; Winnipeg, October 28, 29; Halifax, November 15; Vancouver, to be confirmed. Local NFB offices will have details of place and time.

[Janis Cole and Holly Dale] produced a documentary so honest it makes the National Film Board's Not a Love Story: A Film About Pornography look even sicker than it is.
—Adele Freedman, *Globe & Mail*, September 10, 1981.

It was unfortunate that the festival scheduled *P4W* and *Not a Love Story* opposite each other, unforgivable that the press used that error of judgement to play one film against the other, praising *P4W* at the expense of *Not a Love Story*, with not a shred of recognition that the subject matters interrelate, that it is the same system which imprisons and isolates women unjustly, which objectifies and degrades us for profit. We need many films about the issues which concern us, many films expressing our different viewpoints.

Within a feminist context, there are some valuable lessons to be learned from a comparison of the two films. The women in *P4W* clearly knew and trusted the film makers (all women, minimal crew), but the film makers are never shown on camera—their experience is not central to the film. Had neither film makers nor theorists been shown in *Not a Love Story*, and had their perspective been more clearly conveyed by the film, I think much of the critics' ammunition for derision would have been defused.

The filmmakers give us...Robin Morgan bawling (literally) about how hard it is for her—a thinking, sensitive, radicalized woman—to get along in society.

—Jay Scott, *Globe & Mail*

If it was contemptible of Jay Scott to sneer at Robin Morgan's tears, and I think it was contemptible, it was not wise of the film makers to include her tears in their film, not that emotion in unacceptable, but that the grounds for her emotion haven't been built filmically. Robin Morgan cries for an idea, and her husband and son hold her hands for support. The image is at variance with the mood necessary to sustain the rest of the film; it can be accepted only by those of us who have shared her experience of battle, and that experience has not been shown by the film. Women cry in *P4W*, and the audience cries too—the women cry for their lost children, their lost lovers, their imprisoned lives, and we, having just seen how they live their lives, having witnessed their courage and grace, willingly share their grief.

I was angry at the end of *Not A Love Story*, and while the true focus of my anger should have been directed at the patriarchal makers of porn, somehow lacking a clear channel, lacking a sense from the film of how to direct my anger, I found myself turning it back onto the film makers—why didn't you make a better film, why no Canadians, why why? No wonder the little boys exploded. Anger is a dangerous weapon—like most weapons it can be turned against its owner.

WHO DID MARX'S LAUNDRY?

Reviewed by Mariana Valverde

Volume 3, No. 1 (October 1981), p. 14

Meg Luxton, *More than a Labour of Love: Three Generations of Women's Work in the Home*. Toronto: The Women's Press, 1980.

Bonnie Fox, ed., *Hidden in the Household: Women's Domestic Labour under Capitalism*. Toronto: The Women's Press, 1980.

Housewives are—so the television tells us—by nature stupid and gullible creatures, endlessly worrying about the whiteness of their sheets or the flakiness of their pastry, and always ready to consume whatever product promises to solve these worries. Even in the literature of the women's movement, they have often been portrayed purely as passive victims (of domestic violence, of the advertisers' ploys). Other people have spoken about their problems, but they have seldom been encouraged to speak for themselves. Meg Luxton's recent book, *More than a Labour of Love*, does an excellent job of debunking these myths and stereotypes.

The reader quickly becomes absorbed in the stories told by these housewives from Flin Flon. Luxton gives us the necessary statistics and tables, but only the strictly necessary; mostly, she just lets us enjoy the anecdotes and the half-finished thoughts. And, although her own prose is rather colourless, she has a brilliant way with quotes. For example, here's a woman explaining how she manages to obtain the money she needs from her husband:

> Men are such sucks. They have this big fat ego and it needs feeding. When I need money I have to go through this whole song and dance about how wonderful he is and how big and strong and how I'd be lost without him. And it works. He coughs up.

Luxton's book is a work of sociology, but it actually shows caring and concern, and even a great deal of respect, for the people whose lives are being dissected. The women speak in what sound like unconstrained voices: the researcher is clearly not just an academic, but also a neighbour and friend. Even the last chapter, consisting of political conclusions and strategies, relies as much on these women's opinions as on the perspectives of the author herself. For example, when considering the failings of the Wages for Housework movement, Luxton simply refers us to the views expressed by these women:

> Well, whenever they want us to make more babies, they increase the baby bonus or change the family tax laws. So the government could decide to pay women according to how good a wife and mother they are. Then we'd all have to have dozens of kids and keep spotless houses and do home baking and never complain.

The book deals with such topics as a quick history of the town of Flin Flon, changing relationships among family members, and of course, detailed analyses of how these women spend their hours at home. Such topics as the impact of technology on housework, the various methods of managing the family's finances, and the relationship between the husband's work and his attitude to the home are explored in minute detail, but without boring repetitions or pedantic elaborations of the obvious.

This book, then, is an important contribution to the small but growing literature of the Canadian women's movement. Despite its value both as a work of empirical sociology and as an analysis of housework under capitalism, however, there are some problems concerning its theoretical framework. First, Luxton happily tells us that the experiences of these Flin Flon housewives are "typical." Now, these women live in an isolated, one-industry town where there is virtually no paid work for women. In larger urban centres, however, nearly all single women and about 60% of married women work for wages: the full-time housewife is increasingly *not* typical. Also, Flin Flon is the kind of place where doctors won't give birth control to unmarried women, where abortions are simply unavailable, and where everyone knows your business. Under such repressive social conditions, women are bound to be less independent than they might be in other places: it's very difficult to leave your husband, it's nearly impossible to be gay, etc.

This does not in any way invalidate the thoughts and experiences of these women, but their situation in a town where it's extremely difficult to be independent of men does have some bearing on their approach to housework, men, and life in general.

Secondly, Luxton is not very precise about how her analysis of domestic labour affects the Marxist concepts of labour and value, which she uses in an ambiguous way. Her approach is to legitimize women's work in the home by giving it the status of "production," a word which Marx would never apply to what feminist theoreticians call 'tension management', or to women's sexual services to men. Such an extension of Marxist categories requires more justification than Luxton provides. But she is, it seems to be, relying not only on her own rather brief arguments: she is part of a major current within Marxist-feminism, and is implicitly relying on a whole series of arguments devised by others. It is thus appropriate to now turn to an evaluation of this current by examining another book on domestic labour also published by Women's Press, *Hidden in the Household: Women's Domestic Labour Under Capitalism*.

In the mid-seventies, Marxists in Europe and North America began to develop an analysis of women's oppression that, among other things, provided an understanding of women's work in the home from the point of view of Marxist economics. It was recognized that this seemingly private, non-economic activity was really work; and feminist historians pointed out that capitalism greatly affected women's work in the home. Marxists then set out to analyze housework in its relationship to the capitalist economy. Many different views emerged on this debate, an early one being that proposed by Wages for Housework; and there is as yet no consensus on what the "correct" socialist-feminist theory of domestic labour is.

Wally Seccombe, an early Canadian, contributor to this debate, has two important articles in the anthology under review, and the other writers make a point of either agreeing or disagreeing with his position, so it is to his contribution that we now turn. Also, Seccombe and Luxton have worked together very closely, and the theoretical problems which I see in her work are by and large problems she shares with him.

Seccombe is by no means a vulgar Marxist. He recognizes the importance of the autonomous women's movement, and is willing to reconsider the validity of certain tenets of orthodox Marxism in the light of feminist theory. But his theoretical framework, it seems to me, has not advanced at the same pace as his political ideas; he tends to validate the experience of women in the home by describing it in Marxist terms. Sometimes this is indeed useful, but at other times it amounts to a stretching of the old wineskins of Marxism to contain the new feminist wine.

Seccombe wants to vindicate housewives by proving that their work is crucial for the capitalist economy, in that it produces the strange, intangible commodity which workers sell on the labour market, i.e., "labour-power." (Marx defined labour-power as a person's ability to create and do things, an ability which takes the form of a commodity—something which is bought and sold—only under capitalism.) Women take are of their husbands and they bring up their children, hence producing and reproducing labour-power. Women's work is thus validated as "productive" because it produces a certain saleable commodity—labour-power—which is then exchanged in the market as the worker goes to work. The price of this commodity is then obtained in the form of wages, which then have to be transformed by the housewife into cooked food, clean clothes, etc. The food and the clothes help to reproduce the wage-earner's labour-power, thus setting the cycle in motion once more.

This explanation shows that women are tied into capitalist production even when they do not work for wages, but it goes a little too far in seeing *everything* that women do in the home through the eyes of abstract economic theory. First of all, the housewife performs an endless series of tasks in her daily routine, including such activities as playing with the kids or making love with her husband, which can only be seen as economically productive by stretching the meaning of these words quite considerably. Even if it is true that both her husband and her children will likely proceed to the labour market, there is no direct and immediate connection between her activities and their selling of labour-power. The concrete housewife does not directly produce labour-power, which, as Marx pointed out, is an abstract economic category. The concrete activities of domestic labour—activities which bourgeois housewives also carry out—cannot be reduced to a simple abstraction like "reproduction of labour power."

This emphasis on the housewife's services to the capitalist economy tends to ignore the ideological and cultural components of women's oppression in the family. Luxton tends to explain male miners' domination of their wives in terms of the men's exploitation at work; and similarly, Seccombe tends to explain sex stereotypes in terms of the needs of the capitalist system of production. (They of course allow that there is such a thing as sexism in the working class, but they tend to explain it away with economic theory). Now, even if it is true that domestic labour fulfills an essential function for capitalism, there is nothing in the nature of capital that determines that it shall be *women* who perform this work, or that there will be certain expectations about cleanliness or privacy, or that a married couple is expected to have children.

Finally, the Seccombe-Luxton analysis does not deal with women's oppression *as women* in the labour-force, and how discrimination and job-stereotyping relate to their role as mothers and housekeepers. Marxist economic theory can explain how workers in general are exploited, but it does not explain the concrete ways in which workers are divided according to gender, race, and so on; again, it is necessary to take into account political, ideological, and cultural factors when doing concrete analyses.

In an original contribution to the debate, Linda Briskin's article "Domestic Labour: A Methodological Discussion" also provides a critique of the Seccombe framework. She shows why the categories of "labour," "value," "production," and so on cannot be directly applied to the sphere of domestic labour; and in general, she argues that the oppression of women under capitalism cannot be studied with the tools of political economy alone. At the same time, she recognizes that the abstract dynamic of capital and labour—a dynamic which, as she puts it, is "sex-blind"—does influence and shape all areas of capitalist society, including the home.

This perspective, which recognizes that domestic labour is tied to, but at the same time remains outside of, the "inner dynamic" of capital and labour, is a fruitful one. (A similar, much more systematic analysis is provided by Michèle Barrett in her recent book *Women's Oppression Today*, published by New Left Books). The inner dynamic of capitalist production, i.e., the extraction of surplus-value and subsequent reproduction of capital, is a central one in our society, but it is not a magic solution to all questions of social theory.

In order to concretely understand women's oppression today, analyses of the ideology of domesticity and of gender-stereotyping are as important as abstract economic explanations. Feminism is not simply an addition or revision of Marxism, it is an independent component. A socialist feminism that is not unduly weighted toward socialism would recognize that there are more things in Heaven and on Earth than fit in Marxist economics, while recognizing that this economic theory can indeed provide the key to *some* aspects of women's oppression both on the job and in the family.

VOICES OF THE NISEI
by Jean Wilson
Volume 3, No. 5 (March 1982), p. 14

Joy Kogawa, *Obasan*. Toronto: Lester & Orpen Dennys, 1981.

Takeo Ujo Nakano, with Leatrice Nakano. *Within the Barbed Wire Fence: A Japanese Man's Account of His Internment in Canada.* Toronto: University of Toronto Press 1980.

Ann Gomer Sunahara, *The Politics of Racism: The Uprooting of Japanese Canadians during the Second World War.* Toronto: James Lorimer & Co., 1981.

One of the worst manifestations of racism in Canada occurred between 1942 and 1946. In that period, approximately 21,000 Japanese Canadians—nationals, naturalized Canadians, and Canadian-born—were forced to abandon their homes, businesses, property, and in many cases their birthplaces in order to comply with federal government orders to leave the BC coast. It is a shameful part of Canadian history, and one little discussed in print until the last six years or so.

Three recent books document that history very well, particularly *Obasan*, the fine first novel by Joy Kogawa, who is better known as a poet. Her novel, read in conjunction with a unique first-hand account of internment in a POW camp and a well-documented study of the people and policies involved, makes the story of the Japanese-Canadian uprooting vivid.

In effect, Japanese Canadians during World War II were victims of virulent racism among certain sectors of the BC population and especially among a few highly placed BC civic and federal politicians who influenced dominion policy in this matter. There was also a significant racist streak expressed more subtly by William Lyon Mackenzie King and some of his cabinet colleagues and advisors who were *not* from the west but who held equally strong views about the Japanese "menace."

As Ann Gomer Sunahara points out in her disturbing book, *The Politics of Racism*, it was the Japanese attack on Pearl Harbor in December 1941 that encouraged a traditionally intolerant and extremely vocal minority of British Columbians to resurrect every racist charge ever made against Japanese Canadians. Before that date, military and police authorities had kept a watchful eye on Japanese Canadians, but there had been no attempt to confine them or dispossess them of their property and rights, such as they were — in 1941, Japanese Canadians were denied their right to vote and so had little voice in determination of their own affairs.

Following the attack on Pearl Harbor, however, it took only 12 weeks for anti-Japanese opinion to persuade the federal Liberals that drastic action was needed to prevent collaboration between Japanese in Canada and in Japan. Rather than take the advice of most senior RCMP and military officers, who opposed uprooting, and simplistically assuming that men like rabidly anti-Asian Ian Alistair Mackenzie, MP for Vancouver Centre from 1930 to 1948, represented public opinion generally in BC, King's government devised a hasty and insensitive plan to deal with the problem.

Initially, the government tried to reassure the BC public by arresting 38 Japanese previously suspected of being security threats, closing Japanese cultural centres, and seizing the valuable Japanese fishing fleet. Soon, though, because of public and private pressure, it was decided to intern all Japanese Canadians in BC. By February 1942, it was announced that all so-called enemy aliens — only Japanese Canadians, not those of Italian or German descent — were to be removed from the coast. They were to be removed and resettled as economically as possible, which meant that most — some 12,000 — ended up in hastily constructed, flimsy shacks in the cold BC interior and many others went to equally inadequate shelter and new lives as labourers on sugar beet farms in southern Alberta and Manitoba. Some men were interned in camps north of Lake Superior and families with enough money and influence resettled themselves even further east than Manitoba or in the BC interior.

To pay for removing Japanese Canadians from their homes and confining them in detention camps, the federal government forced sale of all their property and possessions left behind, including all of the fishing fleet and many prosperous Fraser Valley unless the seed flowers with speech, farms which were then bought at below-market value and reserved for war veterans. Few property sales anywhere were fair compensation for economic losses suffered, though proceeds from these sales were supposed to enable Japanese Canadians to survive in their new homes and indeed to relocate east of the Rockies. By April 1945, too few had voluntarily relocated, so a deportation policy was enforced. Inmates of camps were obliged to choose between "immediate, but not necessarily permanent, resettlement in eastern Canada, and repatriation to Japan at some unspecified date. To keep their jobs, to avoid another move, to hide from hostile Caucasians; in despair, in confusion, and in igno-rance, 6,884 Japanese Canadian (males) over the age of 16 signed repatriation requests. With their 3,500 dependents, these potential deportees represented 43 per cent of Canada's Japanese minority" (Sunahara, p. 163).

When Japan capitulated in August 1945, the government tried to enforce these repatriation requests by order-in-council under the since infamous War Measures Act. By then, about two-thirds who had made the requests had changed their minds. King's government at first was immovable, but Canadian public opinion finally was aroused, in BC and elsewhere, on the side of Japanese Canadians and after a sustained public campaign and a long court struggle, led by CCF-ers such as Andrew Brewin and Stanley Knowles and other civic and political leaders across the country, the government was forced to back down.

Because of news censorship, most Canadians apparently were ignorant of Japanese Canadians' plight until after the war. According to Sunahara and people I've spoken to, most had believed that Japanese Canadians were a national security risk, as they'd been told by their federal government, and most were unaware of the sale of

Japanese Canadian property. Once aware of these facts and of the impending enforced deportation of 10,000 people, opposing public opinion increased dramatically. Ultimately, only 4,000 people repatriated to Japan, all of them voluntarily. Most other Japanese Canadians resettled on the prairies or in eastern Canada. By 1949, only 30 per cent of the original population still lived in BC.

One Issei (first-generation Japanese in Canada) who eventually settled in Toronto was Takeo Nakano. Based on diaries he kept at the time, Nakano in *Within the Barbed Wire Fence* describes his own experience of being uprooted. Before Pearl Harbor, he lived in a small lumber town north of Vancouver with his wife and small daughter. In the next 9 months, he was separated from his family, worked in road camps near Jasper, and then was interned in a former POW camp near Angler, Ontario, for resisting resettlement apart from his family. There Nakano was something of an outsider in that most men there were *gambariya*, the small proportion of Japanese in Canada who remained loyal to Japan after Pearl Harbor and most of whom did repatriate.

Although he was not that fiercely loyal to Japan, it was Nakano's homeland and he was naturally more sympathetic to it emotionally than to Canada, where he had come as a young man to earn his fortune but not necessarily to settle as a citizen. Only men were confined at Angler, and they were free to leave if they accepted work from Canadian authorities in designated places like Toronto. Women and children obviously were not considered a threat, just a nuisance. They were left behind to cope as best they could in the absence of the family wage-earner. Nakano was one of the few men who left Angler. His story is told simply and dispassionately and provides some insight into what must have been an anguishing and frightening experience.

To best understand that experience and the effect of internment, the outstanding book to read is *Obasan*. This is an excellent novel, not only because it recreates an event in Canadian history so vividly, but also because it is so well-written. As well, it is a much more rounded story than that told by either Sunahara or Nakano in that the experience of women and children is given its due. The novel is based on Joy Kogawa's own experiences and on contemporary letters and documents.

The story is centred on the narrator's *obasan*, meaning "aunt," and is told by a woman who is 5 when her world falls apart. In a series of well-co-ordinated flashbacks between the present in southern Alberta and the past of BC internment camps and southern Alberta sugar beet farms, Kogawa effectively describes the various responses to internment that occurred even within one family. The language she uses is so evocative that you *know* what it was like to leave a beloved father behind in Vancouver and live in shacks with other remnants most of a once close-knit community in a resurrected ghost town in the BC interior, to be forced to move again with part of your family to the hostile physical and social environment of a sugar beet farm near Lethbridge, and gradually to establish a new way of life in an alien place.

At the beginning of *Obasan*, there is this declaration, which suggests the richness and force of Kogawa's language:

> There is a silence that cannot speak.
> There is a silence that will not speak....
> Unless the stone bursts with telling, unless the seed flowers with speech, there is in my life no living word. The sound I hear is only sound. White sound. Words, when they fall, are pock marks on the earth. They are hailstones seeking an underground stream.
> If I could follow the stream down and down to the hidden voice, would I come at last to the freeing word? I ask the night sky but the silence is steadfast. There is no reply.

Obasan releases the hidden voice. It *is* a reply to too many years of silence.

A ticket to No Frills, one of the bands in the burgeoning women's music scene, 1981.

SUN, FUN, AND GEORGIA O'KEEFFE
by Deena Rasky
Volume 3, No. 6 (April 1982), p. 14

Deena Rasky describes the highlights of her recent trip through the American Western Sunbelt:

What is Berkeley, California like? Try to imagine the crowd from the recent International Women's Day taking over a whole town. No matter where you go, a political sign or message is within eyesight. Buildings are draped with flags criticizing foreign policy: "US Out of El Salvador!" Turn around the corner and you are in front of graffitti condemning the President: "Reagan shoots Geritol!" The parade of car bumper stickers adds to this street dialogue: "Question Authority!" "Try the Solar Solution to the Nuclear Problem!" "Witches Heal!" Even the standard grocery stores have been taken over by Natural Food Co-ops.

No wonder women-run businesses here are thriving. On a typical Sunday morning, the Brick Hut—made famous by Mary Watkins on her *Something Moving* funk/synthesizer album—has a waiting list that would make many a restaurateur cry. This simple, unpretentious restaurant offers standard fare—eggs, pancakes, sandwiches, etc.—but the low prices and the little extras that go into the preparation, such as the use of whole wheat flour in the waffles, or onions, green pepper and a dollop of sour cream with the home fries, make the difference. Not to mention the people who go there…You can find an Amazon Kung-Fu teacher sitting next to an oil-stained trucker at the counter eating an identical breakfast.

> *"It's always crowded, got to wait for a*
> *seat*
> *but watching the people is some kind of*
> *treat.*
> *They got hippies, hoboes, Jims and Pegs*
> *Everything from drinks to scrambled*
> *eggs*
> *Just the place to shake your gloom*
> *Like being in a shrink's waiting room."*
> —Brick Hut © 1978 Mary Watkins

Even though it was hard to locate, ICI: A San Diego Woman's Place, it was worth the visit. This bookstore is well-stocked, designed for wheel-chair access with spacious aisles, and has a special bin of periodicals with the proceeds going to women in prison. You could spend hours alone reading the announcements covering hundreds of square feet in the lounge and then plunge into an old sofa and chat with whoever's there.

The lounge converts into a workshop on certain evenings. As part of Black History Month, Mary Watkins spoke about her life and work there. She spoke candidly about her personal story and encouraged women to tell their own. Her upcoming album consists of full-scale orchestrations, so perhaps Womynly Way Productions can book her with the Toronto Symphony next season!

Within walking distance of where I was staying with my travelling companion was La Peña, the Third World Cultural Centre, bar/restaurant and lecture/concert hall. The building is decorated by a 3-dimensional mural found on the cover of Grupo Raiz's album, the Latin American instrumental folk band that performs with Wallflower Order Dance Group. Inside the building Grupo Raiz were now collecting tickets and stamping hands for the Adrienne Torf/Linda Tillery/Adele Chandler concert. No day care was provided for the concert but it didn't matter since the children were lovingly passed around the capacity audience. During intermission, Linda Tillery became a babysitter.

Not all our time was spent in Berkeley. San Franciso is only a Bay Bridge away. All those wonderful things you've heard about San Francisco being a lesbian/gay/feminist haven are true. Just as Castro Street is known for being a gay male centre, Vallencia Street is becoming known for its women-run businesses. On this street there are two women's bars, a couple of gay /lesbian-run restaurants, a woman's bathhouse, Old Wive's Tales — the woman's bookstore, and a lesbian-owned beauty salon. I fell in love with the décor of one of the restaurants, The Artemis Society Café, with its deep avocado green walls, luscious floral prints and ornate walnut piano.

The further south one travels from San Francisco, the further one gets from political consciousness. Southern California is the perfect breeding ground for the likes of President Reagan. The car bumper stickers now read: "Guns, Guts and God Give Us Freedom."

Certain "feminist" places we visited in Los Angeles were disappointing because the women's movement seemed to be the "in" thing. Feminism can be more trendy, fashionable and profitable to certain people than a lifelong commitment to the betterment of women. It bothered me that the woman running a woman's bookstore was rude to us as customers, the goods were overpriced and she wouldn't give me a receipt in return for copies of *Broadside*.

San Diego wasn't much better. A café listed as feminist turned out to be more of a place for heterosexual men looking for a liberated fuck. But the town offered some bright spots. I met a friendly, balding transsexual who was an expert at winning the brass rings on a Merry-Go-Round. There was also the extraordinary sight of an Amazon Sweet Shoppe, "Home of Ice Cream Without Sugar Blues," right in the heart of the most banal suburban plaza. Imagine Mr. and Mrs. America with their 2.3 children walking into a natural ice cream store complete with spears, shields and the names of hundreds of women-loving-women on the walls!

There was actually a purpose to our trip besides sunning and funning and that was to meet the American artist Georgia O'Keeffe. Yes, young supplicants make quest to meet the Old, Prolific, Wise One. But how do you find her? Abiquiu, New Mexico is a very small town not known for its tourist motels, golfing and discothèques. The town is so tiny that our Ontario Motor League map of the southwest United States located it in the wrong spot. Luck was on our side because we found a motel owner—an artist himself—who not only knew the town but also precisely where O'Keeffe's home was.

It was an adobe castle on top of a hill. The view was gorgeous— in one direction you could see cow pastures, farmland, and rolling hills, and in another dark red badlands.

Once there, the challenge was how to meet this legendary figure when Gloria Steinem and Judy Chicago have failed. She is known for being abrupt to strangers at her door. Once she opened her gate to a stranger who asked to see Georgia O'Keeffe. "Front side!" she declared, then turned and announced, "Back side!" Then she turned again and briskly said to the speechless stranger, "Goodbye!" and slammed the gate.

Her place is not inviting to visitors. It is surrounded by a 6-foot adobe wall tipped with barbed wire, and signs on the door proclaimed in large type: BEWARE OF DOG. We found a raised trap door, probably leading to a cellar, which we stood on to see into the garden. A face appeared on the other side in one of the house windows, then disappeared. I decided then it was time to put my camera away and get out my violin.

I'm only an amateur violinist, but we knew Georgia O'Keeffe once played the instrument herself and for many years allowed the Santa Fe Chamber Music Festival to reproduce her works for advertising posters. It was the only negotiating tool we had. We decided to wait until someone came out by a grouping of three stumps near a door. Sure enough, a young woman soon opened a gate, took a look at me and sternly asked, "What do you want?"

I had rehearsed my reply over and over again in my head. Hesitatingly, I asked, "Would Miss O'Keeffe like to hear some tunes on the violin?" She asked for my name, then quickly darted back into the house. A few moments later she returned, nodding and told us to wait five minutes while she attended to some chores. We whooped with delight.

When Georgia O'Keeffe finally came out of the house, I convinced myself it was all a dream. Otherwise I wouldn't have been able to function at all. She was dressed like she was in a 1948 photo except she now wore a black bandanna, black pants and carried a cane.

She had aged. Her eyes were a brighter red than the nearby badlands, her face weathered, liver spotted and lightly covered with downy facial hair, but her 95-year-old presence was as strong as ever. I started to explain who composed the violin pieces. She raised her hand to silence me and said it didn't matter. While I played she sat on a nearby stump with her head down and eyes shut. Afterwards, our conversation was brief but her replies were witty and filled with a youthful innocence. When I told her that I had only been playing the violin for a few years she told me I was very brave. I mentioned that one piece really needed a piano accompaniment. She raised an eyebrow and said a piano would be very difficult to carry about. I asked about her health. She paused, raised her head and gazed at me. "*I'm* healthy, don't I look it?" she replied with mock indignation.

Looking at my companion, she asked if her job was to follow me about. "No, I have a profession of my own. I'm an artist." Georgia O'Keeffe gave her nurse a knowing glance, then spoke: "An artist. Well, good luck to you." She must have believed me to be a wandering musician. "Who are you going to play for next?" she asked. I was taken aback. There isn't anyone that I'd rather play for.

SATISFACTION GUARANTEED
Reviewed by June Callwood
Volume 4, No. 3 (December 1982/January 1983), p. 11

Maureen Fitzgerald, Connie Guberman, and Margie Wolfe, eds. *Still Ain't Satisfied: Canadian Feminism Today.* Illustrated by Gail Geltner. Toronto: The Women's Press 1982.

The Women's Press, a sturdy collective which for ten years has been a quality publisher of pro-women authors and topics, is celebrating its tenth anniversary with *Still Ain't Satisfied*, which provides a panorama and a platform for feminists in the eighties.

The quality of *Still Ain't Satisfied* is a testament in itself of the progress of women. Liz Martin's cover and design are confident and stunning, Gail Geltner's tender, powerful illustrations stop the show, the editing is top-of-the-line professional, and the contributors responded to their commitment by researching and writing their heads off, plus providing bibliographies. There's a sureness about the tone throughout which flows from the jaunty title and gives several of the writers the nerve to push back the boundaries of conventional feminist wisdom.

The Women's Press collective's existence almost exactly spans the current era of women's liberation which began with the oceanic euphoria of the early all-women conferences, workshops, and consciousness-raising groups. Women found they liked women, and therefore could like themselves; we all felt invincible because we perceived that we had logic and numbers on our side. *Still Ain't Satisfied* explores the gaps, errors, and gains since those heady days.

Notable in this parade of observation and analysis is Kathleen McDonnell's chapter on abortion, "Claim No Easy Victories," in which she attempts to deal with the rigidity which has seized both sides of the bitter debate. She makes an offering, a confession, that there is much pain and ambivalence within the pro-choice movement. "It is possible by *not* acknowledging women's mixed emotions about abortion," she reflects, "we are skipping over some very important steps in helping them come to terms with it, both personally and as a political issue."

That's a major statement of principle that is overdue. In our anxiety not to give the opposition a morsel to make into a meal, many of us on the pro-choice side have kept secret that vast relief we will feel when unwanted, unplanned pregnancies no longer occur. McDonnell suggests a beginning of *détente* by working with the left-wing of the self-styled pro-life movement in such common causes and daycare.

Myrna Kostash examines another divisive topic, pornography. Her crackling style and clarity of vision make her one of the country's most consistently interesting writers. This time out she marches right up to the topic, kicks it soundly in very sensitive places, and refuses all easy solutions. Joanne Kates, another who has congenital inability to stand back from reality, gives one of the most remarkable pieces of her writing career in the chapter on the conflicts that rage when a heterosexual feminist is in love. Similarly, Eve Zaremba with honour and insight explores the various shapes of lesbian sexuality and relationships.

There are fine, well-documented chapters on daycare, sexual harassment, hazardous jobs, rape, collectives, and women in unions. Naomi Wall has the opening spot with a comprehensive historic review of the feminist movement in the past decade and Nancy Adamson co-ordinated a rousing final chapter which pulls together some thoughts on strategy. Between those two buttresses there are such good deeds as Meg Luxton's examination of housewives, whose jobs are shown to be hazardous to their health but whose commitment is mainly to anti-feminist undertakings. And Susan G. Cole contributes a treasure about the national pastime of woman-battering.

The introduction mentions that space did not allow for articles on such topics as "the special problems of welfare, older, adolescent and disabled women." The decision is understandable because no one volume could present solidly all the issues that engross feminists, but women make up the majority of the poor and the omission is sad. The lack of interest some feminists show in women who live below the poverty line is unattractive.

Still, as *Still Ain't Satisfied* amply demonstrates, women are gathering at last into the political force that we fondly believed ten years ago was at hand. A politician, Lloyd Axworthy, saw his leadership hopes destroyed when he tangled with the now-worthless federal Advisory Council on the Status of Women. And women, in a fast, furious, and brilliant campaign, rewrote the constitution in the eleventh hour.

Still Ain't Satisfied chronicles all such good news, doesn't flinch from the agony of the process, and gets the documents in order so that feminists can see where they have been and where they are going. There's a shoulder-to-shoulder feel about the collection which is pure heaven. The Women's Press collective has done itself, and all of us, proud.

June Callwood is a writer and long-time activist in the abortion, women's shelter, and other movements.

BODY BLOW TO ART HISTORY
Reviewed by Susan Crean
Volume 5, No. 3 (December 1983/January 1984), pp. 12 and 13

Norma Broude and Mary D. Garrard, eds. *Feminism and Art History: Questioning the Litany*. New York: Harper & Row, 1982.

It's over ten years since I left the field of art history, after 7 years of study and 2 teaching at York University. Ten years since I've looked back to see whether the events of the real world have had any effect on the charmed existence of the Fine Arts and those elegant creatures—like Anthony Blount and Kenneth Clark[1]—who interpret them for us.

Art history, as I knew it, was mainly about the art of the Western world since ancient times; the pyramids to Picasso in one long-winded heroic tale of progress glorifying the accomplishments of the patriarchs, popes and princes who commissioned the monuments, and the technical prowess of the artists who made them. Like all such tales there are plots and subplots and cautionary notes. Ostensibly, the Fine Arts are about aesthetics: the formal and intellectual qualities that denote excellence in the visual arts. Actually, like all history, the history of art is a mixture of fact, conjecture and hearsay, laced with megalomania. It too boils down to the story from a particular point of view—that of white, middle class, first-world males, though in the case of the arts this has to be qualified. For the males in question are middle class with upper class pretensions. They are the gatekeepers of Official Culture and responsible for devising an aesthetic which legitimizes the values of the modern artistocracy—the mandarins, tycoons and idle rich who hold the purse, strings and govern the policies which control the arts. Excellence, it turns out, is in the eye of the beholder and from experience we know that it is rarely either female or Canadian.

Ten years ago, I would not have put it in such bold terms. But I certainly was aware that art history was in the business of classifying things; establishing where on a predetermined scale particular artefacts belong. Moreover, it was clear that the arts of some people are, by definition, finer than everybody else's. And some couldn't be considered art at all. So art history first of all had to distinguish between greater and lesser forms of art; for example, between art that is merely decorative (the "minor arts") and art that is major league material. You guessed it, the pyramids and Picasso. The Great Masters, you'll notice, weren't quilt makers. They worked in oil paint and marble, and these materials have acquired a special status that automatically puts them in a class apart.

Having drawn these definitions, the job of the curator/art historian is then to patrol the frontiers of art, making sure no one slips in who isn't invited. This is not, as you might imagine, a simple task; for the borders are constantly changing, following the demands of the art market, which is ever-hungry for new styles, new artists and new forms of art for collectors and museums to speculate in. In this the visual arts are unique, for no other art form is so directly tied to a monetary value system in which the whole idea is for the artists to create capital assets for others to turn into wealth. Degas said it for all artists when he remarked after one of his paintings was resold for 900 times the price he'd originally received, that he felt like the horse who wins the Grand Prix and is rewarded with his usual feed of oats. Whatever else the art critics or curators may think they are doing, part of their job is providing stock evaluations for investors.

However, they don't tell you this in art school. Along with all the other cultural assumptions and clichés about Truth and Beauty and Art being its own justification comes the myth that excellence is absolute and universal. It is a matter of discernment, not debate. Thus art (and the whole question of its biases) can be neatly abstracted from life and the social and political circumstances surrounding its creation. And in such an exalted atmosphere the contradictions and omissions are not immediately apparent. But contradictions there are, and it was, I think, inevitable that a new generation of scholars influenced by the women's movement would notice half of humanity is missing and demand an explanation.

Feminism and Art History: Questioning the Litany is the result of serious boat-rocking that's been going on in academic waters in the United States. Ever since Linda Nochlin wrote an essay in 1971 called "Why Are There No Great Women Artists?"[2] and answered it by saying that the question itself falsifies the nature of the issue, which is not whether or not women possess genius ("If Giotto, the obscure shepherd boy and Van Gogh, the epileptic, could make it, why not women?") but how the pressures and expectations placed on women "simply made total devotion to professional art production out of the question and unthinkable," the intellectual floodgates were open. The activity touched off by Nochlin, as this collection of articles demonstrates, has been fast and furious. Several of the contributions here were originally presented as papers at special sessions of the prestigious College. Art Association meetings in 1978 and 1979 (the CAA being the learned society for art historians in the USA). Most of them are scholarly and ponderously written, but all of them are irreverent and intended to contribute to what the co-editors call the feminist revision of art history.

Surveying the record of male/American art history, feminists have attempted to do three things. First, to retrieve the names of women artists from the dark corners of history (Germaine Greer's book *The Obstacle Race* has been the main corrective effort so far): and second, to conduct a reevaluation of the litany from a feminist perspective, adjusting for the distortions built into masculine art criticism. Undertaking this latter work has implied a completely new notion of historical time than we have been used to. To wit: "Just as Renaissance humanists were able to define the Dark Ages for the first time as a separate transitional age bounded at either end by differing cultures, and could therefore understand it as a distinct period with cultural characteristics that were unique to it rather than universal, so feminists have named as 'patriarchal' that period of more than 5,000 years which reach down to the present and which began with the gradual replacement of a long standing Goddess-worshipping culture by patrilineal and God-worshipping civilizations." When you think of it, this is indeed a profound difference. It totally broadens and alters the context in which art is seen and understood. The third objective of the feminist revision has been to take such revelations and turn ait history back on itself; to question the very canons of art theory and methodology, opening up possibilities for entirely new avenues of investigation.

Mary Garrard's article on Artemisia Gentileschi is a wonderful example of the feminist rescue from oblivion. (Gentileschi, incidentally, was one of the elect invited to Judy Chicago's Dinner Party.) Garrard does an amazing piece of detective work using a feminist critique to attribute an early seventeenth-century painting of *Susanna and the Elders* to the hand of a very young but already extremely proficient artist who also happened to be the daughter of the northern Italian minor master Orazio Gentileschi. Orazio is, of course, known to art history; but so is Artemesia, though arguably more because of the historical gossip about her rape by a colleague of her father's than because of her extraordinary achievement as a woman and an artist. When Tassi (the attacker) refused to marry Artemisia—this being the customary "way out" for a respectable rapee—Orazio brought suit and at the end of a five-month trial, Tassi was sentenced to prison. During the trial it was Tassi's word against Gentileschi's; only her word was put to the torture test with thumbscrews, and eventually even that wasn't good enough. Tassi was finally acquitted and Gentileschi was meanly and unjustly branded a hussy.

The apocryphal story of Susanna and the elders also involved a rape—or a suggested rape. The two elders didn't stop at propositioning the young Susanna; they tried to coerce sexual favours from her by threatening to expose her as an unfaithful wife. Susanna resists; the elders denounce her and once again it's her word against the men's. Like Artemisia, Susanna was eventually vindicated but that hasn't stopped history from thinking the worse of her. Tellingly, Garrard notes, there are very few painting either of Daniel's judgement or the stoning of the elders. Painters and their patrons through the ages have preferred the scene where the elders surprise Susanna at her bath and make their lewd suggestion. Although the elders are usually depicted as aging lechers, and despite Susanna's uncommonly self-assured rejection, she is habitually shown as a half-willing participant in the affair, wavering in her resolve to, turn down the two dirty old men—*not* through fear but because of temptation! Her, strength in the face of danger is completely ignored as the male artists seize on a church-sanctioned opportunity to indulge in a bit of soft-core. Susanna, like Artemisia, Garrard remarks, has been the butt of one long historical dirty joke. She goes on to explain exactly why the exceptional painting dated 1610 (and in a private collection in Germany) has to have been painted by a woman; by Artemisia, and not her father as scholars have decreed. For it shows Susanna reacting to the pressure of a threatened rape, not posing as a sex object in a decorative and half distracted manner. She is a person, not a sexual fantasy.

Most of the essays in *Feminism and Art History* are examinations of similar such moments in recorded art history. They are reports of return visits to familiar territory by scholars, mostly women, who've gone back armed with a new set of glasses. They have a feminist's sensibility, a different sense of time and are frankly sceptical of what the male perspective has established as fact. Nancy Luomala's "Matrilineal Reinterpretation of Some Sacred Egyptian Cows" is a good case in point. She points out that while the implications of matrilineal descent are well understood by anthropology, art history has misrepresented Egyptian art and life by wilfully applying its own patri-cultural standards.

A statue from the 4th Dynasty (2470 BC) of Queen Khamerernebty and King Mycerinus standing together side-by-side in the heraldic pose typical of Egyptian sculpture nevertheless shows the Queen making an unusual gesture, embracing the King (her right hand at his waist, and left hand touching his left arm). Art historians have taken this as an indication of the weakening of the concept of the pharaoh as an unapproachable and divine being. A woman has dared to touch him! The truth of the matter is quite the contrary. No Egyptian king inherited his throne. He occupied it, and exercised its power because of being related to, or married to, the Queen who had inherited it. The women transferred the power and delegated it to the men; and they received it through their connection to the supreme power of life, the Great Mother Goddess, who was worshipped throughout the Mediterranean in pre-dynastic times. The Egyptian tradition was a holdover from earlier days and that has been entirely misunderstood by male art history for centuries. So much for objectivity.

Co-editor Norma Broude's article on "Degas's Misogyny" offers another fascinating angle on the Feminist Revision. The irony here is that the French Impressionist painter, renowned for his pictures of ballet dancers, was labelled a woman-hater by some of his contemporaries, and the reputation stuck. Quite unfairly, as it happens. The reason has to do with the artist's unconventional compositions, his candid, slice-of-life interiors depicting women about their everyday activities; unceremonious and unidealized. The critics looked and cried "ugly." Anyone who could paint such unappealing pictures of women must detest them. Degas's bachelorhood corroborated the gossip. Well, it is true that Degas never married. But he did have some abiding friendships with women, including Berthe Morisot and Mary Cassatt, whom he supported and admired as fellow artists. The same cannot be said for Degas's contemporary Renoir, who it was said was only interested in women likely to become his models. It is sometimes breathtaking to behold the lengths male history goes to prop up the male perspective.

Turning to modern art and its antecedents in German Expressionism, there are two essays which deliver a body blow to art history, and begin to offer an explanation as to why it was necessary to savage such a benign sexist as Degas. Alexandra Comini's "Gender or Genius?" explores the careers of three powerful women artists: Käthe Kollwitz, Paula Modersohn-Becker and Gabrielle Munter, whose existence has been grudgingly recognized by art history but whose true contribution has never been properly acknowledged. The second punch in the combination, by Carol Duncan, is demurely and perhaps slightly satirically titled "Virility and Domination in Early 20th Century Vanguard Painting." This is really the *pièce de résistance* of the book, which I guarantee will change the way you think about Picasso forever.

Duncan begins by pointing out that (American) avant garde art, which is to say the Official Art of these very sexist times, is based on ideals of artistic freedom and rugged individualism established at the turn of the century, ideals which found boldest expression in the painting of female nudes. It is no mere coincidence, Duncan notes, that so many of the works of that period singled out by the critics as being particularly important are of naked women who are rendered as powerless and passive under the gaze of the artist's virility. (Today we'd say machismo.) The female model serves not as a subject of the painting but as the object of the artist's sexual domination, which is the real subject of the work. That holy icon of modern art which graces the covers of so many art books—Picasso's brothel scene *Les Demoiselles d'Avignon*—says it all; but Duncan puts it into words for the first time: "No other modern work reveals more of the rock foundation of sexist anti-humanism or goes further and deeper to justify and celebrate the domination of women by men."

Now think again about what was happening during those years when Picasso and the boys were inventing the avant garde. The suffragettes were making the first serious challenge to male political domination; Kollwitz and her colleagues were making the first concerted challenge to the male monopoly of artistic images. The first achievement of twentieth-century Art, it now has to be understood, was to masculinize it. Not only did Picasso and the others paint images of women which are truly degrading, they masterfully sideline all women artists by learning to paint with their penises and declaring that authentic art could only by made by people who possessed the right technical equipment. Small wonder that once the collectors and critics got over the shock of Picasso's assault on traditional images they lined up, cash in hand, to buy the work. For if the new Art was outrageous in the disregard for perspective and human form, it was absolutely conventional in its attitude to women. Picasso always said that women were either goddesses or doormats; in life and art he celebrated the subjugation of women. Now, freed from the fetters of religious or history story-telling, he conceived an art that could be about what interested him most: naked submissive women. In short, he invented the Playboy centrefold long before Hugh Hefner, and battalions of male critics were sent in to cover up the evidence with formalist art theory.

Feminism and Art History has been a revelation for me—but also something of a disappointment. The reader does have to wade through thick pads of academic prose to uncover what I have described. It is worth it, but I suspect only for those who have some familiarity with the argot—and have the patience to follow the scholars through their rituals of minutiae. Unhappily, few of the writers are up to the wonderful paradoxes and insights their material hands them on a platter. Most of them are still trapped in the conventions and manias of the discipline, and really are addressing their profession rather than feminists or a general readership. In questioning the litany, they only go so far. Their radicalism only serves one purpose, and they don't think their positions all the way through. In assailing the sexist assumption, the collection actually brings down the whole house of cards, though no one seems to notice. The editors do talk about re-thinking the whole of art history, but no one takes on the full implication of sexist bias in art history which is, of course, that if American art history has been guilty of promoting chauvinism and the oppression of women, it has also had a hand in classism, racism and imperialism.

I came away from the book pleased to know that some winds of change have gusted through the discipline and given a few elders in the field cause for unease. And it has given me a couple of insights of my own. First, that a feminist critique clearly can be used effectively to demystify art and inject a down-to-earth, humanist approach back into the interpretation of the arts. Canadian art history could do well with some re-interpretation along these lines. I am also reminded of the session I attended at the Women and Words conference in Vancouver last July. It was on feminist criticism (is there or isn't there one?) and I recall the two academics on the panel giving lectures to the audience which were somehow patronizing and abstract at the same time. Here was an audience of receptive and well-informed women and the two academics deliberately talked to an in-crowd of other academics who weren't there. There has to be another way! Feminist academics have to break with that confining language or what is the point of our supporting their well-paid positions in the university? This seems to me to touch on another theme which came up at Women and Words and which has to do with whether we should have special expectations of women in the mainstream media covering women's issues. My short answer is, yes. I think it is fair to expect women, wherever they are working, not to behave as if they were men and to criticize them when they do. I think it is fair to criticize, women scholars for talking down to us and for creating theories about our work which only other academics can understand or even want to.

[1] Blount, for many years the Keeper of the Queen's Collection, was recently exposed as the elusive Fourth Man in the Burgess/Philby/Maclean spy ring. Clark became famous by name dropping his way through art history in glorious colour on the TV series *Civilization*.

[2] In *Woman in Sexist Society*, V. Gornick & B.K. Morgan (eds.) New York, Basic Books 1971.

Susan Crean is the author of Who's Afraid of Canadian Culture *and co-author of the recently published* Two Nations.

STREET LIFE: HOOKERS ON DAVIE
by Donna Gollan
Volume 5, No. 6 (April 1984), p. 13

Janis Cole and Holly Dale have made more than a dozen films together, many of them about the troubled lives of women living on the fringes of society. *P4W: Prison for Women* was their most recent documentary. Completed in 1981, it is a sympathetic portrait of women in Canada's only federal prison for women. Perhaps it is inaccurate to describe it as sympathetic; in fact, it simply provides a chance for these women to tell us about their lives. In listening to each woman's story of personal betrayal, foolish decisions, male oppression and often self-destruction, we find ourselves capable of a surprising and unsettling empathy: there but for the grace of God....

Hookers on Davie, a film about Vancouver prostitutes, remains true to the Cole/Dale style of personal interviews and self-exposure which allows us a touch at the truth of more difficult lives, provided we can interpret the words. Cole and Dale purposely avoid heavy-handed tactics which explain the texts or reason out the subjects' lives. There are no voice-overs or experts present to psychoanalyse the prostitutes. There are only people who sell sex for a living who are willing to tell us a little about their lives, their jobs, and their attempts to organize through ASP, the Alliance for the Safety of Prostitutes. The question is, are we capable of listening?

In speaking to Holly Dale and Janice Cole after seeing the film myself, I asked them how they expected their audience to react. They frankly admitted they expected their film to be controversial. Indeed, it is their aim to make unsettling films. The point is not to convince the audience of one particular viewpoint, nor to produce a film that will answer all our questions about prostitution in Canada. The point is to start us thinking.

In order to think, however, it is necessary that we listen. And it is very difficult to listen to what prostitutes have to say about their lives, simply because they represent to us *as women* the crystallization of our prescribed sex role and its ultimate degradation, power and defeat. Prostitutes threaten women who live within the boundaries of "normal" heterosexual society by flirting with those boundaries but rejecting the taboos that prevent us all from overtly demanding payment for services rendered.

Women who sell sex to men, sell a kind of sex in which they themselves receive no pleasure whatsoever. In eliminating the kind of equality of pleasure that our society admits ought to happen between two consenting adults, or at the very least between husband and wife, we have to redress that imbalance with money. Not just a little money, but as much as the market can stand, or put another way, as much as men will pay for it. If we all feel, as women, that pressure to dress for the male gaze, satisfy the male appetite and per-form for the male ego, then it is prostitutes who take those implied rules of our sexist society to their limit. Certainly they acquire power in so doing, since they demand nothing psychically in return for complete submission, but only money, a currency men in our society can clearly afford. Judging by the women in the film, it is a wise-cracking, strutting power that can be taken from them at any minute by a "bad date" with a knife or a gun.

A prostitute may have sexual power over men because she is prepared to play the stereotypically submissive role that supposedly excites them, while faking her own pleasure, in any kinky form which he demands. But power based on submission lasts only as long as he will allow. We have already seen how this power relation does not work for nice, gently bred, "good girls" through feminist analysis of women's roles in our society. We see now it does not work on the street much faster, where according to one character, "it gives the male population a license to murder."

As each of the hookers on Davie Street tells her story directly to the camera, we are required to look closely for the pain and listen between the lines. Joey, a quiet, dignified woman with a drug habit to support, explains that at fourteen, she wanted to hurt her father, but she wound up hurting herself. Bev, an outspoken, energetic woman, explains that she has never found a job that paid as well as much as just "being a woman." Bev has a seven-year-old son to support, and as we hear her story unfold throughout the film we discover that she has been a prostitute for six and a half years. None of these women speak emotionally of their beginnings. It is up to us to hear the quiet desperation or to ignore it, as we choose.

Ricky perches beside a bathroom mirror, her image reflected from all angles as though she has nothing to hide. She explains that when she accepted money for turning her first trick at thirteen, it took a school friend to point out to her that she was a whore. Where do the boundaries begin? "It had nothing to do with my upbringing," she explains over and over again, "I had a very strict upbringing." Can we hear something she can't?

If there is one thing in this film that really points up female sex role stereotyping, it is the men who appear in it at varying stages of their sex changes in order to become women. Jackie has completed her sex change and explains to us how hard it was to make her mother understand her desire for such an operation. She claims to have felt all along that she had been born into the wrong body, that she has always been a woman at heart. She is the only prostitute who cries while telling her story. She is soft and "feminine" and a little bit more helpless than the women who tell of their troubled lives with a steely-eyed cynicism. Jackie had internalized a role, not a gender, long before her sex change was completed. When asked why she still works the streets, she counters with a question: "Who will hire me at forty-one?" We hear this same cry often enough from newly divorced women, worried that their "wifely" skills have no market value.

While Jackie responds to "bad dates" (i.e., men with knives and guns who demand their sex free of charge) with terror and profound relief that she came out alive, Michelle responds with a knife she keeps concealed on her person. Michelle has hormone-induced breasts and is working to get the money for the rest of her sex change. Michelle is the prostitute we see most often at work. She is brassy and outspoken, extremely proud of her breasts, and the most effective ASP organizer that Davie Street has. Michelle has not internalized either standard sex role, but maintains a kind of flirtatious aggression that "dates" obviously find very appealing.

Unfortunately the lifestyle and the sexual ambiguity are wearing a bit thin on Michelle's nerves. Life is a lot easier for all of us if we just slip into that realm of what's expected of us, rather than attempting to carve out new roles for ourselves. Michelle works the street despite a loving and supportive mother who would like to see "Mark" put his three years at UBC or fine artistic talents to work. Michelle is on the street because she feels she is a freak. In fact, she is a pioneer and I wish, like her mother, she would work on her art and so tell us more.

Finally there is Curtis, who worked the streets as a boy for two months, then became Tiffany when he realized there was better money in it. Nobody is denying that prostitution pays well, though the film stresses that hard economic times have hit everyone. The point is, it pays well for women in a way that few other jobs which are traditionally women's jobs do. It does not take much training, just the training most of us have got by the age of fourteen. As Michelle's mother does not hesitate to tell us: "They're not doing it for fun."

Go and see *Hookers on Davie* on April 5 at the Bloor Street Cinema, catch it at Cineplex during its Toronto run or at the

Vancouver film festival in May. But don't go expecting a film about a group of women organizing with ASP and shouting feminist slogans. These women are aware of the kinds of things they have internalized, but they see them as survival skills.

There are a lot of mums and dads who suffer from terminal smugness because their sons stay sons and manage a certain discretion in their use of prostitutes and pornography. They're smug too because their daughters fake their sexual pleasure within the boundaries of marriage, which makes it perfectly legitimate. Smug people do not have great listening skills. When "Mark's" mom turned to the police for help, frantic about the kind of danger her son was putting himself in and unable to understand his desire to change sex, they responded kindly: "Don't worry, he'll never reach 21."

STRAIGHTFORWARD STEINEM

by Susan G. Cole

Volume 5, No. 3 (December 1983/January 1984), pp. 4 and 5

She would hate it said this way, but it's hard to deny the fact that Gloria Steinem is a star of contemporary feminism.

As a founding mother of *Ms.* magazine, she could be called a heroine on the one hand, a brave soul responsible for carting the feminist message to the most unlikely places in America. Then again, she could be called a bona fide sell-out, someone who had to dilute feminist precepts in order to maintain a readership for the magazine. As an activist she has been a presidential appointee of Jimmy Carter, so maybe she's a reformer. But as a writer, she coined the phrase "reproductive freedom" and is that movement's articulate and outspoken advocate. By any theorist's standard, this makes her a revolutionary. Some of her admirers thank mother nature for having bestowed upon her the good looks that have defined her public persona in a hyper-sexualized culture that is critical of feminists who supposedly "couldn't attract a man." Her detractors will forever distrust a pretty face, no matter what she does.

Her recent book, *Outrageous Acts and Everyday Rebellions*,

and her visit to Toronto in November to promote it, provided a rare opportunity to find out first-hand who she really is. The scene was the Medical Sciences Building at the University of Toronto. The auditorium was packed. She spoke plainly with a bit of a Midwestern twang and only the slightest trace of her confessed fear of public speaking. She spoke about how feminism had changed the language. She gently argued that a class analysis was not quite adequate for women. She answered questions, and while the audience juggled the labels that so many are anxious to affix to high profile personalities, Steinem did what she does best. She communicated.

She is first and foremost a writer and a good one. Her book is a collection of the best work she's produced over two decades as a reporter and commentator. The first two articles, "pre-feminist," as she calls them, one on life as a Playboy Bunny and the other on campaigning with McCarthy, McGovern, Rockefeller and Nixon, are proof that Steinem was a first-rate journalist.

"I Was a Playboy Bunny," written unbelievably in 1963, is state of the art reporting, a feminist *Black Like Me* in which Steinem describes the entire process — interview, bra stuffing, physical examination, the works — of becoming a Playboy Bunny. In an interview with *Broadside* she complained that the Playboy piece was superficial, that it had no analysis and that she almost regrets its apparent naïveté (though it is still the lead piece of the book). "I knew I was humiliated," she says, "but I didn't really know why." She also confesses that at the time she was wary of doing "women's pieces," and tried to avoid them in order to be guaranteed a serious spot in the media establishment.

But it's precisely the distance she puts between her own nascent consciousness and her experience that makes "I Was a Playboy Bunny" so effective. That distance (some call it objectivity) obliges her to be precise about detail — the three-inch heels the bunnies had to wear, the little fur jacket she was "allowed" to have on at the door to the Playboy Club, a jacket that still left her cleavage open to full view, and all the rest of the nasty tidbits that expose Hugh Hefner as a crypto-pimp. Any further analysis would have been heavy-handed.

Her strongest material comes out of the mouths of other people: you simply cannot be a reporter without a good ear. "Here bunny, bunny, bunny" are the first words she hears as she enters the

Playboy Club for her job interview, and her dehumanization to pet status is instantaneous. Steinem occasionally pauses just to listen, and hears one Bunny complain, "I told him our tails were asbestos and he tried to burn it to find out."

A good eye is just as important as a good ear. Steinem notices a sign on the bunny dressing room door; "Knock!" it reads, then underneath: "Come on guys, please cooperate." We get an immediate image of flunkies barging in on women who have no privacy at all.

The terrific assessment of Richard Nixon's speaking style, in "Campaigning," rings almost too true:

> For the phrase "we must reach up"…he may stretch both arms downward; for "the whole world" he may gesture close to his chest, or tick off the first two points on the third finger; for the one arm thrust that marks important statements, he may find himself with his arm raised too soon, and pause visibly to get coordinated….

Good luck helps as well. At the end of a painful interview with Pat Nixon (one of five interesting profiles in the book), in which the then first lady has been responding in near monosyllables, Nixon suddenly spews out a pathetic confession. She can't answer the questions; no one's ever asked her anything to indicate that she might have ideas of her own. What starts off badly turns into the kind of encounter writers pray for.

Steinem even manages to be prophetic. On the campaign trail with Richard Nixon she remarks wryly, "We who learned who Kennedy was only after he died may find out who Nixon is only after he's president." And unfortunately we did.

We will never know what other gems Steinem the reporter might have furnished had she not chosen to come out feminist and to write about women. Except for the articles on *Playboy*, "Campaigning," the profile of Pat Nixon and a moving and personal account of her relationship with her mother ("Ruth's Song," written especially for the book), *Outrageous Acts and Everyday Rebellions* is a compendium of pieces written for *Ms.* magazine. Except for "Networking and "Houston and History," which are both a little too glib and a few others ("In Praise of Women's Bodies" and "The

Time Factor") which don't seem important enough to re-print, the articles are models of clarity, either shedding light on the goals of the women's movement or providing analyses of issues and events that help us understand how the world works.

For example, transsexualism is a phenomenon feminists have viewed with discomfort, though many of us haven't been able to pin down exactly why. In her article on the subject, Steinem helps us understand why we find transsexualism so threatening. Put simply: If a man wants so much to be a woman, why can't biological females be happy with what they've got? And something is awry, she says, when Renée Richards can garner so much sympathy by going through a sex change when draft resisters, many of whom embody a real challenge to the old gun-toting image of machismo, receive no sympathy at all.

In the mid-seventies, the press pronounced the death of the women's movement, taking most of their evidence from observation of conservative women in college. The *New York Times Magazine* in particular seemed to make endless treks to universities in order to trumpet the news. For the sake of feminists who were wringing their hands in distress over their invisibility, Steinem counters with "Why Younger Women Are Conservative," where she explains that women, unlike men, grow more radical with age and that it's important to "educate reporters who announce feminism's demise because its red-hot centre is not on campus."

In her article on genital mutilation, she shreds the arguments belonging to those apologists for clitorectomy, expressing outrage that the opponents of genital mutilation in Africa are called cultural imperialists, and scoffs at other assumptions: "The fact that women in the Middle East who are prostitutes also have clitorectomies is cited as proof that it doesn't reduce pleasure—as if women become prostitutes out of desire."

But her arguments in favour of reproductive freedom are the most useful and should be required reading for us here in Canada, where the issue is coming to the crunch in the courts. She answers the question "If Hitler were alive whose side would he be on?" in an article so titled, and discusses the Nazi policy on women and reproductive freedom. As is often the case with Steinem, one sentence says it all: "Who decides, and where the authority lies, are never discussed in these emotional comparisons between abortion and death camps."

She has the valuable gift of making radical ideas understandable and this is her crucial contribution to development of a broad-based movement in the US. She is, for instance, a friend, admirer, and associate of Andrea Dworkin, whom she considers the "great prophet of modern feminism." Steinem? The apparent moderate, conciliator, America's best PR agent for the women's movement, in the same room as Dworkin, that outrageous raver who inspires radicals but scares just about everybody else to death? The idea seems preposterous.

Steinem admits that her "editing" relationship with Dworkin consists of her saying "Do you have to say *all* men? Couldn't you say *most* men? Or you shouldn't say thus and so, and her ignoring me altogether." Steinem revels in the energy at the radical end of feminism's spectrum and takes equal relish in pitching it to the middle. It's almost fair to say that part of her role is providing feminists with the tools for good argument. Another vital part of her role is to interpret feminism for the "I am a feminist but…" contingent.

Frankly, Steinem is not a master prose stylist. She has an irritating habit of listing events or observations, and these catalogues often seem to be an avoidance of having to organize her thoughts. But she does have a flair for one-liners that can make her work appealing. On pornography: "the preaching of sexual fascism"; or on making the ERA a constitutional amendment: "like reconstructing the entire nation's phone system to get one message across." For the most part, though, her desire to convince is revealed in prose that is often flat, even pedestrian. Steinem is not an elegant writer who soars, but rather one who likes to have her feet planted firmly on the ground. Hers is a style that does not like ambiguity.

Of course, while avoiding ambiguities she tends to skirt the complexities of an issue and this is bound to provoke readers who, from the inside of the women's movement, know that the differences in some areas are sharp and that Steinem has left some things out. She is decidedly unconfrontational in her approach, and this poses problems in one or two of the weaker articles in the book.

"Networking" is the worst offender. It begins by reporting on "women and everything" conferences that brought ambitious and career-oriented women together. This "networking" Steinem describes as important for developing contacts. Behind all of this is the assumption that if women took their places in the board rooms of the great American multi-nationals, things would improve immeasurably—a sentiment which will bother many who insist that more profound changes in the economy are required to make much difference. She tries to assuage these critics in the same article, by turning "networking" into political organizing against the system. At some point one wishes to remind Steinem that she simply can't have it both ways. In many ways, the article on networking reflects the worst of *Ms.* magazine when it tries to be all things to all women.

As an appointee of Carter's presidential commission and an organizer and sponsor of the National Conference in Houston in 1977, Steinem had a hard time wearing both the hat of the organizer and the hat of the reporter. She starts out in "Houston and History" as if to write a puff piece about a conference whose success is still the subject of a heated debate. Then she deftly sidesteps most of the contemporary issues by writing that the Houston conference was not the first of its kind, and that we should rescue from obscurity Seneca Falls and other conventions like it, giving them their rightful place in history.

She speaks glowingly in the same article about the emerging coalition between black and white women. It is a most optimistic analysis. It's easy to agree that the potential for mutual self-interest is there among white women and women of colour, but it's a bit premature to remark on an effective coalition.

But her continued optimism is vintage Steinem. She's a quintes-sentially American writer. She doesn't mind being called American, as if it were more a state of mind than an adjective connoting place of birth. "Yes, I do feel American and positive about it," she said in our interview. "I guess it's because I was able to move out of a working class background. There's a crazy kind of class mobility in the States and a multi-cultural experience that doesn't exist anywhere else."

She still harbours confidence in America's institutions. Even advertising, she argues, can be a forum for consciousness-raising. Her response to criticism of *Ms.* ads was unblinking: "*Ms.* couldn't exist without advertising," she insists. "Advertising constitutes about 40% of the information we get. So we use *Ms.* magazine as a forum to teach advertisers the appropriate images of women. We get them to imagine women driving sports cars and men taking kids to the dentist."

Her confidence in American political institutions is similarly intact. She writes in "Far from the Opposite Shore" about how she and other feminists worried that the ERA amendment would be a drop in patriarchy's bucket of sexist institutions: "The slowly revealed cumulative potential of mass movement pressure has made a lot of us change our minds. So has the right wing backlash and its implicit testimony to the importance of a constitutional principle of equality." She said in the interview that her primary agenda and her gift to Canada will be to get rid of Ronald Reagan, and one of the outrageous acts she recommended to her audience at U of T was simply to vote.

If the point of Steinem's work is to make sense out of feminism, then she's very good at it. In fact, she has done more to raise the collective consciousness of American women (and men) than just about anyone else. She couldn't have done it without travelling the country, talking to women and making sure she stayed involved in a struggle with them. She couldn't have done it by being anything other than what she is—a plain-talking Midwesterner who has a lot in common with her potential constituency and who makes sure she speaks the same language as the people she's trying to reach.

And reach them she does.

THE STORY OF VALERIE VAPID

Reviewed by Margaret Atwood

Volume 6, No. 4 (February 1985), p. 10

Margaret Ann Jensen, *Love's $weet Return*. Toronto: The Women's Press, 1984.

Love's $weet Return is about everything you ever needed to know about Harlequin Romances but were too bored to ask. However, according to Margaret Ann Jensen, your dismissive lack of interest is in itself a symptom: in a society in which women's culture and writing are per se undervalued, Harlequins—unlike male forms of pop culture, such as Westerns—have been literally beneath notice. Jensen is not (luckily) trying to make a case for Harlequins as great literature; but she is saying, quite rightly, that a form consumed in such huge quantities, by, world-wide, such enormous numbers of women, is worthy of examination, at least from a sociological standpoint. Who reads these things, and why? Is the audience for Harlequins really composed of brainwashed subliterate frontal lobotomy cases, as we tend to believe? Do the readers end up believing that some dashing millionaire is going to waft into their lives and upgrade their wardrobes? Do they long for melted knees and a master-doormat relatioship? Are Harlequins—especially from a feminist viewpoint—*dangerous*?

The answer to all these questions are the same: in a word, No. But in order to arrive at this answer, Jensen takes us, statistic by statistic, interview by interview, over every bit of terrain Harlequins have ever set glass slipper on. I guess she figures we'll need a lot of convincing, and she's right about that, too. So we get a history of Harlequin Enterprises, its corporate structure (missionary position: men on top, women supplying the material, the editorial pool, the readers and therefore the cash flow), its marketing attitudes (book as product, with a heavy reliance on consumer surveys; that is, what they get is what they want), its fiction formula, its black velvet painting prose style, its reader profiles, its reader motivation—they *like* predictability—and, most interestingly, its relationship to feminism and the changes that have taken place in Harlequins since I myself last dipped into the adventures of Valerie Vapid, fifteen years ago, and found them just too tedious to go on with.

Jensen's book started life as a thesis, and a whiff of sociological academia lingers on. The prose style is a little cardboardy, the points are sometimes overly made. But on the whole this is a thoughtful and worthwhile book, and a must for anyone pondering the problems of female genre fiction, pop cultch and related fields. I agree with a number of its contentions. For instance, the stand on masochism. Some say that the heroine's engagement to the older, richer, more powerful and rather domineering hero at the end of the book is symptomatic of the female will to lose and represents failure and defeat. Not so, says Jensen. The heroine—who is not rich and powerful—undergoes a hundred and eighty pages of struggle, which embody in symbolic form the struggles encountered by the readers themselves. Life for most women is not easy; the smorgasbord still contains a somewhat limited selection of goodies, even for new-style North American women with jobs.

"Women represent fifty percent of the adult world population, one-third of all working hours, receive only one-tenth of world income and own less than one percent of world property." That's not from Jensen's book, it's from a U N statement on the status of women, but it puts things into perspective. Harlequins are about doing the best you can under the circumstances, which are not dandy. Harlequins are about Beauty and the Beast. Harlequins are about lion taming: if you can't be a lion yourself, at least you can domesticate one. If you can't get power any other way, you make the best available trade-off: your body, with melted knees, for his eternal devotion to you. Your melted knees have to be real, of course: Harlequin readers are not cynics. This is hardly total masochism. Harlequins are, among other things, how-to books on the fantasy level, for women who experience daily their own lack of power. This among other things may explain why there are no Lesbian Harlequins, although there now are some for teenagers and divorcees: if only men have external power, you can't acquire it by annexing another woman.

This point could have been made a little more clearly by contrasting Harlequins and their ilk, which derive from *Pride and Prejudice*, with other forms of female-consumed pop literature: Gothics, for instance, in which the threat is not the failure of romance but death; or Barbara Cartland-style cocktease epics, in which the threat to the heroine is rape; or True Confessions, grittier in texture, in which the driving energy is supplied by guilt; or even True Romance comics with their teardrop covers, which are a lot closer to plain old snivelling. By comparison, Harlequins come out rather practical and down-to-earth. They play Plain Jane to the more extravagant Brontë and Radcliffe progeny of the other sub-genres. What all have in common, of course, is the proposing of individual solutions to what are, in the big picture, social problems: get your heart straight, win the hero. It is your own life that must be adjusted, not the general condition of women. That there aren't enough handsome millionaires to go around is not supposed to trouble you, because Harlequins are, after all, escape fantasy. That there are no longer any stagecoaches doesn't perturb the readers of Westerns, either.

Judging from the samples provided by Jensen, Harlequins are still difficult to read; that is, the style is still as ornate, cliché-ridden and euphemistic as ever. But things are changing. In response to reader demands, more sex is creeping in, disguised in polysyllabic verbal verdure but sex nonetheless. Heroines are becoming more real: they aren't always virgins, they've sometimes had bad experiences. The women's movement has had an impact: the heroines can have erotic feelings of their own, they have better jobs, they sometimes have opinions on things other than what colour of belt goes best with their toe polish. Valerie Vapid has been replaced by Samantha Semi-liberated, who demands and gets better terms. For instance, she doesn't have to give up her job at the end of the book, not always. And sometimes the hero makes concessions. The men are depicted as possessing even greater phallic energy, and sometimes engage in what in any other context would be called sexual harassment. There's even a bit of slapping around, and those versed in the lore of wife-beating would do well to suspect the extremely possessive, bossy, traditional sex-role addict hero, however mad his passion, hard his thighs and fat his pocketbook. As a corollary to the increased bargaining power and active sexuality of the women, there's an increase too in male coyness. It's the hero, not the heroine, who is inscrutable and mysterious and plays peek-a-boo and c'mere-gettaway. As the women display more autonomy, the men display more hostility, in one form or another. It was hard to be hostile to poor Valerie, so delicate and innocent a touch could turn her to Cream of Wheat, but Samantha, in response to reader preferences, is made of sterner stuff.

Thank heavens, I say, and good on her. Keep going, Samantha. Hold out for your job in interior decoration, if that's what you want; it's a step up from Valerie's eternal secretarial drudgery. After three years of marriage you can send Mr. Darcy off to a self-help group so he can learn more adult ways of expressing his emotions, and in another fifteen years I'll check in on you, via the next book by Margaret Ann Jensen, to see how you're doing. As you go, so goes the inner life, and therefore a little bit of the outer life, of a great many women: if you aren't prepared to settle for rock-bottom crummy terms, maybe they won't either. And I agree with Jensen that this fact is far from negligible.

Margaret Atwood's latest book of poetry is Interlunar.

PLEASURE AND DANGER RUNS HOT AND COLD
Reviewed by Sherrill Cheda
Volume 6, No. 8 (June 1985), p. 14

Carole Vance, ed. *Pleasure and Danger: Exploring Female Sexuality*. Boston, London, Melbourne, and Henley: Routledge & Kegan Paul, 1984.

Proceeding from Emma Goldman's *The Traffic in Women and Kate Millet's Sexual Politics*, *Pleasure and Danger* breaks new ground and is one of the most thought-provoking anthologies since *Sisterhood is Powerful* (1971). Carole Vance, in her thoughtful and comprehensive introduction, asks difficult questions about female sexuality and urges us to keep asking these questions. Neither pop psychology nor a sociological text, the articles, first presented at the Scholar and Feminist IX conference held at Barnard College in New York in 1982, have excellent notes.

Contrary to what previous reviewers have led us to believe, this collection is not a study of pornography. It is, however, about the erotic in women's lives. The book eschews an analysis of women's traditionally dangerous efforts to gain pleasure—such as marriage, adultery, pick-ups in bars, dating clubs or placing classified advertisements. Instead, *Pleasure and Danger* explores butch-fem, top and bottom, fat, fantasy, fear as a form of self-censorship, Hispanic and Black women's experience, assumptions about disabled women and sex manuals as conservative information. There are no Ann Landers cuddles here.

Beginning with "Seeking ecstasy on the battlefield," Ellen Carol Dubois and Linda Gordon try to connect contemporary anti-pornography feminists to 19th century social purity politicians. In "The taming of the Id: Feminist sexual politics, 1968-83," Alice Echols suggests that all anti-pornography women are anti-sex and all anti-censorship women are pro-sex. While Echol's points may be more true for the States, in Canada, as Lynda Hurst noted in the *Toronto Star* (April 30, 1985), "The Fraser Committee clearly saw through the current myth that feminism and traditional conservatism coincide." The anti-porn group in Canada includes women from various backgrounds, as does the anti-censorship group. Echols uses pornography as an all inclusive word with no definition and no distinction made for violence and hate literature against women. Rather than being anti-sex (pleasure), the anti-porn women I know are convinced that women can experience no pleasure when being raped, genitally mutilated, or drawn and quartered. The distance between danger and violence is a wide gap. Violence against women is not erotic. To be against violence against women is not to be anti-erotic.

Echols confuses a lot of issues, overstates her case and blurs lines:

> "Although cultural feminists blame the sexual revolution for destroying the old sexual order, radical feminists' attack on marriage, romantic love, puritan morality, and respect certainly hastened its downfall."

Wait a minute. How did "respect" get into that sentence? Respect for whom or what? She overlooks the fact that radical feminism is a method of analyzing reality from a political point of view. Marriage, romantic love, *et al*. were already in great disarray before the second wave of feminism. Her efforts to connect the anti-abortion movement to the anti-pornography movement ultimately fail because most anti-porn feminists are pro-choice.

Other major contributions are "everything they always wanted you to know: the ideology of popular sex literature" by Meryl Altman, "Above and beyond politics," a sensitive and sensible approach to sex education by Mary Calderone, and "Politically correct? Politically incorrect?" by Muriel Dimen. And it is good to see a familiar radical feminist name such as Kate Millett writing about children and sexuality from a power politics point of view.

Esther Newton and Shirley Wallton make a valiant effort to present a more precise sexual vocabulary but end up with some sweeping generalizations, spurious arguments and confusing statements.

"Cunnilingus was satisfying, but since fellatio had been implicity [sic] condemned by feminism, Shirley had almost no sex life."

"'Egalitarian sex' assumes functionally interchangeable partners and acts."

"Thinking sex: notes for a radical theory of the politics of sexuality" by Gayle Rubin represents the 'erotic-tastes-are-like-gastronomic-tastes' school of thought. And the fallacy that sex with children is somehow in the forefront of sexual thought creeps into this contribution to the point that the author attempts to link lack of sympathy with boy-lovers to right-wing anti-communism. The term "intergenerational sex" should receive the Euphemism of the Year award.

Nevertheless, Rubin raises many important issues about sexuality as social construct. She rightly points out that sexual acts are burdened with an excess of significance. She doesn't suggest that the reasons for this could be because of the vulnerability of intimacy, risk of pregnancy, responsibility, jealousy, or even, one of the themes of this book, danger. She does define a democratic morality:

"A democratic morality should judge sex acts by the way partners treat one another, the level of mutual consideration, the presence or absence of coercion, and the quantity and quality of the

pleasures they provide. Whether sex acts are gay or straight, coupled or in groups, naked or in underwear, commercial or free,
with or without video, should not be ethical concerns."

One of the best written articles in the collection is Sharon
Thompson's "Search for to-morrow; on feminism and the reconstruction of teen romance," which is based on fifty life histories
and the author's wise analysis of the quest for romance, juxtaposed
against the reality of teenage sexual experience. The bargains girls
can strike have changed and they are left even more powerless than
when sex equalled marriage.

An underlying theme in the articles by Echols, Rubin and
Thompson is that radical feminists did not change the world as
they promised they would, and unfortunately made way for cultural
feminists, those anti-sex women, mostly lesbian separatists, who
now bring you censorship. The motif that feminism has failed runs
underground throughout this book; some authors go so far as to
blame feminism for their lack of sexual fulfillment.

Generally speaking, according to this collection, there *are* no
misogynists, pimps, pornographers, wife abusers or rapists. Women
seem to exist almost by themselves on a planet where violence has
been scooped out of the landscape—in its own way, a separatist
space. If women are occasionally victims, it is of unknown assailants.

Many of the writing styles seem exaggerated but perhaps this
is because the selections were first verbal presentations, surrounded
by controversy. The controversy continues and reading this book is
guaranteed to stretch your mind.

Sherrill Cheda is a Toronto arts administrator.

THE CLICHETTES: OUT OF THIS WORLD

by Susan G. Cole

Volume 7, No. 2 (November 1985), p. 14

In the early 60s, an array of what became known as "girl groups" released pop records about bad love and mad love. Tragic romance, along with the "dulang dulang"—"de-doo-run-run" back-up vocals, became the thematic and musical signatures for these groups and they repeated the formula with such regularity that the sensibility itself, even within the space of just five years, became something of a cliché. Lip-synching—mouthing the words to recordings- became popular when Dick Clark's American Bandstand featured these pop singers who lip-synched to their own records, pretending to perform live, and not in the least convincingly. Thus lip-synching became a laughable cliché of early 60s music promotion.

Johanna Householder, Louise Garfield and Janice Hladki, all of them devoted to the icons of culture, especially the girls in those groups, knew this. They donned improbable wigs, so that they would look like their role models (remember the 60s beehive look?) and began to lip synch, tearing apart the conventions of sex stereotypes and sexual oppression/repression of the 50s and 60s. They called themselves the Clichettes.

In performance, the Clichettes have always been out of this world, literally and figuratively. Literally speaking, audiences not familiar with the Clichettes brand of comic mayhem could not be sure whether it was a send-up or a put-down, and even the judges in the US may have missed the joke when, faced with the Clichettes' technical brilliance, they bestowed them first prize at the national lip-synching contest in Houston last year. Figuratively speaking, the Clichettes' theatre has always taken them into the realm of science fiction and inter-planetary travel where the implications of sexist ritual can be developed without constraint, dissected and of course, parodied.

She Devils of Niagara is the latest of their theatrical offerings, at the Factory Theatre in Toronto, and admirers who have had to settle for just snippets of Clichette hilarity at benefits can now take in a full two hours of frenzied satire. The time: 1998; the place: Earth, at Niagara Falls (Canadian side of course). Jan, Lou and Jo, three

The fabulous Clichettes in She Devils of Niagara: (from left) Janice Hladki, Johanna Householder, and Louise Garfield.

intergalactic travellers, alight to discover that the "great sperm male" is an endangered species. The gender police are implementing a ten-year plan to preserve male culture, and martial law commands that everyone behave like men. This means that women have to lower their voices, learn to play football and make it appear as if they have a jock-strap-full between their legs. It also means that when the trio lands a gig at Club Over the Falls, their act must denigrate female-ness and celebrate machismo in all its forms. This is the set-up for most of the lip-synch routines.

Jan, Lou and Jo have their own personal preoccupations in a script, co-written with Marni Jackson, that careens with one-liners. Jan misses sex. She won't settle for the fast-food version available at the SCBO (complete with a cigarette afterwards) and so she tries the ultimate subversion: cooking up the right chemical solution for gender differentiation. Lou wants love and finds it with a turtle. Jo is more practical and looks for more work so that she can pay off fines incurred by violating the laws of mono-gender. She does a stint at the wax museum where only one half of history is on display; female heroines have been relegated to the basement. There is a happy ending to all this, all the more wonderful because the Clichettes wind up with a superb change of musical gears.

As is usually the case with comedy that has to try *everything*, the play lacks the kind of structural tension that might make it work for more conventional theatre goers. The gender police appear too many times, so that the suspense they might have generated never seems to materialize. The pleasure in the performance derives more from one-liners than from plot. And the Clichettes are more innovative as performers—lip-synchers and dancers—than as actors. In the end, the Factory Theatre stage seems to overwhelm the performance, and the problem is exacerbated by a nebulous set and flat lighting that never really captures all the potential of a Clichette performance. The spectacular costumes often make up for the technical problems, but She Devils' episodic nature makes it more a revue than capital-T Theatre, which might explain Toronto critics' antipathy to the work.

But these are a matter of form (who cares about critics anyway? Certainly the Clichettes don't) and misses the essence of the Clichettes' vision. They have always been on the brink of a pop epiphany in which mainstream music wails out the pleasure and pain of sex and romance. In past performances, their idiosyncratic tastes held them back from the ultimate revelation. Half Human, Half Heartache, their first full-length theatre piece (about the other side of the gender dilemma: a how to come back to earth and behave like girls without going crazy) often missed because of the Clichettes' purist zeal. They selected obscure material, little known songs by well-known girl groups, appearing to avoid on purpose material that would bring a flash of recognition to an audience. This time, they let go of some of their obscurantism and give us a long-awaited rendition of the Shangri Las' "You Can Never Go Home Anymore," while still finding amazing tid-bits, especially a spoken piece on the (male) I virtues of quail hunting, that sustain their reputations as archivists.

But lip-synching is really the hook here, and it is vintage Clichettes. Every nuance counts, the tug of a crotch, the stroking of a chin, all performed with that award-winning perfect unison. So if the name Clichette evokes something feminine and diminuitive, don't be fooled. There is nothing diminutive about *She Devils of Niagara*. And feminine? Not on planet Earth, not in 1998, and not when the Clichettes "Walk like a man."

A FERTILITY TALE

Reviewed by Carroll Klein

Volume 7, No. 3 (December 1985/January 1986), p. 13

Margaret Atwood, *The Handmaid's Tale*. Toronto: McLelland and Stewart, 1985.

Margaret Atwood's latest novel, *The Handmaid's Tale*, is a nightmare vision of the ascendency of the fundamentalist Christian right in America. In time, it is the near future; in place, the United States, which has become the Republic of Gilead, a theocracy compared, in the historical notes at the end of the book, with Iran in its late 20th century Muslim fundamentalism.

It is a world both bizarre and chillingly possible; "it could never happen here" sounds a hollow, unconvincing whisper. Everything in this novel responds to, or logically extends from, the trends, attitudes and events of the 1980s. The forces of righteousness have risen up to combat what they see as the work of the devil: the rights of individuals to make choices in their lives; women's liberation; the rights of minorities, sexual and otherwise; the epidemic of sexually transmitted diseases; rampant and readily available pornography and prostitution.

Gilead has suffered some devastating nuclear accidents. Fertility has become a major issue, though it is never considered in anything but patriarchal, Biblical terms: this is not a man's problem; women are either fruitful or they are barren. Those few who do manage to bear children, however, have no guarantee that their offspring will be normal; "unbabies" or "shredders" are horribly common.

To offset the dying population, the rulers of Gilead have devised a scheme that, at once, creates a rigid order that keeps women in their place and at the same time provides the most viable breeding pool possible. The Handmaids, women who have successfully borne children or who are young and potentially fertile, are placed in the homes of those men who are in charge of the Republic. Here they are expected to keep their bodies in good order and attempt to become pregnant at each ovulation. They are supervised by Wives, who have much greater status being married to men of power, and cared for by Marthas, who cook and clean and appear to resonate the most simple-minded Christian belief in the righteousness of the existing hierarchy.

Econowives, women married to poor or powerless men, are expected to behave as both Handmaids and Marthas, but they are of no interest in the existing order. The sinister Unwomen are a collection of rebels, feminists and intellectuals who, in official terms, no longer exist. The luckiest of the Unwomen have been sent to the Colonies to work in the agricultural sector; the least lucky sweep tailings of nuclear waste, clean up the toxic pollutants that have devastated the land, or burn the bodies of the soldiers who die protecting Gilead from the rebel forces—Quakers, Baptists, those who would keep alive the dream of a free country.

Women are thus diminished, their roles as utilitarian and subservient as could be wished for by any fundamentalist whose greatest desire is to punish the daughters of Eve for their mother's sin.

Offred, (a brilliant choice of name on Atwood's part: it has a harmless enough Anglo-Saxon look until it is juxtaposed with other Handmaids' names—Ofglen, Ofwarren—and its intent is made clear.) is the central character of the novel, the Handmaid whose tale is being narrated. She has just been assigned to a new Commander for whom she is an "ambulatory chalice," having proven her fertility in her old life, before the revolution and the creation of Gilead.

Offred has never cultivated the "poverty of spirit" that Aunt Lydia, one of the Handmaids' keepers preaches, but she has suppressed her outrage and confusion and defies the existing order only in small and secret ways. It is clear that Offred, in her other life, was intelligent and well educated; she was also complacent and apolitical, unlike her mother who was a feminist and has subsequently disappeared, an Unwoman.

Offred is filled with memories of a time when she had a male partner, a daughter, a house and a cat, an outrageous friend from university days and an unreconstructed radical for a mother. But there is a horrifying aspect to Offred's memory: the old order seems to be dimming, becoming less real; she offers her recollections with a perspective that is at once curious and distant, as if she were remembering a life that belonged to someone else. But there remain glimmers of hope:

> My name isn't Offred, I have another name, which nobody uses now because it's forbidden. I tell myself it doesn't matter, your name is like your telephone number, useful only to others; but what I tell myself is wrong, it does matter. I keep the knowledge of this name like something hidden, some treasure I'll come back to dig up, one day. I think of this name as buried. This name has an aura around it, like an amulet, some charm that's survived from an unimaginably distant past. I lie in my single bed at night, with my eyes closed, and the name floats there behind my eyes, not quite within reach, shining in the dark.

The terrible, oppressive boredom of Offred's life, the month-by-month waiting in hope of fulfilling the role given her, the sensory deprivation of her cloistered life, begin to break down as the story slowly reveals itself. Offred has lost touch with, or never knew how to contact, others who, like her, see Gilead as a perverse and dangerous regime. Somehow, through the cracks, under the deadly watch of the Eyes, Offred discovers resistance and the possibility of escape—or death.

Atwood, at her literary best in this novel, peels back in tantalizing, sometimes maddeningly slow fashion, the layers of history that illuminate the present and reveal the inevitability of the decisions that Offred must make when she is given, once more, the terrible possibility of choice.

LYNNE FERNIE'S LESBIANS FLY CANADA: SAVE ME A SEAT!
by Susan G. Cole
Volume 7, No. 8 (June 1986), p. 10

For a fleeting week, anyone in Toronto standing on the corner of Yonge and Wellesley could face north and see something truly astonishing. Electromedia's giant Pixel board, that computerized dot matrix that usually flashes a version of "buy this or that," was saying, and in very bright lights, "LESBIANS FLY CANADA: Private Desire Public Sins." There was even a twinkling map of Canada to drive the point home. The message was written by visual artist Lynne Fernie as part of an artists project called Some Uncertain Signs.

But this was not Fernie's original submission. Her first version was "Lesbians Fly Air Canada: Private Desires Public Sins." The story of how and why Fernie's contribution had to change sheds some strong light on what happens when feminist artists try to occupy corporate territory.

The Public Access artists collective had put together Some Uncertain Signs to explore the implications of artists working in advertising venues. The Pixel board was donated by Electromedia, an advertising company which controls various billboards and display spaces. When Fernie was asked to contribute, her text was thoughtful and straightforward: She chose "Lesbians" because Electromedia's

Pixel Board is located in the heart of the gay commercial district, and the word "gays," according to Fernie has been too gentrified by media; "Fly" because she wanted to avoid the word buy, the most blatantly consumer-oriented word; "Air Canada" because it is a crown corporation, publicly owned, with the word Canada in it. And essentially, Fernie wanted to state a fact. Hence "Lesbians Fly Air Canada." The phrase, "Private desires, Public sins" captures Fernie's conviction that stating difficult truths is something Canadians avoid, especially if the truth has something to do with sex.

"I expected a problem, and I *had* called it my 'bad girl' project," Fernie said. "But as the work of an artist and a lesbian, by not questioning an absence in culture—particularly in advertising culture—the piece would have lacked integrity. I felt I had to address the inhabitation of a corporate sector which would rather die than associate themselves or their image with a particular group."

She was right. The message went right to the collective corporate solar plexus, and Electromedia didn't like it at all. The company rejected the submission. Fernie had expected this, and had already strategized a fallback position. She would have settled for "Lesbians Fly Air____" followed by the twinkling map of the country. Rejected.

Bad girl project or not, Fernie had never set out to trash the corporate community, only to question its values. "I knew I was pushing the boundaries," she admitted, "but I had worked on it very carefully. I didn't want it to be an attack. I wanted it to be a critique of the absence of lesbians in advertising. It definitely was not corporation bashing. But apparently, the people at Electromedia kept insisting that I should address lesbians directly without making reference to anything else, which is homophobic."

Fernie had only three options in the wake of the first rejection: "I could withdraw from the project, in which case the absence would have been noticed by maybe 100 local artists; I could delay the project; or develop a new one in three weeks." Fernie finally settled for the final version: Lesbians Fly Canada: Private Desires Public Sins. "I always said that if compromises were going to be necessary, it is important that we examine exactly what the compromise will be and that we articulate the boundaries of the acceptable. I personally never had the killer attitude, but I do know now what is allowable in public space."

It's interesting to note what Electromedia had considered acceptable before Fernie had challenged those boundaries. Electromedia had already had their progressive values tested through the submission of Les Levine. His text, "Rape Hate Kill Lie Steal," was considered too provocative until the collective convinced the corporate donors that he had the proper artistic credentials. Showing them another text of Levine's which had been mounted in New York's Times Square helped considerably. Fernie, though, was not so fortunate. She hasn't made the right New York connections yet. And besides, her previous work connecting lesbian visibility with

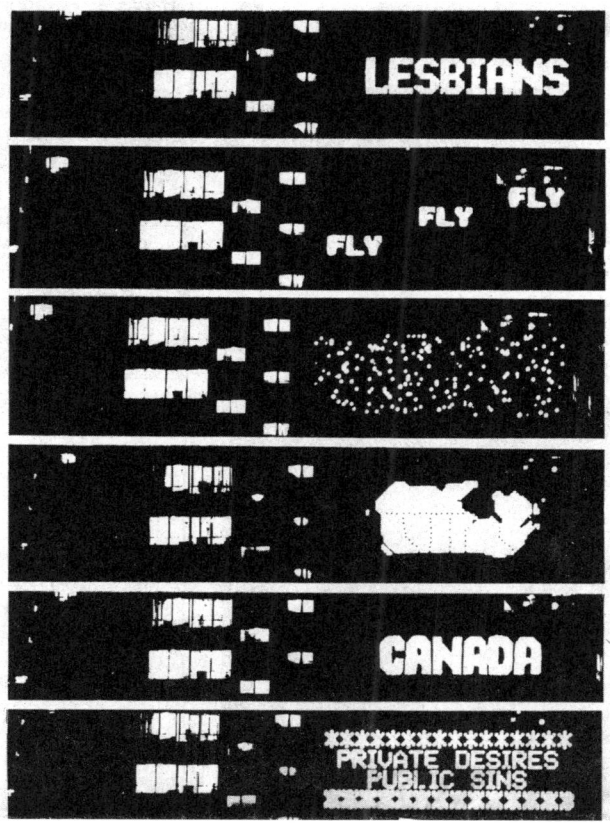

Artist Lynne Fernie's 1986 pixel billboard Lesbians Fly Canada—Private Desire, Public Sins put the word lesbian in lights for the first time.

feminist theory—particularly her paintings and drawings in Sparkes Gallery's Unparallel Views and the YYZ Gallery's Gay Gaze—doesn't have the Levine cowboy/artiste stance that might appeal to a corporate sensibility.

So who allows the expression, and why, continues to be the issue. Notice that the word lesbian was not the problem with Fernie's work. It was the connection between Air Canada and lesbians that counted. And it wasn't Air Canada who complained about the submission. Air Canada is not even one of Electromedia's clients. When a spokesman for Electromedia rejected the first ideas, he mentioned concern over a *potential* client, not a current account. If the object of Some Uncertain Signs was to investigate the relationship between advertising and the corporation, Fernie's project was a complete success. It uncovered what Fernie calls the phenomenon of corporate citizenship. Even without a formal relationship with Air Canada, Electromedia was determined to do the right thing as a member of the corporate fraternity.

The Public Access artists collective, torn between principle and whatever good faith had been generated between the collective and Electromedia, could only give Fernie so much support. They wound up caught in the awkward position of appearing to approve of control of artistic expression. Mark Lewis, one of the collective members, tried valiantly to make the distinction between state and corporate censorship, but Fernie's anti-censorship politics were too sophisticated for Lewis's fine lines, and her earlier work shows it. Fernie's contribution to the A Space show Issues of Censorship was called Altering Image. Using the found art of Vogue photographs and a dense text, Fernie widened the discourse on censorship to take in anorexia and the way women's bodies are shaped and censored. Having done that much, she was not about to buy Lewis' argument that Electromedia had not really "censored" anything. "True, it's not state censorship," she allowed. "But it *is* the corporate control over what can appear in certain public space. Canada is a country where people don't like to talk about what's going on, and anything that threatens Victorian sensibilities gets swept under the carpet."

"And Canada's carpets," Fernie concludes, "are very lumpy."

NO FIXED ADDRESS

Agnès Varda's Vagabond
Reviewed by Donna Gollan
Volume 7, No. 9 (July 1986), p. 8

"By being the filmmaker I am, I feel I'm making a natural statement for feminism," says Agnès Varda; and, after seeing her latest film *Vagabond*, I have to agree with her. The film is no feminist manifesto (as *One Sings, The Other Doesn't* was considered), but it is competently made, as interesting artistically as it is sociologically, proving beyond question Varda's rank as one of the top filmmakers working in France today, male or female. *Vagabond* won the Golden Lion Award (Venice) and its young star, Sandrine Bonnaire walked off with this year's César (France) for best actress, at the tender age of eighteen.

Vagabond is the final chapter in the story of Mona, a young drifter whose journey through the bleak wintry landscape of the South of France ends abruptly when she freezes to death in a ditch. This end is not, however, the final scene of a suspenseful film, but rather the very first image we must deal with—her corpse rudely stuffed into a body bag, despite its awkward frozen state. From here on we retrace her steps, interviewing the people she came in contact with and hearing their often vague and hazy recollections of her, coloured by their own personalities, rather than by Mona's.

Mona is a rude, dirty, objectionable rebel who nonetheless demands our attention, if not our sympathy. Varda takes care not to psychoanalyze her—we are given no pat answers to explain why she hit the road in the first place.

"I like my position as a screenwriter who doesn't know everything)," explains Varda. "I wish to know more about her too."

When I said I had not liked the character, nor her vast negativity, Varda seemed surprised. "You're not supposed to like her…She's not a free woman, she's a rebel. She says 'No.' She goes so far in that word 'No' and 'leave me alone' that she is, in the end, left alone to die." This is the nucleus of what makes Mona so interesting. She is a character with no motivation. She wants nothing. When she is asked to stay, she leaves. When she is given land, she neglects it. Above all, it is crucial for her sense of self to reject the rules. It seems that there are many more rules for a woman than for a man and therefore many more to reject. She wastes no energy on her appearance, her cleanliness, her manners and absolutely rejects the subtle flirtations that might have made getting food and money easy. It is against this rebellion that she measures herself and tests her own strength. This strength is so absolute that it is surprising, in a way, that she ever gives up and dies. We listen eagerly to the people she met along the way, hoping for some clues that would explain this desolate end.

Each character in the film—and they come from all classes, from landowners and their servants to academics and the poorest immigrant farm labourers—projects onto Mona what he or she needs to see in a young woman travelling alone. Mona becomes an empty canvas with nothing to protect her image from being re-painted every time she meets someone, except her insurmountable rebellion. She rejects their sentimentality, protecting herself with a prickly rudeness and a determination to free herself from all entanglements. An over-educated dropout shepherd gets preachy, explaining to us straight through the eye of the camera that she was "withering, not wandering." Mona, however, sneers at his gruelling way of life and scorns his over-educated state: "If I had a degree in philosophy, I sure wouldn't be herding goats."

One rich old woman presumed blind and senile proves to be happily affected by Mona's spirit of rebellion. Together they drink and laugh until the old woman's maid to put an immediate stop to such unprecedented behaviour. Yolande, the maid, is a fascinating character herself; victimized by her criminal boyfriend as well as the rich old woman, she is unable to break out of her role as doormat even though Mona has just shown her that it is entirely possible. Instead, she projects a lovely sentimental fantasy onto is Mona and a young man squatting in an old chateau. While Yolande is busy weaving the ultimate romance around the two, Mona is happily smoking the young man's entire grass supply. And when it is completely finished? Mona leaves, of course. "I thought she was the staying kind," explains the young man, mournfully. We are left wondering what on earth would lead him to think so.

While numerous characters reveal more to us about themselves and their places in society than they do about Mona, there is one woman who attempts to take the wanderer exactly as she finds her.

An academic who specializes in tree diseases picks up Mona as a hitchhiker and comes to enjoy her company, despite the powerful odour she finds initially upsetting. She feeds Mona and allows her to sleep in the car. She does not push for conversation nor search for answers once she discovers that Mona has no intention of letting down her barriers. When she lets her off, eventually, after several days of travelling, Mona seems somehow softened and slightly more vulnerable. It is no coincidence that the following scene finds Mona raped in the woods. The academic is left with a sense of loss and a vague uneasiness about the safety of her odd protégé. We are left with no such uncertainty. A woman alone is sexual prey. This is a danger of the road. Mona has faced this as she faces everything—with a fight, and with defeat which in no way breaks her spirit, that enormous "No" which characterizes her.

When I spoke to Agnès Varda, I asked her about her own feelings towards Mona. She replied that she researched the film by picking up hitchhikers and always found the women that much more fascinating than the men. "A woman alone is more interesting because it is understood that she is without-a-man. How will she manage?" When I told her that many journalists had assumed she spoke through the philosophy of the shepherd or the sorrowful regret of the academic who saw Mona as a reproach to her own comfort, she smiled and said: "Of course there's a little of me in each of the characters—but I would rather be the old woman who drinks and laughs."

The first signs of Mona's spirit breaking begin physically, with the breaking of her boots, and mentally, with a Moroccan farm labourer who lures her with false promises of care and dependence. She agrees to stay with him while he is alone in the vineyards, trimming vines. He accepts her absolutely as lazy, useless, dirty and in turn cares for her without exercising any power over her. When his fellow Moroccans return he bows to the higher authority of their closed society and tells her she must leave. She is furious. For the first time she is being thrown out of a society she has not chosen to reject.

In time she is lured into a world of wine and drugs, squatters and train station begging. She loses her last possessions in a fire—her tent and sleeping bag—and struggles into town for food. She stumbles into a wine ritual in which frightening villagers dressed in masks and leaves douse unsuspecting victims in wine sediment. Mona has nowhere to go to dry off, and dies, crying in the ditch. The story has come full circle. Connections are made between all the people she has met which gives us a sense of narrative closure. The filth she has espoused has finally killed her, so has the wine and the entire wine growing region in bitter wintertime. Mona has travelled from ocean to earth. She dies shortly before dawn and, ironically, just before spring.

Vagabond is rich in imagery, the textures of poverty and, incongruously, beautiful to watch. It is vibrant and strong in the statements it makes about women's lives and their sometimes inescapable roles. Finally, it is desolate and negative in its analysis of absolute freedom and absolute loneliness. Varda set out to make a film about the horror of the possibility of a person dying of the cold in this modern world. She has done far more than that. She has shown us what this cold consists of.

JOYCE WIELAND: INDISPUTABLE SPLENDOUR

by Ingrid MacDonald
Volume 8, No. 7 (May 1987), p. 11

Heralded as Canada's foremost woman artist, Joyce Wieland, now 56 years old, recently opened a major retrospective show at the Art Gallery of Ontario in Toronto. This exhibition, which will travel to Charlottetown, Fredericton, and Regina in the next year, brings together more than 25 years of work in painting and film.

The pleasure of a retrospective is that one can observe the progression of change and growth: abstracts give way to filmic sequences, give way to pop art, to quilting, to pencil drawings, to landscapes, to large bold mythological canvasses.

Wieland's retrospective begins with large canvasses exploring the intensities of colour. Shapes like big bubbles are chalked out against a colour-drenched background in *Hallucination* (1961). 1961 was an extremely prolific year for Wieland: it was the year before her move to New York, and the year that she produced the work that established her prominence as an artist. *Hallucination, Balling*, and *Time Machine Series* brought a new subjectivity to the dominant motif of the post-war period, abstract expressionism. Balling is literally a splash of green paint inside a large circle, and *Time Machine Series* is an organic wheel on a field of turquoise, that conveys time and motion in a static medium.

Given her success and her obvious accomplishments, it is interesting to note that Wieland did not further pursue abstract expressionism. Fascination for film creeps into: her work, as do sexual politics and the desire to get a message across in a popular format.

Solidarity/Art/Organic Foods (1963) and *Penis Wallpaper* (1963) predate Kate Millett's *Sexual Politics* by several years, making Wieland an early sister of the current feminist political wave. The former seems to be a statement on marital vows, the latter a humorous appropriation of the male organ. (At this time, Wieland was married to another prominent Canadian artist, Michael Snow.)

Solidarity/Art/Organic Food is delicately written over a red heart replacing romantic love as the basis of marital unity; below that, air man's hand tweaks a woman's nipple; and below that, two entwined wedding bands shimmer. Penis Wallpaper is a fleet of penises delicately painted on a mauve background. Other works in this period play with the visual pun of the male finger as penis, the hot dog as penis and the erect penis as "new power." We see the beginning of Wieland's use of the filmic sequence—another way of conveying time in a static medium—with *Sailboat Tragedy*. Wieland goes so far as to put cartoon speech bubbles to the people in her paintings, making them look like stills from television commercials.

Sinking sailboats and ocean liners, and: crashing airplanes are the subjects of several works—more playful than morbid—which nonetheless reveal a dismay with reality. Perhaps it is the repeated logical conclusion of a younger Wieland, orphaned and left to provide for herself at age 10, this painful repetition of the great failure of objects in motion. Even in a recent piece, *Early One Morning* (1986), a fuchsia and turquoise landscape seems to represent pastoral calm. Except of course for one Wielandesque aberration: in the corner a barn is tipped on its side, and a tiny woman rages with pots and pans held to the sky: oh the world, it is not quite right.

At the same time, Wieland was working with anti-Vietnam politics and commenting on American military involvements. *Betsy Ross, Look What They Done To The Flag That You Made With Such Care* (1966) is an American flag sewn inside pink plastic bags. A hole in the fabric is sewn up with a Band-Aid and the newspaper photo of a slain soldier. The title refers to the way women's handiwork is co-opted by dominant social values, like militarism, to which women, like Betsy Ross who designed the American flag, would object.

While living as an ex-patriot in New York, Wieland became in touch with her own feelings of nationalism. Back home Trudeaumania was peaking, the Liberals (remember them?) were in power, children got commemorative Centennial coins at school, station wagons full of baby boomers went to Expo '67 in Montreal, and Joyce Wieland, in 1971, opened a show at the National Gallery of Canada called True Patriot Love. The frankness of Wieland's nationalism seems now somewhat pollyannaish. Political animals that we are, I cannot help but feel that her nationalistic works were a product of the times. It would be difficult to stand up in 1987 and blurt out "I love Canada" without also bringing up a few items for the political agenda.

Is it really that times were so different 16 years ago that nationalism now must seem the product of naivete, or was Wieland making a romantic statement of love for a country's history and geography, in spite of the political climate? Was her work an honest translation of the political climate? For me it remains an enigma. I will agree, though, that there is an indisputable splendour, a grandness to the huge beauty of Canada that Wieland was intending. And without a doubt, her nationalism is in reaction to the burgeoning threat of American technical and cultural imperialism. Nine years spent in New York between 1962 and 1971 brought her true expatriated love to the boil and, like James Joyce writing of his home, Dublin, while in his self-imposed Parisian exile, some of her most deliberately Canadian work was done during this period.

Her work in this period is all done in fabric, painting on cloth which is sewn into a quilt, or done in pure quilting. One spectacular piece conveys the Arctic ecosystem by linking paintings of many Arctic waterfowl together in a circle of connected pillows.

Wieland, fey with tangled hair and soft eyes, uses a self-reflexive female figure in occasional early cartoons (such as *Canadian Liberation*, 1972), but mostly in her later works. In traditional art analysis, this would place the majority of Wieland's work within the masculine realm, amongst artists who work with hard concepts and ideas as opposed to autobiography and the "commonplace," the designated traditional female realm. The feminist process of art criticism works against this dichotomy: with the declaration of the quilt as high art in the seventies came the reclamation of women's work as viable creative genius. No doubt Wieland's venture into quilting, as with Judy Chicago with whom Wieland is inevitably compared, was done to deliberately elevate the social value of quilting and embroidery. Like Chicago, Wieland relies on the skill of other women in the execution of her work, while getting credit for the design: much of the quilting is done by Joan Stewart Prowd and the embroidery, which is exquisite, by Joan McGregor.

A dancing nymph figure appears throughout her 1981 series of drawings: flowers and fauna in Fauvian splendour is the subject for these pencil crayon pieces. The crayon is used to such a point of translucence that it is almost vanishing. Although pretty, the pieces as a whole and the figures in them are held back by a tentativeness.

That tentativeness was certainly overcome by 1983, the year that saw the making of three large confrontational canvasses, *Experiment with Life*, *The Artist on Fire*, and *Paint Phantom*. Using colour with the vividness that characterized her first abstracts, these canvasses explore the mythological identity of the artist, and deal for the first time directly with the subconscious. *The Artist on Fire* for example, gives a semi-autobiographical glimpse of Wieland. A woman stands before a canvas, one of her hands is cloven, another holds a paintbrush from which a plume of a fire bird stretches. Flames are coming off her back, and on her canvas a Pan figure with an erect penis is painted.

This review has yet to mention Wieland's work in film, which is extensive, mostly in the experimental genre. In 1976, Wieland released her first feature film for a mass audience, *The Far Shore*. A slow pretty film, sonorous at times and intensely romantic, *The Far Shore* is a hypothetical fiction loosely based on the life and mysterious disappearance of landscape painter, Tom Thompson. Tom, in the movie, is a rugged and noble painter who attracts the love of a Quebecoise beauty, Eulalie. She, alas, is married to an Upper Canadian corporate type, Ross, whose wealth and culture serves only to suffocate her. Although melodrama and symbolism weigh down the film, and the conclusion is disquieting, it is a thoughtful presentation of a woman who seeks love and independence despite dominance and obligation.

To look at the retrospective as a whole, one sees a tremendous body of work, both ambitious and sensitive in its scope. A trickling off of confidence may imbalance the show at times, especially in the years after *The Far Shore*, when pastel whimsy seems to have stolen focus from the larger themes that Wieland conquered: politics, nature, motion, national identity. Wieland as an artist has been able to incorporate the political significance of the past three decades. If the sixties were for Wieland a time for politics, and the seventies a consideration of nature within the context of nations, then the eighties seem a time for personal mythologies and introspection. This show continues until June 28 at the Art Gallery of Ontario, before touring the country.

LORING & WYLE: CAST IN A UNIQUE MOLD
by Ingrid MacDonald
Volume 9, No. 2 (November 1987), pp. 10 and 11

Before the Loring and Wyle sculpture show could be mounted at the Art Gallery of Ontario in Toronto, a great deal of restoration had to happen. Busts and figures were unearthed from the cobwebs of basements and garages; missing toes had to be carefully restored; one piece had been inadvertently splattered with paint; another had been painted over in a thick black paint that had to be removed. A good portion of the work of Loring and Wyle had gone the way of the non-important artists, sculpture with little resale value that had been kept but forgotten.

Frances Loring and Florence Wyle as sculptors represent 19th century principles kept alive in the 20th. Their portraits, friezes, busts and figures could lead one to believe that The Girls, as they were known, were much older than they actually were. In fact, born in the 1880's, they were chronological contemporaries to modernists— people like Gertrude Stein and Pablo Picasso, to movements like surrealism and Dada. While Toronto before and between the wars might not have been a hotbed of contemporary trends in art, the Girls clung to their classicism with spirit and spunk. One can almost hear Florence Wyle saying "Bah, Humbug" to Henry Moore, whose work she called "distortions that pass for sculpture nowadays."

It is not surprising that the kind of work that Loring and Wyle are best known for is either decorative (i.e., birdbaths and friezes for bank building lobbies) or commemorative (i.e., war memorials, busts of the Group of Seven, the Robert Borden sculpture in Ottawa). Many important public commissions went to Frances Loring in her career. Many of them are still in place and worth the visit although the fascination may be as much historical as aesthetic. When we whiz past Loring's Queen Elizabeth Way lion in the car, we don't exclaim, "My what wonderful art!' we usually shout "The Girls did that!"

Throughout their careers Loring, who preferred the monumental scale, was considered the more successful of the two. Her commissions, although they did not provide much money beyond the costs of production, brought profile. "She doesn't like to do pieces unless she has to climb a ladder to get at them," Florence said of Frances. Loring broke ground not only because she was a woman doing a masculine art. She championed the scene as a sculptor in a market that had been hitherto dominated by tombstone builders.

Despite their sharing of a studio and a home for almost as long as they were artists, Loring and Wyle worked separately on individual pieces. Occasionally Frances would call Florence in to do an aspect of a larger piece (like the portrait of Queen Elizabeth and the Duke on the Queen Elizabeth Monument), but that was the extent of it. Apparently they were unfettered by competition between the two, as one might expect in an artistic partnership. They claimed to have distinct approaches and styles that compelled the one not to bother the other one with her work.

This however is not the most obvious thing about their work. At first viewing of their show, I found I needed constant prompting from the display cards to distinguish their works. With further study, it was apparent that the collection showed Florence Wyle to an advantage. Wyle, who worked in general on a smaller scale than Loring, was better represented by a number of works. Her female torsos stole the show, especially *Study of a Girl* (painted plaster, 1931) send Mother of the Race (marble, 1930). *Mother of the Race* was said to be the Finest example of carving of its day and proved Wyle's skill in an extremely difficult medium. Wyle felt the nude was the most expressive way of conveying character through form. Aesthetically Loring and Wyle champion the nude as a by-women-and-for-women phenomenon. Loring and Wyle's nudes are inhabited by a resolute presence of the self, being naked not as men portray women but as women see themselves, whole and sovereign. (Their nudes were a welcome if unintended antidote to another show that was running concurrently at the AGO. American pop artist David Salle brought new meaning to the words "female degradation" with his paintings hung in a gallery upstairs.)

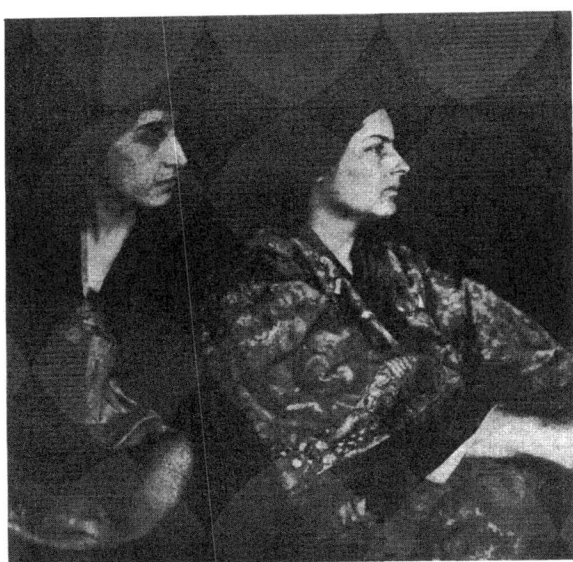

Sculptors Loring and Wyle at the AGO SEE STORY PAGE 10.

Groundbreaking Toronto sculptors Frances Loring and Florence Wyle received a major retrospective at the Art Gallery of Ontario in 1987.

Frances Loring did however work on a small scale (in between monuments no doubt) and with success. *Girl with Fish* (painted plaster, 1932) shows a woman with thick features and great prowess holding a large fish across her shoulders. If the woman's origins are mythological, this is not clear: she represents an epic figure of strength and defiance.

Although Loring worked well in the epic form—as memorials must inevitably be—her strongest piece in the show is a document of the war effort at home called *Noon Hour* at the *Munitions Plant*, (bronze relief, 1918–1919).

Noon Hour shows a line of weary saddened women walking away from their work for lunch. The women have long muscular arms that would glorify an Amazon but their faces are raw with grief. Some look at the ground as they walk while others stare distantly. As a tribute to workers *Noon Hour* represents the hardship of women's work while inverting the typical Art Deco portrait of the worker as an invincible physical champion.

Loring and Wyle lived most of their lives in proud poverty in a converted church in north Toronto. Their studio-home was cluttered with the plaster originals of their many pieces which remained unsold. As companions and artists, they lived the very picture of romantic life. Had I known of them as I grew up, I would have wanted to be them. This show, called a *Sculptors' Legacy*, was a long awaited opportunity to go beyond the legend of The Girls and see the thing most fundamental to their lives: their sculpture.

LORING & WYLE: A SHARED LIFE

by Ingrid MacDonald
Volume 9, No. 2 (November 1987), p. 10

Much the same way that Gertrude Stein and Alice B. Toklas are considered the archetypal lesbian couple without the benefit of their saying so, Frances Loring and Florence Wyle have long been a part of the oral tradition of Toronto lesbian culture. Their house at 110 Glenrose Avenue is a sightseeing stop for as many lesbians as art students—perhaps more, because their relevance is being revived by the current search for a lesbian history.

They were colourful characters. They broke new ground as women artists. They championed sculpture as an art in Canada, and some of their work was the finest of its day. However, their work did not embrace going trends, nor did it anticipate the future; much of their work never sold. As modernism and post-modernism influence contemporary sculpture, classical works by Loring and Wyle recede from importance. Yet for the lesbian historian, Loring and Wyle represent and ideal relationship from a time about which we know very little of the lesbian life. The Loring-Wyle relationship is, as they say, a hot property in an expanding market.

Nonetheless, to the lesbian reader, the text accompanying the show, the catalogue, and a biography by Rebecca Sisler written in 1972 will be disappointing: none confirm the presumption that we dare to make of the Loring-Wyle connection.

One is left playing "does she or doesn't she" with secondary sources and this simply isn't good enough. Both Christine Boyanoski in the catalogue and Sisler in her book are, to their credit, generous with domestic details: one can and one does march right in and draw one's own conclusions. Yet I find it frustrating not to have confirmation in a primary source, such as a journal, a letter, a poem—anything. And reading Sisler's *The Girls* makes it especially apparent that a definitive biography of the girls, as they were called, will not be written until a proper lesbian context can be given to their lives.

What does "a lesbian context" entail? It certainly has much more to do with how they lived their lives, as one woman in relation to another woman, than whether sexual relations can be proved. If we look at this question in reverse, "What does a heterosexual context entail?" the Sisler biography becomes rather interesting reading: it is a text which attempts to describe the life of two lesbians without letting on about this terrible fact. No mean feat considering that we are speaking of women who lived together in an enviable working companionship for sixty years, of women who died within three weeks of each other.

Sisler is most ingenious when she writes of men who appear and then mysteriously disappear from their lives. For example, one of Frances' (Sisler calls her a "compulsive flirt") alleged romances was with a German. During wartime, a German suitor was unacceptable to Frances' father. Sisler says it was he that terminated the affair: "(He) put his foot down on Frances' romantic involvement with a young German—a most unacceptable match, viewed against the background of a nation at war with Germany. He came and went from her life before she had made close ties in Toronto, so that friends of later years knew nothing of him. But the memory of the affair remained within the family as a sort of myth." A myth it would have to remain: is it not possible that the young man in question disappeared because he simply was not romantically important?

While Frances—being of an upper middle class background, of certain beauty and being perhaps the more feminine of the two—can be more easily misconstrued as a heterosexual, Sisler's work is cut out for her when trying to account for the absence of men in Florence's life. Independent Florence was openly critical of men in general. "Florence always pretended to dislike men," Sisler writes. She wore trousers and suits, did her own carpentry, was navigator and mechanic to the car, and was, Sisler admits, a prototypical feminist: "Florence very early developed a sense of the inequalities of women's opportunities." In these ways, Florence is the more stereotypically "lesbian" of the two—that is, she is easier to detect as a lesbian using the crude measurements of a heterosexual environment. The more we learn about lesbian history, the more we develop ideas based on individual lives and the more obsolete stereotypes become.

When lesbianism is mentioned, it is in the context of a slander. When Frances and the Florence moved from Chicago to New York's Greenwich Village (a notoriously Bohemian and gay environment), they had hoped to find work as studio assistants with an established sculptor. Despite the availability of work and the level of their skill, the sculptor brushed them off. Sisler writes that Laredo Taft, a former teacher of Florence's, had blocked their way, "...self-persuaded that she had not fully appreciated all he had done for her, (Taft) had written French warning him that Florence and Frances were not only inconsequential sculptors but a couple of lesbians to boot. It was their first brush with this innuendo."

Where Sisler would call lesbianism a mere innuendo, a lesbian historian would investigate the difference between being a satisfied self-identified lesbian and being a victim of homophobic prejudice. And living as a lesbian but not being able to tell anyone this is one aspect of homophobia. (As is living openly as a lesbian but having this fact subtly omitted from the history books when one's life is recorded.)

The book's most prejudiced moment occurs on the final page when Sisler reports their deaths in a manner that is simply too pat to be believed. "They ended their days in a nursing home in Newmarket where, separated after nearly sixty years together, they seldom inquired for one another." I rage against the lack of analysis in such a statement. It seems to suggest that lack of interest kept them from bothering to ask if the other was well. Why were they not in the same room at the nursing home? Are we to imagine that the Greenacres Home for the Aged in 1967 had support staff specialized in the care of elderly lesbian couples?

In the exhibition catalogue, Boyanoski at least attributes their inability to ask after each other to illness. "They had both been admitted to the Greenacres Home for the Aged in Newmarket in 1967. Sadly, as senility advanced, neither was able to recognize the other."

Loring and Wyle shared a life, a studio, a politic, a craft for 60 years. A new biography based on primary sources that can give an accurate telling of their lives lived in relation to each other certainly seems an idea whose time has come.

NEW FOCUS ON RAPE IN FILM

Reviewed by Brettel Dawson

Volume 10, No. 3 (December 1988/January 1989), p. 8

Shame, directed by Steve Jodrell, 1987: Barron Films released by SKOURAS1987; *The Accused*, directed by Jonathan Kaplan: Paramount Films, 1988.

During October two powerful and essentially women-empowering films grappling with sexual assault, were released in Ontario. *Shame*, hailing from Australia had a relatively short run; *The Accused* was introduced with all the hoopla of Hollywood. One is "fictional"; the other is loosely based on the New Bedford bar gang rape of 1983. Both are "must-see" movies (preferably with a woman friend). The comparison between them is also thought-provoking.

In many ways, *Shame* is a feminist thriller. It has a strong woman lead, Asta Caudell (Deborah Lee Furness) who enters on a Suzuki 750, wears leather and can fix her own bike; an articulate barrister, skilled in self-defence and adept at one line replies to arrogant men. Our feminist hero is forced to cool her heels in a small rural Australian town, which she discovers to be a bastion of male power and of systematic trivialization and abuse of women. She quietly galvanizes the local women who need only her role model to nurture their own empowerment and resistance. But *Shame* is more than a thriller. It offers no simple reassurances and no comforting conclusion.

Lise (Simone Buchanan), the young woman empowered to lay charges against the local louts who raped her and various of her contemporaries, is abducted; her father (Tony Barry), who came to believe and support her is brutally beaten by the local louts charged with the rape and out on bail, and her grandmother is terrorized before a last minute rescue. In the final grief-stricken scene, the local constable, who has wavered between being one of the boys and one of the establishment outraged at the breach of the legal code, accusingly asks Asta if "she is satisfied now." It is one of the local women who replies that "no," they are not, "not by a long way." In its way then, Shame is about an unrelenting reality, about ambivalences of formal legal protection, and the brutality of challenging established power. This places it within the dramatic genre of many Australian films, but this time without the male macho.

Shame reverses the pornographic script of the gang rape scenario. It depicts no overt sexual aggression, only the devastation to women of forced sex, of self-blame and no support. The silence of women and their fragmentation from one another is viewed as being not by choice, but enforced by male power. Male bravado is replaced by cheap rationalizations and lame excuses: "a few kids acting like nature intended" in relation to "sluts" and "little factory girls." Not only are the sexual assaults not shown in the film, but there is no objectification of women, and little scope for voyeuristic gratification in violence. Often through the film, the local louts are made to look extremely foolish and truly vulnerable when their assumed power is challenged or disregarded. No gods these.

The dilemma of the film is that this power has often not been challenged, and that the abuses it produces have been regarded as normal. One of the metaphors of Asta's role is that of security, safety and autonomy. At one point, Lise asks her why she "isn't careful." Asta's reply is that she supposes that she "has never had to be." When Lise looks to Asta for strength, Asta makes a point of teaching her that no-one except yourself can be relied on for security. And even Asta's impromptu self defence lesson is given pause when Lise asks, "but what if there are six of them?"

My dread that Asta would herself end up being inevitably raped or beaten was, mercifully, unrealized. Of course, she is attacked by four youth and single-handedly consigns several of them to medical care, using Wen-Do techniques. Her subsequent confrontation with the constable in the pub, when he regards the incident as some "boys having a bit of fun," provides a platform and a forum for the truth to be spoken. From there, in a non-imperialist vision, the film refocuses on the local stories. Here it is those women, their relationships and their possibility of choice, that are the real focus. And the ultimate message is that challenging male power is fraught with double-speak, split allegiances and socialized self doubt. More even than this, it costs. The higher cost, though, is to do nothing.

Unlike the sexually assaulted young women in *Shame* who never got to the court room, much of the drama in *The Accused* revolves around the trial of three men charged with soliciting and persuading the commission of a crime—the brutal gang rape of Sarah Tobias (Jodie Foster) in the pinball room of a bar. Prosecuting the men who chanted and cat-called and taunted, was unprecedented. The rapists themselves avoided trial by plea bar- gaining and pleading guilty to "reckless endangerment" carrying a similar prison term, but making their crime invisible. Struggling to make it visible, to establish that a wrong had been done, and that Sarah should be believed is what the film is all about. Jodie Foster gives a flawless performance as a raw-edged woman who does not conform to sex role stereotypes of the "good woman." Kelly McGillis as Katherine Murphy, the tough and tenacious prosecutor and "good woman," is powerful. The film is well crafted and intense. In the end, justice is done.

Yet, I'm left with some nagging questions about whether the film is ultimately empowering for women and whether it really is an un-alloyed breakthrough in Hollywood's women's issues bureau. First, although the impression is given that Sarah Tobias feels vindicated and hence healed of the scars of rape, you should know that the real victim of the gang rape is now dead. She was killed in an alcohol related traffic accident over a year ago. Second, again in real life, the convictions were appealed and her death was used to support an argument that she was drunk and consenting to the rape. In April 1988, the convictions were, thankfully, upheld on appeal. Third, the "good woman" prosecutor, Kelly McGillis, again in real life, was herself raped about ten years ago. That said, let's move back into the movie.

Unlike *Shame*, which was shown from the perspective of women, *The Accused* focuses on the men involved: What is it to be a man? what is it to breach the male bond? A central dream is whether the male friend of one of the rapists and who saw the rapes occur, would testify against the men accused of encouraging the rapes. To do so would keep his friend in jail longer and attach the rape to his criminal record. In the depiction of the rape, there is ambivalence— did she ask for it? Was it really a rape? Should the rapists really be held responsible for circumstances that got out of control. Thus one of the rapists is shown as being taunted with begin a faggot if he refused to "take his turn." Is that what it takes to be a man? Perhaps it is a useful social comment.

The rape scene is also problematic. Sarah verbally describes the scene but it is visually evoked through the recollection of the male bystander. It is what he saw. Admittedly he was horrified, did know it was rape and Sarah is shown as resisting; and, of course, how could Sarah describe the actions on the "periphery." But this perspective of gaze slides easily into objectification. The ambivalent edges and male perspective of the film produce another issue with the film—it seems to put its energy into getting it across to the men what they did wrong. In *Shame*, that it was a wrong was never presented as a dilemma; that women are to be believed was not a question.

Where the relationship of women was a priority in *Shame*, this is muted in *The Accused*. Little warmth or human contact is explored. The male characters and the women characters are both drawn in simple lines. Sarah is not shown as receiving any support from other women—not from the rape crisis worker, not from her best friend and only grudgingly initially from Katherine Murphy. This lack of contact is not problematized. Finally, I found the assumptions about the role of law and the legal process in *The Accused* to be limited and perhaps offering dangerous comfort. In *Shame*, there is an ambivalence about legal intervention and the focus is on the realities in women's lives and contacts with legal authority. This is not so clear in *The Accused*. Admittedly, the film, focussing on "the accused" explores the extent to which a victim is herself put on trial. But the power of men is shown as being constrained by the formal legal process and the issues are shown as being mediated by the law. It's not that easy. Conviction doesn't resolve the effect of rape. And, of course, conviction is not the norm with a rape being reported in the United States every six minutes. Challenging male power does cost. What makes it imperative and effective to challenge it is not really (and not really surprisingly) left unformed in *The Accused*.

For all these points, though, the film is an important beginning. The message that coerced sexual aggression is not okay is finally hitting the big time.

ABUSIVE AMUSEMENT

by Susan G. Cole

Volume 10, No. 2 (November 1988), p. 10

Sitting at the Festival Theatre in Stratford, I found myself watching *My Fair Lady* with deep ambivalence. The production values were superb, as is usually the case with Canada's most prestigious drama festival, the music familiar, the transformation of the thrust stage to a venue for musical theatre, ingenious. But the story itself is fraught with political problems. Henry Higgins bets he can pass off the flower girl Eliza as a duchess at the next Embassy ball. All he needs is six months to work on her speech problems and to clean up her manners. During the course of her tutelage he submits her to all manner of abuses including verbal assault, starvation and sleep deprivation. All of this is contextualized—and invariably interpreted by audiences—as diverting amusements followed by the happy ending in which after bolting from Higgins' household, Eliza returns, presumably to take up a romantic relationship with her tormentor.

At the same time, the Stratford Festival has mounted a wildly inventive production of Shakespeare's ode to female oppression, *The Taming of the Shrew*. Here the theme of female makeover at the hands of a tyrannical male is played to the hilt as Petruchio tames Kate with many of the same tactics as Higgins has used to cow Eliza. There are differences, of course. Petruchio triumphs over Kate, turning her into the "perfect" submissive wife—boy wins girl keeps her—whereas Higgins loses Eliza and then gets her back— boy, or rather man, wins girl, loses her and then gets her back. But either way, the plays bring up the thorny problem of whether major theatre companies ought to bother with revivals of obnoxiously unenlightened works.

My Fair Lady is based on George Bernard Shaw's play *Pygmalion* and certainly the socialist and cynic cannot be blamed for the regressive romanticism of the musical comedy Lerner and Loewe fashioned out of his play. The play's title refers to the myth in which the misogynist artist Pygmalion sculpts what he thinks is the perfect woman, only to fall in love with a creation which, voiceless and immobile, can provide him with no emotional sustenance.

Interestingly enough, Shaw wrote his *Pygmalion* without the creator Higgins falling in love with his own artwork. The play ends with Eliza leaving Higgins while the professor scoffs at the idea of Eliza marrying Freddie Eynsford-Hill, thus emphasizing that although Higgins may have wanted to continue to control Eliza, he never wanted her as a lover. This may be inconsistent with the Pygmalion myth but it is perfectly consistent with Shaw's inveterate distaste for romantic relationships whether in his own life or among his plays' characters.

Not surprisingly, audiences were not very satisfied with the ending of *Pygmalion*, but Shaw stuck to his guns, and as Stratford's excellent program notes detail, wrote at some length of why he ended his story there. The play's happy ending, he insisted, hinges on Eliza's escape from Higgins' tyranny, and if audiences wanted something else, they had missed the point. He could not imagine a worse relationship than that between a middle-aged, middle class man with a mother fixation and a nineteen year old flower girl. Better for Eliza to have found someone her own age who was crazy about her. A film version made in the thirties created a romantic link between Higgins and Eliza, but the author never approved.

Imagine how outraged he would have been at Lerner and Loewe's version of the story. Browbeaten for six months and then ignored after she triumphs at the Embassy Ball, Eliza walks out on Higgins, goes out on a date with Freddy and then goes to visit Higgins' mother. The professor finds her there but when he implores her to return she tells him to go to hell. Ah, but not for long. As he edges up the path to his house he realizes that "he's grown accustomed to her face," the audience melts and then thrills as Eliza turns off the tapes of her voice he has unearthed to announce that she's back. Higgins reverts immediately to his old ways, and the final line of the play, "Eliza, where the devil are my slippers?" does not augur well for equality.

Most everything great about *My Fair Lady*—its commentary on language, class and morals—is Shaw's (two thirds of the book come directly from the play), and what greatness is left, namely in the lyrics, is sorely wasted. The brilliance of "I'm an Ordinary Man" ("Let a Woman in Your Life") and "Why Can't a Woman be More like a Man?" both written to categorize Higgins as a staunch woman-hater, fades with the sentimental strategy of turning Higgins into a salvageable love object. The Stratford production, a faithful and gorgeous revival of the original musical, does very little to reinterpret the work, leaving the play with its nagging problems. To be fair, it would be tough to do anything else. The play is time-specific, intended to evoke the particular class conflicts of Edwardian England. But perhaps a company at some theatre will find a way to present the story's happy ending without evoking a wince from any self-respecting women in the audience.

When it comes to the works of William Shakespeare, the dilemma is slightly different. Many feminists have insisted that *The Taming of the Shrew* should be shredded and never presented on our national stages. The story is viciously anti-woman and the dynamics of the play create pleasure in what amounts to violence against women. Scholars counter that Shakespeare was a product of his time and that nothing from the mind of the greatest English language poet should be tossed aside; even with its egregious celebration of woman abuse, the play has redeeming social values.

This year's Stratford production presents another argument, namely that the works of Shakespeare can be reinterpreted in the light of what we know now so that the play can convey some meaning even to twentieth century audiences. It's been done before. Zefferelli's film version offered a conventional reading but audiences tended to be amused by what they thought was a metaphor for the passionate relationship between the two stars, Elizabeth Taylor and Richard Burton. A version of *Shrew* presented in the mid-seventies, just as feminist awareness was increasing, was extremely self-conscious about the play's misogyny. That production, done in modern dress, presented the taming of Kate not as a comedy but as a horror show so grotesque that even Petruchio is repelled at the end by the submissive woman he has created.

The 1988 production does not tamper with the meaning of Shakespeare's text in the same way. Instead, it sets the play in the 1950's, the same repressive decade that spawned *My Fair Lady*, so that the female oppression is given a reasonable historical context. This is an inspired strategy, for Shakespeare's male characters, with their preening and posturing and their unquestioned ownership of women, would have been right at home in the fifties. And the ingenue Bianca, presented as a blonde bimbo reminiscent of the icon (not the person) Marilyn Monroe, would have been in her prime in that decade of saddle shoes and cashmere blouses. If you hate the text and subtext of *Taming of the Shrew*, you definitely hated the fifties and director Richard Monette creates a breathtaking marriage of the two.

But many women will tell you that the technical fireworks (literally—there's even a motorcycle on the set) and other clever ploys (Shakespeare's sonnets sung to Louis Applebaum's fifties rock score) cannot salvage the actual experience of having to watch Kate being abused by Petruchio. If you have an ounce of awareness of the real horror of wife assault, it is difficult to stomach it presented as a comic divertissement. Yet (and this too we have to face, according to the program), The *Taming of the Shrew* is especially popular among female viewers. Why? Is it the classic fantasy of the tall, dark, stranger subduing the feisty female that is so appealing? Or are women so well socialized that they too find women being tortured a source of entertainment. Perhaps it's both.

In the end, the Stratford production provides all of the material for a rollicking debate on whether *The Taming of the Shrew* should be tolerated on stage. It contextualizes the play in a way that can be read as wholly sympathetic to the changing status of women, it breathes new life into a work that is in desperate need of a makeover, but it still keeps the abuse intact. If you are not sure what you think about all of this, and if you are unable to get to Stratford to see this extraordinary production, watch out for it during the Christmas season when CBC will televise Stratford's 1988 version.

And keep aware of the ongoing question of what to do with Stratford's virulent sexism and racism. It is bound to surface again next year, especially in the Jewish community, when the Stratford Festival presents *The Merchant of Venice*.

CONCLUSION

Looking Back on *Broadside*

by Philinda Masters

In putting together a book based on a feminist newspaper from the 1980s, we felt that it was crucial to not only explore *Broadside*'s impact on second-wave feminism, but also to both look at what we thought was important to women at the time and the repercussions of those issues, opinions, and ongoing debates for the future. Typical of the newspaper's overarching themes were feminist politics, group organizing, workplace issues, law, health, welfare, reproductive rights, violence against women, and what's come to be known as intersectionality—the interactions between various different social locations. It has become evident to us that *Broadside*'s content, which reflected the activism of the 1980s, is still being echoed now with #MeToo and other social justice protest groups of the 2010s.

Accordingly, in *Inside Broadside*, we've tried to provide a context for the newspaper's themes and the many issues and debates we covered, and, where possible, to make connections to the debates and issues that are part of our current reality, highlighting the ways in which they have changed or, in some cases, have not changed very much at all. The issues brought up by the #MeToo movement, for example—the prevalence of the sexual harassment of women and the need for men to be accountable—appeared in the pages of *Broadside* in the 1980s and the concerns then are almost indistinguishable from those now. The book's choice of articles, we hope, will also demonstrate the work involved in feminist publishing, the feminist cultural milieu that informed the content decisions we made, and why, and the reasons for the existence of so many vibrant periodicals in the 1980s (at least forty Canadian feminist magazines and newspapers flourished at the time).

Although our politics were mainly a strain of radical feminism, the chronological framework for the book is second-wave feminism, which came to the fore in the 1960s and held sway until the 1990s, when postmodernism and third-wave "sex positive" feminism took hold. At this point, second-wave feminism began to develop a bad rep among younger feminists, who saw it as anti-sex, essentialist, and lacking in analytical sophistication. It was not cool. What we've hoped to do here is to not only enter some of the feminist activism of the second wave into the historical record, but to resurrect some of that lost reputation by showing who we actually were. Future feminists may find this concern with the relative sophistication of second-wave feminism to be extremely dated, but we think that it's important to current feminists—the ones who will carry the history of the movement forward to future feminists, whatever their particular concerns may be—that we highlight the significance of the work done in the 1960s, 1970s, and 1980s.

Many of the feminists who initiated the second wave—and that includes the women who created *Broadside*—came from working in the civil rights movement in the US and the labour movement in Canada. Some came from the peace movement and some even came from a background in liberation theology. In other words, the early second-wave feminists were deeply involved in social justice activism. They weren't neophytes, or politically unsophisticated. They were forced to carve out a space for women in the face of sexist and misogynist resistance from their colleagues in these social justice movements, a space that would take them beyond the "acceptable" roles of adjunct and helpmate. Just the presence of feminism in the political discourse had a huge impact on the social structure and culture of the entire globe. The birth of the women's liberation movement in the 1960s came from a long history of political activism, which is why so much of this book is devoted to the reproduced articles of the 1980s rather than to our current take on the state of feminism back then. We want the voices of those women to be foregrounded, so current and future feminists know where we came from, and where we can go.

One of the main questions that arose while we were putting this book together was about change: How have things changed? Have things actually changed? If not, why not? One good example of change is, again, the #MeToo movement that rose out of today's strong reaction to men's constant sexual harassment and assault of women, particularly women who were in a subordinate position to a more powerful man. Sexual harassment and assault have been with us for millennia, but the fact that men are now being forced by the voices of a critical mass of women to suffer the consequences of their bad behaviour is new. *Broadside* wrote about this issue many, many times over the years, but it is only now that women have been able to hold men accountable, often by threatening them with jail.

There is another example of some changing attitudes: In the 1990s, *The Globe and Mail* ran a centre-spread feature on domestic violence for International Women's Day. It was a thoroughly researched article that covered many aspects of the violence women experience at home—what they suffer, who they get help from, family reactions, self-esteem issues, and so on. But the article did not once mention men. The women in the article were beaten or killed, but apparently no one did it. The current news coverage—on the murder of Indigenous women and girls and on police forces' frequent use of the "unfounded" conclusion to a rape accusation—is quite different. The work of feminist activists, feminist social workers, and feminist lawyers has changed the definition and treatment of rape and sexual assault. And with that has come a changing sense of what's acceptable. Women's reactions to sexism and misogyny is becoming more public and effective. Men are being forced to listen to women and, as a result, often for the first time, they are beginning to understand what women have been telling them for decades.

So there is hope. And now the challenge for women who come after us will be to confront the extreme right. Second-wave feminists fought tooth and nail to change the laws on abortion, on sexual assault, on family and custody practices, on education, on architecture, on public spaces. But we are in danger of losing much of what we worked for in the past four or five decades. We cannot allow ourselves to be derailed by the regressive misogyny and racism that is seeing a resurgence around the globe right now. We cannot afford to ignore the past victories of the second wave of feminist politics and activism, nor how we achieved those victories.

FREE
Join
THE QUOTE OF THE
MONTH CLUB

GET ONE EVERY MONTH FREE IN *Broadside* WHEN YOU SUBSCRIBE

"Quote of the month"

"Quote of the month"

"Quote of the month"

DARTS

Women's Studies — Does that involve macramé?

SUBSCRIBE TO BROADSIDE

name _____

address _____

city_____ postal code_____

$16/10 issues $30/20 issues
Institutions: $24/10 issues, $42/20 issues

Make cheques payable to
Broadside,
PO Box 494, Station P,   ☐ **new**   ☐ **renew**
Toronto, Ontario
M5S 2T1

Clip and mail this coupon today.

ACKNOWLEDGEMENTS

Broadside's operating structure during its decade of publishing, 1979 to 1989, was a collective, a group of about ten dedicated volunteers (with only one paid staff member for half its life). Over the years, a few collective members left and others joined us, but the core remained the same for ten years and beyond. Every collective member was involved in *Broadside* decisions, and decision-making was by consensus throughout the life of the newspaper. When we decided to go digital in 2012, we welcomed several long-time supporters as collective members when we created and launched broadsidefeminist.com online. We've now come back together for this book, and the collective structure is still in place. Which means, we've worked together, made collective decisions about format and content, and presented them to the publisher and its imprint, the Feminist History Society (FHS), for approval.

Our first heartfelt acknowledgment goes to the current members of our collective: Eve Zaremba, Susan G. Cole, Lisa Freedman, Donna Gollan, Ottie Lockey, and Ann Holmes. With me functioning as editor, trying to pull it all together, these women helped select and compile the articles to be included in the book. This meant each of us taking on a couple of volumes (two years' worth of issues) and reading everything in them. Overall, we whittled the content down from about four thousand articles published over ten years to what you now see in the book. Quite the task! We then discussed, over a period of several months, the framework of the book, and the themes and categories we wanted to be addressed. We met as a collective at least once a month to keep on top of the process, and we all participated in the various aspects of publishing this book. I want particularly to express my thanks to Natasha Bozorgi, our editor at Second Story Press. She was with me all along the way with suggestions and corrections and general overall help. She is very much part of this book, and she's a great editor!

My personal thanks, though, must go to Susan G. Cole. She jumped right in and helped me throughout the past summer and fall with the final choice of articles (a lengthy and difficult task); she wrote the small introductions to each of the chapters—and they are a very good read—and she joined in the process of assigning the photos and other images to pages of the book as it was going into the typesetting phase, and writing the cutlines, or photo captions. Thanks also should go to Lisa Freedman for her lawyerly eye and her considerable proofreading skills. But thanks should also go to previous members of the collective who helped provide the material we have now drawn on for this book. Their names are to be found in our Collective Members list below.

The Feminist History Society is the organization that, through Second Story Press, has published a series of books in the past several years with the express purpose of recording second-wave feminism to ensure its inclusion in the historical record. Current feminist activities and thinking can be—and often are—recorded online, but for much of feminist history before the digital age, if it isn't written down, usually in a book, it will be lost to future generations forever. Even now, there is widespread misunderstanding of what second-wave feminism entailed, and the FHS series of books is extremely useful for setting the record straight. So our thanks go to the Feminist History Society for giving us the opportunity to publish this book and to record the history of our particular patch of second-wave feminism.

And, for our last word: If reading these pages makes you yearn for more, remember that the entire run of *Broadside* articles, images, ads, and games is posted online at www.broadsidefeminist.com. Enjoy!

Broadside gratefully acknowledges receipt of a Recommender Grant to Writers from the Ontario Arts Council/Conseil des Arts de l'Ontario 2019, for the book *Inside Broadside: A Decade of Feminist Journalism*.

PHOTO CREDITS

page 2: Pamela Harris @ 1984. Used with permission.
page 41: Sarah MacKenzie
page 64: Illustration by General Idea's Jorge Zontal
page 93: Moira Armour
page 119: Susan Sturman
page 120: Moira Armour
page 121 (top): Deena Rasky
page 121 (bottom): Catherine Maunsell
page 122 (top): Lyons
page 204: Kathy Shaw

CONTRIBUTORS AND COLLECTIVE MEMBERS

CONTRIBUTORS

Margaret Atwood
June Callwood*
Anne Cameron
Sherrill Cheda*
Susan Crean
Pat Daley
Brettel Dawson
Karen Dubinsky
Valerie Edwards
Sarah Eliot (pseud.)
Lynne Fernie
Lilith Finkler
Robin Gerland
Jane Hastings
Maryon Kantaroff*
Joanne Kates
Carrroll Klein
Myrna Kostash
Judith Lawrence
Helen Lenskyj
Ingrid MacDonald
Catherine Mackinnon

Kay Macpherson*
Daphne Marlatt
Barbara Martineau*
Sheila McIntyre
Melanie Randall
Deena Rasky
Sarah Sheard
Janet Silman
Susan Sturman
Susan Ursel
Mariana Valverde
Vickie Van Wagner
Eleanor Wachtel
Betsy Warland
Jean Wilson
Ellea Wright
Hewan Yang
José Zontal*

COLLECTIVE MEMBERS
1979–2019

Beverley Allinson*
Heather Brown*
Susan G. Cole
Debra Curties
Brettel Dawson
Jean Deeth
Jackie Edwards
Lisa Freedman
Jacqueline Frewin*
Donna Gollan
Amanda Hale
Jane Hastings
Ann Holmes
Carroll Klein
Judith Lawrence
Helen Lenskyj
Alex Maass
Ingrid MacDonald
Philinda Masters
Catherine Maunsell
Layne Mellanby
Ottie Lockey
Maureen Phillips
Deena Rasky
Judy Stanleigh
Susan Sturman
Jean Wilson
Eve Zaremba

* deceased

INDEX

Note: Page numbers in italics indicate illustrations.

Comini, Alexandra, 326
communism, 62, 91, 155
Conde, Carole, *297*
Conger, Lauri, 47
consciousness, 252–53, 255, 289
consent, 138, 148, 156, 168
    to sexual contact, 97, 147, 174, 176
conservatism, among women, 336
Constitution, 97, 98, 164. *See also*
Charter of Rights and Freedoms
Cooper, Beverly, 47
Coulter, Clare, 243, 244–49
Cow Café Committee, 98, 188–90
Crean, Susan, 180, 288, 321
Cummings, Gail, 108, 109
custody, 110
Customs, pornography at, 73

Daigle, Chantal, 56
Dale, Holly, 298, 299, 302, 329–30
Dallas, 76
Damnée Manon, Sacré Sandra
(Tremblay), 247
daycare. *See* childcare
Dear Enemies (Graham), 59
Degas, Edgar, 322–23, 326
Delauney, Sonia, 273
Dempsey, Shawna, 10, 287
Desert Hearts (film), 287
Dewar, Marion, 100, 189
Dinner Party, The (Chicago), 104,
192–95, 273, 324
disabled persons, 134
discrimination
    in hiring, 202
    in legislation, 200–201, 202
distinct society, 34
divorce, 132, 150, 152, 265
Dodd, Barbara, 56
domestic labour, 104, 134, 307–8. *See
also* homemakers and homemaking
Donna (prostitute), 233, 235, 238
Downtown Hookers Association,
232
Dubois, Ellen Carol, 344
Duncan, Carol, 327
Dworkin, Andrea, 69, 71, 72, 77, 156,
242, 337
Dynasty, 76

Echols, Alice, 344–45, 346
editing, 4, 8, 28–29, 205, 208
education, 134
Edwards, Jackie, 11–12
Electromedia, 353, 354, 355, 356
Emperor's Virgin, The (Fraser), 242,
257–58, 266–67, 291, 292, 293–95
employment equity, 135
equality rights, 179
equal pay, 97, 132, 150
Equal Rights Amendment, 94, 97,
339
Erola, Judy, 153

families, 156
family and families, 132, 155–56
family law, 200–201
Fanny (Jong), 291–92
Farrow, Jane, 47
Far Shore, The (film), 363–64
fascism, 90
FBI, 15, 211
Fear of Flying (Jong), 289–90, 292
Feinstein, Sarah, 114
feminism
    cultural, 317, 346
    Marxist, 306, 308–9
    radical, 78, 344, 346
    and the ruling apparatus, 146–48
    second wave, 15, 17, 223, 224, 379,
    380, 381, 392
    theory, 286
    third wave, 380
Feminism and Art History, 323–29
feminist, self-identification as, 186
Feminist Party of Canada, 92–97,
186
Feminists Against Anti-Semitism,
111–12
Femme de l'hôtel, Le (film), 281
Fernie, Lynne, 277, 287, 353–54,
355–56
Festival of Festivals, 287, 298–99,
301
fetal rights, 168–73
film, women in, 274, 281–83, 287,
288, 298–303, 357–60
Fireweed, 46, 255
Forget Commission on
Unemployment Insurance, 155

Forum (Penthouse), 48–50, 69, 70, 73
Fox, Frances, 220
Francophone women, 99, 100
Fraser, Paul, 137
Fraser, Sylvia, 242, 257–67, 291, 293–96
Fraser Report on Pornography and Prostitution, 137–48, 344
Fraticelli, Rita, 288
Freedman, Adele, 302
freedom of speech, 215–16
freedom of the press, 202
Freeman, Jo, 8–9
free trade, 30–33, 50–51
Freud, Sigmund, 106–7
Frewin, Jacqueline, 6
Frye, Marilyn, 177
FUSE, 46

Garfield, Louise, 347, *348*
Garrard, Mary D., 324, 325
gay and lesbian rights, 153
gay marriage, 153
gay men, harassment of, 141–42
Geltner, Gail, 319
gender, as category of analysis, 74
genital mutilation, 82, 84–88, 336
Gentileschi, Artemisia, 324
Globe and Mail, The, 91, 187, 381
Gollan, Donna, 2, 11, 287
Gordon, Linda, 344
Graham, Gwethalyn, 58–59
grants, 11–13, 55, 206–7, 209
Greene, Gael, 290
Greenspan, Brian, 109–10
Greer, Germaine, 323
Griffin, Susan, 301
Guilbault, Luce, 252

Hacker, Pat, 189
hair, 259–60
Handmaid's Tale, The (Atwood), 152, 350–53
Harlequin romances, 225, 295, 340–42
Hartman, Grace, 22, 30–33
Healthsharing, 12
Hemlow, Mary, 23
Herizons, 53, 82, 153
heterosexuality, forced, 224, 225

Hidden in the Household, 306–7, 308
Hite Report, The, 105
Hladki, Janice, 347, *348*
Hoffman-LaRoche, 43, 44
Hogg (judge), 169–70, 171
homemakers and homemaking, 104, 152, 181, 304–5, 306–9, 320
Hookers on Davie, 329–33
Hosken, Fran, 82, 85, 86–87, 88
Householder, Johanna, 347, *348*
Hubbard, Ruth, 130
Hughes, Patricia, 94
humour, sense of, 22–23, *124*
Hurst, Lynda, 344
Hustler, 72, 212
Hysteria, 53

immigrant women, 27–28, 134
imperialism, 29–30, 75–76, 78
incest. *See* child abuse, sexual
income inequality, 104, 133–36
indecent exposure, 159–61
Indian Act, 163–67
Indigenous peoples, 75, 164, 165
Indigenous women, 76, 100, 134, 167, 277
    in the feminist movement, 27–28, 101
    rights of, 163–67, 201
    violence against, 165, 381
International Women's Day, 53, 94, *119–21*
International Women's Day Committee, 3
International Women's Week, 151, 153
Israel, 53, 112–17
"I Was a Playboy Bunny" (Steinem), 334–35

Jackman, Nancy, 180
Jackson, Marni, 349
Jane Doe case, 180
Japanese Canadians, 309–13
Jensen, Margaret Ann, 340, 342, 343
Jewett, Pauline, 99, 101, 188
Johnson, Bertha, 86
Jong, Erica, 289–90, 291–92, 293
journalism, 182–88

Kantaroff, Maryon, 95–96, *124*
Kates, Joanne, 83, 102, 320
Khaled, Leila, 116
Khamerernebty (queen), 325–26
Kinesis, 53, 153
King, William Lyon Mackenzie, 310, 311
Kirkland, D. K., 169
Kitzinger, Sheila, 125
Knight, Andrea, 66–67, 68
knitting, 273
Kogawa, Joy, 309, 312–13
Kollwitz, Käthe, 326, 327
Kostash, Myrna, 320
Kramer, Hilton, 193
Kuhn, Annette, 147

labour movement, 380
Landers, Ann, 230
Landolt, Gwen, 154
Landsberg, Michele, 6, 300
Langer, Felicia, 115
language, 252, 253, 279–80
language, colonialism and, 29–30
Lansberg, Michelle, 189
Laurendeau, Ghislaine, 59
Lavell, Jeannette, 166–67
Lawrence, Judith, 6
Lawson, Darlene, 171
Leetutu, Soro, 270, 271
Lenskyj, Helen, 83
Lerner, Alan, 375
lesbian activism, 224
lesbian baiting, 153
lesbian history, 367–68, 370
lesbianism
　Broadside and, 53, 54, 55, 83
　in media, 237, 277
　sexual ideology in, 225
　and writing, 253–54, 255–56
Lesbian Lives, 111
Lesbian Nuns, 49–50
Lesbian Organizaiton of Toronto, 3
lesbian separatism, 114, 346
Lesbians Fly Canada (Fernie), 353–56
Letocha, Louise, 192
Levine, Les, 355, 356
Lewis, Mark, 356
liberation theology, 380
lifestyle feminism, 157

Lilith, 111
Lippard, Lucy, 193–94
literature
　sex in, 289–93
　women in, 340–43
literature, women in, 249–67, 278–80, 285–86, 288, 350–53
Lockey, Ottie, 11
Loewe, Frederick, 375
Longino, Helen, 219
Loring, Frances, 287, 364–67, *366,* 367–68, 369–70
Lovelace, Sandra, 167
Love's Sweet Return (Jensen), 340–42
Luomala, Nancy, 325–26
Lushington, Kate, 288
Luxton, Meg, 304, 307–8, 320

Maass, Alex, 6
MacDonald, Ann-Marie, 47
MacDonald, Dawn, 189
MacDonald, Flora, 99, 101, 153, 188
MacDonald, Ingrid, 11, 360, 364, 367
MacDonnell, J., 168, 173
MacGuigan, Mark, 219–20, 221–22
MacKinnon, Catharine A., 69, 72, 73
Macpherson, Kay, 59, 60–61, 101
magazines and journals
　fashion, 225
　feminist, 203–11
mainstream media, 181, 182–88
male gaze, 76, 330
Mandela, Winnie, 78
Manitowabi, Edna, 301
Marcuse, Herbert, 15–16, 106
Marlatt, Daphne, 29, 242, 278
Martin, Liz, 319
Martineau, Barbara (Sara Halprin), 287
Marxism, 306, 308–9
massage parlours, 232, 233
Massi, Julie, 47
mass media, 76–77, 230, 277, 282
Masters, Philinda (Phil), *2,* 6, 19, 20, 181, 205
Masters and Johnson, 105
Maunsell, Catherine, *2,* 11
McDonnell, Kathleen, 319–20
McEwen, Thomas J., 108

Riverdale Walkabout, 159–60
Riverdale Women's Action Committee, 158, 161
Rock Against Racism (RAR), 88, 89–91
Rock Against Sexism (RAS), 90–92
rock music, 88, 229
Rogers, Sandra, 170
romantic fiction, 280, 340–42
Room of One's Own (journal), 53, 255
Roy, Marcel, 45
Royal Commission on Bilingualism and Biculturalism, 59
Royal Commission on Equality in Employment, 133–36
Rubin, Gayle, 227–28, 229, 345–46
Russell, Diana, 81
Ruth, Nancy Jackman, 180
Ryan Nye, Linda, 99, 189

Sabia, Laura, 96, 186–87, 188, 189
sadomasochism, 228, 266
Salle, David, 366
Sand, Cy-Thea, 46
Saskatchewan Action Committee on the Status of Women, 209
Saskatchewan Advisory Council on the Status of Women, 101, 190
Saulis, Eva, 165
Sauvé, Jeanne, 45
Schlafly, Phyllis, 132
Scime, Lynne, 151
Scott, Jay, 300, 303
Scott, Valerie, 171
Seccombe, Wally, 306–7, 308
Second World War, 309–13
Secretary of State Women's Program, 12–13, 54–55, 151, 153, 209
Segato, Lorraine, 47
sex, 26, 102–7, 181, 222–31
    in language, 280
    in literature, 289–93, 294, 295
    and obscenity laws, 221
    and pornography, 295–96
Sex and Love, 223
sexual abuse and assault, 81, 141, 146, 158–63, 179, 232, 262, 381. *See also* child sexual abuse; spousal abuse and assault
    in art, 324–25, 371–74

consent and, 97
    in the justice system, 162–63, 174–76
    myths about, 159
sexual liberation, 156, 223–24, 236, 289
Sexual Politics (Millett), 361
Sexual Revolution, 102–3, 104
sexual subordination, 224–25
sex work. *See* prostitutes; prostitution
Shame (film), 371–72, 373, 374
Shaw, George Bernard, 375, 376
Sheard, Sarah, 22, 23
She Devils of Niagara (Clichettes), 347–50
shelters, 45, 132
Silvera, Makeda, 46
Sisler, Rebecca, 368, 369–70
Smart, Carol, 174, 176
Smith, Dorothy, *120,* 148, 298, 301
Smothers Sisters, 47
socialist feminism, 78, 309
Sopinka, John, 128–29, 130
Spector, Norman, 33–34
Spender, Dale, 279–80
sports, women in, 108–9, 127–31
spousal abuse and assault, 45–46, 81, 152, 213, 229, 381
    in the justice system, 174–77
spousal support, 200–201
status of women councils, 3–4
Steed, Judy, 274
Steele, Lisa, 74, 227, 230
Stein, Gertrude, 333–39, 367
Steinem, Gloria, 317
Still Ain't Satisfied: Canadian Feminism Today, 319
St. James, Margo, 232, 237
Stratford Festival, 288, 375–78
strippers, 239
Studio D (NFB), 287, 300, 301
Sturman, Susan, 5, 6, *119*
Sunahara, Ann Gomer, 310, 311, 312
Supreme Court of Canada, 107–8, 109–10, 166, 167, 172
surnames, 200
Susanna and the Elders (Gentileschi), 324–25

Tabor, A.H., 87
Take Back the Night, *121*
Talese, Gay, 102–3
Taming of the Shrew, The
(Shakespeare), 288, 375, 377–78
tampons, 83, 287
television, 282
Têtes de Pioche, Les (newsletter), 252
theatre, women in, 244–49, 286–87,
288, 347–50
This Magazine, 46
Thompson, Sharon, 346
Tiger Lily, 53
Tillery, Linda, 316
Tobique First Nation, 164–65
    women of, 163, 165, 166, 241
Toike Oike, *122*
Toklas, Alice B., 367
Tomlinson, Lizzie, 92
Tom Robinson Band, 89
Toronto, 89, 92, 94, 97, 145, 367–68
    sexual assault in, 158–62
Toronto Rape Crisis Centre, 158
Toronto Star, 91, 187
Toronto *Sun*, 103
Toronto Women's Bookstore, *122*
transgender people, 331–32, 333, 336
Trudeau, Margaret, 268
Trudeau, Pierre Elliott, 101, 220
Tucker, Helen, 58, 59, 60
Two-Axe Earley, Mary, 166

UNICEF, 87
United Kingdom, 88–89, 90
United Nations, 112, 167
Ursel, Susan, 180

Vagabond (film), 287, 357–60
Valium, 43, 44
Vance, Carole, 227, 228, 229, 343
Vanier, Pauline, 59
Van Wagner, Vicki, 81–82
Varda, Agnès, 357–58, 359
Veltmeijer, Anjele, 90
Vidal, Gore, 290
Vie en Rose, La (magazine), 53
violence. *See also* child abuse; sexual
abuse and assault; spousal abuse
and assault
    against Indigenous people, 164

against Indigenous women, 165,
381
    sex and, 225–26
against women, 45–46, 81, 132,
141, 146, 152, 213
virginity, 85, 103
Voice of Women (VOW), 58, 59, 61
Voices of the Nisei, 286
Voiz des Femme, La, 58
volunteers, 209

Wachtel, Eleanor, 5–6, 242
Wages for Housework, 305
Wall, Naomi, 320
Walton, Shirley, 226, 345
Warland, Betsy, 29, 242, 278–79
Watkins, Mary, 315, 316
We're Talking Vulva (Dempsey), 10,
287
white middle-class feminism, 27–28,
55–56, 194
    and racism, 75, 78
"Why Are There No Great Women
Artists?" (Nochlin), 323
Wieland, Joyce, 268–76, 287, 360–64
Willis, Ellen, 227, 228, 229
Wilson, Bertha, 107–11, 172
Wilson, Michael, 12–13
Within the Barbed Wire Fence
(Nakano), 312
Wolfenden Report (UK), 147–48
Womanist, The, 53
Women Against Violence Against
Women (WAVAW), 3, *41*, 158, 161, 179
Women and Words conference, 27,
46, 207, 328
women of colour
    in the feminist movement, 27–28,
46, 56, 338
    in pornography, 74, 75, 77–78
Women's Cultural Building, 192, *297*
Women's Fire Brigade, 220
Women's International Network,
87–88
Women's Legal Education and
Action Fund (LEAF), 168, 173
women's movement
    failures of, 156–57
    in mainstream media, 182, 183,
184, 186–87

ABOUT THE AUTHOR

PHILINDA MASTERS has long been involved in Canadian feminist activism, starting with volunteering at the Toronto women's centre. She came to *Broadside* after several years of journalism, first at *The Varsity*, University of Toronto student newspaper, as reporter and section editor, then the *Financial Post Magazine* as editorial assistant. In the early 1970s she worked at The Women's Place as co-coordinator, helped found the Toronto Rape Crisis Centre (and did the first shift there) and the Toronto Women's Credit Union. She was one of the founders of *Broadside*, and as editor of *Broadside* she was involved in pretty well every aspect of the paper. On leaving *Broadside* after ten years, she went to the Ontario Institute for Studies in Education (OISE) where she was editor of Resources for Feminist Research, president of the union local representing researcher officers, and chair of the equity and diversity committee of OISE's faculty council. She has since been involved in the digitizing of the entire run of *Broadside* (at broadsidefeminist.com) and is a member of the current Broadside Collective.

THE FEMINIST HISTORY SOCIETY SERIES

The Feminist History Society is committed to creating a lasting record of the women's movement in Canada and Québec for the fifty years between 1960 and the year of the Society's founding, 2010. Feminism has a history that predates the 1960s and continues long after 2010.

The energy that women brought to their quest for equality in these decades is beyond dispute, and it is that energy that we capture in this series. Our movement is not over and new campaigns are upon us. But the FHS series presents an opportunity to take stock of the wide-ranging campaigns for equality that occurred in Canada between 1960 and 2010. There was much transformative social, economic, civil, political, and cultural change.

We maintain an open call for submissions (https://secondstorypress.ca/submissions/) across a full range of approaches to the period, including autobiographies, biographies, edited collections, pictorial histories, plays and novels. There will be many different authors as all individuals and organizations that were participants in the movement are encouraged to contribute. We make every effort to be inclusive of gender, race, class, geography, culture, dis/ability, language, sexual identity, and age.

Beth Atcheson, Constance Backhouse, Lorraine Greaves, Diana Majury, and Beth Symes form the working collective of the Feminist History Society. Margie Wolfe, Publisher, Second Story Feminist Press Inc. and her talented team of women, are presenting the Series.